THE BOOK OF GOING FORTH BY DAY

THE EGYPTIAN BOOK OF THE DEAD

THE BOOK OF GOING FORTH BY DAY

BEING

THE PAPYRUS OF ANI

(ROYAL SCRIBE OF THE DIVINE OFFERINGS)

WRITTEN AND ILLUSTRATED CIRCA 1250 B.C.E., BY

SCRIBES AND ARTISTS UNKNOWN

INCLUDING THE BALANCE OF CHAPTERS
OF THE BOOKS OF THE DEAD KNOWN AS THE
THEBAN RECENSION
COMPILED FROM ANCIENT TEXTS, DATING BACK TO
THE ROOTS OF EGYPTIAN CIVILIZATION

TRANSLATED BY

DR. RAYMOND O. FAULKNER

WITH ADDITIONAL TRANSLATIONS AND A COMMENTARY BY

DR. OGDEN GOELET, JR.

WITH ORIGINAL COLOR ILLUSTRATIONS BASED ON THE FACSIMILE
VOLUME PRODUCED IN 1890 UNDER THE SUPERVISION OF
P. LE PAGE RENOUF AND E.A. WALLIS BUDGE

INTRODUCED BY

CAROL A.R. ANDREWS

EDITED BY

EVA VON DASSOW

IN AN EDITION CONCEIVED AND PRODUCED BY

JAMES WASSERMAN

CHRONICLE BOOKS

SAN FRANCISCO

THIS EDITION PUBLISHED BY CHRONICLE BOOKS LLC IN 2008.
THE EGYPTIAN BOOK OF THE DEAD © 1994, 1998 BY JAMES WASSERMAN.
ALL IMAGES © 1994, 1998 BY JAMES WASSERMAN.
DR. GOELET'S TRANSLATION AND COMMENTARY © 1994 BY OGDEN GOELET, JR.
DR. FAULKNER'S TRANSLATION © 1972 BY LIMITED EDITIONS CLUB, NEW YORK, NY.
MISS ANDREW'S PREFACE © 1994 BY CAROL A. R. ANDREWS

FIRST EDITION, 1994
SECOND REVISED EDITION, 1998

ISBN: 978-0-8118-6489-3

THE LIBRARY OF CONGRESS HAS PREVIOUSLY CATALOGED THIS BOOK AS:

BOOK OF THE DEAD. ENGLISH & EGYPTIAN.
    THE EGYPTIAN BOOK OF THE DEAD: THE BOOK OF GOING FORTH BY DAY:
    BEING THE PAPYRUS OF ANI (ROYAL SCRIBE OF THE DIVINE OFFERINGS) . . .
    / TRANSLATED BY RAYMOND O. FAULKNER; WITH ADDITIONAL TRANSLATIONS
    AND A COMMENTARY BY OGDEN GOELET; INTRODUCED BY CAROL A. R. ANDREWS;
    EDITED BY EVA VON DASSOW; IN AN EDITION CONCEIVED BY JAMES WASSERMAN.
        P. CM.
    "WITH COLOR ILLUSTRATIONS FROM THE FACSIMILE VOLUME PRODUCED IN
    1890 UNDER THE SUPERVISION OF . . . E. A. WALLIS BUDGE."
        ISBN 0-8118-0767-3 (PB) — ISBN 0-8118-0792-4 (HC)
        1. INCANTATIONS, EGYPTIAN.   2. FUTURE LIFE.   I. FAULKNER, RAYMOND
    OLIVER, 1894– . II. GOELET, OGDEN.   III. VON DASSOW, EVA.
    IV. WASSERMAN, JAMES, 1948– .   V. PAPYRUS OF ANI.   VI. TITLE.
    PJ1555.E5F38   1991
    299'.31 — DC20   93-51261
                                                                       CIP

PRODUCED UNDER SPECIAL AGREEMENT WITH INTRINSIC BOOKS,
THE BOOK PACKAGING PARTNERSHIP BETWEEN
SPECIALTY BOOK MARKETING, INC., AND STUDIO 31, INC.

MANUFACTURED IN CHINA

10 9 8 7 6 5 4 3 2

CHRONICLE BOOKS LLC
680 SECOND STREET
SAN FRANCISCO, CA
94107

WWW.CHRONICLEBOOKS.COM

WWW.BOOKOFDEAD.COM

TABLE OF CONTENTS

FOREWORD by James Wasserman   9

PREFACE by Carol A. R. Andrews   11

INTRODUCTION by Dr. Ogden Goelet   13

THE PAPYRUS OF ANI   (Plates 1–37)   19

MAP KEY TO THE PAPYRUS   94

THE BALANCE OF THE THEBAN RECENSION   99

COMMENTARY by Dr. Ogden Goelet   137

SELECTED BIBLIOGRAPHY   171

GLOSSARY OF TERMS AND CONCEPTS   173

This book is dedicated to

TAHUTI

(Djehuty)

The Lord of Wisdom and of Utterance
The God who cometh forth from the Veil

And to
BILL CORSA
Without whose intelligence and integrity
it would have remained a dream

FOREWORD

So compelling an influence has this book exercised upon me, for fully one-third of my life, that I write these words with a profound sense of gratitude and relief. I began working at Samuel Weiser's Bookstore in New York in 1973. During my lunch hours I loved to study the many rare and beautiful books kept in the basement, and there I came upon the "elephant folio" (14 3/4 × 21 inches) facsimile of the Papyrus of Ani. Published by the British Museum in 1890, this magnificent volume overwhelmed me with the intensity and beauty of its mysterious imagery. My interest in occult philosophy naturally led me to study the text of the Egyptian *Book of the Dead*. I first used the virtually unreadable 1895 translation by Budge in the ubiquitous Dover reprint. The original edition had been released as a companion to the facsimile. One was expected to view the images in the facsimile while reading the separate translation.

In January of 1979, I purchased the facsimile from Donald Weiser. Soon after, I found myself literally "watching" a vision of the book you are now holding in your hands taking shape — that is, the exquisite papyrus in full color running along the top of the page, with a readable, uncluttered English translation below. When in 1985 the color edition of Faulkner's translation of the Theban Recension was published by Macmillan, I initially thought my idea might have been accomplished. But examination of the book quickly revealed that it did not correspond to the majestic volume I had envisioned.

Now that vision has been realized — the rendition of an ancient Egyptian papyrus that comes the closest in 3500 years to approximating the feeling of the original, where the words and images are again treated as a unity.

Three key issues regarding the creation of this book need to be discussed. The first is the text. My original idea, developed in detail over several years, was to follow the Ani Papyrus word for word. I planned to use Budge's translation, with his excellent key to the hieroglyphics as my guide, to present the text and images together on the same page. The Map Key to the Papyrus, which appears here on pages 94–97, was developed from that research. Dr. Goelet, however, made clear, first, that Budge's translation falls far short of modern standards, and second, that the hieroglyphic text of the Ani Papyrus itself is of uneven quality, often much inferior to the excellence of its vignettes. He proposed that we use Faulkner's translation of the "ideal text" of each chapter below the images of the Ani Papyrus, supplemented by his own translations where necessary. Our text would then represent the best translation from the best Egyptological sources for the specific chapter of the *Book of the Dead* illustrated in the Ani Papyrus.

Thus this volume combines the finest modern scholarship with the most beautifully illuminated surviving ancient papyrus.

The second concern is my "recutting," or electronic reorganization of the papyrus. The medium of a scroll is vastly different from that of a book, and I have sought to restore the integrity of the images at all costs. Budge unfortunately cut the original papyrus using the basic "yardstick" method — dividing it into thirty-seven sheets of relatively even length. The result was to disfigure the flow of the original scroll. On the other hand, the facsimile volume he published looks more like a book, with images of uniform width across pages of uniform width. In this edition, you will find some few images occupying just over a third of the page in width, while others have necessitated the trouble and expense of gatefold spreads (originally suggested by my colleague Bill Corsa) to properly accommodate the ornately bordered art. (The original papyrus measured 78 feet long by 1 foot 3 inches deep. It is displayed here at 59% of its original size.)

The third issue to address is my decision to use the 1890 facsimile as the primary artistic reference for this edition, rather than the original Papyrus of Ani in the British Museum. The reason is simple — the condition of the 3500-year-old original. *Codices Selecti* Volume LXII (Akademische Druck und Verlagsanstalt, Graz, 1979, ed. E. Dondelinger) presented photographs of the original papyrus.

Budge's facsimile was much closer to what the original would have looked like when it was first created. The sole purpose of the extensive electronic retouching that we have devoted to the papyrus, has been to bring the images even closer to their original form — in fact, to recreate the original Papyrus of Ani in book form three and a half millennia after the scroll was first painted. The advent of color computer technology in the last fifteen years has at last caused me to appreciate that the project took so long to achieve; my original concept of working with the papyrus was greatly inhibited by the technique of manual dot etching available in 1979. We have literally spanned the ages by making use of state-of-the-art modern electronic technology to reclaim one of the most beautiful treasures of antiquity.

A final word: I believe the power, wisdom, and spiritual vision offered in the following pages can be greatly beneficial to our modern culture. Perhaps in searching out our spiritual roots, we can rediscover the golden thread all but lost today. The ancient Egyptians taught that the individual who led a pure life and persevered against deadly trials would then feast with the Gods. This is an altogether refreshing assessment of our inherent human divinity. Were we, as a culture, to be reminded of such an elevated spiritual condition, might not the true pride so engendered help end the irresponsibility endemic to our world? After all, *noblesse oblige!*

I wish to express my gratitude to Donald Weiser, who carefully preserved the rare facsimile from which this book was created; Henry Suzuki, who knew it was mine when once I had almost forgotten; Jane Nelson and Harry Smith, who helped me to appreciate beauty; Gerry Burstein, who taught me how to make a book; Wileda Wasserman, whose tenacious faith in this project carried me through many dark days. Thanks also go to my father, Arnold Wasserman, my friends Larry Barnes and Kanya Vashon McGhee, and to Gene Keiffer, all early supporters. Ari Caratzas first made it clear that Budge's translation was not going to work. William Breeze introduced me to Ogden Goelet, whose quiet faith in this book extended over a decade. Ehud Sperling reaffirmed the necessity of accredited scholars. Alan Miller and Avo Kubar echoed the ancient precept "Know thyself." James Curran and Gary Isenstadt helped restore my faith. Elise Douglas stressed not to give up before the miracle. I also thank Joe Kulin, whose kindness and generosity brightened the process; Jane Stroll, who saw the point one day; Peter Sherred, whose lighthearted genius and encouragement were valued gifts; and Del Riddle, Michael Mann, and Larry Abramoff for their efforts. Thanks to Sidney and Shawn Shiff of the Limited Editions Club for granting us the use of Faulkner's superb translation. Eva von Dassow, our editor, and Dr. Goelet engendered in me the greatest respect for the critical intellectual integrity of the scholarly method used to investigate ancient culture. Carol Andrews's enthusiastic reaction to my work on the papyrus is deeply appreciated. Caroline Herter's professional acumen and courage have brought this book to fruition. Werner Mark Linz, representing the American University in Cairo Press, completed the circle by publishing an edition of *The Book of the Dead* in the land of its origin. Finally, I am grateful for the support of my son, Satra, who literally grew to young manhood on this project; and to my wife, Nancy, without whose assistance I never could have come this far. And thanks once again to Bill and Maryann Corsa.

Most importantly, thanks to the nameless Masters, who bequeathed this treasure to humanity, and to the living Gods of Ancient Egypt, who have guided this book to publication.

James Wasserman
New York City

PREFACE

The funerary papyrus known as the *Book of the Dead of Ani* is one of the most famous of all the ancient artifacts held by the Department of Egyptian Antiquities at the British Museum. It is certainly one of the most complete of its kind, being some seventy-eight feet in total length. As the papyrus has been segmented, only one of its thirty-seven sheets lacks a vignette of some kind. Most sheets have a frieze of vignettes running in a band along the top of the text; others have vignettes which span the whole height of the papyrus. Sheets 3, 4, and 37, containing the Weighing of the Heart, the Introduction to Osiris, and the Western Theban Mountain, comprise nothing but a vignette which encompasses the whole height and width of the sheet in question.

And therein lies Ani's fame, for many of its highly colorful, almost impressionistic scenes have been used as illustrative material in numerous publications and other media. However, exigencies of exhibition space have allowed only a relatively small number of sheets of the Ani Papyrus ever to be displayed to the public at any one time, and consequently it is these vignettes which have become well known. But that is not to say that those other sheets which are not exhibited are any less finely decorated. Indeed, many of them are of great importance to scholars and would be of certain interest to the public. Thus, in spite of Sir Peter Le Page Renouf's mammoth, full-color facsimile publication of the Papyrus of Ani in 1890 and the better-known corrected second edition by Sir E. A. Wallis Budge, for the last hundred years only scholars have been aware of its hidden riches.

This magnificent publication will rectify that lack of awareness, and I am sure the public will be amazed not only at the quality of the original paintings so superbly reproduced in it but at their number, the range of subject matter that they contain, and the great wealth of detail for their small size.

The text of the Papyrus of Ani, however, is far from careful, being full of repetitions, errors, and omissions. Yet even this is instructive in providing proof that the quality of the vignettes is no indication of the quality of textual content and that it was perfectly possible for a master draftsman to work alongside mediocre scribes. Interestingly enough, it is known from internal evidence that the papyrus was not specially commissioned for Ani, let alone written by him, in spite of the important scribal offices he held. Despite its flawed nature the hieroglyphic text remains of great importance, but apart from its original publication in the facsimile, it has only been relatively easily accessible in Budge's 1895 and 1910 editions, which reproduced the linear hieroglyphs in horizontal rows using a printed font and without the accompanying vignettes.

This superb publication not only reproduces for the first time in a single volume the original facsimile edition, with hieroglyphic text and vignettes together once more, it also juxtaposes them with an English translation of each chapter on the same page that the Egyptian text occurs. The translation used is that produced by the distinguished British Egyptologist the late Dr. R. O. Faulkner, generally agreed to be one of the best translations available. The up-to-date emendations in light of recent scholarship, additional material such as the provision of a translation of Chapter 64, one of the most interesting in the *Book of the Dead* (not included in Ani's papyrus), and a full commentary, which will be of use to the public and scholars alike, are the work of Dr. Ogden Goelet.

One of the most valuable features of this fine new publication is the reassembly on the plates of the original papyrus roll, which for the sake of convenience of storage and display was divided into thirty-seven framed and glassed sheets, varying in length from 52 cm to 76 cm, the norm being between 65 cm and 70 cm. Budge was sometimes influenced in cutting the roll by what he considered a natural break in the frieze of vignettes — even if this led to the text of a chapter being on different sheets. At other times the layout of the text was considered of greater importance, and as a result vignettes have been segmented, some even separated from their relevant chapter. Moreover, as the divisions progressed there came points where, unless the sheets produced were to be abnormally short or long large-scale vignettes were cut in two.

The most damaging example of this process is the division of Sheets 33 and 34 which cuts in two the elaborate and important vignette of Chapter 151A and its schematized representation of the burial chamber with the mummy surrounded by protective deities and magical objects. In this volume, the rejoined sections now form Plate 33. In a similar way the text of Chapter 110 at the end of Sheet 34 is now reunited with its vignette depicting the activities in the Field of Reeds from Sheet 35 to form the contents of Plate 34. The elements of the vignette of Chapter 148 comprising the seven celestial kine and bull of heaven and the four rudders representing the cardinal points are reassembled from Sheets 35 and 36 to form Plate 35. The splendid figures of Ani and his wife and the Iwnmutef priest on Sheet 12 are now seen on Plate 12 to be directing their address to the squatting ranks of the great gods of Egypt. Plate 23 restores the doorway from Sheet 22 to its corresponding vignette on Sheet 23. Plates 19 and 30 restore the magnificent full-height vignettes of Osiris and Isis to the same scene as the figures of the deceased and his wife in adoration from Sheets 19 and 29. Falcon-headed Sokar-Osiris, extracted from the vignette of the Western Mountain, is correctly located as the object of their veneration on Plate 36. The fourth Son of Horus alone at the beginning of Sheet 9 is restored to the company of his brothers on Plate 8. The vignette accompanying the hymn to the rising sun has been moved from Sheet 2 to rejoin the text on Plate 1. The reamalgamation of Sheets 11 and 12 by means of fold-out Plate 11 reunites all the Gates and Portals of the Underworld, that of Sheets 31 and 32 reassembles on another fold-out Plate (31) the shrine with open doors containing the deities to whom all forty-two sections of the Negative Confession are addressed. From a textual point of view, the last column of Sheet 3 is moved to join its vignette on Sheet 4, forming Plate 4. The last column of Sheet 15 is reunited with the beginning of Sheet 16, and thus Chapter 27 regains its vignette depicting Ani's heart on Plate 15. The last column of Sheet 16 is restored to the start of Sheet 17 to reassemble Chapter 93 on Plate 16. The beginning of Chapter 92 on Sheet 17, a spell for opening up and leaving the tomb, is restored to the remainder of the text and its vignette on Sheet 18, forming Plate 17. The last column of Sheet 18, which represents the beginning of Chapter 15, is reunited with the remainder of the text on Sheet 19, forming Plate 18.

Without doubt this single beautiful volume will become a prized possession for those with any interest in the world of ancient Egypt and an accessible tool for those engaged in study and research.

Carol A. R. Andrews
Dept. of Egyptian Antiquities
British Museum

INTRODUCTION

The Egyptians lived in a world of allusions." This statement of Helmut Brunner, one of the greatest historians of Egyptian religion, is a profound observation regarding the language and imagery of Egyptian religious texts. We enter Ani's *Book of the Dead* as we might enter a contemporary tomb, flanked by hymns to the sun god Re and then by eloquent invocations to Osiris. Passing through these hymns, so to speak, the deceased arrives at the central metaphor of the papyrus and the critical moment of the passage from this world to the next: the weighing of the heart. Here the visual image symbolically represents the judgment of a person's moral worth as the balancing of his heart against the feather of Maat, the goddess who personified truth, justice, and order.

How evocative is this Egyptian metaphor! For all humanity, male or female, mightily rich or wretchedly poor, the delicacy of the necessary equipoise of moral worth contained in the heart meant that one's sins must be feather-light; the criterion of judgment was as unbiased, fair, and impersonal as a marketplace scale. During the New Kingdom, weighing scenes like this were placed near the beginning of a papyrus. The implication was clear — virtue was necessary in procuring passage beyond this point and into a successful afterlife.

In many passages of the *Book of the Dead* we can almost hear the voice of a modern symbolist poet. Like the metaphor of the scales of judgment, the rich imagery of Egyptian texts was derived from the concrete world of daily life and the natural environment of Egypt. For example, the locus of the afterlife in the Field of Reeds (an Egyptian version of the Isles of the Blessed) emerged from a vision of an infinitely vast and peaceful expanse of golden reeds, much like the wide tracts of the Delta and the thickets along the Nile banks. The Egyptian hoped to find in the next world marshes like those in which he had hunted during life, and fields like those he had plowed.

The Nature of the *Book of the Dead*

The pyramids and the Sphinx, the mummies and the hieroglyphs, and the *Book of the Dead* have become the most popular symbols of Egypt in the public imagination; they are icons summarizing that ancient culture.

Consider the Great Pyramid of Khufu (Cheops) at Giza. Rising 484 feet above ground level, its 780-foot sides were oriented so accurately that there was a deviation of only a half degree of arc from true north along one edge. This massive structure contains approximately 2.5 million blocks weighing on the average a ton and a half apiece, some so finely dressed that it is barely possible to insert a playing card between adjacent stones. It would be easy to be over-whelmed merely by the engineering achievement and miss the corollary informa-tion about Egyptian society. If we assume that Khufu reigned for fifty years and that his builders worked at a breakneck pace ten hours a day, one enormous block had to be added to the pyramid every four minutes or so — every day for fifty years, inexorably. Only the precision scheduling, rigorous planning, and careful organization of an efficient, honest, and clear-thinking bureaucracy could complete a project like this.

Icons, however, can also become stereotypes, which are at best oversimplifi-cations and often involve misinterpretations. In the case of the *Book of the Dead,* we can literally look up its misinterpretation in library catalogues. The idea that the *Book of the Dead* was like a bible goes back to the Middle Ages and Renaissance, long before the papyri could be read. Since all that was known about these mysterious documents was that they came from coffins and cemeteries, it was assumed that they were the one religious text that the deceased wished to take into the next world, and such a text must have been the Egyptian equivalent of the Bible. With Champollion's decipherment of the hieroglyphs in 1822, Egyptology changed dramatically from a speculative exercise to a scholarly discipline. Although specialists soon realized that the *Book of the Dead* was not an Egyptian "Bible," that notion has persisted in the public imagination.

The Bible and the Koran, each of which transmits the revealed messages of a single supreme deity to humanity, are fundamental to their respective religions. These books articulate the bases of faith: the nature of the deity and the theological underpinnings of man's relationship to the deity; the obligations of god to man and man to god; the moral code by which adherents should conduct themselves; and, especially in the case of Islam, even the social and political thought by which the believers should organize their societies. The *Book of the Dead,* on the other hand, is chiefly concerned with the afterlife. Its purpose was not to set forth the basic tenets of Egyptian religion, nor to guide the faithful through a religious life, but rather to assist its owner in the next world. Moreover, rather than serving as a fundamental text, the *Book of the Dead* was part of a larger body of religious literature (discussed in the next section). And, as the more speculative and eclectic product of a polytheistic culture, the *Book of the Dead* was never formalized into a canon. It is a collection of texts from which the individual was able to choose for his or her particular scroll, based often on a combination of what could be afforded and the current religious views of the period. Certain chapters were loosely considered to be essential, others were completely discretionary.

Egyptian religion was not one of revelation; its doctrines were not ascribed to any one divinely inspired intermediary and teacher comparable to Christ, Mohammed, or the Buddha. Only in the genre we call *Wisdom Literature* — Egyptian collections of moral teaching, proverbial maxims, and worldly guidance — are texts attributed to (almost certainly pseudepigraphic) teachers of the past. Egyptian *Wisdom Literature* was strongly didactic, and the moral tone of these texts is more reminiscent of biblical texts than other Egyptian literature is. Just as the language of our daily life is filled with phrases and images drawn from the Bible, Egyptian literature and biographical texts continually allude to *Wisdom Literature.*

The origins of the *Book of the Dead* may be traced to the *Pyramid Texts,* which appear at the end of the Fifth Dynasty in Egypt's Age of the Pyramids (ca. 2400 B.C.E.). As their name implies, the *Pyramid Texts* were originally intended solely for the benefit of the king and his family. Over the next few centuries these texts were adapted for private use and incorporated into a group of new spells called the *Coffin Texts,* which could be employed by anyone who could afford a sarcophagus. By the early New Kingdom (ca. 1550 B.C.E.), the *Coffin Texts* were slowly being replaced by the work which we know as the *Book of the Dead.* Like a line of shingles, these groups of texts follow each other, partially overlapping and partially presenting innovative material.

Although the *Book of the Dead* focuses on the afterlife, some of its chapters are said to be equally efficacious in this world; similarly, its moral content applies to this life. Each statement of the so-called Negative Confession, which the deceased proclaimed before the weighing of his or her heart, implied a code of behavior to be followed during life. Every "I did not . . ." reflects an unexpressed "Thou shalt not . . ." Without an exemplary and moral existence, there was no hope for a successful afterlife.

Egyptian Religion

Egyptian religion was fundamentally polytheistic, although there were tendencies to view certain deities as implicit in other gods and in the universe. The multiplicity of Egyptian gods and their many manifestations is probably the greatest source of modern conceptual problems with Egyptian religion. Monotheism and polytheism have become more than merely descriptive terms today; they imply a value judgment as well. We tend to look at the belief in many gods as primitive, and therefore intellectually weaker. Polytheistic religions, however, have certain strengths, particularly from a political standpoint. In a polytheistic society, the state does not have to enforce a theological conformity on its citizens.

With many gods and cults, there is less reason for attempting to make religious beliefs wholly consistent. Differing opinions on the nature of the divine need not be seen as conflicts or heresies; they are simply alternative interpretations. Without the compulsion of dogma, polytheistic religions allow the individual greater freedom to define his or her own relationship with the divine.

The borderline between various deities and beliefs was constantly blurred, for it was easy to find some characteristic of one god present in another. Many features which appear contradictory or illogical at first glance are actually accommodations of contrasting viewpoints. In the polytheistic context, logically stated dogma was essentially unnecessary. Theological literature is often aimed at convincing the reader of a unique truth, but such argumentation would be foreign to the purpose of most Egyptian religious literature. Egyptian theology tended more toward inclusion than exclusion. It was not expressed fanatically — except for the brief appearance of a virtual monotheism during the reign of the "heretic" pharaoh Akhenaten (1379–1362 B.C.E.). If, however, theology can be defined as meditations on the nature of the divine, then nearly all Egyptian religious texts are theological. The great Egyptian hymns of the New Kingdom, dedicated to Osiris, Ptah, Amun, and Re, are more than collections of laudatory epithets; they delineate the characteristics of those gods in such detail, they likely represent the collected and reasoned products of priestly associations. The Great Hymn to the Aten, in particular, contains an unusually detailed statement of the uniqueness of Akhenaten's god as well as his place and function in the cosmos.

The Egyptian afterlife, like many Egyptian conceptions, was characterized by a contrasting duality: a chthonic netherworld presided over by Osiris, Lord of Resurrection, and a solar/astral existence, in which the sun god Re was supreme. But neither god was exempt from the struggle against nonexistence. At the moment of creation the forces of chaos were overcome but not eliminated from the earth. Most of "that which does not exist" was consigned to the fringes of the world, namely foreign lands, deserts, and particularly the underworld, but order and disorder continued to exist side by side both in this world and beyond it. If the *Book of the Dead* often appears surreal and confusing, let us remember that it describes what happens after death, the moment when one left the orderly world of Egypt and confronted nonexistence and chaos. The notion that the next world might be perilous, confusing, and unpredictable is hardly unique to Egyptian culture, but the Egyptians universalized the irrationality: not only mortals but the gods themselves had to contend with the same perils. The purpose of the mortuary literature was to enable the deceased to emerge victorious from these trials.

Because of our unfamiliarity with much of its mythical and allegorical underpinnings, Egyptian mortuary literature is often unfairly described as a collection comprised mostly of magical spells. Egyptologists today are just beginning to deal with the complex interaction of myth, ritual, and magic in Egyptian religion. Magic played an important part in the *Book of the Dead,* but its role should not be exaggerated. Magic is a word which is very easy to use carelessly. One man's magic is apt to be another man's religion, especially if the symbolic nature of ritual is overlooked. One wonders what a jaundiced Egyptian observer would have said about the role of bread and wine in the Christian church, or the function of food in the Jewish Passover seder; magical, perhaps?

WORD AND IMAGE

While several generations of Egyptologists have dismissed the *Book of the Dead* as a degraded expression of Egyptian religion, the work continues to fascinate the public. The lure of the book's mysterious language is heightened by the colorful and elegant vignettes, which surmount the hieroglyphic text with its odd and appealing symbols. Modern observers feel a semiotic saturation. Browsing through the plates in this volume or walking past an unrolled *Book of the Dead* in a museum, we are struck by the calm conviction with which the complex and bizarre aspects of the Egyptian afterlife are presented. The serenity of the

Egyptian imagery conveys the impression that these people really knew about life after death.

Art historians remark constantly on the hieroglyphic nature of much Egyptian art, in which text and scene seemingly engage in constant conversation. We have come to realize that word, image, and reality were a unity in Egyptian thought. So close is this identification in the Egyptian language that "idea" and "word" can be expressed by the same term. This conceptual association persisted after Egypt had converted to Christianity, when the most popular book of the Bible was the Gospel of John, which begins, "In the beginning was the Word, and the Word was with God . . ." By means of a word or an image, thought could be actualized. In the past decade scholars have consequently turned more attention to the vignettes in hope of a fuller understanding of the text.

THE PRESENT TRANSLATION AND COMMENTARY

At the top of each sheet of every *Book of the Dead* papyrus stand the illustrations, essential to the understanding of the text beneath. Only a few papyri from the vast corpus of extant *Books of the Dead* can compare with the beauty of the Papyrus of Ani. This magnificent manuscript was purchased by Sir E. A. Wallis Budge, to whom the British Museum owes many of the most important pieces in its collection. The beautiful color facsimiles that he produced, to accompany the translation which he released in a separate volume, did much to bring this masterpiece to public attention and to popularize an important work of Egyptian religion.

The images will always retain a timeless quality, but advances in the field of Egyptology have rendered Budge's translation quite antiquated. We have replaced it for this publication with one of the best available today, that of the late Raymond O. Faulkner. Professor Faulkner, whose career was too wide ranging to summarize here, was a great translator; he had a flair for rendering difficult Egyptian texts into clear English, including the most problematic religious materials. I have personally "loved to death" four copies of his *Concise Dictionary of Middle Egyptian,* a completely indispensable book for Egyptologists. His insights have made his work on the *Pyramid Texts* and the *Coffin Texts* classics, and he produced wonderful renderings of the masterpieces of Egyptian literature. Unfortunately, Faulkner died before he could complete his work on the *Book of the Dead,* so it appeared without any commentary. My commentary, wherein many of the themes introduced here are treated at greater length, is my main contribution to the present volume. Although the Ani Papyrus is a masterpiece of Egyptian book illustration, its text is frequently inferior to that of many contemporaneous manuscripts; therefore the translation presented here does not precisely represent the hieroglyphic text shown. Like most modern translations of the *Book of the Dead,* Faulkner's translation was drawn from a composite of several manuscripts, resulting in an "ideal text" rather than representing one specific papyrus. When, in the case of certain chapters or passages, the version found in the Ani Papyrus and Faulkner's version are too much at variance, I have substituted a new translation based on the text of the Ani Papyrus; the more significant of such alterations have been noted in the second section of the commentary. In the case of a small number of chapters which were not included in his work, but are present in the Ani Papyrus, my translation is given. Finally, scholarly opinion has changed on some minor points, and I have altered Faulkner's translation accordingly. It is a testament to Faulkner's deft touch that so few changes were required twenty years after his translation was done.

Egyptian texts present the translator with greater technical problems than most ancient tongues. The Egyptians left behind none of the usual (and invaluable) aids to translation. There are no contemporaneous dictionaries of Egyptian; bilingual texts are few and brief; and no well-known sister tongue survives. For the most part, philologists have been forced to get a sense of the vocabulary using Egyptian material alone. This often leaves lexicographers in the unenviable position of comparing the obscure and unknown with the merely uncertain. Like modern Hebrew and Arabic, Egyptian was written without vowels, so that only the consonantal structure of the language has been preserved. Its vital organs of sound and rhythm are gone, leaving behind dry bones. Much of the poetry and word play that surely characterized the *Book of the Dead* is lost forever.

Lexicography remains today, more than a century and a half after Champollion, the Achilles' heel of Egyptian translation. For instance, we know many Egyptian words that express some degree of fear or happiness. But which one of these expresses dread, anxiety, or worry; how do we distinguish between ecstasy, delight, joy, and jubilation? The Egyptians composed their inscriptions carefully, delighting especially in synonymous and contrasting parallels, playing on sounds, alluding to other texts and genres. A translator can feel the skill and balance of a text, feel the breath of words, and sense allusions, but so much simply eludes us. As a result, we render Egyptian rainbows into monochromatic arcs; our translations may be accurate, but often have a colorless, affectless tone, bereft of the vivacity and tonal nuances of the original.

When dealing with the intricate and often convoluted imagery of Egyptian mortuary texts and their vignettes, it would be very easy to produce the Egyptological equivalent of *Pale Fire,* Vladimir Nabokov's brilliant satire of academic writing, in which the footnotes and the commentary swell up and overwhelm the original work. These texts are notoriously obscure. In my commentary I try to explain where I can and summarize opinions in other places. The vignettes receive particular attention; I have attempted to show how these images interact with the text beneath them, and vice versa.

It should be borne in mind that there often can be more than one interpretation, and we should beware of overconfidently imposing our conceptions upon Egyptian religion. The *Book of the Dead* was never meant to be a unity. The fact that it envisions both an Osirian and a Solar afterlife demonstrates the impossibility of seeking a single message. The commentary is designed to introduce the non-specialist to the aspects of Egyptian religion which are relevant to the *Book of the Dead*. It does not pretend to be all-inclusive or the final word on the subject.

The Modern Relevance of the *Book of the Dead*

Man is a historical as well as a social animal. In order to understand where we are today and to sense where we are headed, we must know where we have been; an awareness of past and future makes us uniquely moral beings. Egypt, non-European, yet neither wholly African nor wholly Near Eastern, makes us aware of our multicultural heritage. We are only beginning to realize the extent to which Ancient Egypt and Mesopotamia influenced European civilization. The cultures of the eastern Mediterranean were the crucible of Judeo-Christian and Islamic values, in whose development Egypt played a significant role. Mosaic law and many aspects of Judaism show evidence of positive and negative reactions to the sojourn in Egypt. Contemplating the delightful interaction of image and word in the *Book of the Dead,* along with its multiplicity of gods, can help us to understand both why the deity of the religions of the Book is abstract in nature and why monotheistic creeds should prohibit graven images so strongly. Greece and Rome, too, were simultaneously fascinated and repulsed by Egypt. The worship of deities in animal form, for instance, appeared naive to them. But Egypt's great intelligence, elegance, and antiquity demanded the attention of the classical world, which normally dismissed civilizations other than its own.

The poetry and allusions of the *Book of the Dead* enhance its relevance for modern readers, for poetry and great literature can refocus our thoughts and beliefs. The Egyptians' striking integration of symbol, art, and language compares favorably with our society's obsession with imagery, political and otherwise. Examining their approach to life helps us see our society in a different light; the contrast combats fossilization of thought. Certainly the high sophistication of ancient Egyptian culture is a marvelous curative for the arrogant notion of our modern world that less technically advanced peoples are perforce intellectually inferior.

The *Book of the Dead,* at turns so familiar and so alien to our beliefs, offers a unique vantage point for examining Egyptian religion and its worldview. The *Book of the Dead* promised resurrection to all mankind, as a reward for righteous living, long before Judaism and Christianity embraced that concept. The Egyptians believed in a moral judgment of the dead, but even virtue triumphant would be compelled to contend with dangerous irrationality. The gods too had to struggle against the enemies of universal order. Here, the Egyptians seem to have anticipated Jefferson's remark that the price of freedom is eternal vigilance. The notion that the deceased shared in the perils and rewards of the afterlife on a nearly equal footing with the deities reveals a striking sense of human dignity, for the Egyptian hoped to become a companion and equal of the gods.

Dr. Ogden Goelet
New York University

CONVENTIONS

The numbering system used for the chapters of the *Book of the Dead* was originated by Richard Lepsius in his 1842 publication of the papyrus of a Ptolemaic official named Iuwefankh, which is now in the Turin Museum. Since he believed that this lengthy and well-illustrated manuscript would represent a "standard edition" of the text, Lepsius divided the work into 165 chapters, assigning the numbers on the basis of the dividing lines and rubrics of that document. Additional chapters were identified over the years by such scholars as Willem Pleyte, Édouard Naville, Budge, T. G. Allen, and others. At present the number of chapters stands at 192.

Small caps indicate explanatory interpolations added to the translation by either Faulkner or Goelet to clarify the sense. The use of italics in the translation essentially follows Faulkner's usage in the Macmillan edition. Italics indicate where the hieroglyphic text is rubricized, that is, written in red ink. However, for the sake of consistency in design, the use of italics has been expanded somewhat in passages that are characteristically, but not consistently, rubricized in the Egyptian. Thus, all "chapter headings" are entirely italicized even if red ink is not used throughout the corresponding text of the Ani Papyrus; and, while the Egyptians did not normally write the name of a god or the name of the deceased in red, when such names occur within a rubric they are italicized here. Conversely, in some cases the Ani Papyrus includes rubricized text within the body of a chapter, while Faulkner's translation (based on an "ideal text" and thus not precisely representing the Ani Papyrus) does not italicize the corresponding passage. Italics are used in the commentary both to indicate rubricized text and, in the standard way, to identify untranslated foreign words, titles, and emphasized words.

N	denotes the name of the deceased person, in the Theban Recension chapters
[. . .]	missing word or passage
. . .	illegible or incomprehensible word or passage
( )	translator's addition for clarity

Certain Egyptian terms have been left untranslated and the reader may consult the glossary for their interpretation.

E. v.D., O. G., J. W.

PUBLISHER'S NOTE: Rather than imposing our stylistic conventions, the text throughout this work conforms with the style of Dr. Faulkner's translation. In keeping with this choice, Faulkner's transposition of single and double quotation marks has been followed throughout the commentary.

THE
PAPYRUS
OF
ANI

ROYAL SCRIBE
OF THE DIVINE OFFERINGS
OF ALL THE GODS

Introductory Hymn to the Sun-God Re

Worship of Re when he rises
in the eastern horizon of the sky by Ani

He says: Hail to you, you having come as Khepri, even Khepri who is the creator of the gods. You rise and shine on the back of your mother (the sky), having appeared in glory as King of the gods. Your mother Nut shall use her arms on your behalf in making greeting. The Manu-mountain receives you in peace, Maat embraces you at all seasons. May you give power and might in vindication — and a coming forth as a living soul to see Horakhty — to the Ka of Ani.

He says: O all you gods of the Soul-mansion who judge sky and earth in the balance, who give food and provisions; O Tatenen, Unique One, creator of mankind; O Southern, Northern, Western, and Eastern Enneads, give praise to Re, Lord of the Sky, the Sovereign who made the gods. Worship him in his goodly shape when he appears in the Day-bark. May those who are above worship you, may those who are below worship you, may Thoth and Maat write to you daily; your serpent-foe has been given over to the fire and the rebel-serpent is fallen, his arms are bound, Re has taken away his movements, and the Children of Impotence are nonexistent. The Mansion of the Prince is in

festival, the noise of shouting is in the Great Place, the gods are in joy, when they see Re in his appearing, his rays flooding the lands. The Majesty of this noble god proceeds, he has entered the land of Manu, the land is bright at his daily birth, and he has attained his state of yesterday. May you be gracious to me when I see your beauty, having departed from upon earth. May I smite the Ass, may I drive off the rebel-serpent, may I destroy Apophis when he acts, for I have seen the Abdju-fish in its moment of being and the Inet-fish piloting the canoe on its waterway. I have seen Horus as helmsman, with Thoth and Maat beside him, I have taken hold of the bow-warp of the Night-bark and the stern-warp of the Day-bark. May he grant that I see the sun-disk and behold the moon unceasingly every day; may my soul go forth to travel to every place which it desires; may my name be called out, may it be found at the board of offerings; may there be given to me loaves in the Presence like the Followers of Horus, may a place be made for me in the solar bark on the day when the god ferries across, and may I be received into the presence of Osiris in the Land of Vindication. For the Ka of Ani.

INTRODUCTORY HYMN TO OSIRIS

Worship of Osiris Wennefer, the Great God who dwells in the Thinite nome, King of Eternity, Lord of Everlasting, who passes millions of years in his lifetime, first-born son of Nut, begotten of Geb, Heir, Lord of the Wereret-crown, whose White Crown is tall, Sovereign of gods and men. He has taken the crook and the flail and the office of his forefathers. May your heart which is in the desert land be glad, for your son Horus is firm on your throne, while you have appeared as Lord of Busiris, as the Ruler who is in Abydos. The Two Lands flourish in vindication because of you in the presence of the Lord of All. All that exists is ushered in to him in his name of 'Face to whom men are ushered'; the Two Lands are marshalled for him as leader in this his name of Sokar; his might is far-reaching, one greatly feared in this his name of Osiris; he passes over the length of eternity in his name of Wennefer.

PLATE 2   THE BOOK OF GOING FORTH BY DAY

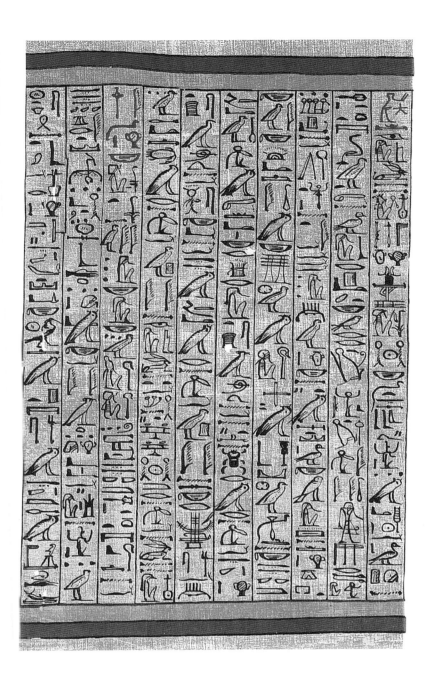

Hail to you, King of Kings, Lord of Lords, Ruler of Rulers, who took possession of the Two Lands even in the womb of Nut; he rules the plains of the Silent Land, even he the golden of body, blue of head, on whose arms is turquoise. O Pillar of Myriads, broad of breast, kindly of countenance, who is in the Sacred Land: May you grant power in the sky, might on earth, and vindication in the God's Domain, a journeying downstream to Busiris as a living soul and a journeying upstream to Abydos as a heron; to go in and out without hindrance at all the gates of the Duat. May there be given to me bread from the House of Cool Water and a table of offerings from Heliopolis, my toes being firm-planted in the Field of Reeds. May the barley and emmer which are in it belong to the Ka of the Osiris Ani.

CAPTIONS ALONG TOP ROW:

Sia and Hu	Hathor-Mistress-of-the-West	Horus, the Great God	Nephthys and Isis	Nut-Mistress-of-the-Sky	Geb

CAPTIONS AROUND WEIGHING SCENE: Meskhenet   Renenutet   Shai

— 30B —

Chapter for not letting Ani's heart create opposition against him in the God's Domain

O my heart which I had from my mother! O my heart which I had from my mother! O my heart of my different ages! Do not stand up as a witness against me, do not be opposed to me in the tribunal, do not be hostile to me in the presence of the Keeper of the Balance, for you are my Ka which was in my body, the protector who made my members hale. Go forth to the happy place whereto we speed; do not make my name stink to Entourage who make men. Do not tell lies about me in the presence of the god; it is indeed well that you should hear!

Thus says Thoth, judge of truth, to the Great Ennead which is in the presence of Osiris: Hear this word of very

PLATE 3   THE BOOK OF GOING FORTH BY DAY

Tefnut   Shu   Atum   Re-in-the-Midst-of-his-Bark

Words spoken by He who is in the Embalming
Chamber: 'Pay attention, to the decision of
truthfulness and of the plummet of the
balance according to its stance.'

truth. I have judged the heart of the deceased, and his soul
stands as a witness for him. His deeds are righteous in the
great balance, and no sin has been found in him. He did not
diminish the offerings in the temples, he did not destroy
what had been made, he did not go about with deceitful
speech while he was on earth.

Thus says the Great Ennead to Thoth who is in Hermopolis: This utterance of yours is true. The vindicated
Osiris Ani is straightforward, he has no sin, there is no
accusation against him before us, Ammit shall not be
permitted to have power over him. Let there be given to
him the offerings which are issued in the presence of Osiris,
and may a grant of land be established in the Field of
Offerings as for the Followers of Horus.

CHAPTER 30B (*continued*)

Thus says Horus son of Isis: I have come to you, O Wennefer, and I bring Ani to you. His heart is true, having gone forth from the balance, and he has not sinned against any god or any goddess. Thoth has judged him in writing which has been told to the Ennead, and Maat the great has witnessed. Let there be given to him bread and beer which have been issued in the presence of Osiris, and he will be forever like the Followers of Horus.

Thus says Ani: Here I am in your presence, O Lord of the West. There is no wrongdoing in my body, I have not wittingly told lies, there has been no second fault. Grant that I may be like the favored ones who are in your suite, O Osiris, one greatly favored by the good god, one loved of the Lord of the Two Lands, Ani, vindicated before Osiris.

PLATE 4   THE BOOK OF GOING FORTH BY DAY

The Osiris Scribe Ani

FROM RIGHT TO LEFT:

Imsety

Hapy

Duamutef

Qebehsenuef

Osiris Lord of Eternity

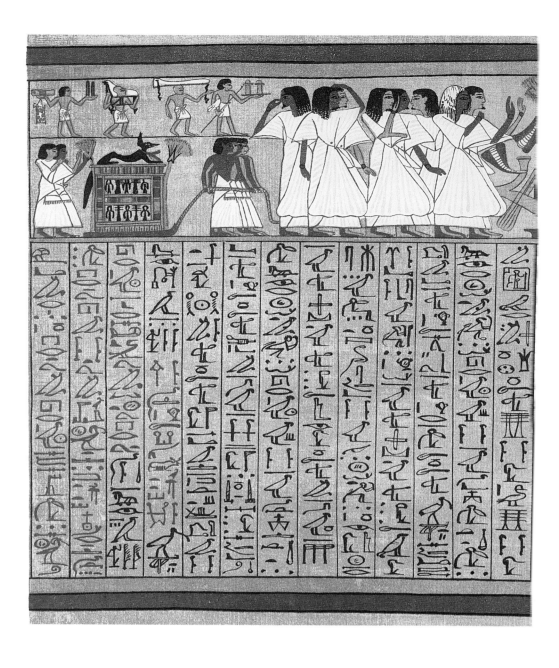

— I —

Here begin the chapters of going out into the day,
the praises and recitations for going to and fro in the
God's Domain which are beneficial in the beautiful
West, and which are to be spoken on the day of
burial and of going in after coming out.

Hail to you, Bull of the West — so says Thoth, the King of Eternity, of me. I am the Great God, the protector. I have fought for you, for I am one of those gods of the tribunal which vindicated Osiris against his foes on that day of judgment. I belong to your company, O Osiris, for I am one of those gods who fashioned the Children of Nut, who slew the foes of Osiris and who imprisoned those who rebelled against him.

I belong to your company, O Horus, I have fought for you and have watched over your name; I am Thoth who vindicated Osiris against his foes on that day of judgment in the great Mansion of the Prince which is in Heliopolis. I am a Busirite, the son of a Busirite, I was conceived in Busiris, I was born in Busiris when I was with the men who

PLATE 5

THE BOOK OF GOING FORTH BY DAY

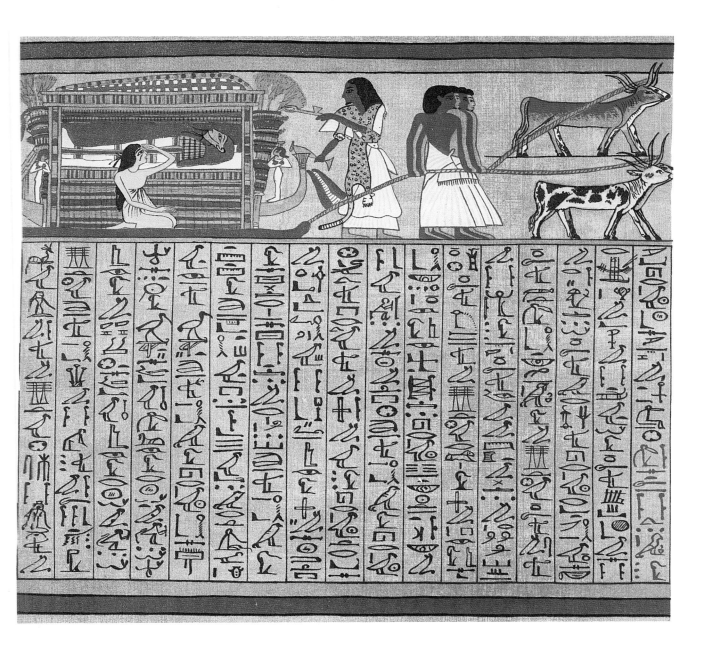

lamented and the women who mourned Osiris on the Shores of the Washerman and who vindicated Osiris against his foes — so they say. O Re, Thoth has vindicated Osiris against his foes — so men say. Thoth has helped me so that I might be with Horus on the day of the clothing of the Dismembered One and of the opening of the caverns for the washing of the Inert One and the throwing open of the door of the secret things in Rosetjau; so that I might be with Horus as the protector of the left arm of Osiris who is in Letopolis. I go in and out among those who are there on the day of crushing the rebels in Letopolis so that I may be with Horus on the day of the Festival of Osiris; offerings are made on the days of the Sixth-day Festival and the Seventh-day Festival in Heliopolis.

I am the priest in Busiris for the Lion-god in the House of Osiris with those who raise up earth; I am he who sees the mysteries in Rosetjau; I am he who reads the ritual book for the Soul in Busiris; I am the Sem-priest at his duties; I am the Master Craftsman on the day of placing the Bark of Sokar on its sledge; I am he who takes the hoe on the day of breaking up the earth in Heracleopolis.

CHAPTER I (*continued*)

O you who cause the perfected souls to draw near to the House of Osiris, may you cause the excellent soul of Ani to draw near with you to the House of Osiris. May he hear as you hear, may he see as you see, may he stand as you stand, may he sit as you sit.

O you who give bread and beer to the perfected souls in the House of Osiris, may you give bread and beer at all seasons to the soul of Ani, who is vindicated with all the gods of the Thinite nome, and who is vindicated with you.

O you who open a path and open up roads for the perfected souls in the House of Osiris, open a path for him, open up roads for the soul of Ani in company with you. May he come in freely, may he go out in peace from the House of Osiris, without being repelled or turned back. May he go in favored, may he come out loved, may he be vindicated, may

his commands be done in the House of Osiris, may he go and speak with you, may he be a spirit with you, may no fault be found in him, for the balance is voided of his misdoings.

— 22 —

*Chapter for giving a mouth to
Ani for him in the God's Domain*

I have arisen from the Egg which is in the secret land, my mouth has been given to me that I may speak with it in the presence of the Great God, Lord of the Duat; my hand shall not be thrust aside in the tribunal of all gods, for I am Osiris, Lord of Rosetjau. I will share with this one who is on the dais, for *I have come for what my heart desires into the Lake of Fire which is quenched for me.*

PLATE 6   THE BOOK OF GOING FORTH BY DAY

— 21 —

Chapter for giving a mouth to
Ani for him in the God's Domain

Hail to you, Lord of Light, preeminent in the Great Mansion, in charge of the twilight! I have come to you spiritualized and pure. Your arms are about you and your portion of food is before you; may you give me my mouth with which I may speak, and may my heart guide me at its hour of destroying the night.

RUBRIC TO CHAPTER 72

As for him who knows this book on earth or it is put in writing on the coffin, it is my word that he shall go out into the day in any shape that he desires and shall go into his place without being turned back, and there shall be given to him bread and beer and a portion of meat from upon the altar of Osiris. He shall enter safely into the Field of Reeds in order to learn this command of Her who is in Busiris, there shall be given to him barley and emmer therein, he shall be hale like he was upon earth, and he shall do what he wishes like those nine gods who are in the Duat. A matter a million times true.

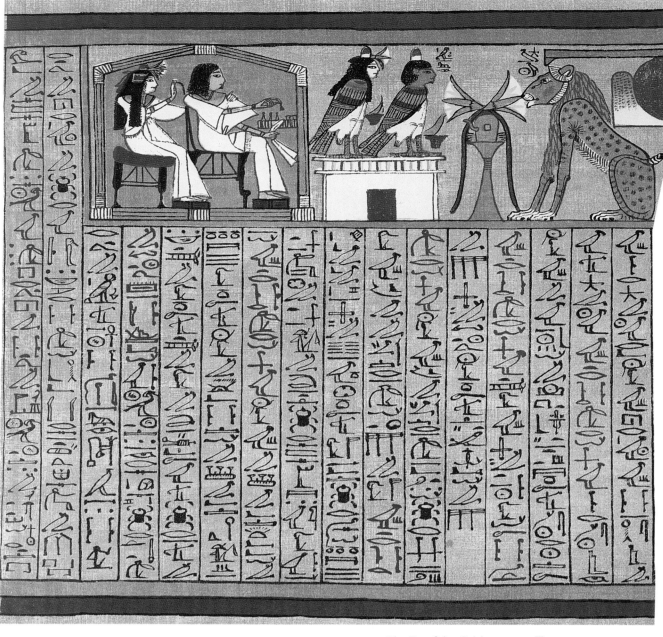

The Ba of the Osiris   Tomorrow

— 17 —

*Here begin praises and recitations, going in
and out of the God's Domain, having benefit in the
beautiful West, being in the suite of Osiris, resting at the
food-table of Wennefer, going out into the day, taking any
shape in which he desires to be, playing at Senet, sitting
in a booth, and going forth as a living soul by the
Osiris Ani after he has died. It is beneficial
to him who does it on earth.*

Now come into being all the words of the Lord of All: I was Atum when I was alone in the Primordial Waters; I was Re in his glorious appearings when he began to rule what he had made.

What does it mean? It means Re when he began to rule what he had made, when he began to appear as king, before the Supports of Shu had come into being, when he was upon the hill which is in Hermopolis, when he destroyed the Children of Impotence on the hill which is in Hermopolis.

I am the Great God, the self-created.

Who is it? The Great God, the self-created, is water, he is Nun, father of the gods. *Otherwise said:* He is Re.

He who created his names, Lord of the Ennead.

Who is he? It is Re who created his names and his members, it means the coming into existence of those gods who are in his suite.

I am he who is not opposed among the gods.

Who is he? He is Atum who is in his sun-disk. *Otherwise said:* He is Re when he rises in the eastern horizon of the sky.

To me belongs yesterday, I know tomorrow.

What does it mean? As for yesterday, that is Osiris. As for tomorrow, that is Re on that day in which the foes of the Lord of All were destroyed and his son Horus was made

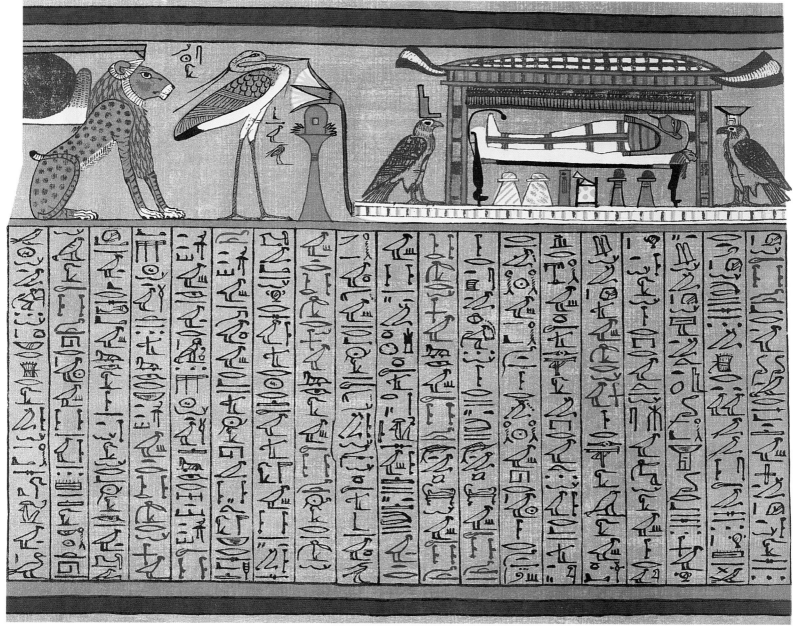

Yesterday   The Benu-bird

to rule. *Otherwise said:* That is the day of the 'We-remain' festival, when the burial of Osiris was ordered by his father Re.

The battle-ground of the gods was made in accordance with my command.

What does it mean? It is the West. It was made for the souls of the gods in accordance with the command of Osiris, Lord of the Western Desert. *Otherwise said:* It means that this is the West, to which Re made every god descend, and he fought the Two for it.

I know that Great God who is in it.

Who is he? He is Osiris. *Otherwise said:* His name is Re, his name is Praise-of-Re, he is the soul of Re, with whom he himself copulated.

I am that great Benu-bird which is in Heliopolis, the supervisor of what exists.

Who is he? He is Osiris. As for what exists, that means his injury. *Otherwise said:* That means his corpse. *Otherwise said:* It means eternity and everlasting. As for eternity, it means daytime; as for everlasting, it means night.

I am Min in his going forth, I have set the plumes on my head.

What does it mean? As for Min, he is Horus who protected his father. As for his going forth, it means his birth. As for his plumes on his head, it means that Isis and Nephthys went and put themselves on his head when they were the Two Kites, and they were firm on his head. *Otherwise said:* They are the two great and mighty uraei which are on the brow of his father Atum.

The Papyrus of Ani   PLATE 7

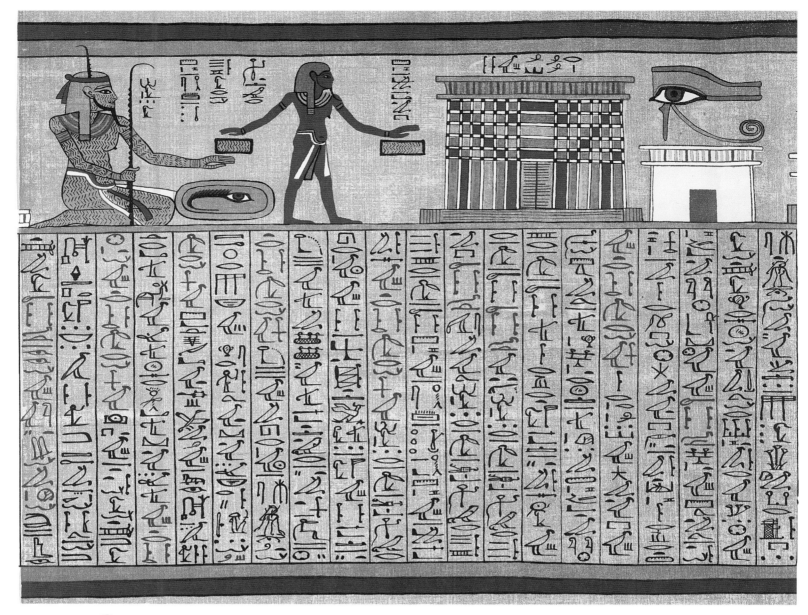

| Heh (Chaos) | The Lake of Natron | River is his Name | Wadj-wer (Ocean) | The Lake of Maet | Rosetjau |

CHAPTER 17 (*continued*)

Otherwise said: The plumes on his head are his eyes.

When I was in my land, I came into my city.

What is it? It is the horizon of my father Atum.

I destroy what was done wrongly against me, I dispel what was done evilly against me.

What does it mean? It means that the navel-string of Ani will be cut.

All the ill which was on me has been removed.

What does it mean? It means that I was cleansed on the day of my birth in the two great and noble marshes which are in Heracleopolis on the day of the oblation by the common folk to the Great God who is in them. *What are they?* 'Chaos-god' is the name of one; 'Sea' is the name of the other. They are the Lake of Natron and the Lake of Maet. *Otherwise said:* 'The Chaos-god governs' is the name of one; 'Sea' is the name of the other. *Otherwise said:* 'Seed of the Chaos-god' is the name of one; 'Sea' is the name of the other. As for that Great God who is in them, he is Re himself.

I go on the road which I know in front of the Island of the Just.

What is it? It is Rosetjau. The southern gate is in Naref, the northern gate is in the Mound of Osiris; as for the Island of the Just, it is Abydos. *Otherwise said:* It is the road on which my father Atum went when he proceeded to the Field of Reeds.

I arrive at the Island of the Horizon-dwellers, I go out from the holy gate.

PLATE 8

THE BOOK OF GOING FORTH BY DAY

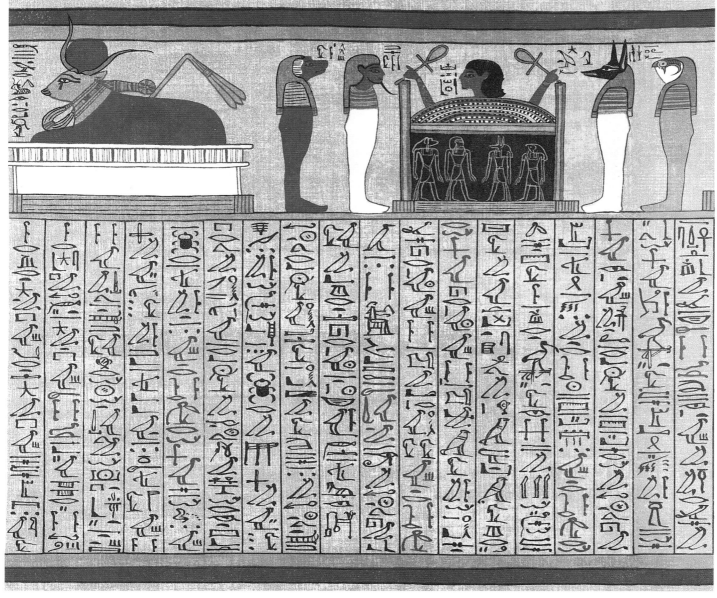

The Great Flood Water,
the Eye of Re

Hapy Imsety The Mound of Abydos Duamutef Qebehsenuef

What is it? It is the Field of Reeds, which produced the provisions for the gods who are round about the shrine. As for that holy gate, it is the gate of the Supports of Shu. *Otherwise said:* It is the gate of the Duat. *Otherwise said:* It is the door through which my father Atum passed when he proceeded to the eastern horizon of the sky.

O you who are in my presence, give me your hands, for indeed I am he who grew up among you.

What does it mean? It means the blood which fell from the phallus of Re when he took to cutting himself. Then there came into being the gods who are in the presence of Re, who are Authority and Intelligence, while I followed after my father Atum daily.

I restored the Sacred Eye after it had been injured on that day when the Rivals fought.

What does it mean? It means the day when Horus fought with Seth when he inflicted injury on Horus's face and when Horus took away Seth's testicles. It was Thoth who did this with his fingers.

I lifted up the hair from the Sacred Eye at its time of wrath.

What does it mean? It means the right Eye of Re when it raged against him after he had sent it out. It was Thoth who lifted up the hair from it when he fetched it in good condition without its having suffered any harm. *Otherwise said:* It means that his Eye was sick

He who sees   He who is under   Horus the   Anubis   Nedjehnedjeh
his father   his moringa tree   Eyeless

CHAPTER 17 (*continued*)

when it wept a second time, and then Thoth spat on it.

I have seen this sun-god who was born yesterday from the buttocks of the Celestial Cow; if he be well, then will I be well, and vice versa.

What does it mean? It means these waters of the sky. *Otherwise said:* It is the image of the Eye of Re on the morning of its daily birth. As for the Celestial Cow, she is the Sacred Eye of Re.

Because I am one of those gods who are in the suite of Horus, who spoke before him all that my lord desired.

Who are they? They are Imsety, Hapy, Duamutef and Qebehsenuef.

Hail to you, Lords of Justice, tribunal which is behind Osiris, who put terror into the doers of wrong, who are in the suite of Her who makes content and protects. Here am I; I have come to you that you may drive out all the evil which is on me just as you did for those seven spirits who are in the suite of the Lord of Sepa, whose places Anubis made ready on that day of 'Come thence.'

| Iakedked | The one in front of his brazier | He who is in his hour | Red-eyed | The Radiant One who sees in the night what he shall bring by day |

Who are they? As for those gods the Lords of Justice, they are Seth and Isdes, Lord of the West. As for the tribunal which is behind Osiris, Imsety, Hapy, Duamutef and Qebehsenuef, it is these who are behind the Great Bear in the northern sky. As for those who put terror into the doers of wrong, who are in the suite of Her who makes content and protects, they are Sobk and those who are in the waters. As for Her who makes content and protects, she is the Eye of Re. *Otherwise said:* She is a flame which follows after Osiris, burning up his enemies. As for all the evil which is on me, it is what I have done among the lords of eternity ever since I came down from my mother's womb. As for these seven spirits, Imsety, Hapy, Duamutef, Qebehsenuef, He who sees his father, He who is under his moringa-tree, and Horus the Eyeless, it is they who were set by Anubis as a protection for the burial of Osiris. *Otherwise said:*

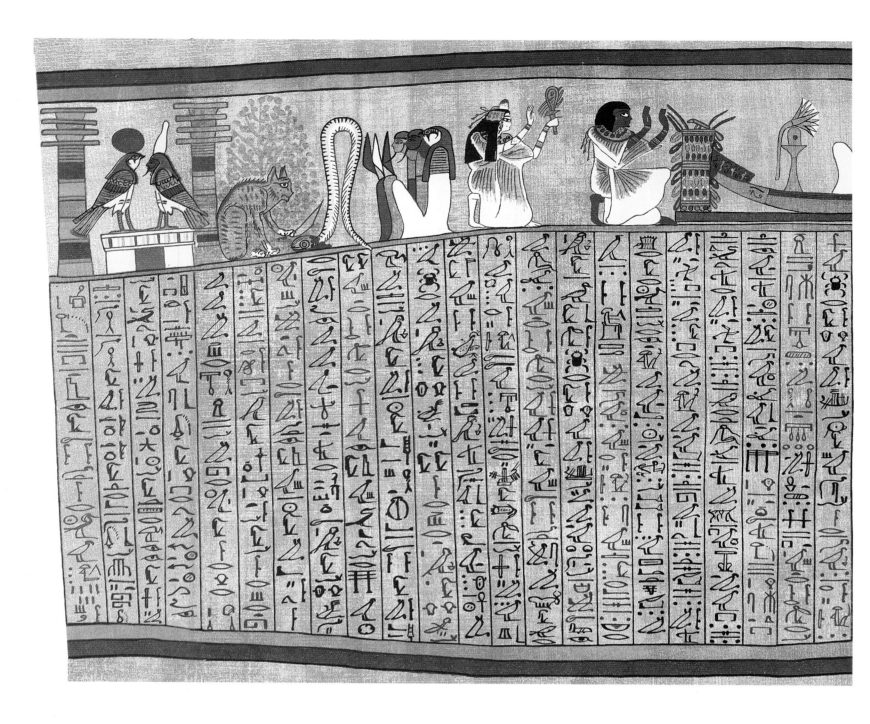

Behind the embalming place of Osiris. *Otherwise said:* As for these seven spirits, they are Nedjehnedjeh, Iakedked, Bull whose flame was set for him in front of his burning, He who entered into him who is in his hour, the Red-eyed who is in the Mansion of Red Linen, the Radiant One who comes out after having turned back, He who sees in the night what he shall bring by day. As for the head of this tribunal, his name is He who subdued the Great One. As for that day of 'Come to me', it means that Osiris said to Re, 'Come to me that I may see you' — so said he in the West.

I am his twin souls which are within the Two Fledglings.

Who is he? He is Osiris when he entered into Mendes. He found the soul of Re there and they embraced each other. Then his twin souls came into being.

[Note: A large section of the chapter is omitted; see Theban Recension.]

Save me from that god who steals souls, who laps up corruption, who lives on what is putrid, who is in charge of darkness, who is immersed in gloom, of whom those who are among the languid ones are afraid.

Who is he? He is Seth. *Otherwise said:* He is the great Wild Bull, he is the soul of Geb.

O Khepri in the midst of your Sacred Bark, primeval one whose body is eternity, save me from those who are in charge of those who are to be examined, to whom the Lord of All has given power to guard against his enemies, who put knives into the slaughterhouses, who do not leave their guardianship; their knives shall not cut into me, I shall not enter into their slaughterhouses, I shall not fall victim to their slaughter-blocks, I shall not sit down in their fish-traps, no harm shall be done to me from those whom the gods detest, because I have passed on, having bathed in the Milky Way, one to whom has been given a meal of the faience which is in the Tjenenet-shrine.

What does it mean? As for Khepri in the midst of his

PLATE 10   THE BOOK OF GOING FORTH BY DAY

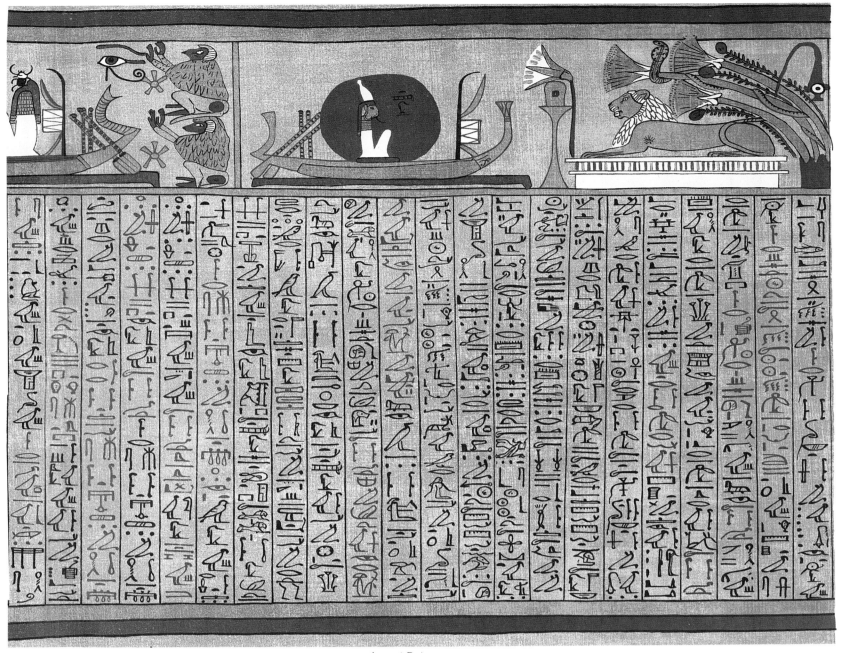

Atum(-Re)

bark, he is Re himself. As for those who are in charge of those who are to be examined, they are the two sun-apes, Isis and Nephthys. As for those things which the gods detest, they are feces and falsehood. As for him who passed on, having bathed in the Milky Way, he is Anubis who is behind the chest which contains the entrails of Osiris. As for him to whom has been given a meal of the faience which is in the Tjenenet-shrine, he is Osiris. As for the meal of faience which is in the Tjenenet-shrine, it is sky and earth. *Otherwise said:* It means that Shu hammered out the Two Lands in Heracleopolis. As for faience, it is the Eye of Horus. As for the Tjenenet-shrine, it is the tomb of Osiris.

How well built is your house, O Atum! How well founded is your mansion, O Double Lion! Run, run to this! If Horus be respected, Seth will be divine, and vice versa. I have come into this land, I have made use of my feet, for I am Atum, I am in my city. Get back, O Lion, bright of mouth and shining of head; retreat because of my strength, take care, O you who are invisible, do not await me, for I am

Isis. You found me when I had disarranged the hair of my face and my scalp was disordered. I have become pregnant as Isis, I have conceived as Nephthys. Isis drives out those who would await me, Nephthys drives off those who would disturb me. The dread of me follows after me, my dignity is before me, millions bend their arms to me, the common folk serve me, the associates of my enemies are destroyed for me, the Grey-haired ones uncover their arms for me, the well-disposed give sweet things to me, those who are in Kheraha and those who are in Heliopolis create things for me. Every god is afraid because so great and mighty is my protection of the god from him who would vilify him. Malachite glitters for me, I live according to my will. As to Wadjet, Lady of the Devouring Flame, she is Re.

[Note: Another section of the chapter is omitted; see Theban Recension.]

from it by the wall of charcoal. Open the way in Rosetjau, so that I might cure the sickness of Osiris, so that I might embrace the one who cut out his own divine standard, who made his way in the valley. O great one, make the path of light for Osiris.'

The second gate: the name of its gatekeeper is 'One who opens up the breast'; the name of its guardian is 'Seqed-face'; the name of the announcer in it is 'Wesed.'

Words spoken by the Osiris Ani, the vindicated, when arriving at the gate: 'He lifts himself up, acting in front of these three, making judgments as a companion of Thoth, and one who protects Thoth. Do not be weary, you just secret ones, you who lived on truth in their years. I am the one weighty of striking power, the one who makes his own way. I have traversed, so make a path for me. May you allow that I pass and rescue. May I see Re among those who make offerings.'

The third gate: the name of its gatekeeper is 'One who Eats the Putrefaction of his Posterior'; the name of its guardian is 'Alert of Face'; the name of the announcer in it is 'Gateway.'

Words spoken by the Osiris Ani, the vindicated, when arriving at the gate: 'I am the secret one of the cloudburst, the one who separated the Two Companions. It is in order that I might drive evil away from Osiris that I have come. I am the one who clothed his own standard, who emerges in the Wereret-crown. I have established offerings in Abydos. Open the way for me in Rosetjau because I have relieved the sickness in Osiris. I have painted his perch. Make way for me so that he might shine in Rosetjau.'

The fourth gate: the name of its gatekeeper is 'One whose Face Repels, One of Multitudinous Voices'; the name of its guardian is 'Alert One'; the name of the announcer in it is 'One who Repels the Crocodile.'

mistress of mankind, the one who distinguishes everyone.' The name of its gatekeeper is 'Child of the Fashioner.'

What is to be said when arriving at the third portal of the temple of Osiris. *Words spoken by* the Osiris Ani, the vindicated: 'O Mistress of Altars, the One Great of Offerings, the one who refreshes every god, who sails south to Abydos.' The name of its gatekeeper is 'Splendid.'

What is to be said when arriving at the fourth portal. *Words spoken by* the Osiris Ani, the vindicated: 'O Mighty of Knives, Lady of the Two Lands, the one who smashes the

enemies of the Weary-hearted One, the one who does what is wise, the one free of wrong.' The name of its gatekeeper is 'Long-Horned Bull.'

What is to be said when arriving at the fifth portal. *Words spoken by* the Osiris Ani, the vindicated: 'O Fiery One, Mistress of Heat, the joyful one, the one to whom the entreaties of the bald-headed do not descend, the one who asks that something be given to her without the swift of glance entering into her.' The name of its gatekeeper is 'One who Spears the Disaffected.'

THE BOOK OF GOING FORTH BY DAY

The first gate: the name of its gatekeeper is 'Inverted of Face, Multitudinous of Forms'; the name of its guardian is 'Eavesdropper'; the name of the announcer in it is 'Hostile-Voiced.'

Words spoken by the Osiris Ani, the vindicated, when arriving at the gate: 'I am the great one who makes his own light. It is so that I might adore you, Osiris, that I have come before you, the one purified by the efflux within you against which the name of Rosetjau was made. Hail to you, Osiris, in your might and power in Rosetjau. Raise yourself up, Osiris, by your might and your power. Raise yourself up, Osiris, in Abydos, so that you might circulate around the sky and that you might row before Re, so that you might see the folk. O you with whom Re has circulated, behold I say, O Osiris, to me belongs the dignity of a god. What I have said happens. My arm shall not be repulsed

What is to be said when arriving at the first portal. *Words spoken by* the Osiris Ani, the vindicated: 'O Mistress of trembling, lofty of enclosure wall, chieftainess and Mistress of Destruction, the one who proclaims words which repel storms, the one who rescues the plundered one who has arrived.' The name of its gatekeeper is 'Terror.'

What is to be said when arriving at the second portal. *Words spoken by* the Osiris Ani, the vindicated: 'O Mistress of the Sky, Lady of the Two Lands, the one who licks, the

PLATE 11

arriving at the gate: 'I have come before you, Osiris, so that I might be pure of evils. May you circulate around the sky, may you see Re. May you see the folk. O unique one, you are in the night bark as he circles the horizon of the sky. I say what I please to his dignity, to his power. It happens just as he says (even if) you repel (me) from him. You have made for me all the goodly paths to you.'

Recitation when reaching the seven gateways. It means that this blessed spirit will be able to enter these portals. He shall not be turned away; he shall not be repelled from Osiris. One shall allow that he be among the blameless blessed spirits in order that he might prevail among the chief followers of Osiris. As to any spirit for whom this is done, he shall be yonder as a lord of eternity in one flesh with Osiris. Do not use for anyone else — take great care!

---

her own lord whose girth is 350 rods, one strewn with Upper Egyptian malachite, the one who lifts up her secret image, who clothes the Weary One, the devourer, the mistress of everyone.' The name of its gatekeeper is 'One who Made Himself.'

What is to be said when arriving at the tenth portal. *Words spoken by* the Osiris Ani, the vindicated: 'O She of Loud Voice, the one whose cries awake, Laugher, Fearsome of Nobility, but whom the one who is in it does not fear.' The name of its gatekeeper is 'Great Embracer.'

PLATE II

Words spoken by the Osiris Ani, the vindicated, when arriving at the gate: 'I am the Bull, the son of the Kite of Osiris. Behold, you witnesses for his father, the possessor of his grace. I have cut off harm from him. I have brought life for him at his nose for eternity. I am the son of Osiris, make a path for me, so that I might pass by in the God's Domain.'

The fifth gate: the name of its gatekeeper is 'He Lives on Worms'; the name of its guardian is 'Shabu'; the name of the announcer in it is 'Hippopotamus-faced, One who Charges Opposite.'

Words spoken by the Osiris Ani, the vindicated, when arriving at the gate: 'I have brought to you the jaws which are in Rosetjau. I have brought to you the backbones. I have united his many parts thereby. I repulsed Apophis for you. I have spat upon his wounds. Make way for me among you, for I am the eldest among the gods, so that I might make purifications for Osiris. I have protected him in triumph. I

have gathered his bones and I have pulled together his limbs.'

The sixth gate: the name of its gatekeeper is 'Seizer of Bread, Raging of Voice'; the name of its guardian is 'One who Brings his own Face'; the name of the announcer in it is 'Sharp of Face, Belonging to the Pool.'

Words spoken by the Osiris Ani, the vindicated, when arriving at the gate: 'I have come today, I have come today. I am the possessor of the Wereret-crown, the assistant of the magicians. I have protected truth. I have protected his eye. I have rescued the eye of Osiris for him. Make way so that the Osiris Ani might go off with you in triumph.'

The seventh gate: the name of its gatekeeper is 'One who Prevails over Knives'; the name of its guardian is 'Great of Triumph'; the name of the announcer in it is 'One who Repels the Demolishers.'

Words spoken by the Osiris Ani, the vindicated, when

What is to be said when arriving at the sixth portal. *Words spoken by* the Osiris Ani, the vindicated: 'O Mistress of Darkness, Loud of Shouting, whose length and breadth cannot be known, whose nature has not been understood since her beginning. There are snakes in it whose number is not known, who were fashioned before the Weary-hearted One.' The name of its gatekeeper is 'United One.'

What is to be said when arriving at the seventh portal. *Words spoken by* the Osiris Ani, the vindicated: 'O Veiling which clothes the Weary One, One who wishes to conceal

the (body).' The name of its gatekeeper is 'Ikety.'

What is to be said when arriving at the eighth portal. *Words spoken by* the Osiris Ani, the vindicated: 'O Heat of Flames, the one who quenches embers, sharp of flames, swift of hand, the one who kills without warning, the one whom no one passes because of the fear of her pain.' The name of its gatekeeper is 'One Who Protects Himself.'

What is to be said when arriving at the ninth portal. *Words spoken by* the Osiris Ani, the vindicated: 'O Foremost One, Mistress of Power, contented of heart, one who bore

The Papyrus of Ani

INTRODUCTION

The praising of Osiris, Lord of Rosetjau, and the Great Ennead which is in the God's Domain by the Osiris scribe Ani. *He says:* Hail to you, O Foremost of the Westerners, Wennefer-dwelling-in-Abydos, I have come before you, my heart bearing truth, without wrongdoing in my body, without saying falsehood knowingly. I have not done a misdeed — (repeat) twice. May you give me bread which comes forth upon the altar of the Possessors of Truth. May I enter into and go forth from the God's Domain, without my Ba being hindered. May I see the sun and may I behold the moon every day.

Words spoken by the Pillar-of-his-Mother Priest, *he says:* I have come before you, O Great Councilors who are in the sky, earth, and the God's Domain, I have brought to you Osiris Ani who is blameless before all the gods, let him be with you every day.

The praising of Osiris, Lord of Eternity, and all the Councilors of Rosetjau by the Osiris scribe Ani, the vindicated. *He says:* Hail to you, King of the God's Domain, Ruler of the Land of Silence, I have come before you, I know your ways, I am equipped with your forms of the Underworld. May you give me a place in the God's Domain in the presence of the Lords of Truth, and a permanent endowment in the Field of Offerings. May I receive offerings in your presence.

Words spoken by the Son-Whom-He-Loves Priest, I have come before you, O Great Councilors who are in Rosetjau, I have brought to you the Osiris Ani. May you give him bread, water and air, and an endowment in the Field of Offerings, like a Follower of Horus.

PLATE 12   THE BOOK OF GOING FORTH BY DAY

O Thoth, who vindicated Osiris against his enemies, vindicate the Osiris Ani, the vindicated, against his enemies in the presence of the council which is with Re and Osiris, and which is in Heliopolis, on that night of the Evening Meal, on that night of battle, at the moment of guarding the rebels, and on that day of destroying the enemies of the Lord of All.

As to 'the Great Council which is in Heliopolis': they are Atum, Shu, and Tefnut.

As to 'the guarding of the rebels': it means the destruction of the gang of Seth when he repeated his offenses.

O Thoth, who vindicated Osiris against his enemies, vindicate the Osiris Ani, the vindicated, against his enemies in the presence of the council which is in Busiris, on that night of erecting the Djed-pillar which is in Busiris.

As to 'the Great Council which is in Busiris': they are Osiris, Isis, Nephthys, and Horus-Avenger-of-his-Father.

As to 'the raising of the Djed-pillar in Busiris': it is the shoulder of Horus-Preeminent-of-Letopolis. They were behind Osiris in binding with cloth.

O Thoth, who vindicated Osiris against his enemies, vindicate the Osiris Ani, the vindicated, against his enemies in the presence of the council which is in Letopolis, on the night of the Evening Meal which is in Letopolis.

CHAPTER 18 (*continued*)

As to 'the Great Council which is in Letopolis': they are Horus-with-no-Eyes-in-his-Forehead and Thoth who is with the Council of Naref.

As to 'that night of the Evening Meal': it is the dawn at the burial of Osiris.

O Thoth, who vindicated Osiris against his enemies, vindicate the Osiris Ani, the vindicated, against his enemies in the presence of the Great Council which is in Pe and Dep, on that night of erecting the Snake Shrine of Horus which was erected for him as an inheritance from the property of his father Osiris.

As to 'the Great Council which is in Pe and Dep': they are Horus, Isis, Imsety, Hapy.

As to 'the erecting of the Snake Shrine of Horus': it means when Seth said to his entourage, 'erect a Snake Shrine for it.'

O Thoth, who vindicated Osiris against his enemies, vindicate the Osiris Ani, the vindicated, against his enemies

PLATE 13   THE BOOK OF GOING FORTH BY DAY

in the presence of the Great Council which is on the Banks of the Washerman on that night of Isis spending the night awake, mourning over her brother Osiris.

As to 'the Great Council which is on the Banks of the Washerman': they are Isis, Horus, and Imsety.

O Thoth, who vindicated Osiris against his enemies, vindicate the Osiris Ani, the vindicated in peace, against his enemies in the presence of the Great Council which is in Abydos on that night of the Haker-festival when the dead are counted and the Blessed Spirits are chosen, when dancing happens in Thinis.

As to 'the Great Council which is in Abydos': they are Osiris, Isis, and Wepwawet.

O Thoth, who vindicated Osiris against his enemies, vindicate the Osiris Ani, Scribe of the Divine Offerings of All the Gods, against his enemies in the presence of the Council who judge the dead on that night of making an accounting of their dead.

CHAPTER 18 (*continued*)

As to 'the Great Council which is at the judging of the dead': they are Thoth, Osiris, Anubis, and Isdes.

As to 'accounting their dead': it means when the offerings were shut off from the souls of the Children of Weakness.

O Thoth, who vindicated Osiris against his enemies, vindicate the Osiris Ani, the vindicated, against his enemies in the presence of the Great Council which is in the hacking up of the earth of Busiris on that night of hacking the earth with their blood and vindicating Osiris against his enemies.

As to 'the Great Council which is in the hacking up of the earth of Busiris': it means the arrival of the Gang of Seth when they made their transformation as goats and when they were sacrificed in the presence of these gods, and the blood which dropped from them was captured and was given to those who are counted among the ones in Busiris. O Thoth, who vindicated Osiris against his enemies, vindicate the Osiris Ani, the vindicated, against his enemies in the presence of the Great Council which is in Naref on that night of secreting of forms.

As to 'the Great Council which is in Naref': they are Re, Shu, and Babai.

As to 'that night of secreting of forms': it was when there was the burial of the forearm, the flanks, and the thighs of Osiris.

PLATE 14   The Book of Going Forth by Day

O Thoth, who vindicated Osiris against his enemies, vindicate the Osiris Ani against his enemies in the presence of the Great Council which is in Rosetjau on that night when Anubis spent the night with his hands upon the offerings about Osiris and Horus was vindicated against his enemies.

As to 'the Great Council which is in Rosetjau': they are Horus, Osiris, Isis and Osiris. The heart of Osiris was pleased, the heart of Horus was gladdened, and the Double Gateway was satisfied with it.

O Thoth, who vindicated Osiris against his enemies, vindicate the Osiris Ani against his enemies in the presence of the Ten Great Councils which is with Re and which is with Osiris, and which is with every god and goddess before the Lord of All when he drives off his enemies and when he drives off every evil which pertains to him.

If one says this Chapter, while pure, it means going forth by day after he has been buried and the assumption of which of his forms he desires. Now as to anyone over whom this incantation is recited, it means being prosperous upon earth; he shall emerge from every fire; nothing evil shall encircle him. A matter a million times true.

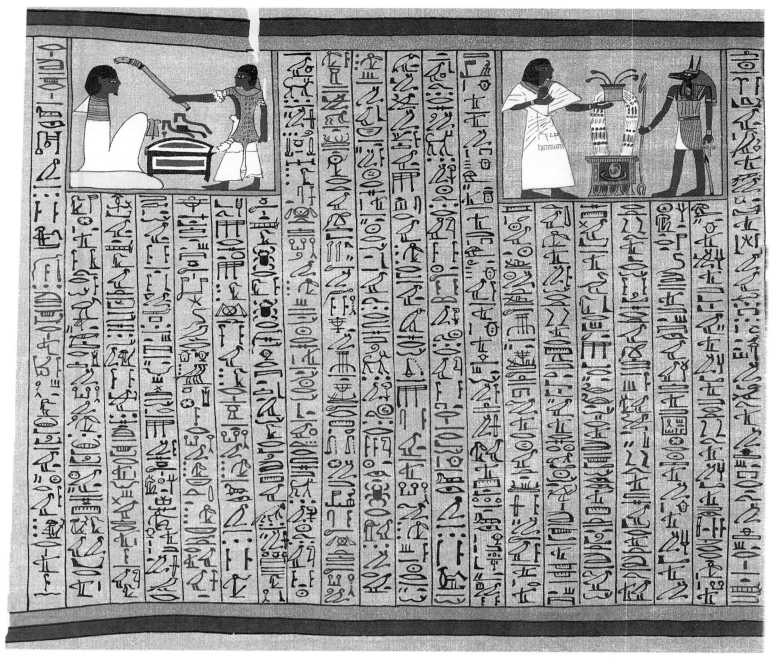

— 23 —
Chapter for opening the mouth of Ani

My mouth is opened by Ptah and what was on my mouth has been loosened by my local god. Thoth comes indeed, filled and equipped with magic, and the bonds of Seth which restricted my mouth have been loosened. Atum has warded them off and has cast away the restrictions of Seth.

My mouth is opened, my mouth is split open by Shu with that iron harpoon of his with which he split open the mouths of the gods. I am Sekhmet, and I sit beside Her who is in the great wind of the sky; I am Orion the Great who dwells with the Souls of Heliopolis.

As for any magic spell or any words which may be uttered against me, the gods *will rise up* against it, even the entire Ennead.

— 24 —
Chapter for bringing magic to Ani

I am Atum-Khepri who came into being of himself upon the lap of his mother Nut, who gave jackals to those who are in the Primordial Waters and hunting-dogs to those who are in the tribunal. *I have collected this magic in every place where it was, from the possession of anyone who possessed it, more speedily* than a hound, more swiftly than a shadow. *O you who bring the ferryboat* of Re, strengthen your rope in the north wind. Ferry upstream to the Island of Fire beside the realm of the dead, *collect this magic* from wherever it may be, from the possession of anyone who may possess it, more speedily than a hound, more swiftly than a shadow. *Transform yourself* into a heron, the mother who created you; the gods are hushed,

your mother has made you warm for the gods. *Now there is given to me* this magic, to whomsoever it may belong, more speedily than a hound, more swiftly than a shadow.

— 26 —
Chapter for giving Ani's heart to him in the God's Domain

My heart is mine in the House of Hearts, my heart is mine in the House of Hearts, my heart is mine, and it is at rest there. I will not eat the cakes of Osiris on the eastern side of the Gay-water in the barge when you sail downstream or upstream, and I will not go aboard the boat in which you are. My mouth will be given to me that I may speak with it, my legs to walk, and my arms to fell my enemy. The doors of the sky are opened for me; Geb, chiefest of the gods, throws open his jaws for me, he opens my eyes which were closed up, he extends my legs which were contracted; Anubis strengthens for me my thighs which were joined together; the goddess Sekhmet stretches me out. I will be in the sky, a command shall be made for my benefit in Memphis, I shall be aware in my heart, I shall have power in my heart, I shall have power in my arms, I shall have power in my legs, I shall have power to do whatever I desire; my soul and my corpse shall not be restrained at the portals of the West when I go in or out in peace.

— 30B —
Chapter for not letting Ani's heart create opposition against him in the God's Domain

O my heart which I had from my mother! O my heart which I had from my mother! O my heart of my different ages! Do

not stand up as a witness against me, do not be opposed to me in the tribunal, do not be hostile to me in the presence of the Keeper of the Balance, for you are my Ka which was in my body, the protector who made my members hale. Go forth to the happy place whereto we speed; do not make my name stink to Entourage who make men. Do not tell lies about me in the presence of the god; it is indeed well that you should hear!

— 61 —
Chapter for not letting a man's soul be taken away from him in the God's Domain

I am he, I am he who came forth from the flood, to whom abundance was given, that I might have power thereby over the River.

— 54 —
Chapter for giving breath to Ani in the God's Domain

O Atum, give me the sweet breath which is in your nostril, for I am this Egg which is in the Great Cackler, I am the guardian of this great being who separates the earth from the sky. If I live, she will live; I grow young, I live, I breathe the air. I am he who splits iron, I go round about the Egg, tomorrow is mine through the striking-power of Horus and the strength of Seth. O you who sweeten the state of the Two Lands, you with whom are provisions, you with whom is lapis-lazuli, beware of Him who is in his nest; the Youth goes forth against you.

— 29 —
Chapter for not permitting a man's heart to be taken away from him in the God's Domain

Get back, you messenger of any god! Have you come to take away this heart of mine which belongs to the living? I will not let you take away this heart of mine which belongs to the living who move about. The gods who rest for me have heard, falling headlong on their faces . . . in their own land.

— 27 —
Chapter for not permitting a man's heart to be taken from him in the God's Domain

O you who take away hearts and accuse bosoms, who recreate a man's heart (in respect of) what he has done, he is forgetful of himself through what you have done. Hail to you, lords of eternity, founders of everlasting! Do not take Ani's heart with your fingers wherever his heart may be. You shall not raise any matter harmful to him, because as for this heart of Ani, this heart belongs to one whose names are great, whose words are mighty, who possesses his members. He sends out his heart which controls his body, his heart is announced to the gods, for Ani's heart is his own, he has power over it, and he will not say what he has done. He himself has power over his members, his heart obeys him, for he is your lord and you are in his body, you shall not turn aside. I command you to obey me in the realm of the dead, even I, Ani, who am vindicated in peace and vindicated in the beautiful West in the domain of eternity.

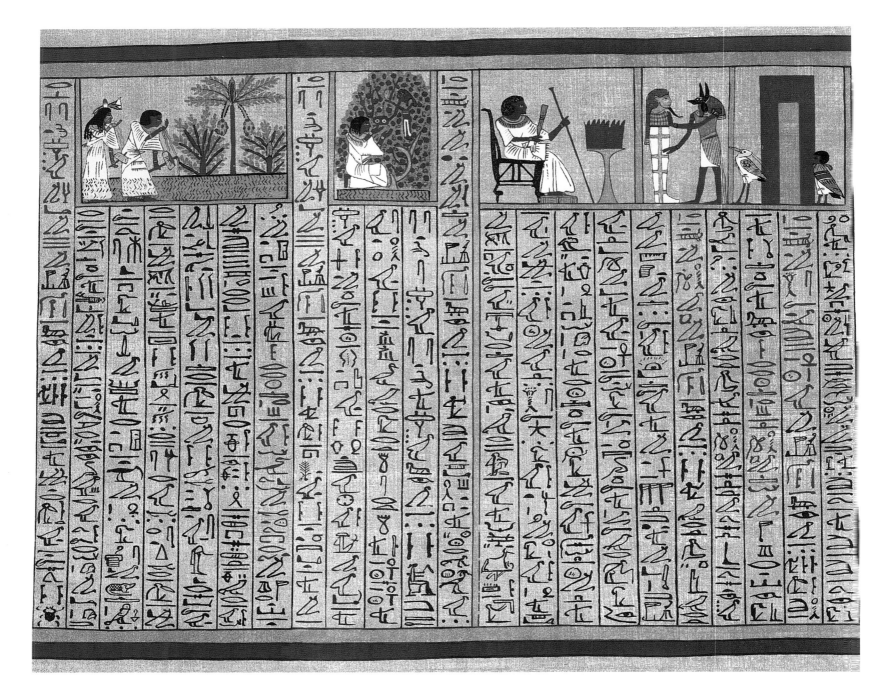

— 58 —

Chapter for breathing air and having
power over water in the God's Domain

Open to me!

Who are you? What are you? Where did you grow up?

I am one of you.

Who is with you?

It is the two Songstress-serpents.

You shall separate head from head when approaching the Milky Way.

I shall cross to the Mansion of Him who finds faces; 'Collector of souls' is the name of the ferryman, 'Tresses of hair' is the name of the oars, 'Thorn' is the name of the bailer; 'Precise and accurate' is the name of the steering oar, like him who smoothed things over when you buried yourself in the waters; you shall give me a jug of milk, a Shens-loaf, a Persen-loaf, a jug of beer, and a portion of meat in the Mansion of Anubis.

As for him who knows this chapter, he will go in after coming
out in the cemetery of the beautiful West.

— 59 —

Chapter for breathing air and having
power over water in the God's Domain

O you sycamore of the sky, may there be given to me the air which is in it, for I am he who sought out that throne in the middle of Wenu and I have guarded this Egg of the Great

Cackler. If it grows, I will grow; if it lives, I will live; if it breathes the air, I will breathe the air.

— 44 —

Chapter for not dying again in the God's Domain

My cavern is opened, the spirits fall within the darkness. The Eye of Horus makes me holy, Wepwawet has caressed me; O Imperishable Stars, hide me among you. My neck is Re, my vision is cleared, my heart is in its proper place, my speech is known.

THE GOD RE SPEAKS: I am Re who himself protects himself; I do not know you, I do not look after you, your father the son of Nut lives for you.

THE DECEASED REPLIES: I am your eldest son who sees your secrets, I have appeared as King of the Gods, and I will not die again in the God's Domain.

— 45 —

Chapter for not putrefying in the God's Domain

Weary, weary are the members of Osiris! They shall not be weary, they shall not putrefy, they shall not decay, they shall not swell up! May it be done to me in like manner, for I am Osiris.

As for him who knows this chapter, he shall not putrefy in
Osiris's God's Domain.

PLATE 16   THE BOOK OF GOING FORTH BY DAY

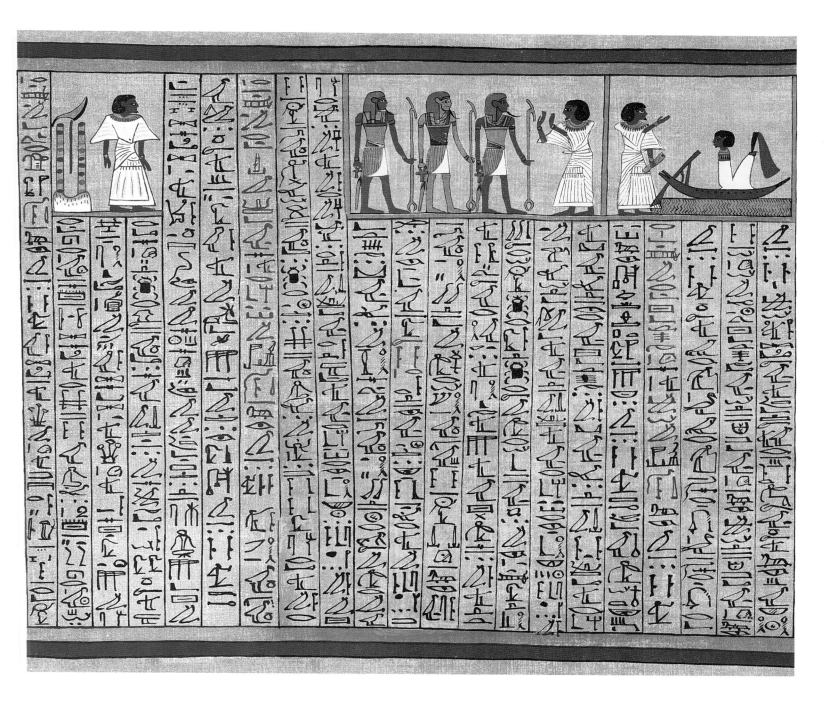

— 46 —
Chapter for not perishing and for being alive in the God's Domain

O you young men of Shu of the morning, who have power over those who flash among the sun-folk, whose arms move about and whose heads sway to and fro; may I move about every day.

— 50 —
Chapter for not entering into the slaughterhouse of the god

The four knots are tied about me by the guardian of the sky. He has made the knot firm for the Inert One on his thighs on that day of cutting off the lock of hair.

The knot was tied about me by Seth, in whose power the Ennead were at first, before uproar had come into being, when he caused me to be hale.

The knot was tied about me by Nut, when I first saw Maat, when the gods and the sacred images had not yet been born. I am a heavenborn, I am in the presence of the Great Gods.

— 93 —
Chapter for not letting a man be ferried over to the East in the God's Domain

O you phallus of Re, this which is injured by uproar, whose inertness came into being through Babai, I am stronger thereby than the strong ones, I am mightier thereby than the mighty ones. If I be ferried over and taken to the East with bound horns, or if any injury be done to me by rebels, I will swallow up the phallus of Re and the head of Osiris, I will be guided to the tomb of the decapitation of the gods in which they make answer; I will bind the horns of Khepri, I will become the stone in the Eye of Atum the Destroyer if I be seized and ferried over to the East, if the festival of the rebels be celebrated over me, or if anything terrible be evilly done to me.

— 43 —
Chapter for preventing a man's decapitation in the God's Domain

I am a Great One, the son of a Great One, I am a flame, the son of a flame, to whom was given his head after it had been cut off. The head of Osiris shall not be taken from him, and my head shall not be taken from me. I am knit together, just and young, for I indeed am Osiris, the Lord of Eternity.

Chapter for letting a soul
rejoin its corpse in the God's Domain

O you who bring, you who run, you who are in the booth of the Great God, let my soul come to me from anywhere it is. If the bringing of my soul to me from anywhere it is be delayed, you will find the Eye of Horus standing up thus against you. O you Osirians, if you do not sleep, then will I not sleep in Heliopolis, the land of thousands of abodes. My soul shall be taken to me, and my spirit shall be vindicated with it wherever it may be.

Come for my soul, O you wardens of the sky! If you delay letting my soul see my corpse, you will find the Eye of Horus standing up thus against you. O you gods who are dragged in the Bark of the Lord of Millions of Years, who bring the Upper Sky to the Duat and who raise up the Lower Sky, who let souls draw near to the noble dead, may your hands be filled with your ropes, may your grip be on your harpoons, may you drive off the enemy. The Sacred Bark will be joyful and the Great God will proceed in peace when you allow this soul of mine to ascend vindicated to the gods, while your buttocks are in the eastern horizon of the sky, so as to follow in peace to the place where it was yesterday, to the West. May it see my corpse, may it rest on my mummy, which will never be destroyed or perish.

To be spoken over a human-headed bird of gold inlaid with semi-precious stones and laid on the breast of the deceased.

Chapter for not restraining
Ani's soul in the God's Domain

O you who are on high, who are worshipped, whose power is great, a Ram greatly majestic, the dread of whom is put into the gods when you appear on your great throne: you shall make a way for me and my soul, my spirit and my shade, for I am equipped. I am a worthy spirit; make a way for me to the place where Re and Hathor are.

As for him who knows this chapter, he shall become an equipped spirit in the God's Domain, he shall not be restrained at any gate of the West whether coming or going. A true matter.

PLATE 17   THE BOOK OF GOING FORTH BY DAY

— 92 —

Chapter for opening the tomb to Ani's
soul and shade so that he may go out into
the day and have power in his legs.

Open and close! O you who sleep, open and close for my soul according to the command of Horus. O Eye of Horus, save me, establish my beauty on the vertex of Re. O Far-strider whose legs extend, make a way for me here, for my flesh is made ready.

I am Horus who protects his father, I am he who brought his father and who brought his mother with his staff; open a way for one who has power in his legs, who sees the Great God within the Bark of Re wherein souls are examined at the beginning of the reckoning of years. Save my soul for me, O Eye of Horus, who fixes ornaments on the vertex of Re. When the dusk is in your sight, you wardens of Osiris, do not restrain my soul or hold back my shade; open a way for my soul and my shade, that it may see the Great God within the shrine on the day of examining souls. May it speak again to Osiris. O you whose seats are hidden, wardens of the limbs of Osiris, who hold back spirits and who shut up the shades of the dead, and who would harm me, you shall not harm me. 'Go far away, because your Ka is with you as a soul,' say the wardens of the limbs of Osiris who hold back the shades of the dead, 'lest you be grasped by the sky and restrained by the earth; may the slayers not be with you, for you have power in your legs. Be far away from your corpse which is on earth.'

Get back, you who guard the tomb of Osiris!

As to one who knows this chapter, he shall go forth by day and his Ba shall not be restrained.

The Papyrus of Ani

PLATE 17

— 74 —
Chapter for being swift-footed when going out from the earth

May you do what you are wont to do, O Sokar who are in your Mansion, possessing a foot in the God's Domain. I shine in the sky, I ascend to the sky; though I am inert, I climb on the sunshine; though I am inert, I walk on the riverbanks . . . in the God's Domain.

— 8 —
Chapter for opening up the West by day

Hermopolis is opened and my head is sealed. O Thoth, the Eye of Horus is unblemished, the Eye of Horus saves me, and splendid are my ornaments from the brow of Re, father of the gods; I am this Osiris here in the West. Osiris knows his day, and if he does not exist in it, then I will not exist in it. I am Re who is with the gods and I will not perish; stand up, Horus, that I may number you among the gods.

— 2 —
Chapter for going out into the day and living after death

O you Sole One who shine in the moon, O you Sole One who glow in the sun, may Ani go forth from among those multitudes of yours who are outside, may those who are in the sunshine release him, may the Duat be opened to him when Ani goes out into the day in order to do what he wishes on earth among the living.

— 9 —
Chapter for going out into the day after opening the tomb

O you Soul, greatly majestic, behold, I have come that I may see you; I open the Duat that I may see my father Osiris and drive away darkness, for I am beloved of him.

I have come that I may see my father Osiris and that I may cut out the heart of Seth who has harmed my father Osiris. I have opened up every path which is in the sky and on earth, for I am the well-beloved son of my father Osiris. I am noble, I am a spirit, I am equipped; O all you gods and all you spirits, prepare a path for me.

PLATE 18   THE BOOK OF GOING FORTH BY DAY

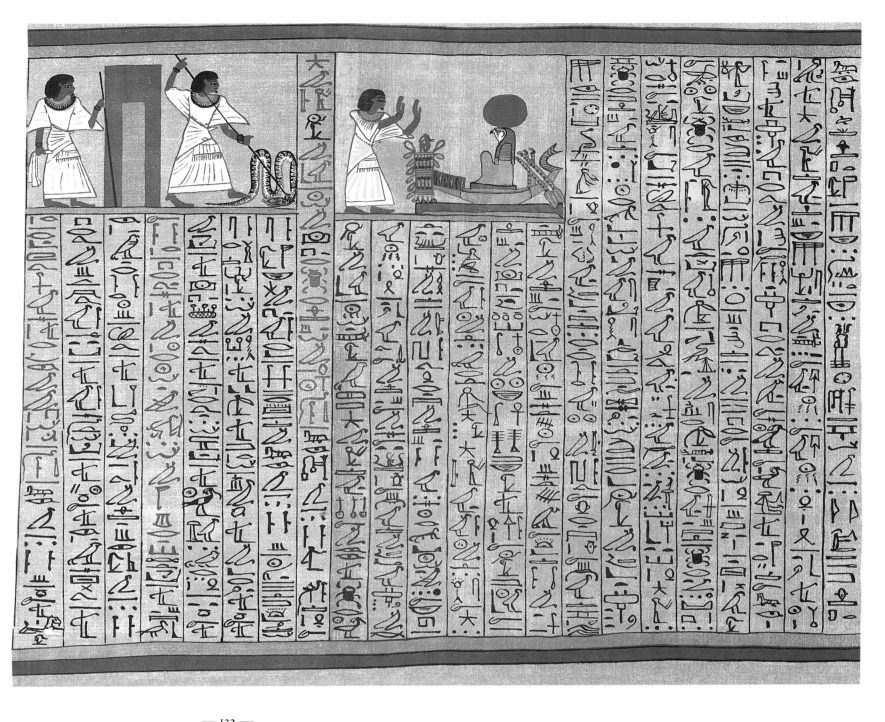

— 132 —
Chapter for causing a man to
turn about in order to see his house upon earth

I am the Lion who went out with a bow, I have shot and I
have . . . The Eye of Horus belongs to me, I have opened
the Eye of Horus at this time, I have reached the riverbank.
Come in peace, O Ani.

— 10 —
Another chapter for a man's going out into
the day against his foes in the God's Domain

I have dug up the sky, I have hacked up the horizon, I have
traversed the earth to its furthest extent, I have taken
possession of the spirits of the great ones, because I am one
who equips a myriad with my magic. I eat with my mouth,
I defecate with my hinder-parts, for I am a god, lord of the
Duat. I have given those things which were established in
the past, I have planned appearance in glory.

— 15 —
Worship of Re when he rises in the horizon
until the occurrence of his setting in life

Hail to you, O Re, at your rising, O Atum-Horakhty! Your
beauty is worshipped in my eyes when the sunshine comes
into being over my breast. You proceed at your pleasure in
the Night-bark, your heart is joyful with a fair wind in the
Day-bark, being happy at crossing the sky with the blessed
ones. All your foes are overthrown, the Unwearying Stars
acclaim you, the Imperishable Stars worship you when you
set in the horizon of Manu, being happy at all times, and
living and enduring as my lord.

Hail to you, O Re when you rise and Atum when you
set. How beautiful are your rising and your shining on the
back of your mother Nut, you having appeared as King of
the Gods. The Lower Sky has greeted you, Justice embraces
you at all times. You traverse the sky happily, and the Lake
of the Two Knives is in contentment. The rebel has fallen,
his arms are bound, a knife has severed his spine, but Re will
have a fair wind, for the Night-bark has destroyed those
who would attack him. The southerners, northerners, westerners, and easterners tow you because of the praise of you,
O primeval god, whose images have come into being. The
voice goes forth, and the earth is inundated with silence, for
the Sole One came into existence in the sky before the plains
and the mountains existed. The Herdsman, the Sole Lord,
who made whatever exists, he has fashioned the tongue of
the Ennead. O you who took what is in the waters, you
issue thence onto the bank of the Lake of Horus. I breathe
the air which comes out of your nose, the north wind which
comes forth from your mother. You glorify my spirit, you
make the Osiris my soul divine. I worship you; be content,
O Lord of the Gods, for you are exalted in your firmament,
and your rays over my breast are like the day.

TEXT ABOVE TUTU:
The Mistress of the House, the
Songstress of Amun, Tutu

TEXT ABOVE ANI:
Osiris, true Royal Scribe, the one
whom he (i.e. the King) loves, the
Scribe of the Divine Offering of
All the Gods, Ani triumphant

CHAPTER 15 (*continued*)

AN ADDRESS TO OSIRIS IN VARIOUS ASPECTS

Hail to you, Starry One in Heliopolis; Sun-folk in Kheraha; Wenti more powerful than the gods; Mysterious One in Heliopolis.

Hail to you, Heliopolitan in Iun-des; Great One; Horakhty the Far-Strider when he crosses the sky: he is Horakhty.

Hail to you, Ram of Eternity, Ram who is Mendes, Wennefer son of Nut: he is Lord of the Silent Land.

Hail to you in your rule of Busiris, the Wereret-crown is firm on your head: you are the Sole One who makes his own protection, and you rest in Busiris.

Hail to you, Lord of the Naret-tree; Sokar is placed on his sledge, the rebel who did evil is driven off, and the Sacred Eye is set at rest in its place.

Hail to you, strong in your power, the great and mighty one who presides over Naref, Lord of Eternity, maker of everlastingness: you are Lord of Heracleopolis.

Hail to you who are pleased with justice: you are Lord of Abydos, and your flesh has enriched the Sacred Land; you are he who detests falsehood.

Hail to you, occupant of the Sacred Bark, who brings the Nile from its cavern, over whose corpse the sun has shone; you are he who is in Nekhen.

Hail to you who made the gods, the vindicated King of Upper and Lower Egypt Osiris, who founded the Two

Lands with his potent deeds: you are Lord of the Two Banks.

May you give me a path that I may pass in peace, for I am straightforward and true; I have not wittingly told lies, I have not committed a second fault.

A HYMN TO OSIRIS

Worship of Osiris, Lord of Eternity, Wennefer.

Horakhty multiple of forms and great of shapes, Ptah-Sokar, Atum in Heliopolis, Lord of the Shetyt-shrine, who enriches Memphis; these are the gods who govern the Duat; they protect you when you go to rest in the Lower Sky. Isis embraces you in peace and drives away the adversary from your path. Turn your face to the West that you may illumine the Two Lands with fine gold. Those who were asleep stand up to look at you; they breathe the air, they see your face like the shining of the sun-disk in its horizon, their hearts are at peace because of what you have done, for to you belong eternity and everlasting.

The Papyrus of Ani

PLATE 19

CHAPTER 15 (*continued*)

ANOTHER HYMN TO THE SUN

Worship of Re when he rises in the eastern horizon
of the sky, when those who are in his following are joyful.

O Sun-disk, Lord of the sunbeams, who shines forth from the horizon every day: may you shine in the face of Ani, for *he worships you* in the morning, he propitiates you in the evening. May the soul of Ani go up with you to the sky, may he travel in the Day-bark, may he moor in the Night-bark, may he mix with the Unwearying Stars in the sky.

The Osiris Ani *says* when he honors his lord, the Lord of Eternity:

Hail to you, Horakhty, Khepri the self-created! How beautiful is your shining forth from the horizon when you illumine the Two Lands with your rays! All the gods are in joy when they see you as king of the sky, the royal serpent being firm on your head and the crowns of Upper and Lower Egypt on your vertex; she (the serpent) has made her seat on your brow. Thoth is established in the bow of your Sacred Bark, destroying all your foes, while those who are in the Duat have come out to meet you and to see this beautiful image.

I have come to you and I am with you in order to see your disk every day; I will not be restrained or repulsed, but my flesh will be renewed at seeing your beauty, like all those whom you favor, for I was one of those who were well esteemed by you on earth. I have arrived at the land of eternity, I have joined myself to the land of everlasting, and it is you who commanded it for me, O my lord.

PLATE 20   THE BOOK OF GOING FORTH BY DAY

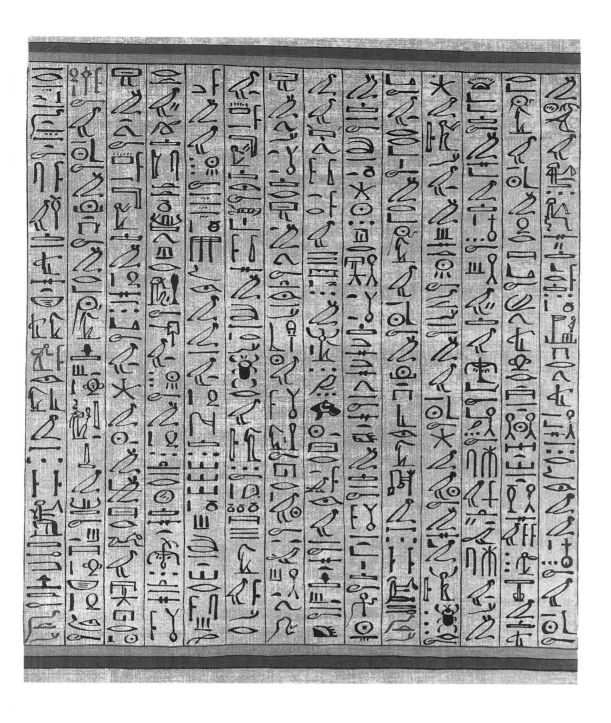

Hail to you when you rise in your horizon as Re who is pleased with justice; when you cross the sky, all men see you, after your movements have been hidden from their sight. You display yourself from morning till evening on the day when celestial navigation with Your Majesty is successful; your rays are in men's faces, and fine gold does not know them, pigment does not report them when you illumine the lands of the gods, and it has not been seen in writing; the mountains of Punt disclose Him who was hidden. You did it alone when Ani's mouth was opened, and your shape was upon the primeval waters. He will travel just as you travel, and there will be no ceasing for him as for Your Majesty, not even for a little day, for you have passed through seasons of millions and hundreds of thousands of moments; when you have spent them you have gone to rest, you have also completed the hours of the night, and you have regulated and completed them according to your regular custom. The land becomes bright when you reveal yourself in your place as Re when he arises in the horizon.

The Osiris Ani *says* when he worships you at your shining, and speaks to you when you rise early to set your shape on high: You appear in glory in magnifying your beauty, creating yourself; you mold your own flesh. One who fashions but is not fashioned, as Re who shines in the sky. May you permit me to reach the eternal sky, the country of the favored; may I join with the august and noble spirits of the God's Domain; may I ascend with them to see your beauty when you shine in the evening.

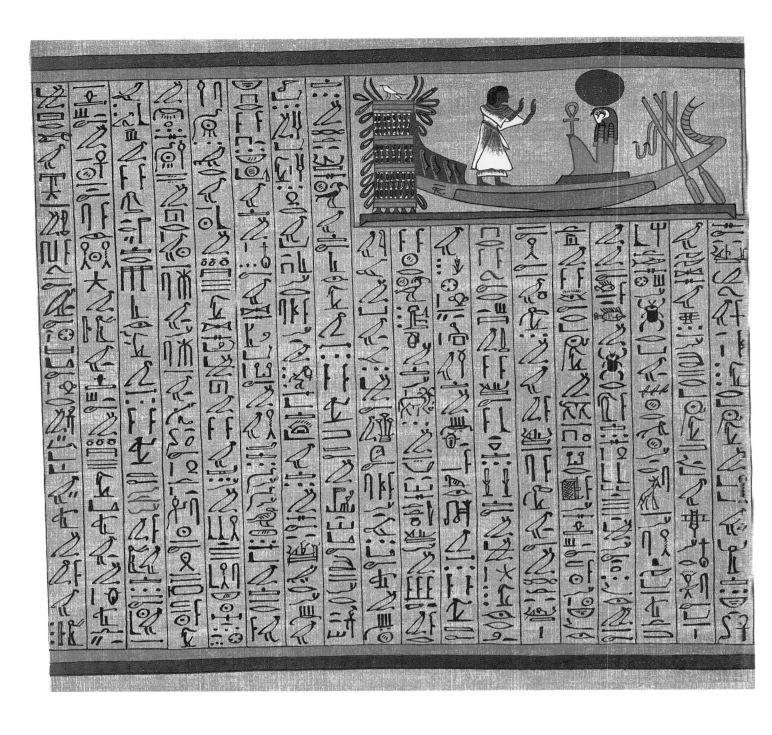

CHAPTER 15 (*continued*)

Your mother traverses for you the Lower Sky when you are placed in the West, and my arms are upraised in adoration at your setting, for you are he who made eternity. I worship you when you set in the Primordial Water, and I set you in my heart which is not inert, O you who are more divine than the gods. Praise to you who rise in gold and who illumine the Two Lands by day at your birth! Your mother Nut has borne you on her hand, and what the sun-disk encircles is bright because of you. Great Illuminator who shines forth from the Primordial Water, who knits his family together in the waters, who makes festal all estates, towns, and households, who protects with his goodness, may your spirit be sustained with food and provisions. Greatly feared, Power of Powers, whose throne is far from the evildoers; greatly majestic in the Night-bark, mightily long-lasting in the Day-bark, may you glorify Ani in the God's Domain, may you cause him to endure in the West, he being devoid of evil. May you ignore my wrongdoing and may you set me as one honored with the spirits; may you protect my soul in the Sacred Land, may it navigate in the Field of Reeds, because I have passed on in joy.

THE GOD REPLIES: You shall ascend to the sky, you shall traverse the firmament, you shall associate with the stars, who shall make acclamation to you in the Sacred Bark. You shall be summoned into the Day-bark, you shall see Re within his shrine, you shall propitiate his disk daily, you shall see the Inet-fish in its shape in the stream of turquoise, you shall see the Abdju-fish in being, the serpent of evil having fallen according as was foretold for him, the sharp knives having cut his spine apart for me. Re shall sail with a fair wind, and the Night-bark shall be wiped clean for me. The crew of Re shall reach him with joy, and the Lady of Life will be happy when the hostile serpent has fallen to her lord. You shall see Horus whose face is kindly, with the standards of Thoth and Maat on his hands; all the gods will be in joy when they see Re coming in peace to vivify the hearts of the spirits, and the vindicated Osiris Ani shall be with them.

PLATE 21   THE BOOK OF GOING FORTH BY DAY

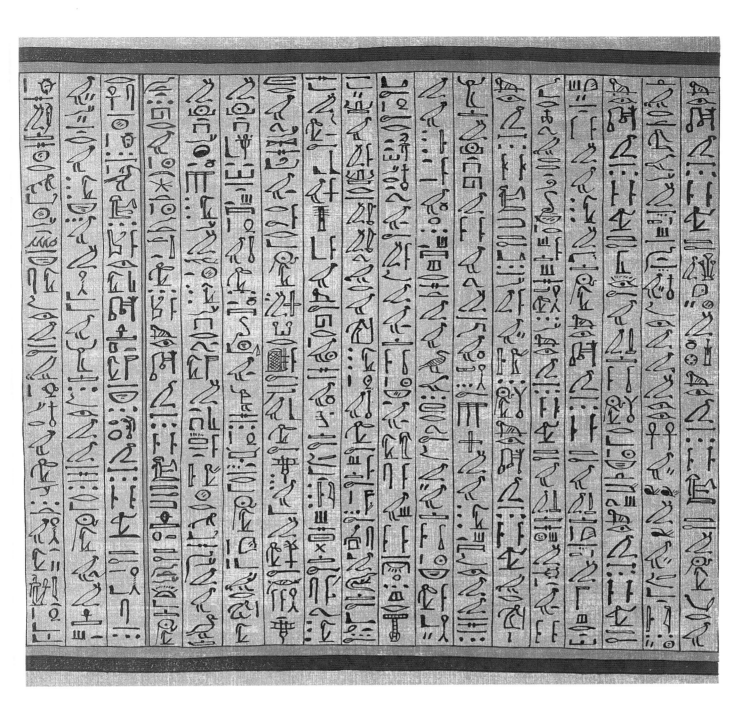

Writing for making a spirit worthy;
to be recited on the first of the month

Re appears in his horizon, his Ennead following after him; the god issues from the secret place, and trembling falls on the eastern horizon of the sky at the voice of Nut; she clears the ways for Re before the Oldest One, who turns about. Raise yourself, O Re who are in your shrine, that you may lap up the breezes. May you swallow the north wind, may you swallow the spine, may you entrap the day, may you kiss Maat, may you divide your suite, may you sail the Sacred Bark to the Lower Sky, may the Elders run to and fro at your voice; may you reckon up your bones, may you gather your members together, may you turn your face to the beautiful West, may you return anew every day, for you are that golden image which bears the likeness of the sun-disk, the sky being possessed with trembling at your recurrence every day. The horizon is joyful, and there is acclamation within your bounds.

As for the gods who are in the sky who behold Ani, they have offered up praise as though to Re, for Ani is a great one who seeks out the Wereret-crown of Re and reckons up his needs; Ani is one alone whose affairs flourish in that first company of those who are in the presence of Re; Ani is hale on earth and in the God's Domain, Ani is hale like Re every day, Ani will run and will not tire in this land forever. How happy are those who see with their eyes and who hear truth with their ears as Re and who ply the oar in the

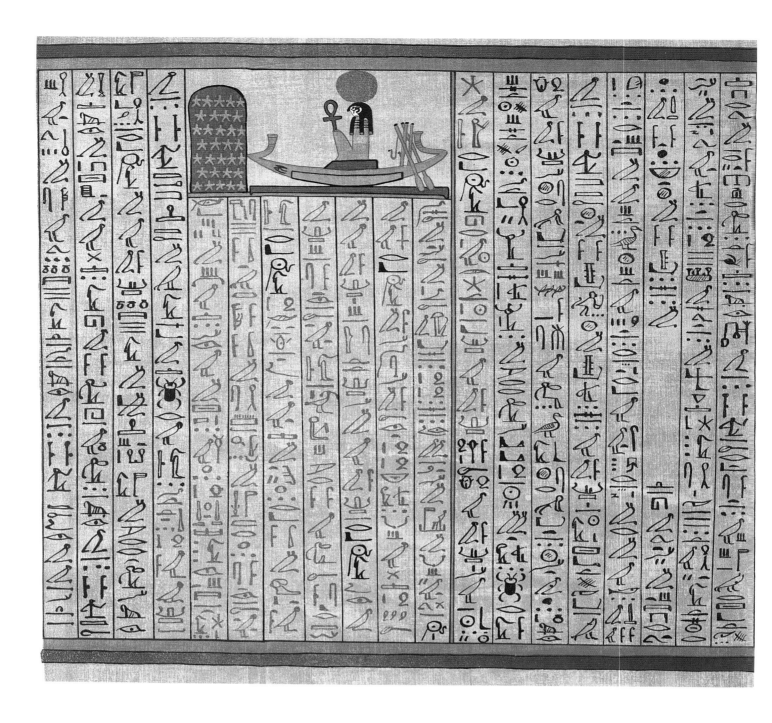

CHAPTER 133 (*continued*)

suite of Nun! Ani will not tell what he has seen nor will he repeat what he has heard of the secret matters, and there is acclamation for Ani. The god's body of Re crosses the Primordial Water among those who propitiate the will of the god with what he has desired, and Ani is a falcon whose shape is great.

To be spoken over a Sacred Bark of four cubits' length made of pieces of malachite, and having upon it the tribunal of the nomes. There shall be made a sky with stars purified with natron and incense. Make an image of Re with ochre in a new bowl placed in front of this bark, and put an image of this spirit which you desire to be made worthy within this bark; it means that he will sail in the Bark of Re, and that Re himself will see him in it. This spirit will be deemed worthy in the heart of Re, he will

be caused to have power over the Ennead, and they will be with him; the gods will see him as one of themselves, the dead will see him, and they will fall on their faces when he is seen in the realm of the dead by means of the rays of the sun.

— 134 —

Praising Re on the (first) day
of the month and sailing in the divine bark

Hail to Him who dwells in his shrine, who rises and shines, who imprisons myriads at his will and who gives commands to the sun-folk, Khepri who dwells in his Bark, for he has felled *Apophis*. It is the children of Geb who will fell you, you enemies of Ani, who would demolish the Bark of Re.

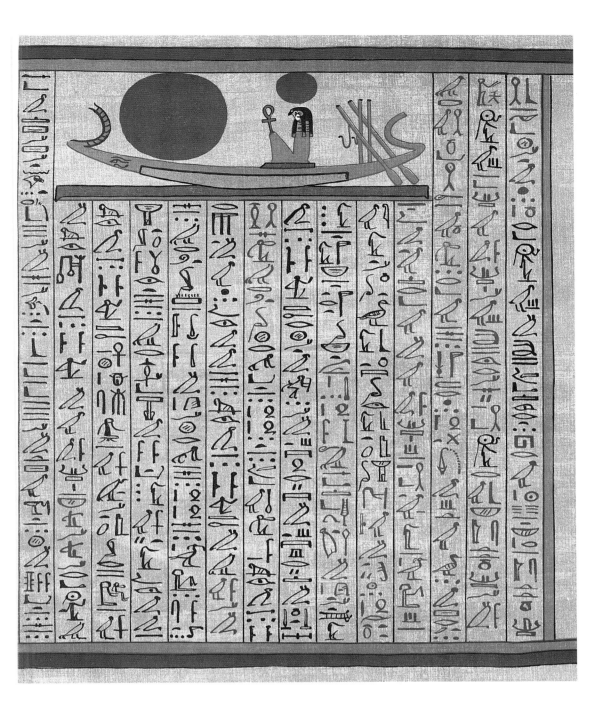

Horus has cut off their heads in the sky like birds, and their goat-buttocks are in the Lake of Fish. As for any male or female adversary who would do harm to Ani, whether he is one who shall descend from the sky or ascend from the earth, who shall come by water or travel in company with the stars, Thoth the son of an eggshell who came out of the two eggshells shall decapitate them. Be dumb, be deaf before Ani! This is Re, this god mightily terrible and greatly majestic; he will bathe in your blood, he will drink of your gore, O you who would do much harm to Ani in the Bark of his father Re. Ani is Horus; his mother Isis bore him, Nephthys nursed him, just as they did for Horus, in order to drive away the confederacy of Seth, and they see the Wereret-crown firm-planted on his head. The spirits of men and gods and the spirits of the dead fall on their faces when they see Ani as Horus, with the Wereret-crown firm-planted on his head; they fall on their faces when Ani is triumphant over his enemies in the Upper Sky and the Lower Sky and in the tribunals of every god and every goddess.

To be spoken over a falcon standing with the White Crown on his head; Atum, Shu and Tefnut, Geb and Nut, Osiris and Isis, Seth and Nephthys being drawn in ochre on a new bowl placed in the Sacred Bark, together with an image of this spirit whom you wish to be made worthy, it being anointed with oil. Offer to them incense on the fire and roasted ducks, and worship Re. It means that he for whom this is done will voyage and be with Re every day in every place he desires to travel, and it means that the enemies of Re will be driven off in very deed. A matter a million times true.

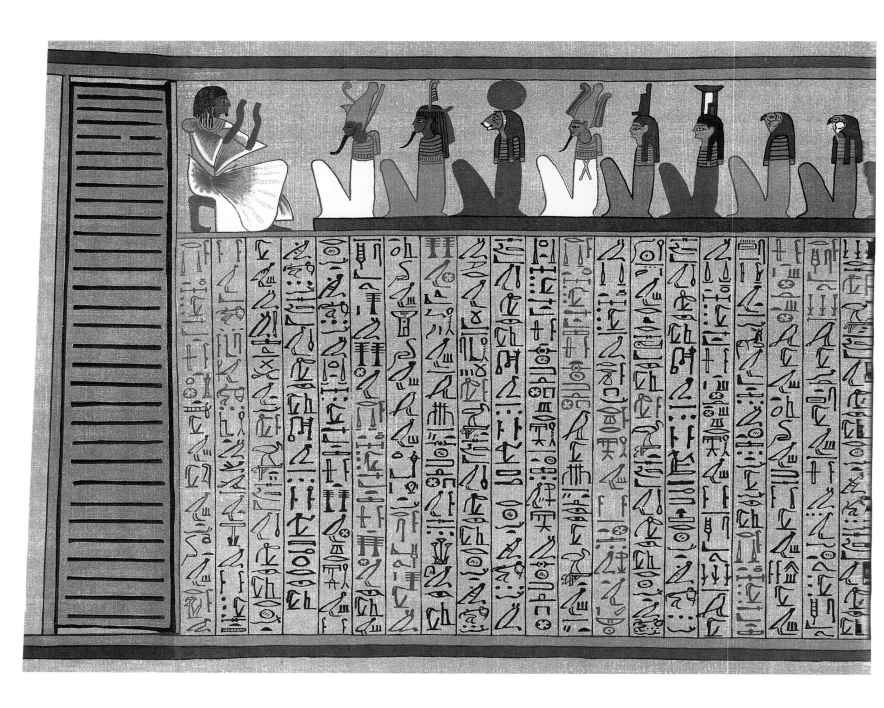

O Thoth, who vindicated Osiris against his enemies, vindicate the Osiris Ani, the vindicated, against his enemies in the presence of the council which is with Re and Osiris, and which is in Heliopolis, on that night of the Evening Meal, on that night of battle, at the moment of performing guarding the rebels, and on that day of destroying the enemies of the Lord of All.

As to 'the Great Council which is in Heliopolis': they are Atum, Shu, and Tefnut.

As to 'the guarding of the rebels': it means the destruction of the gang of Seth when he repeated his offenses.

O Thoth, who vindicated Osiris against his enemies, vindicate the Osiris Ani, the vindicated, against his enemies in the presence of the council which is in Busiris, on that night of erecting the Djed-pillar which is in Busiris.

As to 'the Great Council which is in Busiris': they are Osiris, Isis, Nephthys, and Horus-Avenger-of-his-Father.

As to 'the raising of the Djed-pillar in Busiris': it is the shoulder of Horus-Preeminent-of-Letopolis. They were behind Osiris in binding with cloth.

O Thoth, who vindicated Osiris against his enemies, vindicate the Osiris Ani, the vindicated, against his enemies in the presence of the council which is in Letopolis, on the night of the Evening Meal which is in Letopolis.

As to 'the Great Council which is in Letopolis': they are Horus-with-no-Eyes-in-his-Forehead and Thoth who is with the Council of Naref.

As to 'that night of the Evening Meal': it is the dawn at the burial of Osiris.

O Thoth, who vindicated Osiris against his enemies, vindicate the Osiris Ani, the vindicated, against his enemies in the presence of the Great Council which is in Pe and Dep, on that night of erecting the Snake Shrine of Horus which was erected for him as an inheritance from the property of his father Osiris.

As to 'the Great Council which is in Pe and Dep': they are Horus, Isis, Imsety, Hapy.

As to the erecting of 'the Snake Shrine of Horus': it means when Seth said to his entourage, 'erect a Snake Shrine for it.'

O Thoth, who vindicated Osiris against his enemies, vindicate the Osiris Ani, the vindicated, against his enemies in the presence of the Great Council which is on the Banks of the Washerman on that night of Isis spending the night awake, mourning over her brother Osiris.

As to 'the Great Council which is on the Banks of the Washerman': they are Isis, Horus, and Imsety.

O Thoth, who vindicated Osiris against his enemies, vindicate the Osiris Ani, the vindicated in peace, against his enemies in the presence of the Great Council which is in Abydos on that night of the *Haker*-festival when the dead are counted and the Blessed Spirits are chosen, when dancing happens in Thinis.

As to 'the Great Council which is in Abydos': they are Osiris, Isis, and Wepwawet.

O Thoth, who vindicated Osiris against his enemies, vindicate the Osiris Scribe of the Divine Offerings of all the Gods, Ani against his enemies in the presence of the Council who judge the dead on that night of making an accounting of their dead.

As to 'the Great Council which is at the judging of the dead': they are Thoth, Osiris, Anubis, and Isdes.

As to 'accounting their dead': it means when the offering were shut off from the souls of the Children of Weakness.

O Thoth, who vindicated Osiris against his enemies, vindicate the Osiris Ani, the vindicated, against his enemies in the presence of the Great Council who are at the hacking up of the earth of Busiris on that night of hacking the earth with their blood and making true the voice of Osiris against his enemies.

As to 'the Great Council which are at the hacking up of the earth of Busiris': it means the arrival of the Gang of Seth when they made their transformation as goats and when they were sacrificed in the presence of these gods, and the blood which dropped from them was captured and was given to those who are counted among the ones in Busiris.

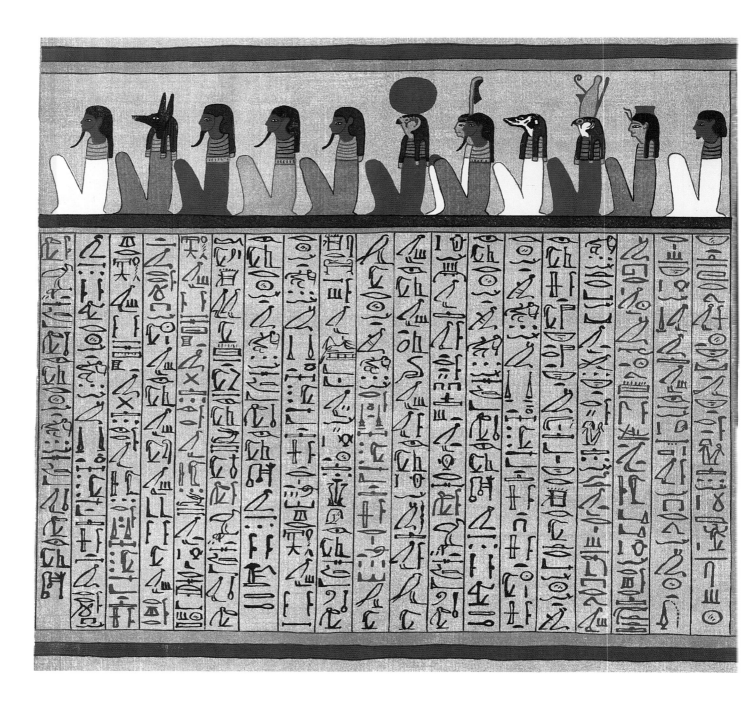

CHAPTER 18 (*continued*)

O Thoth, who vindicated Osiris against his enemies, vindicate the Osiris Ani, the vindicated, against his enemies in the presence of the Great Council which is in Naref on that night of secreting of forms.

As to 'the Great Council which is in Naref': they are Re, Shu, and Babai.

As to 'that night of secreting of forms': it was when there was the burial of the forearm, the flanks, and the thighs of Osiris.

O Thoth, who vindicated Osiris against his enemies, vindicate the Osiris Ani against his enemies in the presence of the Great Council which is in Rosetjau on that night when Anubis spent the night with his hands upon the offerings about Osiris and the voice of Horus was made true against his enemies.

As to 'the Great Council which is in Rosetjau': they are

Horus, Osiris, Isis and Osiris. The heart of Osiris was pleased, the heart of Horus was gladdened, and the Double Gateway was satisfied with it.

O Thoth, who vindicated Osiris against his enemies, vindicate the Osiris Ani against his enemies in the presence of the Great Council of Ten which is with Re and which is with Osiris, and which is with every god and goddess before the Lord of All when he drives off his enemies and when he drives off every evil which pertains to him.

If one says this Chapter, while pure, it means going forth by day after he has been buried and the assumption of whatever of his forms which he desires. Now as to anyone over whom this incantation is recited, it means prosperous upon earth; he shall emerge from every fire; nothing evil shall encircle him. A matter a million times true.

PLATE 24   THE BOOK OF GOING FORTH BY DAY

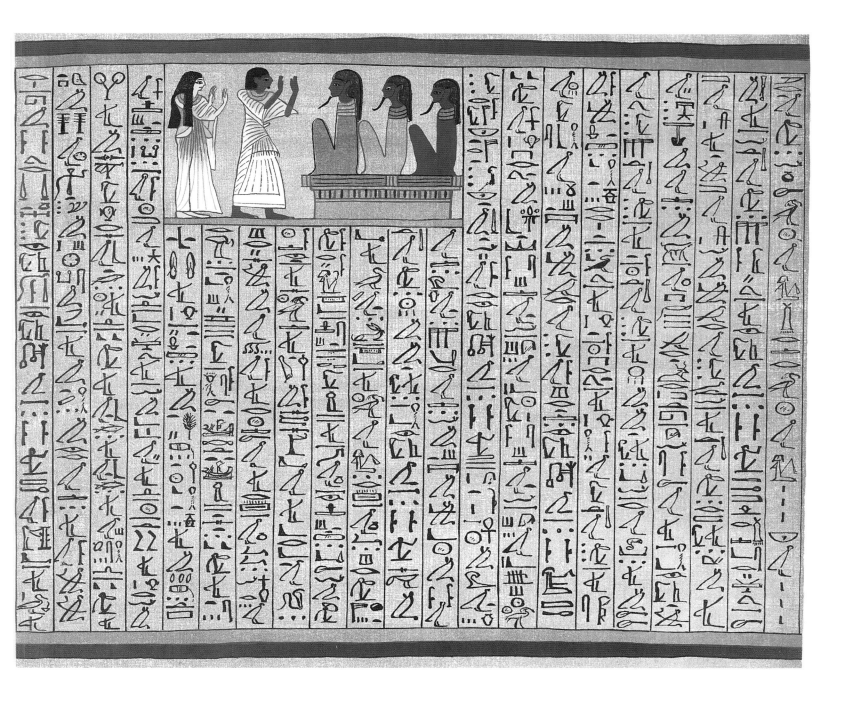

Chapter for going down to the Tribunal of Osiris

My soul has built an enclosed place in Busiris, and I am flourishing in Pe; I plow my fields in my own shape, and my dom-palm is that upon which Min is.

What I doubly detest, I will not eat; my detestation is feces, and I will not eat it, I will not consume excrement, I will not approach it with my hands, I will not tread on it with my sandals, because my bread is of white emmer and my beer is of red barley. It is the Night-bark and the Day-bark which bring it to me, and I will eat beneath the branches, for I know the bearers of what is good. Then I will recite glorifications of the White Crown, and I will be raised aloft by the uraei. O you door-keepers of Him who pacified the Two Lands, bring me those who prepare offerings and let the branches be raised for me; may the sunshine open its arms to me, may the Ennead be silent when the sun-folk speak to me. May I guide the hearts of the gods, and may they protect me, may I be mighty among those who suspend themselves on high. As for any god or any goddess who shall oppose themselves to me, they shall be handed over to those who are in charge of the year, who live on hearts, while the preparation of Senu-bread is before me; may Osiris eat it when going forth from the East, may it be allotted to those who are in the presence of Re, may it be allotted to those who are in the presence of the Sunshine-god who covers the sky among the great ones who belong to it.

Place bread in my mouth; I will go in to the Moon-god, so that he may speak to me, that the followers of the gods may speak to me, that the sun may speak to me, and that the sun-folk may speak to me. The dread of me is in the twilight and in the Celestial Waters which are his on his forehead; I am there with Osiris, and my mat is his mat among the Elders. I have told him the words of men, and I have repeated to him the words of the gods. My spirit comes equipped, for I am an equipped spirit and I have equipped all the spirits.

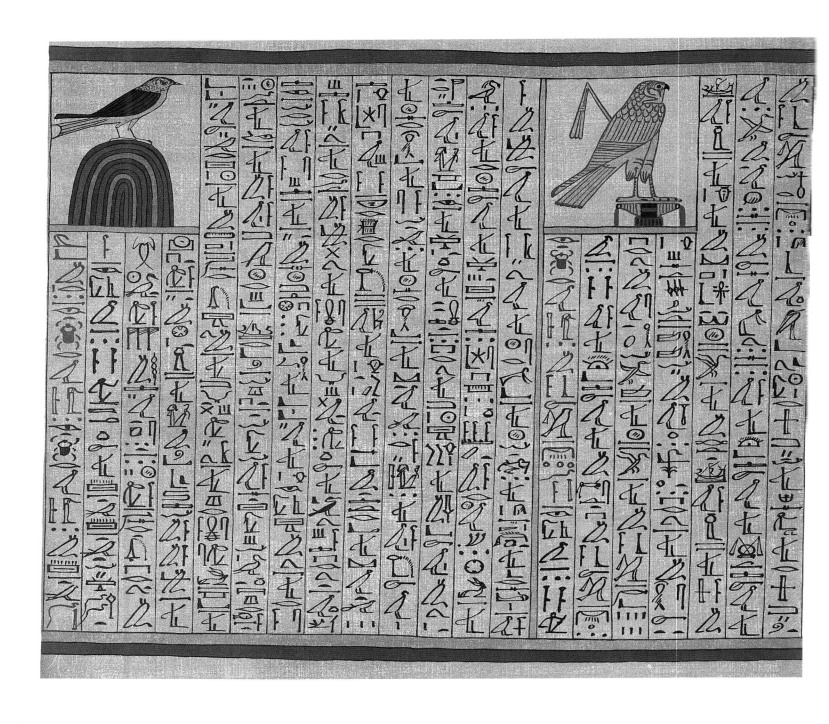

— 86 —

Chapter for being transformed into a swallow

I am a swallow, I am a swallow, I am that Scorpion-goddess, the daughter of Re. O you gods, may your savor be sweet; a flame has gone up from the horizon. O you who are in the city, I have brought him who guards his coils; give me your hands, for I have spent the day in the Island of Fire, I have gone on an errand and I have returned with a report. Open to me; then I will tell what I have seen. Horus is in command of the Sacred Bark, and the throne of his father Osiris has been given to him, while that Seth the son of Nut is in bonds because of what he has done. What is in Letopolis has been allotted to me, and I have made obeisance to Osiris. I have gone to make inspection and I have returned to speak; let me pass, that I may report on my errand. I am one who goes in esteemed and who goes out distinguished at the portal of the Lord of All; I am pure on that great tomb-plateau, for I have got rid of my evil, I have discarded my wrongdoing, I have cast to the ground the ills which were on my flesh. O you keepers of the gate, make a way for me, for I am one like you. I go out into the day, I walk on my feet, I have power in my strides. O You of the sunshine, I know the secret ways of the portals of the Field of Rushes. See, I have come, having felled my enemies to the ground, and my corpse is buried.

As for him who knows this chapter, he shall go out into the day, and he shall not be turned away at any portal in the realm of the dead, and he shall assume the shape of a swallow. A matter a million times true.

— 77 —

Chapter for being transformed into a falcon of gold

I have appeared as a great falcon, having come forth from the Egg; I have flown up and alighted as a falcon of four cubits along its back, whose wings are of green-stone of Upper Egypt; I have gone up from the coffer into the Night-bark, I have brought my heart from the eastern mountains, I have alighted in the Day-bark, there are brought to me those of ancient times bowing down, and they give me worship when I appear, having been reassembled as a fair falcon of gold upon the pointed stone. Re

PLATE 25   THE BOOK OF GOING FORTH BY DAY

comes in daily to give judgment, and I sit among those elder gods of the Lower Sky; He of the Field of Offerings bows to me in the Presence, and I eat of him and have power over him, I have abundance to my desire. The grain-god has given me smoked barley, and I have power over what appertains to my head.

— 78 —

Chapter for being transformed into a divine falcon

OSIRIS SPEAKS: O Horus, come to Busiris, clear my ways for me, and go all over my house, that you may see my form and extol my shape. May you inspire fear of me, may you create awe of me, that the gods of the Duat may fear me, that the gates may beware of me. Do not let him who has done me harm approach me, so that he sees me in the House of Darkness, and uncovers my weariness which is hidden from him.

THE GODS: 'Do thus,' say the gods, who hear the voices of those who go in the suite of Osiris.

HORUS: Be silent, you gods; let a god speak with a god, let him hear the true message which I shall say to him. Speak to me, Osiris, and grant that what has come forth from your mouth concerning me be revoked. See your own form, form your shape, and cause him to go forth and to have power over his legs that he may stride and copulate among men, and you shall be there as the Lord of All. The gods of the Duat fear you, the gates beware of you. You move along with those who move along, while I remain on your mound like the Lord of Life. I ally myself with the divine Isis, I rejoice on account of him who has done you harm. May he not come so that he sees your weariness which is hidden from him. I shall go and come to the confines of the sky, that I may ask the word from Geb, that I may demand authority from the Lord of All. Then the gods shall fear you, even they who shall see that I send to you one of those who dwell in the sunshine. I have made his form as my form, his gait as my gait, that he may go and come to Busiris, being invested with my shape, that he may tell you my affairs. He shall inspire fear of you, he shall create awe of you in the gods of the Duat, and the gates shall beware of you.

CHAPTER 78 (*continued*)

THE MESSENGER: Indeed I am one who dwells in the sunshine, I am a spirit who came into being and was created out of the body of the god, I am one of those gods or spirits who dwell in the sunshine, whom Atum created from his flesh, who came into being from the root of his eye, whom Atum created and with whom he made spirits, whose faces he created, in order that they might be with him, while he was alone in the Primordial Water, who announced him when he came forth from the horizon, who inspired fear of him in the gods and spirits, the Powers and Shapes. I am one of those serpents which the Sole Lord made, before Isis came into being that she might give birth to Horus. I have been made strong, I have been made young and vigorous. I am distinguished above the other beings who dwell in the sunshine, the spirits who came into being along with me. I have made my appearance as a divine falcon, Horus has invested me with his shape in order that I might take his affairs to Osiris, to the Duat.

THE DOUBLE LION RAISES AN OBJECTION: The Double Lion who is in his cavern, warden of the House of the Royal Nemes Headdress, said to me: How can you reach the confines of the sky? Indeed you are equipped with the form of Horus, but you do not possess the Nemes Headdress. Do you speak on the confines of the sky?

THE MESSENGER: I am indeed he who takes the affairs of Horus to Osiris, to the Duat. Horus has repeated to me what his father Osiris said to him in the . . . on the day of burial.

THE DOUBLE LION: Repeat to me what Horus has said as the word of his father Osiris in the . . . on the day of burial. Then shall I give you the Nemes Headdress — so said the Double Lion to me — that you may come and go on the roads of the sky. Then those who dwell in the horizon shall see you, and the gods of the Duat shall fear you.

THE MESSENGER: You may jubilate concerning him, he has been initiated into the world of these gods, the Lords of All, who are at the side of the Sole Lord — so said he who is high on his dais, who dwells in holiness, concerning me.

THE DOUBLE LION IS SATISFIED: Take out the Nemes Headdress for him — so said the Double Lion concerning me.

THE MESSENGER, NOW POSSESSED OF HIS PASSPORT, THE ROYAL NEMES HEADDRESS, CONTINUES HIS JOURNEY: O Heret, clear my way for me. I am high in the form of Horus, and the Double Lion has taken out the Nemes Headdress for me, he has given me my wings, he has established my heart on his great standard. I do not fall on account of Shu, I am he who pacifies himself with his own beauty, the Lord of the two mighty royal serpents. I am he who knows the roads of Nut, the winds are my protection, and the raging bull shall not drive me back. I go to the place where dwells He who sleeps, being helpless, who is in the Field of Eternity, who was conducted to the painful western darkness, even Osiris. I come today from the House of the Double Lion, I have come forth from it to the House of Isis, to the secret mysteries, I have been conducted to her hidden secrets, for she caused me to see the birth of the Great God. Horus has invested me with his shape in order that I might say what is there, in order that I might say . . . which shall drive back the fearful attack. I am the falcon

PLATE 26   THE BOOK OF GOING FORTH BY DAY

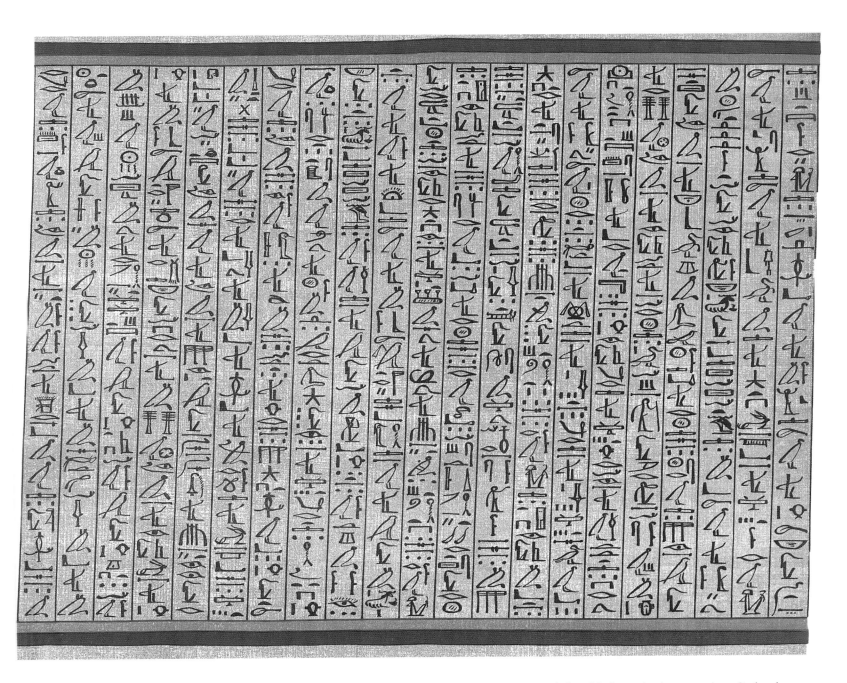

who dwells in the sunshine, who has power through his light and his flashing. I go and come to the confines of the sky . . . There is none who thwarts me . . . Horus to the confines of the sky. Horus is upon his seats and his thrones, and I am he who is in his form. My arms are those of a divine falcon, I am one who has acquired (the position of) his lord, and Horus has invested me with his shape. I come forth to Busiris that I may see Osiris, I land at the Mansion of the Great Dead One; I inspire fear of him and create awe of him among the gods. I belong to the great shrine, even I the holy one of . . . in front of whom one walks to and fro, and Nut shall walk to and fro when she sees me. The hostile gods have seen that she incites the Eyeless One against those who shall stretch forth their arms against me. The Powerful One stands up against the earth-gods, the holy roads are opened for me when they see my form and hear what I shall say. Down on your faces, you gods of the Duat, whose faces are . . . whose necks are outstretched, and who hide the face of the Great Demolisher! Clear the road of . . . towards the majestic shape.

THE MESSENGER QUOTES THE COMMAND OF HORUS: Horus has commanded: Lift up your faces and look at him; he has made his appearance as a divine falcon, the Double Lion has taken out the Nemes Headdress for him, he has come with the word of Horus to Osiris. The Grey-haired Ones have . . . he has united himself with the Powers. Get out of the way, you wardens of your gates, for him in front of me, clear the way for him. Let him pass by, O you who dwell in your caverns, wardens of the House of Osiris.

THE MESSENGER RESUMES HIS OWN SPEECH: I say: How mighty is Horus! I cause them to know that the terror of him is great, and that his horn is sharp against Seth; that Horus has taken authority and that he has acquired the might of Atum. I have followed Horus, the Lord of All.

THE GODS GIVE THE MESSENGER PERMISSION TO PASS: Pass by in peace — so say the gods of the Duat to me. The wardens of their caverns, the wardens of the Mansion of Osiris rise up.

THE MESSENGER REPLIES: See, I come to you as an equipped spirit. The wardens of the gates walk for me, the Powers clear the roads for me, I have fetched the Grey-haired Ones whom Nenet has defied. The great ones who dwell in the horizon fear me, even the wardens of . . . in the sky, who guard the roads. I make firm the gates for the Lord of All, I have cleared the roads towards him; I have done what was commanded, for Horus invested me with his shape. Let my wisdom be granted, for I desire triumph over my enemies. May the mysteries be uncovered for me, may the secret caverns be opened to me, may I enter into the Lord of Soul, greatly majestic, may I come forth to Busiris and go all over his mansion, may I tell him the affairs of his son whom he loves, while the heart of Seth is cut out. May I see the Lord of Weariness, who is limitless, that he may know how Horus regulated the affairs of the gods without him.

THE MESSENGER ATTAINS HIS AIM AND ADDRESSES OSIRIS: O Lord of the Soul, greatly majestic, see, I have come, the Duat has been opened for me, the roads in the sky and on earth have been opened for me, and there was none who thwarted me.

Be high upon your seat, O Osiris.

— 87 —

Chapter for being transformed into a snake

I am a long-lived snake; I pass the night and am reborn every day. I am a snake which is in the limits of the earth; I pass the night and am reborn, renewed, and rejuvenated every day.

— 88 —

Chapter for being transformed into a crocodile

I am a crocodile immersed in dread, I am a crocodile who takes by robbery, I am the great and mighty fish-like being who is in the Bitter Lakes, I am the Lord of those who bow down in Letopolis.

— 82 —

Chapter for becoming Ptah, eating bread, drinking beer, purifying the hinder-parts, and being alive in Heliopolis

I have flown up as a falcon, I have cackled as a goose, I have alighted on yonder road of the Mound of the Great Festival. What I doubly detest, I will not eat; what I detest is feces, and I will not eat it; what I detest is excrement, and it shall not enter my body.

'What will you live on?' say the gods and spirits to me.
'I will live and have power through bread.'
'Where will you eat it?' say the gods and spirits to me.
'I will have power and I will eat it under the branches of the tree of Hathor my mistress, who made offering of bread, beer, and corn in Heliopolis. I will don a loincloth from the hand of Tayt, I will dwell in the place where I wish to be.'

My head is that of Re who is united with Atum, the four suns of the length of the land; I have gone forth, for my tongue is that of Ptah, my throat is that of Hathor, for I have recalled with my mouth the speech of Atum to my father when he destroyed the majesty of the wife of Geb, whose head was broken at his word. Be afraid thereat and report it, the outcry at my strength. There shall be assigned to me the heritage of the Lord of the Earth, namely Geb, and I shall be cared for thereby; Geb shall refresh me, for he has given to me his appearings in glory. Those who are in Heliopolis bow their heads to me, for I am their lord, I am their bull. I am mightier than the Lord of Terror; I copulate and I have power over myriads.

PLATE 27   THE BOOK OF GOING FORTH BY DAY

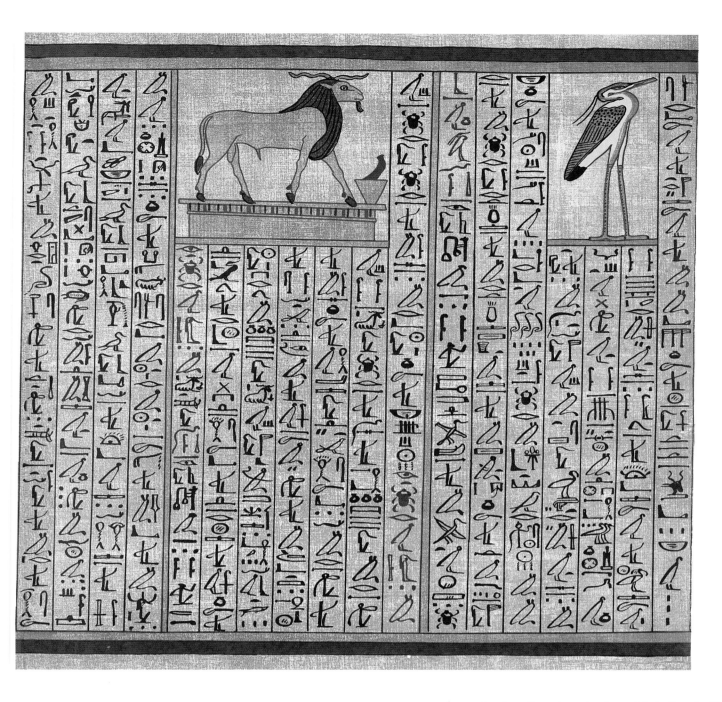

— 85 —

Chapter for being transformed into the soul of Atum and not entering into the place of execution. He who knows it will never perish.

I am the soul of Re who issued from the Primordial Water, that soul of the god who created authority. Wrongdoing is my detestation, and I will not see it; I think about righteousness, and I live by it; I am Authority which will never perish in this my name of 'Soul.' I came into being of myself with the Primordial Water in this my name of Khepri, and I come into being in it daily.

I am the Lord of Light; death is my detestation, and I will not enter into the place of execution of the Netherworld. It is I who cause Osiris to be a spirit, and I have made content those who are in his suite. I desire that they grant fear of me and create respect of me among those who are in their midst, for I am lifted aloft on my standard, on my throne, and on my allotted seat.

I am Nun, and the doers of wrong cannot harm me. I am the eldest of the primeval gods, the soul of the souls of the eternal gods; my body is everlasting, my shape is eternity, Lord of Years, Ruler of Everlasting. I am he who created darkness and who made his seat in the limits of the sky. I desire to reach their limits, and I walk afoot, I go ahead with my staff, I cross the firmament of those who . . ., I drive away the hidden snakes which are upon my march to the Lord of the Two Regions.

I am the soul of the souls of the eternal gods, my body is everlasting, I am he who is on high, Lord of Tatjebu, I am young in my city, I am boyish in the field, and such is my name, for my name will not perish. I am the soul who created the Primordial Water, who made his seat in the realm of the dead. My nest will not be seen, my egg will not be broken, I have got rid of my ills, I have seen my father, the Lord of the Evening, and whose body it is which is in Heliopolis; I govern those who are in the dusk upon the western Mound of the Ibis.

— 83 —

Chapter for being transformed into a Benu-bird

I have flown up like the primeval ones, I have become Khepri, I have grown as a plant, I have clad myself as a tortoise, I am the essence of every god, I am the seventh of those seven uraei who came into being in the West, Horus who makes brightness with his person, that god who was against Seth, Thoth who was among you in that judgment of Him who presides over Letopolis together with the Souls of Heliopolis, the flood which was between them. I have come on the day when I appear in glory with the strides of the gods, for I am Khons who subdued the lords.

As for him who knows this pure chapter, it means going out into the day after death and being transformed at will, being in the suite of Wennefer, being content with the food of Osiris, having invocation-offerings, seeing the sun; it means being hale on earth with Re and being vindicated with Osiris, and nothing evil shall have power over him. A matter a million times true.

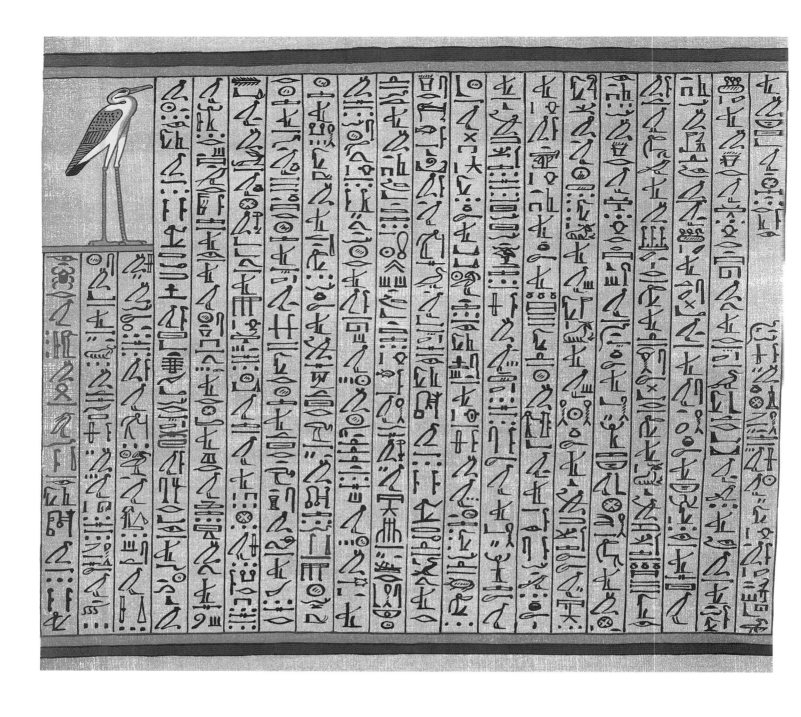

Chapter for being transformed into a heron

I am the mightiest of the bulls, I am the forceful one among them, I am the twin braided locks which are on the head of the shorn priest, whom they of the sunshine worship, whose stroke is sharp. I am vindicated on earth, and the terror of me is in the sky — and vice versa; it is my strength which makes me victorious to the height of the sky, I am held in respect to the breadth of the sky, my strides are towards the towns of the Silent Land. I have gone and reached Wenu; I have ejected the gods from their paths, I have struck down those who are wakeful within their shrines. I do not know the Primordial Water, I do not know the emerging earth, I do not know the red ones who thrust with their horns, I do not know the magician, but I hear his words; I am this Wild Bull who is in the writings.

Thus said the gods when they lamented the past: 'On your faces! He has come to you while the dawn lacks you, and there is none who will protect you.' My faults are in my belly, and I will not declare them; O Authority, wrong-doing is of yesterday, but righteousness is of today. Righteousness runs on my eyebrows on the night of the festival 'The Old Woman lies down and her land is guarded.'

PLATE 28   THE BOOK OF GOING FORTH BY DAY

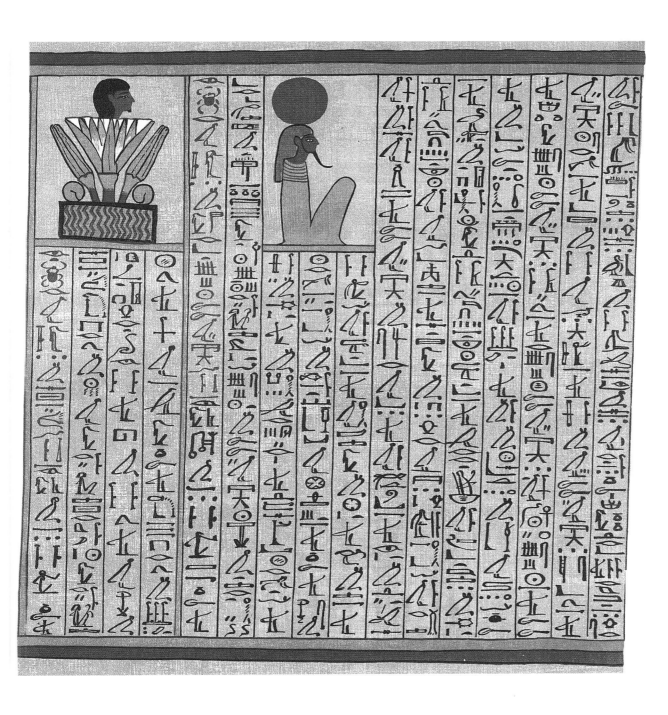

— 81A —

Chapter for being transformed into a lotus

I am this pure lotus which went forth from the sunshine, which is at the nose of Re; I have descended that I may seek it for Horus, for I am the pure one who issued from the fen.

— 80 —

*Making transformation into a god
and giving light and darkness*

I am he who donned the white and bright fringed cloak of Nun which is on his breast, which gives light in darkness, which unites the two companion-goddesses who are in my body by means of the great magic which is on my mouth. My fallen enemy who was with me in the valley of Abydos will not be raised up, and I am content. The remembrance of him is mine, I have taken authority in my city, for I found him in it, I have brought darkness by means of my power, I have rescued the Eye from its nonexistence before the festival of the fifteenth day had come, I have separated Seth from the houses of the Above because of the Elder who was with him, I equipped Thoth in the Mansion of the Moon before the festival of the fifteenth day had come, I have taken possession of the Wereret-crown, and right is in my body, also the turquoise and faience of its monthly festival, and my field of lapis-lazuli is there on my riverbank. I am the Woman who lightens darkness, I have come to lighten the darkness, and it is bright. I have lightened the darkness, I have felled the evil spirits, those who were in darkness have given praise to me, I have made the mourners whose faces were hidden to stand up, even though they were languid when they saw me. As for you, I am the Woman of whom I do not permit you to hear.

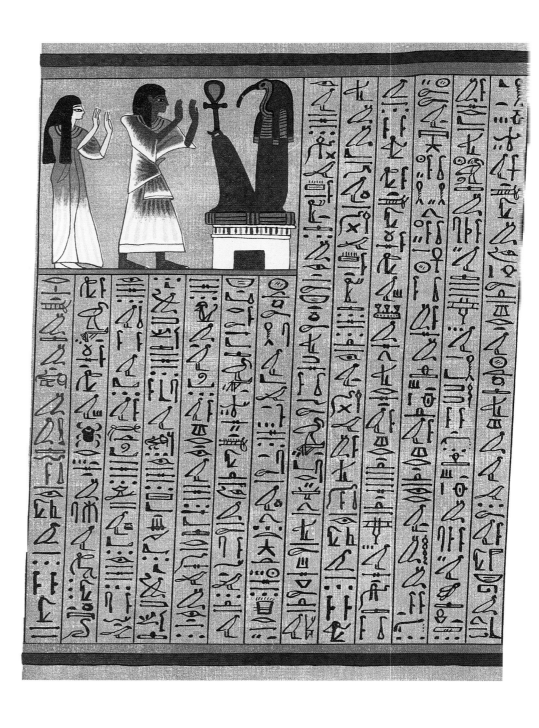

Chapter for not dying again

O Thoth, what is it that has come about through the Children of Nut? They have made war, they have raised up tumult, they have done wrong, they have created rebellion, they have done slaughter, they have created imprisonment, they have reduced what was great to what is little in all that we have made; show greatness, O Thoth! — so says Atum. You shall not witness wrongdoing, you shall not suffer it! Shorten their years, cut short their months, because they have done hidden damage to all that you have made. I have your palette, O Thoth, I bring your inkpot to you; I am not among those who have done hidden damage, and none will work harm on me.

Thus says Ani: O Atum, how comes it that I travel to a desert which has no water and no air, and which is deep, dark, and unsearchable?

ATUM: Live in it in content!

ANI: But there is no love-making there!

ATUM: I have given spirit-being instead of water, air, and love-making, contentment in place of bread and beer — so says Atum. Do not be sorry for yourself, for I will not suffer you to lack.

ANI: But every god has taken his place in the Bark of Millions of Years!

ATUM: Your seat now belongs to your son Horus — so says Atum — and *he* will dispatch the Elders, he will rule from your seat, he will inherit the throne which is in the Island of Fire.

ANI: Command that I may see his equal, for my face

will see the face of the Lord of All. What will be the duration of my life? — so said he.

ATUM: You shall be for millions on millions of years, a lifetime of millions of years. I will dispatch the Elders and destroy all that I have made; the earth shall return to the Primordial Water, to the surging flood, as in its original state. But I will remain with Osiris, I will transform myself into something else, namely a serpent, without men knowing or the gods seeing. How good is what I have done for Osiris, even more than for all the gods! I have given him the desert, and his son Horus is the heir on his throne which is in the Island of Fire; I have made what appertains to his place in the Bark of Millions of Years, and Horus is firm on his throne in order to found his establishments.

ANI: But the soul of Seth will travel further than all the gods.

ATUM: I have caused his soul which is in the bark to be restrained, so that the body of the god may be afraid.

ANI: O my father Osiris, do for me what your father Re did for you, so that I may be long-lived on earth, that my throne may be well founded, that my heir may be in good health, that my tomb may be long-enduring, and that these servants of mine may be on earth; let my enemies be split open, may the Scorpion be on their bones, for I am your son, O my father Re; do this for me for the sake of my life, welfare, and health, for Horus is firmly established on his throne, and let my lifetime come to attain to the blessed state.

Chapter for entering into the Hall of the Two Truths and a chapter of praising Osiris, Foremost of the Westerners.

Words spoken by the Osiris scribe Ani, the vindicated: I have come here in order to see your beauty, my two arms raised in exaltation to your real name. I have come here before the fir-tree came into being and the acacia was born, before the earth created the tamarisks. If I enter the secret place, I shall speak with Seth and I shall be friendly with the one who approaches me. The one whose face is veiled falls because of the secret things. He enters into the house of Osiris and he sees the secrets which are therein. The Councils of the Portals are the Blessed Dead.

Words spoken by Anubis in the presence of his entourage:

A man has come from Egypt who knows our roads and our towns, and I am satisfied with him. I smell his odor as belonging to one among you. He has said to me: I am the Osiris scribe Ani, the vindicated, in peace and in vindication. I have come here to see the great gods and so that I might live upon the offerings which are their victuals, while I am the limits of the Ram, the Lord of Mendes. He allows me to fly up as a Benu-bird at my saying so, when I am in the river. I make a presentation of incense and I conduct myself in my kilt to the children, while I am in Elephantine in the house of Satis. I have sunk the bark of the enemies, I have crossed over to the pool in the Neshmet-bark, I have seen the nobles of Athribis, while I was in Busiris, whom I have silenced. I have caused that the god have power over

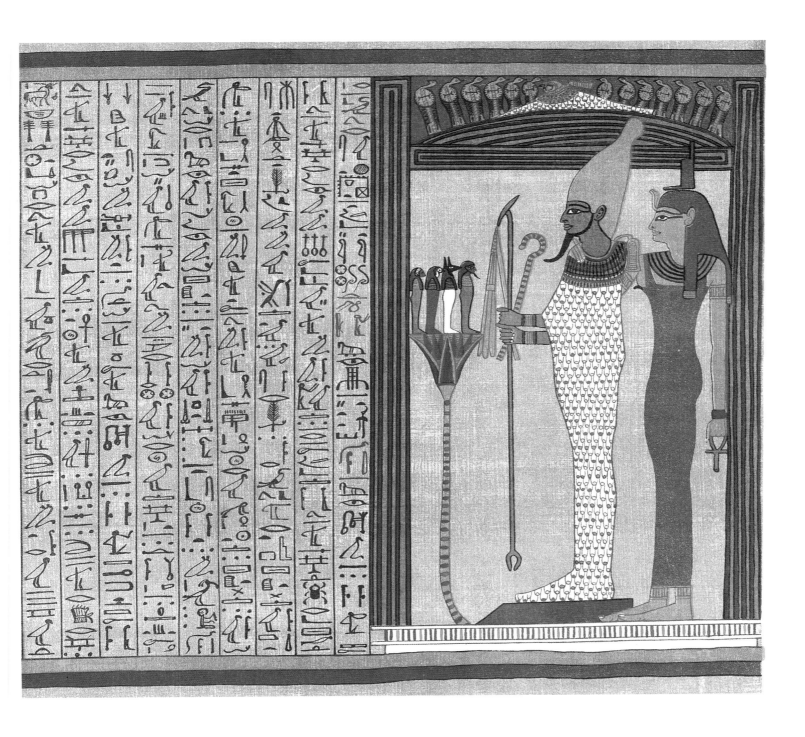

his two legs, while I was in the house of He who is upon his Mountain (Anubis). I have seen the One Preeminent of the Embalming Tent. I have entered into the house of Osiris, I have stripped off the bag-wigs of those who are yonder. I have entered into Rosetjau and I have seen the secrets which are therein. I have hidden the one whom I found missing. I have descended to Naref and I have clothed the one who was there naked. I have given incense to the women in the retinue of the commoners.

Behold, these things have been told to me concerning the one to whom I shall speak when he shall be weighed in our midst.

Then shall say the Majesty of Anubis concerning this: Do you know the name of this gateway, as many say to me?

Then the Osiris, the Scribe Ani, the vindicated, shall say: In peace and in vindication: 'You Dispel Light' is the name of this gate.

Then shall say the Majesty of Anubis: Do you know the names of the upper and lower portions of the door?

'Lord of Truth, Master of his Two Legs' is the name of the upper portion; 'Lord of Strength, the One who Commands the Cattle' is the name of the lower.

Pass you on then, for you know, O Osiris, Scribe of the Accounting of the Divine Offerings of all the Gods of Thebes, Ani, the vindicated, possessor of reverence.

The Papyrus of Ani

PLATE 30

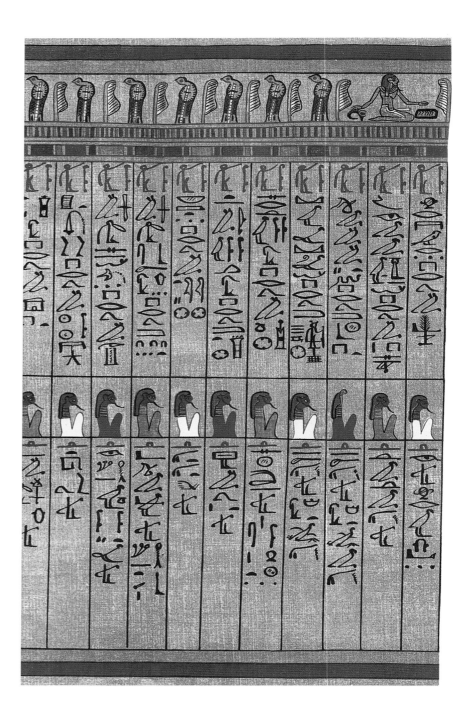

O He-of-the-Cavern who came forth from the West, I have not fornicated with the fornicator.

O He-whose-Face-is-behind-him who came forth from his hole, I have not caused (anyone) to weep.

O Anointed One who came forth from the chapel, I have not dissembled.

O Hot-Legs who came forth at twilight, I have not transgressed.

O He-who-is-Blood who came forth from the place of slaughter, I have not done grain-profiteering.

O Eater of Entrails who came forth from the Council of Thirty, I have not robbed a parcel of land.

O Lord of Truth who came forth from Hall of Two Truths, I have not discussed (secrets).

O Strayer who came forth from Bubastis, I have brought no lawsuits.

O Planter(?) who came forth from Heliopolis, I have not disputed at all about property.

O Doubly Evil One who came forth from the Busirite Nome, I have not had intercourse with a married woman.

O *Wammety*-serpent who came forth from the place of execution, I have not had intercourse with a married woman.

O He-who-Sees-what-he-has-brought who came forth from the House of Min, I have not (wrongly) copulated.

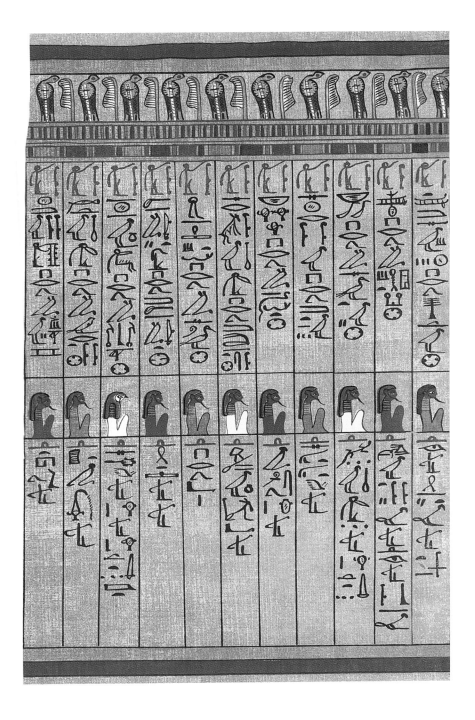

O He-who-is-over-the-Great-Ones who came forth from -?-, I have not struck terror.

O Demolisher who came forth from -?-, I have not transgressed.

O Proclaimer of Speech who came forth from Weryt, I have not been hot(-tempered).

O Youth who came forth from the Double Scepter Nome, I have not been neglectful of truthful words.

O Dark One who came forth from darkness, I have not cursed.

O He-who-Brings-his-Offering who comes forth from Asyut, I have not been violent.

O Proclaimer of Voice who came forth from Wenis, I have not confounded (truth).

O Possessor of Faces who came forth from Nedjefet, I have not been impatient.

O Captain who came forth from Weten, I have not discussed.

O Possessor of Two Horns who came forth from Asyut, I have not been garrulous about matters.

O Nefertum who came forth from Memphis, I have not done wrong, I have not done evil.

O He-who-does-not-(allow)-Survivors who came forth from Busiris, I have not disputed the King.

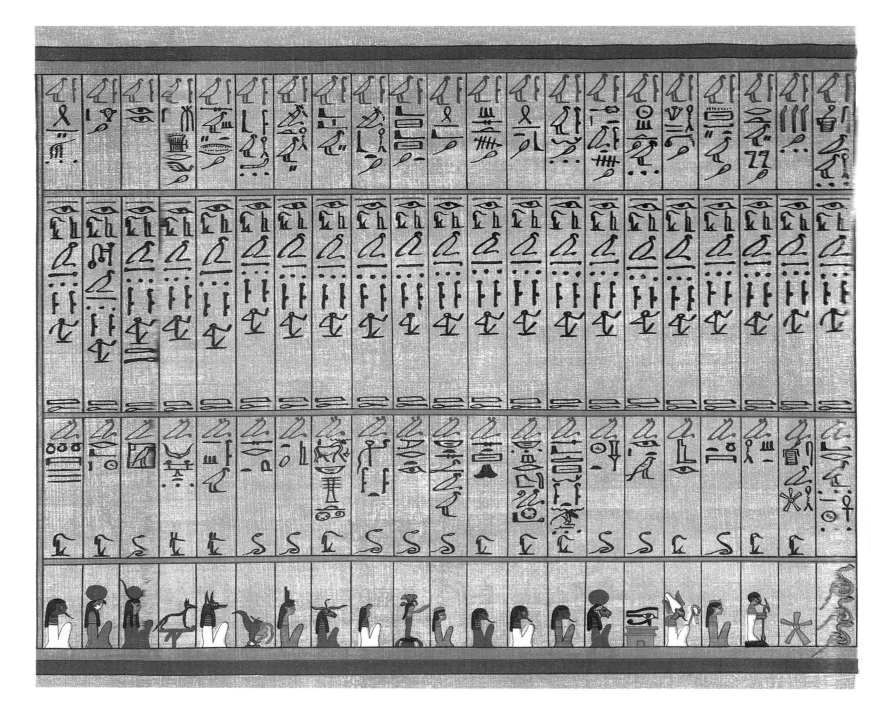

My hair is Nun; my face is Re; my eyes are Hathor; my ears are Wepwawet; my nose is She who presides over her lotus-leaf; my lips are Anubis; my molars are Selket; my incisors are Isis the goddess; my arms are the Ram, the Lord of Mendes; my breast is Neith, Lady of Sais; my back is Seth; my phallus is Osiris; my muscles are the Lords of Kheraha; my chest is He who is greatly majestic; my belly and my spine are Sekhmet; my buttocks are the Eye of Horus; my thighs and my calves are Nut; my feet are Ptah; my fingers are Orion; my toes are living uraei; there is no member of mine devoid of a god, and Thoth is the protection of all my flesh.

[Note: The remainder of this chapter is found in the Theban Recension.]

RUBRIC TO CHAPTER 125

The correct procedure in this Hall of Justice. One shall utter this chapter pure and clean and clad in white garments and sandals, painted with black eye-paint and anointed with myrrh. There shall be offered to him meat and poultry, incense, bread, beer, and herbs when you have put this written procedure on a clean floor of ochre overlaid with earth upon which no swine or small cattle have trodden. As for him who makes this writing, he shall flourish and his children shall flourish, he shall not be in need, he shall be in the confidence of the king and his entourage, and there shall be given to him a Shens-cake, a jug of beer, a Persen-cake, and a portion of meat from upon the altar of the Great God; he shall not be turned back from any gateway of the West, but shall be ushered in with the kings of Upper Egypt and the kings of Lower Egypt, and he shall be in the suite of Osiris. A matter a million times true.

— 155 —

Chapter for a Djed-pillar of gold

Raise yourself, O Osiris, place yourself on your side, that I may put water beneath you and that I may bring you a Djed-pillar of gold so that you may rejoice at it.

To be said over a golden Djed-pillar embellished with sycamore-bast, to be placed on the throat of the deceased on the day of interment. As for him on whose throat this amulet has been placed, he will be a worthy spirit who will be in the realm of the dead on New Year's Day like those who are in the suite of Osiris. A matter a million times true.

PLATE 32   THE BOOK OF GOING FORTH BY DAY

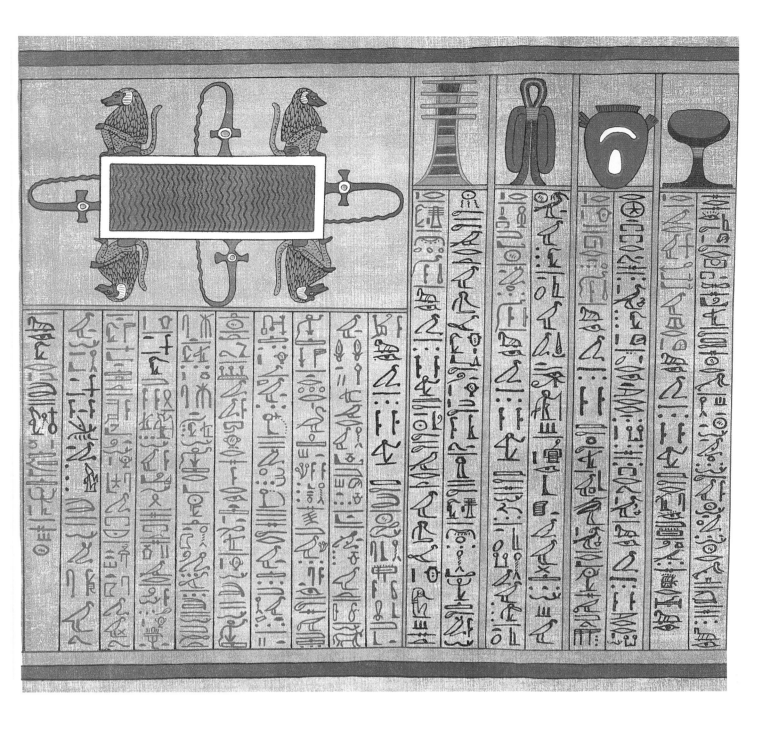

— 156 —

Chapter for a knot-amulet of red jasper

You have your blood, O Isis; you have your power, O Isis; you have your magic, O Isis. The amulet is a protection for this Great One which will drive away whoever would commit a crime against him.

To be said over a knot-amulet of red jasper moistened with juice of the 'life-is-in-it' fruit and embellished with sycamore-bast and placed on the neck of the deceased on the day of interment. As for him for whom this is done, the power of Isis will be the protection of his body, and Horus son of Isis will rejoice over him when he sees him; no path will be hidden from him, and one side of him will be towards the sky and the other towards the earth.

A true matter; you shall not let anyone see it in your hand, for there is nothing equal to it.

— 29B —

Chapter for a heart-amulet of Seheret-stone

I am the Benu-bird, the soul of Re, who guides the gods to the Duat when they go forth. The souls on earth will do what they desire, and the soul of Ani will go forth at his desire.

— 166 —

Chapter for a headrest

May the pigeons awaken you when you are asleep, O Ani, may they awaken your head at the horizon. Raise yourself, so that you may be triumphant over what was done against you, for Ptah has felled your enemies, and it is commanded that action be taken against those who would harm you. You are Horus son of Hathor, the male and female fiery serpents, to whom was given a head after it had been cut off. Your head shall not be taken from you afterwards, your head shall not be taken from you forever.

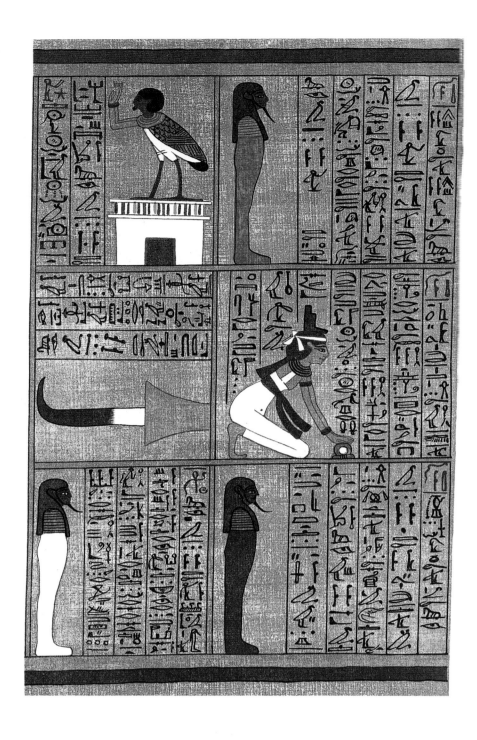

Praising Re when he rises on the eastern horizon of the sky by the Osiris Ani, the vindicated. [Note: Rest of text omitted by scribe.]

Words spoken by Hapy: I am Hapy, your son, O Osiris Ani, the vindicated. I have come that I may be your protection and that I may knit together your head and your limbs. I have smitten down your enemies beneath you for you. I have given you your head eternally — (repeat) twice — O Osiris Ani, the vindicated — (repeat) twice. In peace.

SPEECH FOR THE PRESENTATION OF A FLAME: I am your protection of this fire, I drive him away from the valley, I drive it, namely the sand from your two feet. For I am the one who drags the sand in order to stop up the hidden place. I ward off the arm of the one who would oppose himself against the flame of the desert. I have set fire to the desert, I have deflected the path, for I am the protection.

Words spoken by Isis: I have come that I may be your protection. I fan air at your nostrils for you, I fan the north wind which comes forth from Atum for your nose. I clear your windpipe for you. I cause you to be a god with your enemies fallen under your sandals. May you be vindicated in the sky and may your flesh be powerful among the gods.

TEXT FOR THE SHABTI FIGURINE: (Said by the) *Illuminated One*, Osiris Ani, the vindicated. O shabti, if the Osiris Ani is accounted to do any work in the God's Domain, while obstacles have been erected against him there, as a man to his duties, to the irrigation of the fields, or to water the banks, or to row sand of the east to the west, I will do it. Here I am.

Words spoken by Qebehsenuef: I am Qebehsenuef, your son, O Osiris Ani, the vindicated. I have come that I may be your protection. I assemble your bones, I pull together your limbs. I have brought your heart to you. I have put it in its place in your body for you. I have caused that your house flourish after you. May you live eternally.

PLATE 33

THE BOOK OF GOING FORTH BY DAY

SPELL FOR THE DJED-PILLAR AMULET: I have come seeking, that I may reverse the steps of the One Hidden of Face and that I might illuminate his hidden place. I am one who stands behind the Djed-pillar on that day of repelling the doomed. I raise up in your protection, O Osiris.

Words spoken by Imsety: I am Imsety, your son, O Osiris Ani, the vindicated. I have come that I may be your protection. I have caused your house to flourish enduringly — (repeat) twice. Just as Ptah has commanded me and Re himself has commanded.

Praising Re *when* he sets on the western horizon of the sky by the Osiris Ani, the vindicated, in peace and in the God's Domain. I am an equipped Ba.

Words spoken by Nephthys to the Osiris Ani, the vindicated: I have gone about my brother Osiris. I have come that I may be your protection. My protection is about you, my protection is about you eternally. Your call has been heard by Re, and you have been vindicated by the gods.

Raise yourself up, so that you may be vindicated because of what has been done against you. Ptah has overthrown your enemies for you, for you are Horus, the son of Hathor.

ANOTHER SPEECH FOR THE PRESENTATION OF A FLAME: *Words spoken by* the Osiris Ani, the vindicated. O you who come to me in order to disarray, I shall not be disarrayed, I will not allow that you disarray me. I come in order that I deal harm. You shall not deal harm against me. I am your protector.

Words spoken by Duamutef: I am your beloved son Horus. I have come that I may protect my father Osiris from the one who does injury to him. I have placed him under your two feet eternally, eternally, enduringly, enduringly, O Osiris Ani, in vindication — (repeat) twice.

Words spoken by the Osiris Ani, the vindicated. I am an equipped Ba who is in this egg of the Abdju-fish. I am the Great Cat who is in the Place of Truth in which the light shines forth.

*Here begin the chapters of the Field of Offerings
and chapters of going forth into the day; of coming
and going in the God's Domain; of being provided for
in the Field of Reeds which is in the Field of Offerings,
the abode of the Great Goddess, the Mistress of Winds;
having strength thereby, having power thereby, plowing
therein, reaping and eating therein, drinking therein,
copulating therein, and doing everything that
used to be done on earth by Ani.*

He says: The Falcon has been taken by Seth, and I have seen the damage in the Field of Offerings; I have released the Falcon from Seth, I opened the paths of Re on the day when the sky was choked and stifled, when the Rejected One panted for breath in vivifying Him who was in the Egg and took Him who was in the womb from the Silent Ones.

Now it befell that I rowed in the bark in the Lake of Offerings; I took it from the Limbs of Shu, and his northern stars, his Limbs, were set in due order; I rowed and arrived at its waterways and towns, I fared southward to the god who is in it, because I am he who would rest in his fields. I control the two Enneads whom he loves, I pacify the Combatants on behalf of those who are in the West; I create what is good, I bring peace, I pacify the Combatants on behalf of those who belong to them, I drive away mourning from their elders, I remove turmoil from their young; I wipe away harm of all kinds from Isis, I wipe away harm of all kinds from the gods, I remove turmoil from the Rivals, I separate the Authoritative One from his light, and I give abundance to souls and spirits; I have power over them.

I am one whom Hotep knows, I row on its waterways, I arrive at its towns. My utterance is mighty, I am more acute than the spirits, and they shall not have power over me.

[Note: The remainder of this chapter is found in the Theban Recension.]

PLATE 34   THE BOOK OF GOING FORTH BY DAY

TOP REGISTER:

IN FRONT OF THE THREE SEATED DIVINITIES:
The two enneads.

FAR RIGHT, BEHIND STANDING MUMMIFORM FIGURE:
Being in the Field of Offerings, breath at the nose (i.e. breathing).

SECOND REGISTER:

FAR LEFT, CAPTION BEHIND FIGURE OF ANI REAPING WITH A
SICKLE: Osiris harvesting .

FAR RIGHT, BETWEEN OVALS AND MOUNDS OF GRAIN:
The victuals of the blessed dead.

THIRD REGISTER:

CAPTION BEHIND FIGURE OF ANI PLOWING: Plowing.

CAPTION ABOVE TEAM OF OXEN: The Field of Reeds.

TWO LONG LINES OF TEXT IN FRONT OF PLOWING SCENE:
Speech (var. pool) of the White Hippopotamus: 'It is a [thousand]
river-measures in its length and its breadth cannot be said. There are
no fish at all in it and there are no serpents in it.'

BOTTOM REGISTER:

FAR LEFT, THREE LINES OF TEXT: The place of the blessed dead: its
length is seven cubits long. The emmer is three cubits (high). It is the
effective noblemen who harvest them."

CAPTION ABOVE FLIGHT OF STEPS: Su-djebai.

CAPTION ON RIGHT SIDE OF LOWER LOOP OF WATER: Ishet.

CAPTION ON LEFT SIDE OF SNAKE-HEADED BOAT:
The god who is within is Osiris.

CAPTION ON RIGHT SIDE OF SNAKE-HEADED BOAT:
The holy shore.

CAPTION OVER FAR RIGHT BOAT: Abundance.

*Spell for making provision
for a spirit in the God's Domain*

Hail to you, You who shine in your disk, a living soul who goes up from the horizon! I know you and I know your name; I know the names of the seven cows and their bull who give bread and beer, who are beneficial to souls and who provide daily portions; may you give bread and beer and make provision for me, so that I may serve you, and may I come into being under your hinder-parts.

THE NAMES OF THE CATTLE ARE:

Mansion of Kas, Mistress of All.
Silent One who dwells in her place.
She of Chemmis whom the god ennobled.
The much Beloved, red of hair.

She who protects in life, the particolored.
She whose name has power in her craft.
Storm in the sky which wafts the god aloft.
The Bull, husband of the cows.

May you grant bread and beer, offerings and provisions which shall provide for my spirit, for I am a worthy spirit who is in the God's Domain.

THE NAMES OF THE
FOUR STEERING-OARS OF THE SKY:

O Good Power, the good steering-oar of the northern sky;

O Wanderer who guides the Two Lands, good steering-oar of the western sky;

PLATE 35

THE BOOK OF GOING FORTH BY DAY

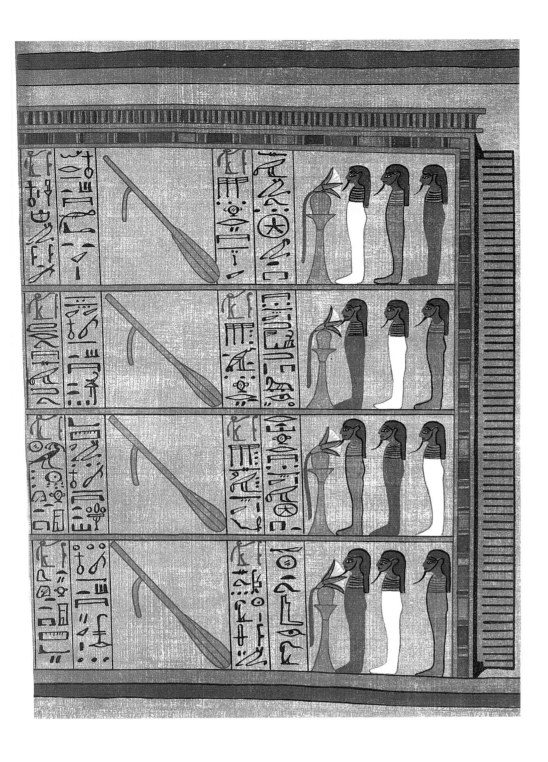

O Shining One who dwells in the Mansion of Images, good steering-oar of the eastern sky;

O Preeminent who dwells in the Mansion of the Red Ones, good steering-oar of the southern sky;

May you grant bread and beer, offerings and provisions which are beneficial to my spirit, may you grant me life, prosperity, health, joy, and long duration on earth; may you grant to me sky and earth and what is beneficial in Heliopolis and the Duat, for I know them all; may you do the like for me.

O fathers of the gods and mothers of the gods who are over sky and earth and who are in the God's Domain, save me from all kinds of harm and injury, from the trap with painful knives and from all things bad and harmful which may be said or done against me by men, gods, spirits, or the dead, by day, by night, in the monthly festival, in the half-monthly festival, in the year, or in what appertains to it.

To be spoken by a man, when Re manifests himself, over these gods depicted in paint on a writing-board. There shall be given to them offerings and provisions before them, consisting of bread, beer, meat, poultry, and incense. The invocation-offering for this spirit shall be made to them in the presence of Re; it means that this soul will have provision in the God's Domain; it means that a man will be saved from anything evil. Do nothing on behalf of anyone except your own self, for it is the Book of Wennefer. As for him for whom this is done, Re will be his helmsman and his protection, and none of his enemies will know him in the God's Domain, in the sky, on earth, or in any place where he may walk; it means that this spirit will be provisioned in very deed. A true matter.

Praising Osiris, Foremost-of-the-Westerners, Wennefer
dwelling in Abydos, by the vindicated Osiris Ani.

He says: O my Lord who passes eternity repeatedly, he who
shall endure everlastingly, Lord of Lords, King of Kings,
Sovereign and Horus of the Horuses (i.e. Kings). Those
who have ever existed, behold, they are in your presence,
namely those gods and men, you having made their seats
preeminent in the God's Domain, so that, assembled together, they might make supplication to your Ka, those

PLATE 36   THE BOOK OF GOING FORTH BY DAY

Sokar-   Lord of the   The Great God,
Osiris   Secret Place   Lord of the
                                God's Domain

who come in millions and millions, reaching and mooring with you. And they who are in the womb, they too have their faces towards you, for a tarrying (forever) in the Beloved Land (Egypt) shall never happen. Cause that they all come to you, the great as well as the small. May he allow a going forth and a reentry from the God's Domain without hindrance at the gateway of the Duat. To the Ka of the Osiris Ani.

— 186 —

Hathor, Lady of the West; She of the West; Lady of the
Sacred Land; Eye of Re which is on his forehead; kindly of
countenance in the Bark of Millions of Years; a resting-place
for him who has done right within the boat of the blessed;
who built the Great Bark of Osiris in order to cross the
water of truth.

PLATE 37   THE BOOK OF GOING FORTH BY DAY

M A P   K E Y   T O   T H E

PLATE 1
Direction of text *(right to left)*
Text columns read top to bottom
Numbers refer to chapters

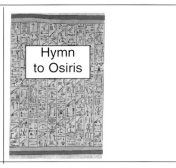

PLATE 2
(right to left)

PLATE 3
Columns 1-15 (above Ani and Tutu) *(right to left)*
Columns 16-25 (above the scale) *(left to right)*
Columns 26-30 (above Ammit) *(right to left)*

PLATE 4
(right to left)

PLATE 5
(left to right)

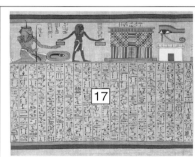

PLATE 6
(left to right)

PLATE 7
(left to right)

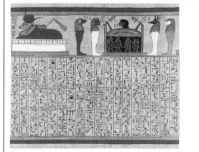

PLATE 8
(left to right)

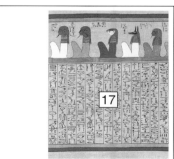

PLATE 9
(left to right)

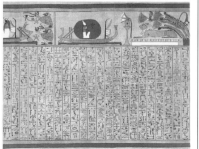

PLATE 10
(left to right)

THE BOOK OF GOING FORTH BY DAY

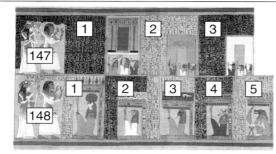
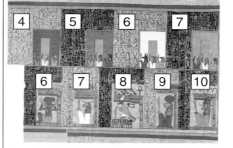
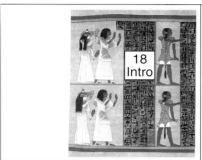
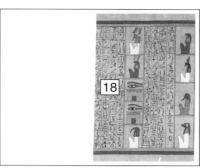

PLATE 11
(all right to left)
The numbers 1–7 refer to the Gates of Chapter 147
The numbers 1–10 refer to the Portals of Chapter 148

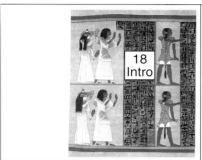

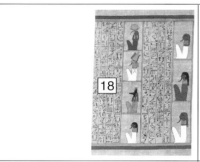

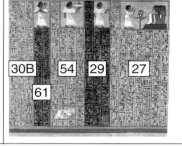
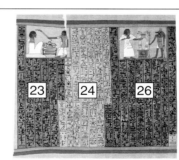

PLATE 12
Introduction *(right to left)*
Chapter text *(left to right)*

PLATE 13
(left to right)

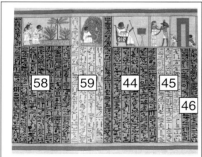

PLATE 14
(left to right)

PLATE 15
(left to right)

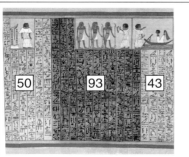
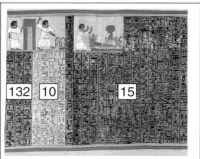

PLATE 16
(left to right)

PLATE 17
(left to right)

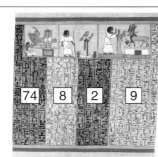

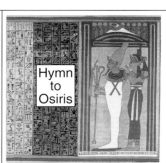

PLATE 18
(left to right)

PLATE 19
(right to left)

Map Key to the Papyrus of Ani

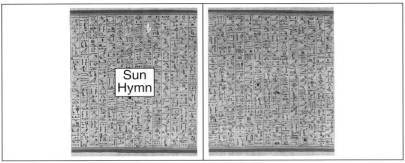

PLATE 20
(left to right)

PLATE 21
(left to right)

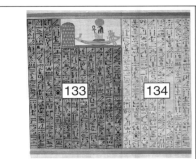

PLATE 22
(left to right)

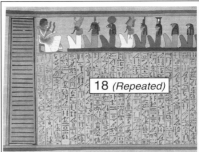

PLATE 23
(left to right)

PLATE 24
(left to right)

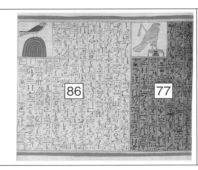

PLATE 25
(left to right)

PLATE 26
(left to right)

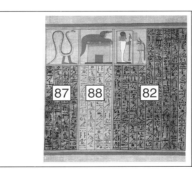

PLATE 27
(left to right)

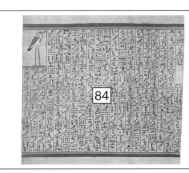 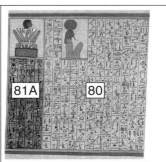

PLATE 28
(left to right)

PLATE 29
(left to right)

THE BOOK OF GOING FORTH BY DAY

PLATE 30
(right to left)

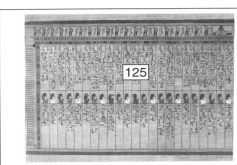

PLATE 31
(left to right)

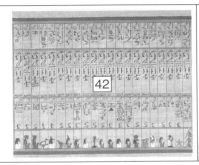

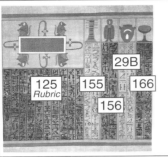

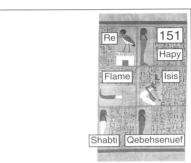

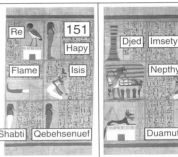

PLATE 32
All except Rubric to 125 are *(left to right)*
Rubric to 125 *(right to left)*

PLATE 33

Re (rising) *(l. to r.)*
Hapy *(right to left)*
Flame *(270° – r. to l.)*
Isis *(left to right)*
Shabti *(left to right)*

Qebehsenuef *(right to left)*
Djed *(right to left)*
Imsety *(left to right)*
Re (setting) *(l. to r.)*

Nephthys *(left to right)*
Flame *(90° – r. to l.)*
Duamutef *(left to right)*
Osiris Ani *(left to right)*

PLATE 34
(right to left)

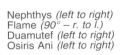

PLATE 35
(left to right)

PLATE 36
(right to left)

PLATE 37
(left to right)

Map Key to the Papyrus of Ani

THE CHAPTERS COMPRISING

The Theban Recension

OF

The Book of Going Forth by Day

WHICH DO NOT APPEAR IN

THE PAPYRUS OF ANI

Chapter for permitting the noble dead to descend to the Duat on the day of interment

Hail to you who are in the sacred desert of the West! N knows you and knows your name; may you save him from those snakes which are in Rosetjau, which live on the flesh of men and gulp down their blood, because N knows you and knows your names.

The First One, Osiris, Lord of All, mysterious of body, gives command, and he puts breath into those frightened ones who are in the midst of the West; what has been commanded for him is the governance of those who exist. May his place within the darkness be opened up for him, may a spirit-shape be given to him in Rosetjau, even to the Lord of gloom who goes down as the swallower of snakes in the West; his voice is heard but he is not seen. The Great God within Busiris, those who are among the languid ones fear him, they having gone forth under report to the slaughterhouse of the god.

I have come, even I the vindicated Osiris N, on business of the Lord of All, while Horus has taken possession of his throne and his father has given to him all those honors which are within his father's sacred bark. Horus has come with a report; he goes in that he may tell what he has seen in Heliopolis. Their great ones on earth wait on him, the scribes who are on their mats magnify him, and there has been given to him the mottled snake in Heliopolis. He has taken possession of the sky, he has inherited the earth, and who shall take this sky and earth from him? He is Re, the eldest of the gods; his mother has suckled him, she has given him a nurse who is in the horizon.

This chapter is to be recited after going to rest in the West, the Tjenenet-shrine being made content with its lord Osiris when going to and fro to the Sacred Bark of Re; his body on his bier shall be reckoned up, and shall be enduring in the Duat, namely that of N.

— 3 —

Another like it

O Atum who went forth as the Great One of the waters, having power as the Double Lion, announce in your own words to those who are in the Presence that N comes as one who is in their midst, and give command on his behalf to the crew of Re in the evening. May N live after death like Re every day. Was Re born yesterday? Then will N be born. May every god be joyful when N lives just as they were joyful when Ptah lived, when he came forth from the great Mansion of the Prince which is in Heliopolis.

— 4 —

Chapter for passing on the upper road of Rosetjau

I am he who fixed the limits of the flood and who judged between the Rivals, I have come and I have removed the evil which was on Osiris.

— 5 —

Chapter for not doing work in the God's Domain

It is I who lift up the arm of Him who is inert; I have gone out of Hermopolis, I am a living soul, I have been initiated into the hearts of the baboons.

— 6 —

Chapter for causing a shabti to do work for a man in the God's Domain

O shabti, allotted to me, if I be summoned or if I be detailed to do any work which has to be done in the God's Domain; if indeed obstacles are implanted for you therewith as a man at his duties, you shall detail yourself for me on every occasion of making arable the fields, of flooding the banks, or of conveying sand from east to west; 'Here am I,' you shall say.

— 7 —

Chapter for passing by the dangerous coil of Apophis

O you waxen one who take by robbery and who live on the inert ones, I will not be inert for you, I will not be weak for you, your poison shall not enter into my members, for my members are the members of Atum. If I am not weak for you, suffering from you shall not enter into these members of mine. I am Atum at the head of the Primordial Water, my protection is from the gods, the lords of eternity, I am He whose name is secret, more holy of throne than the Chaos-gods; I am among them, I have gone forth with Atum, I am one who is not examined, I am hale, I am hale!

— 11 —

Chapter for going out against a foe in the God's Domain

O you who consume your arm, prepare a path for me, for I am Re, I have come forth from the horizon against my foe. He has been given to me and he shall not be taken from me. I have extended my arm as Lord of the Wereret-crown, I have stridden out with the speed of the uraeus when my foe has not been put into my hand for me. Such is my foe; he has been given to me, he shall not be taken from me. I have arisen as Horus, I have sat down as Ptah, I am strong as Thoth, I am mighty as Atum, I walk with my legs, I speak with my mouth in order to seek out my foe; he has been given to me and he shall not be taken from me.

— 12 —

Chapter for going in and out

Hail to you, O Re, guardian of the secrets of the gates which are on this neck of Geb, because of this balance of Re with which he weighs out justice daily. Behold, I have hacked up the earth, and I have been permitted to come, having grown old.

— 13 —

Chapter for going in and out of the West

To me belong all men, I have given everything to myself. I have gone in as a falcon, I have come out as a Benu-bird, the god who worships Re. Prepare a path for me, that I may enter in peace in to the beautiful West, for I belong to the Lake of Horus, I leash the hounds of Horus. Prepare a way for me, that I may go in and worship Osiris, the Lord of Life.

— 14 —

Chapter for removing anger from the heart of the god

Hail to you, you who descend in power, chief of all secret matters! Behold, my word is spoken: so says the god who was angry with me. Wrong is washed away, and it falls immediately. O Lords of Justice, put an end to the evil harm which is in me. O you companions of the God of Justice, may this god be gracious to me, may my evil be removed for you. O Lord of Offerings, as mighty ruler, behold I have brought to you a propitiation-offering so that you may live on it and that I may live on it; be gracious to me and remove all anger which is in your heart against me.

— 17 —

[Note: The following text is the portion of Chapter 17 which is omitted from the Ani Papyrus at the point noted on Plate 10, left-hand column.]

Now as for the Two Fledglings, they are Horus the Protector of his father and Horus the Eyeless. *Otherwise said:* As for his twin souls which are within the Two Fledglings, they are the soul of Re, the soul of Osiris, the soul which is in

Shu, the soul which is in Nut, his twin souls which are in Mendes.

I am that great Cat who split the ished-tree on its side in Heliopolis on that night of making war on behalf of those who warded off the rebels and on that day in which were destroyed the enemies of the Lord of All.

What does it mean? As for that Cat, he is Re himself, who was called 'Cat' when Sia spoke about him; he was cat-like in what he did, and that is how his name of 'Cat' came into being. *Otherwise said:* He will be Shu making an inventory for Geb and for Osiris. As for the splitting of the ished-tree on its side in Heliopolis, it was when the Children of Impotence carried out what they did. As for that night of making war, it means that they entered into the east of the sky, and war broke out in the entire sky and earth.

O Re who are in your Egg, shining in your disk, rising in your horizon, swimming over your firmament, having no equal among the gods, sailing over the Supports of Shu, giving air with the breath of your mouth, illuminating the Two Lands with your sunshine, may you save me from that god whose shape is secret, whose eyebrows are the arms of the balance, on that night of reckoning up the robbers.

Who is he? It is he who uses his hand on that night of reckoning up the robbers, on that night of the flame against the fallen, when the lasso was put on the wrongdoers at the slaughterhouse for killing souls.

Who is he? He is Shesmu, he is the mutilator of Osiris. *Otherwise said:* He is Apophis, he has only one head which bears righteousness. *Otherwise said:* He is Horus, he has two heads, one bearing right and one bearing wrong; he gives wrong to whoever does it and right to whoever comes with it. *Otherwise said:* He is Horus the Great, preeminent in Letopolis. *Otherwise said:* He is Thoth. *Otherwise said:* He is Nefertum, son of Bastet. These are the tribunal who take action against the enemies of the Lord of All.

Save me from those who deal wounds, the slayers whose fingers are sharp, who deal out pain, who decapitate those who follow after Osiris; they shall not have power over me, and I will not fall into their cauldrons.

Who is he? He is Anubis, he is Horus the Eyeless. *Otherwise said:* It is the tribunal who took action against the foes of the Lord of All. *Otherwise said:* He is the master-physician of the Court. Their knives shall not have power over me, I will not fall into their cauldrons, because I know them, I know their names, I know the name of that smiter among them who belongs to the House of Osiris, who shoots with his eye, yet is unseen. The sky is encircled with the fiery blast of his mouth and Hapi makes report, yet he is unseen.

I was one who was hale on earth with Re and who died happily with Osiris; your offerings will not come into being through me, O you who are in charge of your braziers, because I am in the suite of the Lord of All at the edict of Khepri. I fly up as a falcon, I cackle as a goose, I pass eternity like Nehebkau.

What does it mean? It means that as for those who are in charge of their braziers, they are the likeness of the Eye of Re and the likeness of the Eye of Horus.

O Re-Atum, Lord of the Great Mansion, Sovereign of all the gods, save me from that god whose face is that of a hound but whose skin is human, who lives by butchery, who is in charge of the windings of the Lake of Fire, who swallows corpses, who controls hearts, who inflicts injury unseen.

Who is he? 'Swallower of Myriads' is his name, and he dwells in the Lake of Wenet. Now as for that Lake of Fire, it is what is between Naref and the House of the Entourage. As for anyone who treads on it, beware lest he fall to the knives. *Otherwise said:* 'He of the Sharp Knife' is his name, and he is door-keeper of the West. *Otherwise said:* Babai is his name, and he is the guardian of this interior of the West. *Otherwise said:* 'He who is over his affairs' is his name.

O Lord of Terror who is at the head of the Two Lands, O Lord of Blood whose slaughter-blocks are flourishing, who lives on entrails.

Who is he? He is the heart of Osiris, and he devours all kinds of slaughtering.

To whom was given the Wereret-crown and joy in Heracleopolis.

Who is he? As for him to whom was given the Wereret-crown and joy in Heracleopolis, he is Osiris.

To whom was entrusted rulership among the gods on that day when the Two Lands were united in the presence of the Lord of All.

Who is he? As for him to whom was entrusted rulership among the gods, he is Horus son of Isis, who was made ruler in the place of his father Osiris on that day when the Two Lands were united. It means the union of the Two Lands at the burial of Osiris.

Potent Ram who is in Heracleopolis, who gives good fortune and drives off wrong-doers, to whom the way of eternity is shown.

Who is he? He is Re himself.

[Note: The following text is omitted from the end of Chapter 17 in the Ani Papyrus.]

What does it mean? 'Secret of shape, the arms of Hemen' is the name of the fish-trap. 'He who sees what he brings by hand' is the name of the storm-cloud. *Otherwise said:* The name of the slaughter-block. As for the Lion whose mouth is bright and whose head is shining, he is the phallus of Osiris. *Otherwise said:* He is the phallus of Re. As for my having disarranged the hair of my face and having disordered my scalp, it means that Isis was in the shrine of Sokar and she rubbed her hair. As for Wadjet, Lady of the Devouring Flame, she is the Eye of Re. As for those few who approach her, it means that the confederacy of Seth are near her, because what is near her is burning.

If a man speaks this chapter when he is in a state of purity, it means going forth after death into the day and assuming whatever shape he desires. As for anyone who shall read it daily for his own benefit, it means being hale on earth; he shall come forth from every fire and nothing evil shall reach him. It is a matter a million times true; I have seen and it has indeed come to pass through me.

— 20 —

O Thoth, you who vindicated Osiris against his enemies, may you entrap the enemies of N in the presence of the tribunals of every god and every goddess:

In the presence of the great tribunal which is in Heliopolis on that night of battle and of felling those who rebelled.

In the presence of the great tribunal which is in Busiris on that night of erecting the two Djed-pillars.

In the presence of the great tribunal which is in Letopolis on that night of performing the night-ritual in Letopolis.

In the presence of the great tribunal which is in Pe and Dep on that night of confirming the heritage of Horus in respect of the property of his father Osiris.

In the presence of the great tribunal which is in the Two Banks on that night when Isis mourned for her brother Osiris.

In the presence of the great tribunal which is in Abydos on that night of the Haker-festival and of the numbering of the dead and the spirits.

In the presence of the great tribunal which is on the Road of the Dead on that night of making inquiry into him who is nothing.

In the presence of the great tribunal which is in the Great Devastation.

In the presence of the great tribunal which is in Naref.

In the presence of the great tribunal which is in Rosetjau on that night when Horus was vindicated against his enemies.

Horus has become great happily, the Two Conclaves are pleased about it, and Osiris is glad. O Thoth, vindicate N against his enemies in the tribunal of every god and every goddess, and in those tribunals of Osiris which are behind the shrine.

— 25 —

Chapter for causing that N
be remembered in the God's Domain

A name has been given to me in the Per-wer, my name has been remembered in the Per-neser, on that night of reckoning the years and of counting the months. I am this builder, I sit on the eastern side of the sky. As for any god who shall not come following after me, I will declare his name to those who are yet to be.

— 28 —

Chapter for not permitting N's heart
to be taken from him in the God's Domain

O Lion, I am a Weneb-flower; the slaughterhouse of the god is what I abhor, and my heart shall not be taken from me by those who fought in Heliopolis.

— 29A —

Chapter for not taking away the heart of one
whose conduct has been vindicated in the God's Domain

My heart is with me and it shall not be taken away, for I am a possessor of hearts who unites hearts. I live by truth, in which I exist; I am Horus who is in hearts, he who is in the middle of what is in the body. I live by saying what is in my heart, and it shall not be taken away; my heart is mine, and none shall be aggressive against it, no terror shall subdue me. I take it that I may be in the body of my father Geb and of my mother Nut, for I have committed no sin against the gods, and nothing shall be deducted in that respect from my vindication.

— 30A —

Chapter for not letting N's heart create
opposition against him in the God's Domain

O heart which I had from my mother, O my heart which I had upon earth, do not rise up against me as a witness in the presence of the Lord of Things; do not speak against me concerning what I have done, do not bring up anything against me in the presence of the Great God, Lord of the West.

Hail to you, my heart! Hail to you, my heart! Hail to you, my entrails! Hail to you, you gods who are at the head of those who wear the sidelock, who lean on their staffs! May you say what is good to Re, may you make me to flourish, may powers be bestowed when I go forth, having been interred among the great ones who long endure upon earth.

Not dying in the West, but becoming a spirit in it.

A RUBRIC FOR CHAPTER 30A, B

To be inscribed on a scarab made from nephrite, mounted in fine gold, with a ring of silver, and placed at the throat of the deceased. This incantation was found in Hermopolis, under the feet of this god. It was written on a block of mineral of Upper Egypt in the writing of the god himself and was discovered in the time of the Majesty of the vindicated King of Upper and Lower Egypt Menkaure. It was the king's son Hordedef who found it while he was going around making an inspection of the temples.

— 31 —

Chapter for driving off a crocodile which comes to
take away N's magic from him in the God's Domain

Get back! Retreat! Get back, you dangerous one! Do not come against me, do not live by my magic; may I not have to tell this name of yours to the Great God who sent you; 'Messenger' is the name of one and Bedty is the name of the other.

THE CROCODILE SPEAKS: Your face belongs to righteousness. The sky encloses the stars, magic encloses its settlements, and my mouth encloses the magic which is in it. My teeth are a knife, my tusks are the Viper Mountain.

THE DECEASED REPLIES: O you with a spine who would work your mouth against this magic of mine, no crocodile which lives by magic shall take it away.

— 32 —

Chapter for repelling a crocodile which comes to take
away a spirit's magic from him in the God's Domain

The Great One has fallen on his side, but the Ennead have pulled him together. I come, my soul speaks with my father, and I have this Great One from those eight crocodiles. I know them by their names and their lives, and I save my father from them.

Get back, you crocodile of the West, who lives on the Unwearying Stars! Detestation of you is in my belly, for I have absorbed the power of Osiris, and I am Seth.

Get back, you crocodile of the West! The Nau-snake is in my belly, and I have not given myself to you; your flame will not be on me.

Get back, you crocodile of the East, who lives on those who are mutilated! Detestation of you is in my belly, and I have gone away, for I am Osiris.

Get back, you crocodile in the East! The Nau-snake is in my belly, and I have not given myself to you; your flame will not be on me.

Get back, you crocodile of the South, living on feces, smoke and want! Detestation of you is in my belly, and my blood is not in your hand, for I am Sopd.

Get back, you crocodile in the South! I will erase you, for I become a Bebet-herb, and I have not given myself to you.

Get back, you crocodile of the North, living on the . . . which is in the midst of the stars! Detestation of you is in my belly, your poison is in my head; I am Atum.

Get back, you crocodile in the North! A scorpion is in my belly, but I will not give it birth.

I am one whose eyes are green, what exists is in my grasp, what does not exist is in my belly, I am clad and equipped with your magic, O Re, even this which is above me and below me. I am . . . , I am exalted, my throat is wide open in the house of my father the Great One; he has given to me yon beautiful West which destroys the living; strong is its lord, who daily is weary in it. My vision is cleared, my heart is in its proper place, my uraeus is with me every day. I am Re, who himself protects himself, and nothing can harm me.

— 33 —

Chapter for driving off a snake

O Rerek-snake, take yourself off, for Geb protects me; get up, for you have eaten a mouse, which Re detests, and you have chewed the bones of a putrid cat.

— 34 —

Chapter for not being bitten
by a snake in the God's Domain

O cobra, I am the flame which shines on the brows of the Chaos-gods of the Standard of Years. *Otherwise said:* the Standard of Vegetation. Begone from me, for I am Mafdet!

— 35 —

Chapter for not being eaten
by a snake in the God's Domain

'O Shu,' says He of Busiris, and vice versa. Neith is wearing the head-cloth, Hathor makes Osiris glad, and who is he who will eat me? Depart, leave me, pass me by, you snake; it is the Sam-plant which wards you off, this is the leek of Osiris which he asked for when he was buried. The clouded eyes of the Great One have fallen on you, and Maat will examine you for judgment.

— 36 —
Chapter for repelling a beetle

Begone from me, O Crooked-lips! I am Khnum, Lord of Peshnu, who dispatches the words of the gods to Re, and I report affairs to their master.

— 37 —
Chapter for repelling two Songstress-snakes

Hail to you, you two companions, sisters, Songstresses! I have divided you with my magic, for I am he who shines in the Night-bark, I am Horus, son of Isis, and I have come to see my father Osiris.

— 38A —
Chapter for living by air in the God's Domain

I am Atum who ascended from the Primordial Water to the Celestial Waters, I have taken my seat in the West and I give orders to the spirits whose seats are hidden, for I am the Double Lion, and acclamation is made to me in the Bark of Khepri. I eat in it and have become strong thereby, I live in it on air, and I drink in the Bark of Re. He opens a road for me, he throws open the gates of Geb. I have carried off those who are in the net of the Great One, I have governed those who are in their shrines, I have associated with Horus and Seth, the Two Lords. I dispatch the Elders on my own account, I come and go without having my throat cut, I go aboard the Bark of the just, I join those who are in the Day-bark when I attend on Re in his presence in the horizon, I daily live after death, I am strong through the Double Lion and I live after death, even I, N, who fills full the earth, who comes forth as the bloom of the lotus-plant, who makes the Two Lands content.

— 38B —
Chapter for living by air in the God's Domain

I am the Double Lion, the first-born of Re, Atum of Chemmis; those who are in their booths (serve me), those who are in their holes guide me, there are made for me ways which encircle the Celestial Waters on the path of the bark of Atum. I stand on the deck of the Bark of Re, I proclaim his words to the common folk and I repeat his words to these whose throats are constricted; I have judged my forefathers at eventide, I open my mouth, I eat life, I live in Busiris, and I live again after death like Re every day.

— 39 —
Chapter for repelling a Rerek-snake in the God's Domain

Get back! Crawl away! Get away from me, you snake! Go, be drowned in the Lake of the Primordial Water, at the place where your father commanded that the slaying of you should be carried out. Be far removed from that abode of Re wherein you trembled, for I am Re at whom men tremble; get back, you rebel, at the knives of his light. Your words have fallen because of Re, your face is turned back by the gods, your heart is cut out by Mafdet, you are put into bonds by the Scorpion-goddess, your sentence is carried out by Maat, those who are on the ways fell you.

Fall! Crawl away, Apophis, you enemy of Re! O you who escape massacre in the east of the sky at the sound of the roaring storm, open the doors of the horizon before Re, that he may go forth, wearied with wounds. I do what you desire, O Re, I do what is good, I act as one who pleases, O Re, I

cause your bonds to fall, O Re. Apophis has fallen to your destruction, the southern, northern, western and eastern gods have bound their bonds on him, Rekes has felled him, he who is over the partisans has bound him, and Re is content, Re proceeds in peace. Apophis the enemy of Re has fallen down, and what you have experienced is greater than that experience which is in the heart of the Scorpion-goddess; great is what she has done against you with the everlasting pains which are hers. You shall not become erect, you shall not copulate, O Apophis, you enemy of Re. Opposition is made against you, O you whom Re hates when he looks on you.

Get back! You shall be decapitated with a knife, your face shall be cut away all round, your head shall be removed by him who is in his land, your bones shall be broken, your limbs shall be cut off; the earth-god has condemned you, O Apophis, you enemy of Re.

O Re, your crew . . . may you rest there, for your possessions are there. Bring to the house, bring your Eye to the house, bring what is good; may no evil opposition come forth from your mouth against me, being what you might do against me, for I am Seth, who can raise a tumult of storm in the horizon of the sky like one whose will is destruction — so says Atum.

Lift up your faces, you soldiers of Re, and keep Nendja away from the tribunal for me — so says Geb. Make yourselves firm, O you who are on your seats aboard the bark of Khepri. Take your ways and your weapons which are put into your hands for you — so says Hathor. Take your javelins — so says Nut. Come, drive away that enemy of his, namely Nendja, that those who are in his shrine may come and that he may ferry himself in solitude, even he the Lord of All, who shall not be opposed — so say those primeval gods who circumambulate the Lakes of Turquoise. Come, O Great One whom we worship; save us, O you whose shrines are great, from whom the Ennead came forth, to whom what is beneficial is done, to whom praise is given; may someone report it to you and me — so says Nut — for yonder Happy One — so say those who are among the gods. May he go forth, may he find the way, may he plunder the gods, may he rise early in front of Nut, and may Geb stand up — so says the Terrible One. The Ennead is on the move, the door of Hathor has been infringed, and Re is triumphant over Apophis.

— 40 —
Chapter for repelling him who swallowed an ass

Get back, you Male whom Osiris detests, whose head Thoth has cut off! I have done everything in respect of you which was said about you in the Ennead in order to carry out your destruction.

Get back, you whom Osiris in the Neshmet-bark detests when he sails southward with a fair wind! Purify yourselves, all you gods, and fell with shouting the enemies of Osiris, Lord of the Thinite nome.

Get back, you swallower of an ass, whom Ha who is in the Duat detests! I know, I know, I know, I know! Where are you? I am . . .

— 41 —
Chapter for preventing the slaughter which is carried out in the God's Domain

O Atum, spiritualize me in the presence of the Double Lion, the Great God; may he open for me the portal of Geb, that I may do homage to the Great God who is in the realm of the dead; may you induct me into the presence of the Ennead who preside over the Westerners.

O you door-keeper of the City of the Bee which is in the West, may I eat and live by air, may he who is safe and great guide me to the Great Bark of Khepri, and may I speak to the evening crew; may I come and go, may I see who is there; I will raise him up, I will speak my words to him, when my throat is constricted. May I live, may I be saved after sleeping.

O Bringer of offerings who open your mouth, confirm the writings for offerings, establish Maat on her throne for me; confirm the tablets, establish the goddesses in the presence of Osiris the Great God, the ruler of eternity, who reckons up his seasons, who listens to them of the islands, who raises his right arm when he commissions the great ones whom he sends into the great tribunal which is in the God's Domain.

— 42 —
Chapter for preventing the slaughter
which is carried out in Heracleopolis

O Land of the Staff! O Crown of the Statue! O Standard which is rowed! I am the Child! O Great Kid, I speak to you today! The slaughterhouse is equipped with what you know, and you have come to it . . . I am Re, continually praised; I am the knot of the god within the tamarisk. How beautiful is the . . . with him!

I am Re, continually praised; I am the knot of the god within the tamarisk; if I am hale, then will Re be hale today.

[Note: The portion of the chapter which occurs at this point appears in the Papyrus of Ani on Plate 32.]

I am the daily sun, I am not grasped by my arms, I am not gripped by my hands, and there are no men, gods, spirits, dead men, patricians, common folk, sun-folk or robbers who shall harm me. I go forth hale, one whose name is unknown, I am Yesterday; one who views a million years; my name is one who passes on the paths of those who are in charge of destinies. I am the Lord of Eternity; may I be recognized as Khepri, for I am the Lord of the Wereret-crown.

I am he in whom is the Sacred Eye, and who is in the Egg, and it is granted to me to live by them.

I am he in whom is the Sacred Eye, namely the Closed Eye, I am under its protection. I have gone out, I have risen up, I have gone in, I am alive.

I am he in whom is the Sacred Eye, my seat is on my throne, I dwell in my abode with it, for I am Horus who treads down millions, my throne has been ordered for me, and I will rule from it. Behold, my mouth is what speaks and what keeps silence, and I am precise. Behold, my shape is turned upside down. I am Wennefer, season by season, whose attributes (come) into him one by one when he travels around.

I am he in whom is the Sacred Eye, and nothing shall come into being against me, no evil cutting off and no uproar, and there shall be no danger to me.

I am he who opened a door in the sky, who rules from his throne, who adjudges those who are born this day; there is no child who treads yesterday's road, and today is mine. O people on people, I am he who protects you for eons. Are you in being, you sky-folk, earthlings, southerners, northerners, easterners, and westerners, is the fear of me in your bellies? I am he who fashioned with his Eye, and I will not die again. My striking power is in your bellies, my shape is before me; I am . . . and I ignore the wrath in your faces against me; I am joyful, and there can be found no season when he could harm me. Where is the sky? Where is the earth? Their offspring are rebuffed and they are disunited. My name overpasses it, namely everything evil, for great are the spoken words which I speak to you.

I am one who rises and shines, wall of walls, most unique of the unique ones, and there is no day devoid of its duties. Pass by! Behold, I have spoken to you, for I am the flower which came out of the Primordial Water, my mother is Nut. O you who created me, I am one who cannot tread, the great knot within yesterday; my arm is knotted into my hand, I will not know him who would know me, I will not grasp him who would grasp me. O Egg, O Egg, I am Horus who presides over

myriads, my fiery breath is in the faces of those whose hearts would move against me. I rule from my throne, I pass time on the road which I have opened up. I am released from all evil, I am the golden baboon, three palms and two fingers high, which has neither arms nor legs, in front of Memphis. If I am hale, then will the baboon which is in front of Memphis be hale.

— 47 —
Chapter for preventing the taking of N's
place and throne from him in the God's Domain

O Place of mine, O Throne of mine, come and serve me, for I am your lord. O you gods, come in my company, for I am the son of your lord, you are mine, for it was my father who made you.

— 53 —
Chapter for not eating feces
or drinking urine in the God's Domain

I am the horned bull who rules the sky, Lord of Celestial Appearings, the Great Illuminator who came forth from the heat, who harnesses the years; the Double Lion is glad, and the movement of the sunshine has been granted to me. I detest what is detestable, I will not eat feces, I will not drink urine, I will not walk head downward.

I am the owner of bread in Heliopolis, bread of mine is in the sky with Re, bread of mine is on earth with Geb, and it is the Night-bark and the Day-bark which will bring it to me from the house of the Great God who is in Heliopolis. I am loosed from my windings, I make ready the ferry-boat of the sky, I eat of what they eat, I live on what they live on, I have eaten bread in every pleasant room.

— 55 —
Chapter for giving breath in the God's Domain

I am the jackal of jackals, I am Shu who draws the air into the presence of the sunshine to the limits of the sky, to the limits of the earth, to the limits of the plume of the nebeh-bird, and air is given to those youths who open my mouth so that I may see with my eyes.

— 56 —
Chapter for breathing air
among the waters in the God's Domain

O Atum, give me the sweet breath which is in your nostril, for I seek out that great place which is in Wenu, I have guarded that Egg of the Great Cackler. If I be strong, it will be strong; if I live, it will live; if I breathe the air, it will breathe the air.

— 57 —
Chapter for breathing air and
having power over water in the God's Domain

O Hapi, Great One of the sky in this your name of 'The sky is safe', may you grant that I have power over water like Sekhmet who saved Osiris on that night of storm. Behold, the Elders who are before the throne of 'Abundance' have sent to me just as that august god whose name they do not know sent them, and they send me likewise. My nostrils are opened in Busiris, I rest in Heliopolis, my house is what Seshat built for me, Khnum stands up for me on his battlements.

If the sky comes with the north wind, I will dwell in the south; if the sky comes with the south wind, I will dwell in the north; if the sky comes with the west wind, I will dwell in the east; if the sky comes with the east wind, I will dwell in the west. I will pull the skin of my nostrils, I will open up at the place where I desire to be.

— 62 —
Chapter for drinking water in the God's Domain

May the great water be opened for Osiris, may the cool water of Thoth and the water of Hapi be thrown open for the Lord of the Horizon in this my name of Pedsu. May I be granted power over the waters like the limbs of Seth, for I am he who crosses the sky, I am the Lion of Re, I am the Slayer who eats the foreleg, the leg of beef is extended to me, the pools of the Field of Reeds serve me, limitless eternity is given to me, for I am he who inherited eternity, to whom everlasting was given.

— 63A —
Chapter for drinking water and not being burnt by fire

O Bull of the West, I am brought to you, for I am that oar of Re with which the Old Ones are rowed. I will be neither burnt up nor scorched, for I am Babai, the eldest son of Osiris, for whom all the gods have assembled within his Eye in Heliopolis; I am the trusted heir when the Great One is inert, my name will be strong for me, and assuredly you will live daily through me.

— 63B —
Chapter for not being scalded with water

I am that equipped oar with which Re is rowed when the Old Ones are rowed and the efflux of Osiris is upraised at the Lake of Flames which does not burn, I have climbed in the sunshine. O Khnum who is in charge of whips, come, cut away the bonds from him who travels on this road on which I have ascended.

— 64 —
Chapter of knowing all the chapters of going forth by day in a single chapter by N.

He says: Yesterday, which is pregnant with the one who shall give birth to himself at another time, belongs to me. I am the one secret of Ba-spirit who made the gods and gives offerings to the Duat-gods of the West of the sky. I am the steering oar of the East, the possessor of two faces whose rays are seen and the possessor of clouds, one who emerges at twilight, whose forms belong to the House of Mooring. O you two falcons of his, chieftains of their councils, who hear matters, you are the ones who lead the "Moored Ones" to the secret places, who drag in Re, who follows from the upper place, the shrine which is above the firmament, lord of the shrine which stands within the circumvallation of the earth. I am he and he is I. Faience is molded and Ptah is in charge of his minerals.

O Re, laugh. May your heart be sweet with your good truth belonging to this day. Enter from out of Hermopolis, come forth from the East. May the eldest ones and the ancestors greet you. Make pleasant your roads for me, make wide your paths for me, that I may cross the earth according to the fashion of crossing the sky. May your light be upon me, O threefold Ba (i.e. Re). I am one who draws near to the god who speaks in my ears in the Duat. There are no sins of mine towards my mother against me. (Accordingly) may you rescue me, may you protect me from the one who closes his eye in the evening and yet sees in the total darkness.

I am the inundation, my name is 'Great Black Lake,' the one whose back fills what clothes the goat skin. O Eldest One yonder who does not have an island, call out to the ones who are amidst their sedges in that hour of being in attendance on the god. Speak, please, to the one who is in charge of his overflow: Behold the foreleg is tied upon the neck and the hindquarters are atop the head of the West. Give to me what is within you, O greater of the Two Great Ones, as one who is put with me instead. I weep because of what I have seen.

May I sail from the dyke in Abydos, while the doorbolts move the doorways quickly, and their faces are downcast. May your arm be in your skin; your face is that of the greyhound whose nose smells at the shrine. My feet convey me, Anubis having hesitated at "Having no Limits". My two nurses are Tatenen and the Double Lion, so I am healthy. I am the one who goes forth from a part of a door. The sunlight, which his wish made, remains.

I know the depths and I know your name. You have made the portions of the blessed dead — who are millions and hundreds of thousands more — and 1,200 things moreover than those things of theirs. The eddies are more than the hours of the day. That which is upon the shoulders of Orion is examined, being one-twelfth, strewing out what is united, as what one gives to another among them. It is one-sixth which is the due therein which is preeminent, namely the hour of overthrowing the rebel and returning therefrom vindicated. It is these who are in the opening of the Duat, it is these who are provided for Shu.

I have risen as a possessor of life because of goodly Maat of that day of cold blood, fresh wounds, and burial. I split the horns among the ones who were united with the crocodile against me.

O ones mysterious of fashioning, do not repel me. O those upon their bellies, I have arrived with a commission of the lord of lords in order to greet Osiris. Do not cause that the eye swallow its tears.

I am the disarrayed one of the house of him who is in his offering chapel. I have come from Letopolis to Heliopolis in order to inform the Benu-bird about the matters of the Duat.

O land of silence and secrets who is with its companion, which creates forms as Khepri does, may you cause that N go forth so that he may see the sun-disk, and that he may be increased in the presence of the great god. Shu is he who is in eternity.

May I travel in peace, may I tread upon the firmament. May I praise the Fiery One by the light of my eye. May I fly up, that I might see the bright expanses of gloriousness in the presence of Re every day, the one who causes all the common folk to live. He treads upon the tails of the ones who are in the earth.

O shouter, O shouter, who thrusts aside the shadows of the blessed dead from the earth, may a good road to the gateway of the praised ones be given to me, for I am acting because the one who is yonder is weary, so that the one who is pus-filled may pull himself together.

Who, pray, is the one who licks in the hidden place? I am the one who is preeminent in Rosetjau, who enters in his name and goes forth as the one who seeks. The Lord of Millions of the earth is his name.

The pregnant one is putting down her load, Hiyet has borne before the one who is upside-down. The door in the wall is sealed, it being overthrown by your hand. I have made it pleasant for you. The water pot is overturned on the back of the Benu-bird and the two lady confederates. Horus is the one to whom his eye is given, so that his face may be illuminated at dawn. I shall not vomit, but instead I shall become a lion. The affairs of Shu are with me. I am nephrite. How good it is to see the moored one on that good day of the weary-hearted one, when he alights in the marsh. I am the Going Forth by Day, a possessor of life in the presence of Osiris.

Behold, your protection remains every day. I have embraced the sycamore tree, and the sycamore has protected me. The two Sekh-snakes have opened the Duat for me. I have come that I may embrace the Wadjet-eye.

O Ba of mine, where pray are you on the Pesdjet-festival, when the corpse is silent? I have come that I may see Re when he sets, and that I may receive breath at his going forth again. My two arms are pure in praising him. Gather me together, gather me together, that I may soar up and alight upon land. My eye races thereby in my footsteps. I am one who gave birth to myself yesterday, one who created my own name. The

Akeru-spirits of the earth created me and released me in my time.

I am one who is hidden from the one whose arms fight. Come following me, for my Heka-magic is firm and my Akhu-magic is my protection which I inherited. My Ba quivers when it alights, because of my counsel. The Ennead has heard that which I say.

Now as to anyone who knows this spell, it means that he shall be vindicated upon earth and in the God's Domain. He shall do what the living do.

This spell was found in Hermopolis on a brick of the ore of Upper Egypt, written on real lapis lazuli, under the feet of this god in the time of the King of Upper and Lower Egypt, Menkaure, the vindicated, by Prince Hordedef, who found it when he was wandering about to make an inspection of the temples, a troop of the Braves being with him on that account. He requisitioned it by entreaty and brought it back like a marvel to the king when he saw this great secret, unseen and unbeheld.

It should be recited while one is pure, without going near women, without eating goats, without consuming fish.

— 65 —
Chapter for going out into the day and having power over one's enemy

Re sits in his Abode of Millions of Years, and there assemble for him the Nine Gods with hidden faces who dwell in the Mansion of Khepri, who eat abundance and who drink the drinks which the sky brings at dawn. Do not permit me to be carried off as booty to Osiris, for I have never been in the confederacy of Seth, O you who sit on your coils before Him whose soul is strong, let me sit on the throne of Re and take possession of my body before Geb; may you grant that Osiris may go forth vindicated against Seth; may the dreams of Seth be the dreams of a crocodile. O you whose faces are hidden, who preside over the Mansions of the King of Lower Egypt, who clothe the gods in the Sixth-day Festival, who weave forever and who knot eternally, I have seen the Pig put into fetters, but indeed he who was put under ward has been released, the Pig has been loosed. I have been reborn, I have gone forth in the shape of a living spirit whom the common folk worship on earth. O you sick one who would harm me, be driven off from the wall of Re. Let me see Re, let me go forth against my enemies, let me be vindicated against them in the tribunal of the Great God in the presence of the Great God. If you do not let me go forth against that enemy of mine that I may be vindicated against him in the tribunal, then Hapi shall not ascend to the sky that he may live on truth, nor shall Re descend to the waters that he may live on fish. Then shall Re ascend to the sky that he may live on truth, and Hapi descend to the waters that he may live on fish, and the great day on earth shall end its condition. I have come against that enemy of mine, and he is given over to me, he is finished and silent in the tribunal.

— 66 —
Going out into the day

I know that I was conceived by Sekhmet and borne by Satis. I am Horus who came forth from the Eye of Horus, I am Wadjet who came forth from Horus, I am Horus who flew up, I have lighted on the vertex of Re in the prow of his bark which is in the Primordial Water.

— 67 —
Chapter for opening the tomb

The cavern is opened for those who are in the Primordial Water, and those who are in the sunshine are released; the cavern is opened for Shu, and if he comes out, I will come out. I will go down into the earth-opening, I will receive . . . , for I have grasped the lashings in the house of Him who is in

charge of the mooring-posts. I will go down to my seat which is in the Bark of Re; may I not suffer through being deprived of my seat which is in the Bark of Re the great who rises and shines in the waterway of the lake.

— 68 —
Chapter for going out into the day

The doors of the sky are opened for me, the doors of the earth are opened for me, the door-bolts of Geb are opened for me, the shutters of the sky-windows are thrown open for me. It is he who guarded me who releases me, who binds his hand on me and thrusts his hand on to me on earth, the mouth of the Pelican is opened for me, the mouth of the Pelican is given to me, and I go out into the day to the place where I desire to be.

May I have power in my heart, may I have power in my heart, may I have power in my arms, may I have power in my legs, may I have power in my mouth, may I have power in all my members, may I have power over invocation-offerings, may I have power over water, may I have power over air, may I have power over the waters, may I have power over the streams, may I have power over riparian lands, may I have power over the men who would harm me, may I have power over the women who would harm me in the God's Domain, may I have power over those who would give orders to harm me upon earth.

A GOD REPLIES: Surely it will be according to what you say to me. You shall live on the bread of Geb, and you shall not eat what you detest. You shall live on bread of white emmer and beer of red barley of Hapi in the pure place; you shall sit under the branches of the tree of Hathor who is preeminent in the wide solar disk when she travels to Heliopolis bearing the script of the divine words, the book of Thoth. You shall have power in your heart, you shall have power in your heart, you shall have power in your mouth, you shall have power in your arms, you shall have power over water, you shall have power over the waters, you shall have power over the streams, you shall have power over the riparian lands, you shall have power over the men who would harm you, you shall have power over the women who would harm you in the God's Domain, you shall have power over those who would give orders to harm you on earth or in the God's Domain. Raise yourself upon your left side, put yourself upon your right side, sit down and stand up, throw off your dust, may your tongue and your mouth be wise.

As for whoever knows this book, he shall go out into the day, he shall walk on earth among the living and he shall never suffer destruction. A matter a million times true.

— 69 —
Chapter for being the successor of Osiris

I am the Radiant One, brother of the Radiant Goddess, Osiris the brother of Isis; my son and his mother Isis have saved me from my enemies who would harm me. Bonds are on their arms, their hands and their feet, because of what they have done evilly against me. I am Osiris, the first-born of the company of the gods, eldest of the gods, heir of my father Geb; I am Osiris, Lord of persons, alive of breast, strong of hinder-parts, stiff of phallus, who is within the boundary of the common folk.

I am Orion who treads his land, who precedes the stars of the sky which are on the body of my mother Nut, who conceived me at her desire and bore me at her will. I am Anubis on the Day of the Centipede, I am the Bull who presides over the field. I am Osiris, for whom his father and mother sealed an agreement on that day of carrying out the great slaughter; Geb is my father and Nut is my mother, I am Horus the Elder on the Day of Accession, I am Anubis of Sepa, I am the Lord of All, I am Osiris.

O you Eldest One who have come in, say to the collector

of writings and to the door-keeper of Osiris that I have come, being a spirit, fully reckoned and divine; I have come that I myself may protect my body, that I may sit on the birth-stool of Osiris and get rid of his sore suffering. I am mighty and divine upon the birth-stool of Osiris, for I was born with him when he was very young. I uncover those knees of Osiris, I open the mouths of the gods because of them, I sit beside him, and Thoth has gone forth happy with a thousand of bread (and a thousand of beer) upon my father's altar, with my dappled cattle, long-horns, red cattle, geese, and poultry for offering which I gave to Horus and offered to Thoth; my place of slaughter belongs to Him who is over the place of sacrifice.

— 70 —

Otherwise said: My place of slaughter belongs to Him who is over the place of sacrifice, I am happy and pleased with the altar of my father Osiris. I rule in Busiris, I travel about on its river-banks, I breathe the east wind because of its tresses, I grasp the north wind by its braided lock, I grip the south wind by its plaits, I grasp the west wind by its nape. I travel around the sky on its four sides, I give breath to the blessed ones among those who eat bread.

As for him who knows this book on earth, he shall come out into the day, he shall walk on earth among the living, and his name shall not perish forever.

— 71 —

Chapter for going out into the day

O you falcon who rise from the Primordial Water, Lord of the Celestial Waters, make me hale just as you made yourself hale. Release him, loose him, put him on earth, cause him to be loved: so says the One-faced Lord concerning me.

O you falcon within the shrine, may I be revealed to Him on whom is a fringed garment: so says Horus son of Isis.

O Horus son of Isis, make me hale as you made yourself hale. Release him, loose him, put him on earth, cause him to be loved: so says the One-faced Lord concerning me.

O Horus in the southern sky, O Thoth in the northern sky, pacify for me the raging fiery serpent, raise up Maat for me to Him whom she loves: so says Thoth.

O Thoth, make me hale just as you made yourself hale. Release him, loose him, put him on earth, cause him to be loved: so says the One-faced Lord concerning me.

I am the Weneb-flower of Naref, the Nebheh-flower of the hidden horizon: so says Osiris.

O Osiris, make me hale just as you made yourself hale. Release him, loose him, put him on earth, let him be loved: so says the One-faced Lord concerning me.

O you who are terrible on your feet, who are in action, Lord of the Two Fledglings: as the Two Fledglings live, make me hale just as you made yourself hale. Release him, loose him, put him on earth, cause him to be loved: so says the One-faced Lord concerning me.

O you of Nekhen who are in your Egg, Lord of the Celestial Waters, make me hale just as you made yourself hale. Release him, loose him, put him on earth, cause him to be loved: so says the One-faced Lord concerning me.

Rise up, O Sobk, in the midst of your river-bank; rise up, O Neith, in the midst of your riparian land. Release him, loose him, put him on earth, cause him to be loved: so says the One-faced Lord concerning me.

O you seven knots, the arms of the balance on that night of setting the Sacred Eye in order, who cut off heads, who sever necks, who take away hearts, who snatch hearts, who make a slaughter in the Island of Fire: I know you, I know your names; may you know me just as I know your names; if I reach you, may you reach me; if you live through me, may I live through you; may you make me to flourish with what is in your hands, the staff which is in your grasp. May you destine

me to life annually; may you grant to me many years of life over and above my years of life; many months over and above my months of life; many days over and above my days of life; many nights over and above my nights of life, until I depart. May I rise to be a likeness of myself, may my breath be at my nose, may my eyes see in company with those who are in the horizon on that day of dooming the robber.

As for him who shall recite this chapter, it means prosperity on earth with Re and a goodly burial with Osiris; it will go very well with a man in the God's Domain, and there shall be given to him the loaves which are issued daily in the Presence. A matter a million times true.

— 72 —

*Chapter for going out into the day
and opening up the tomb*

Hail to you, you owners of souls, who are devoid of wrong, who exist for all eternity! Open to me, for I am a spirit in my own shape, I have power by means of this my magic, and I am recognized as a spirit. Save me from aggressors in this land of the just, give me my mouth that I may speak with it, let my arms be extended in your presence, because I know you, I know your names, I know the name of that Great God before whom you place your provisions, whose name is Tjekem. He opens up the eastern horizon of the sky, he alights in the western horizon of the sky, he removes me so that I may be hale. The Milky Way will not reject me, the rebels will not have power over me, I shall not be turned away from your portals, the doors shall not be closed against me, because my bread is in Pe, my beer is in Dep, my hands shall be . . . there, there shall be given to me my father Atum, there shall be established for me my houses in the sky and on earth, with uncounted emmer therein; offering shall be made to me there of food by my son of my body, you shall give invocation-offerings of bread and beer, incense and unguent, and all things good and pure whereon a god lives, in very deed forever, in any shape which I desire, and faring downstream and upstream in the Field of Rushes, for I am the Double Lion.

[Note: The standard rubric for this chapter appears on Plate 6 of the Ani Papyrus.]

— 75 —

*Chapter for going to Heliopolis
and receiving a throne there*

I have gone forth from the limits of the earth that I may receive my fringed cloak for the heart of the Baboon; I have razed the Pure Mansions which were in Edfu, I have destroyed the Mansions of Him who beats with a stick, I have attacked the Mansions of Ikhsesef, I have forced the sacred gates, I have passed by the House of Kemkem, the 'knot-of-Isis' amulet has laid her hands on me, and she has commended me to her sister the Accuser by her own mother the Destroyer, she has set me in the eastern sky in which Re appears and in which Re is daily exalted. I have appeared in glory, I have been initiated, I have been ennobled as a god, and they have put me on the sacred road on which Thoth travelled when he pacified the Combatants and proceeded to Pe so that he might come to Dep.

— 76 —

*Chapter for being transformed
into any shape one may wish to take*

I have passed by the Palace, and it was an Abyt-bird which brought you to me. Hail to you, you who flew up to the sky, the white and shining bird which guards the White Crown. I shall be with you and I shall join the Great God; make a way for me that I may pass on it.

Chapter for becoming an elder of the tribunal

I am Atum who made the sky and created what exists, who came forth from the earth, who created seed, Lord of All, who fashioned the gods, the Great God, the self-created, the Lord of Life, who made the Ennead to flourish.

Hail to you, you lords of pure offerings, whose thrones are secret! Hail to you, you lords of eternity, whose forms are hidden, whose shrines are secret, whose place is unknown! Hail to you, you gods who are in the Radiance! Hail to you, you gods who encircle the firmament! Hail to you, you gods who are in the West! Hail to you, Ennead which is in the Lower Sky! See, I have come to you pure, divine, possessing a spirit, mighty, besouled; I have brought to you a measure of incense and natron, that I may drive away slaver therewith from your mouths, I have come that I may remove the ill which is in your hearts, I have removed the evil which is on you. I have brought you what is good, I have raised up to you what is true, for I know you, I know your names, I know your forms which were unknown. I have come into being among you, I appear in glory as that god who eats men and lives on gods, I am mighty among you as that god who is uplifted on his standard, to whom the gods come in joy, at whom the goddesses exult when they see him. I have come to you, having appeared as son of you all; I sit in my seat which is in the horizon, I receive offerings upon my altar, I drink wine in the evening. Those who are in joy come to me, praise is given to me by those who are in the horizon in this my rank of the Lord of All. I am exalted as this noble god who is in the Great Mansion; the gods rejoice when they see him among those who go forth happily on the body of the Lower Sky when his mother Nut has borne him.

Chapter for being transformed into a lotus

O Lotus belonging to the semblance of Nefertum, I am the Man. I know your name, I know your names, you gods, you lords of the God's Domain, for I am one of you. May you grant that I see the gods who lead the Duat, may there be given to me a seat in the God's Domain in the presence of the lords of the West, may I take my place in the Sacred Land, may I receive offerings in the presence of the lords of eternity, may my soul go forth to every place that it desires, without being held back from the presence of the Great Ennead.

Chapter for removing foolish speech from the mouth

O you who cut off heads and sever necks and who put folly into the mouths of the spirits because of the magic which is in their bodies, you shall not see me with those eyes of yours with which you see, (you shall kneel) on your knees, you shall go about with your face behind you, you shall look on the tormentors belonging to Shu who follow after you to cut off your head and to sever your neck at the behest of Him who saved his lord, because of this which you have said you would do to me, namely the putting of folly into my mouth with intent to cut off my head, to sever my neck, and to close my mouth because of the magic which is in my body, just as you did to the spirits because of the magic which was in their bodies. Turn away at the sentence which Isis spoke when you came to put folly into the mouth of Osiris at the desire of his enemy Seth, saying to you: 'May your face be downcast at seeing this face of mine!' May the flame of the Eye of Horus go forth against you within the Eye of Atum, which was injured on that night when it swallowed you. Get you back because of Osiris, for abhorrence of you is in him — and vice versa; get you back because of me, because abhorrence of you is in me — and vice versa. If you come against me, I will speak to you; if you do not come against me, I will not speak to you. Get back to the tormentors belonging to Shu . . .

Chapter for requesting a water-pot and a palette

O you great one who see your father, keeper of the book of Thoth, see, I have come spiritualized, besouled, mighty, and equipped with the writings of Thoth. Bring me the messenger of the earth-god who is with Seth, bring me a water-pot and palette from the writing-kit of Thoth and the mysteries which are in them.

See, I am a scribe; bring me the corruption of Osiris that I may write with it and that I may do what the great and good god says every day, being the good which you have decreed for me, O Horakhty. I will do what is right and I will send to Re daily.

Chapter for being beside Thoth

I am he who gave protection in the tumult, who guarded the Great Goddess in the war. I smote with my knife, I calmed Ash, I acted on behalf of the Great Goddess in the war. I made strong the sharp knife which was in the hand of Thoth in the tumult.

Chapter for being beside Thoth and for causing a man to be a spirit in the God's Domain

I am he who dwells in his Eye, I have come that I may give Maat to Re, I have propitiated Seth with the bodily fluids of Aker and the blood which is in the spinal cord of Geb.

O Night-bark, O Staff of Anubis, I have propitiated those four spirits who are in the suite of the Lord of Offerings, I am an owner of fields through their command. I am the father of Bah who drives away thirst and who guards the waterways. See me, you great, elder, and mighty gods who are at the head of the Souls of Heliopolis; I am high above your heads and I am one potent among you. See, I am one whose mighty, elder, and great soul is respected; I will not be given over to this ill-will which has issued from your mouths, and harm will not turn round over me, for I am pure in the Island of Propitiation . . . in the divine Eye under the tree of the goddess of the sky, which refreshes the vindicated ones, the lords who were aforetime.

Draw near quickly, you righteous ones! I was the most truly precise person on earth, I was an interpreter of speech, the scepter of the Sole Lord, Re the Great God who lives by truth; do not injure me . . .

Chapter for fetching a ferryboat in the sky

Hail to you, you plateau which is in the sky north of the Great Waterway, for whoever sees it will not die. I stand upon you, I appear as a god, I have seen you and I will not die. I stand upon you, I appear as a god, I cackle as a goose, I fly up thence as the falcon upon the branches.

O Dew of the Great One, I cross the earth towards the sky, I stand up as Shu, I make the sunshine to flourish on the sides of the ladder which is made to mount up to the Unwearying Stars, far from decapitation. Bring me those who repel evil when I have passed you by at the polar region of Tepen.

'Where have you come from?'

'O Tepen, I have come from the Lake of Burning in the Field of Fire.'

'What did you live on in the Lake of Burning in the Field of Fire?'

'I lived on that noble tree of Ikaa who brought these boats from the Dried-up Lake for me. The water-jar was on . . . that

I might stand in the Sacred Bark and guide the waters; that I might stand in the Sacred Bark and conduct the god; that I might stand up, my staff being a rod.'

'Go aboard and sail.' The gates are opened for me in Letopolis, the earth is split open for me in Wenu, and the staffs have been given to me in respect of my inheritance.

— 99 —

*Chapter for bringing a ferryboat
in the God's Domain*

I

O Ferryman, bring me this which was brought to Horus on account of his Eye and which was brought to Seth on account of his testicles; there leaps up the Eye of Horus which fell in the eastern side of the sky so that it may protect itself from Seth.

O Mahaf, as you are provided with life, awaken Iqen for me, for see, I have come.

Who are you who comes?

I am the beloved of my father, one who greatly loves his father, and I am he who awakens his sleeping father.

O Mahaf, as you are endowed with life, awaken Iqen for me, for see, I have come.

Do you say that you would cross to the eastern side of the sky? If you cross, what will you do?

I will raise up his head, I will lift up his brow, and he shall make a decree in your favor, and the decree which he shall make for you shall not perish nor become void in this land forever.

O Mahaf, as you are endowed with life, awaken Iqen for me, for see, I have come.

Why should I awaken Iqen for you?

That he may bring me the built-up boat of Khnum from the Lake of Feet.

But she is in pieces and stored in the dockyard.

Take her larboard side and fix it to the stern; take her starboard side and fix it to the bow.

But she has no planks, she has no end-pieces, she has no rubbing-pieces, she has no oar-loops.

Her planks are the drops of moisture which are on the lips of Babai; her end-pieces are the hair which is under the tail of Seth; her rubbing-pieces are the sweat which is on the ribs of Babai; her oar-loops are the hands of the female counterpart of Horus. She is built by the Eye of Horus, who shall steer her to me.

O Mahaf, as you are endowed with life, awaken Iqen for me, for see, I have come.

Who will guard this boat?

Bring the tail of the Senemty-animal and put it in her stern; that will guard her.

O Mahaf, as you are endowed with life, awaken Iqen for me, for see, I have come.

Who will bring her to you and to me?

Bring her to me with the best of the gods and his offspring, namely Imsety, Hapy, Duamutef and Qebehsenuef; he will command her, the Tetwy-animal being placed at her bow, and he will steer her to the place where you are.

What is she?

She is the wings of the Tetwy-animal.

The weather is windy and she has no mast.

Bring this phallus of Babai which creates children and begets calves.

To what shall I make it fast?

To the thighs which open out the shanks.

What about her cable?

Bring this snake which is in the hand of Hemen.

Where shall I stow it?

You shall stow it in her bilge.

What about her sail?

It is the cloth which came out of Sutyu when Horus and the Ombite kissed on New Year's Day.

What about the gunwales?

They are the sinews of Him whom all these fear.

Who is he whom all these fear?

It is he who lives in the night which precedes the New Year.

O Mahaf, as you are endowed with life, awaken Iqen for me, for see, I have come.

Who are you who comes?

I am a magician.

How have you come and how have you gone up?

I have gone up on this . . .

What have you done to her?

I have trodden on her back, I have guided her . . . aright.

What else have you done to her?

My right side was at her starboard, my front was towards her bow, my left side was at her larboard, my back was towards her stern.

What else have you done to her?

At night her bulls were slaughtered and her geese cut up.

Who stands on her?

Horus of the Rulers.

Who takes her cordage?

The Foremost One, the Ruler, the Oldest One.

Who controls her bowls?

The Foremost One, the Ruler, Baty.

What else have you done to her?

I went to Min of Coptos and Anubis the Commander of the Two Lands, and I found them celebrating their festivals and reaping their emmer in bundles of ears with their sickles between their thighs, from which you have made cakes. The god who ascends led me to the goddess who ascends, and the Lady of Pe led me to the Lady of Netjeru. Now as for the gods of Pe who are in front of their houses, I found them washing their head-cloths. They will come bearing the cakes of the gods, and they will make cakes for you when going downstream and bread when going upstream.

O Mahaf, as you are endowed with life, awaken Iqen for me, for see, I have come.

Who are you who comes?

I am a magician.

Are you complete?

I am complete.

Are you equipped?

I am equipped.

Have you healed the limbs?

I have healed the limbs.

What are those limbs, magician?

They are the arm and the leg.

Take care! Do you say that you would cross to the east side of the sky? If you cross, what will you do?

I will govern the towns, I will rule the villages, I will know the rich and give to the poor, I will prepare cakes for you when going downstream and bread when going upstream.

O Mahaf, as you are endowed with life, awaken Iqen for me, for see, I have come.

Do you know the road on which you must go, magician?

I know the road on which I must go.

Which is the road on which you must go?

It is 'Power of Earth', and I shall go to the Field of Reeds.

Who will guide you?

The Royal Twins will guide me.

Who will tell your name to this august god?

He who is content, the elder brother of Sokar.

O Mahaf, as you are endowed with life, awaken Iqen for me, for see, I have come.

He does not wake for me.

You shall say: O Vulture-god who rebuilds a courtyard,

I will break your box, I will smash your pens, I will tear up your books because of Him who is in the Primordial Water. If I see, Shu will see; if I hear, Shu will hear; I will give orders to the Imperishable Stars, and it will be well with me on earth.

II

'What is it?' says Iqen; 'I was asleep.'

O Iqen, as you are endowed with life, bring me this, for see, I have come.

Who are you who comes?

I am a magician.

Are you complete?

I am complete.

Are you equipped?

I am equipped.

Have you taken care of the two limbs?

I have taken care of the two limbs.

What are the two limbs, magician?

They are the arm and the leg.

O Iqen, as you are endowed with life, bring me this, for see, I have come.

Have you power over what I have not brought to you, magician, that is to say this boat? She has no bailer.

Bring that . . . of Khnum through which I am made alive, and put it in her.

O Iqen, as you are endowed with life, bring me this, for see, I have come.

Have you power over what I have not brought to you, magician, that is to say this boat? She has no spars.

What is missing from her?

She has no beams, she has no rigging, she has no mooring-post, she has no wraps.

Go to that god who knows you and all that you would mention to him in respect of her spars; what he has given to you will come.

Who is that god who knows me and all that I would mention to him in respect of her spars, so that what he has given to me will come?

He is Horus with whom is a seal-ring.

O Iqen, as you are endowed with life, bring me this, for see, I have come.

Have you power over what I have not brought to you, magician, that is to say this boat? She has no cable.

Bring that snake which is in the hands of Hemen and of Anubis the Controller of the Two Lands, and put it in her, with its head in your hands and its tail in my hands, and we must pull it tight between us (in) its name of 'Pain' . . . the waterways which are between those two cities; the river is in good order and the Lake of Offerings which connects with that river is in good order.

O Iqen, as you are endowed with life, bring me this, for see, I have come.

What are those two cities, magician?

They are the horizon and the malachite-region, or so I believe.

Do you know those two cities, magician?

I know them.

What are those two cities, magician?

They are the Duat and the Field of Reeds.

O Iqen, as you are endowed with life, bring me this, for see, I have come.

Have you power over what I have not brought to you, magician? That august god will say: 'Have you ferried over to me a man who does not know the number of his fingers?'

I know how to count my fingers; take one, take the second, quench it, remove it, give it to me, be friendly towards me; do not let go of it; have no pity on it; make the Eye bright; give the Eye to me.

III

O you who bring the ferryboat of the Primordial Water to this difficult bank, bring me the ferryboat, make fast the warp for me in peace, in peace! Come, come; hurry, hurry, for I have come in order to see my father Osiris. O Lord of Red Cloth, who is mighty through joy; O Lord of Storm, the Male who navigates; O You who navigate over this sandbank of *Apophis*; O You who bind on heads and make necks firm when escaping from wounds; O You who are in charge of the mysterious ferryboat, who ward off *Apophis*, bring me the ferryboat, knot the warp for me, in order to escape from that evil land in which the stars fall upside down upon their faces and are unable to raise themselves up.

O Henswa who is the tongue of Re; O Indebu who governs the Two Lands; O Mengeb their helmsman; O Power who reveals the solar disk, who is in charge of redness, fetch me, do not let me be boatless, for there comes a spirit, my brother, who will ferry me over to the place I know of.

'Tell me my name,' says the mooring-post.

'Lady of the Two Lands in the shrine' is your name.

'Tell me my name,' says the mallet.

'Shank of Apis' is your name.

'Tell me my name,' says the bow-warp.

'Lock of hair of the mooring post of Anubis in the craft of embalming' is your name.

'Tell me my name,' says the steering-post.

'Pillars of the God's Domain' is your name.

'Tell me my name,' says the mast-step.

'Earth-god' is your name.

'Tell me my name,' says the mast.

'He who brought back the Great Goddess after she had been far away' is your name.

'Tell me my name,' say the halyards.

'Standard of Wepwawet' is your name.

'Tell me my name,' says the mast-head.

'Throat of Imsety' is your name.

'Tell me my name,' says the sail.

'Nut' is your name.

'Tell me my name,' say the oar-loops.

'You have been made with the hide of the Mnevis-bull and the tendons of Seth' is your name.

'Tell me my name,' say the oars.

'The fingers of Horus the Elder' are your names.

'Tell me my name,' says the bailer.

'The hand of Isis which swabs up the blood from the Eye of Horus' is your name.

'Tell me my name,' say the ribs which are in her timbers.

'Imsety, Hapy, Duamutef and Qebehsenuef, Plunderer, He who takes by robbery, He who sees what he has brought, He who helps himself' are your names.

'Tell me my name,' says the hogging-beam.

'She who presides over gardens' is your name.

'Tell me my name,' says the rowing bench.

'Songstress' is your name.

'Tell me my name,' says the steering oar.

'Accurate' is your name. 'That which rises from the water, whose blade is limited (in movement)' is your name.

'Tell me my name,' says the boat.

'That leg of Isis which Re cut off with a knife in order to bring blood to the Night-bark' is your name.

'Tell me my name,' says the skipper.

'Rebuffer' is your name.

'Tell me my name,' says the wind, 'since you are carried thereby.'

'North wind which went forth from Atum to the nose of the Foremost of the Westerners' is your name.

'Tell me my name,' says the river, 'since you ferry over on me.'

'He who sees them' is your name.

'Tell me my name,' says the bank of the river.

'Destroyer of those who stretch out the arm in the pure place' is your name.

'Tell me my name,' says the ground, *'since you tread on me.'*

'Nose of the sky which goes out from the Embalmer who is in the Field of Reeds, from which one goes out in joy' is your name.

What is to be said to them: Hail to you, you whose natures are kind, possessors of offerings who live for ever and ever! I have penetrated to you so that you may give me a funeral meal for my mouth with which I speak, namely the cake which Isis baked in the presence of the Great God, for I know that Great God to whose nose you present provisions, whose name is Tjekem. He reveals himself in the eastern horizon of the sky, he travels in the western horizon of the sky. When he departs, I will depart; when he is hale, I will be hale. You shall not repel me from the Milky Way, and those who are rebellious will not have power over this flesh of mine. My bread is in Pe, my beer is in Dep, your gifts of today shall be given to me, and the gifts due to me are barley and emmer, the gifts due to me are myrrh and clothing, the gifts due to me are life, welfare and health, the gifts due to me are what are issued by day in any shape in which I desire to go out to the Field of Reeds.

As for him who knows this chapter, he will go out into the Field of Rushes, and there will be given to him a cake, a jug of beer and a loaf from upon the altar of the Great God, an aroura of land with barley and emmer by the Followers of Horus, who will reap them for him. He will consume this barley and emmer and will rub his body with them, his body will be like these gods, and he will go out into the Field of Reeds in any shape in which he desires to go out. A matter a million times true.

— 100 —

The book of making a soul worthy and of permitting it to go aboard the Bark of Re with those who are in his suite

I have ferried over the Benu-bird to the East, Osiris is in Busiris, I have thrown open the caverns of Hapi, I have cleared the paths of the solar disk, I have dragged Sokar on his sledge, I have made the Great Goddess powerful in her moment of action, I have hymned and worshipped the solar disk, I have joined with him who is with the worshipping baboons, and I am one of them. I have acted as second to Isis, I have strengthened her powers, I have knotted the rope, I have driven off *Apophis*, I have put a stop to his movements, Re has given his hands to me and his crew will not drive me away. If I am strong, the Sacred Eye will be strong — and vice versa. As for him who shall hold me back from the Bark of Re, he shall be held back from the Egg and the Abdju-fish.

To be said over this written text, which should be written on a clean blank roll with powder of green glaze mixed with water of myrrh. To be placed on the breast of the blessed dead without letting it touch his flesh. As for any blessed dead for whom this is done, he will go aboard the Bark of Re every day, and Thoth will take count of him in daily going and coming. A matter a million times true.

— 101 —

Chapter for protecting the Bark of Re

O you who emerge from the waters, who escape from the flood and climb onto the stern of your bark, may you indeed climb onto the stern of your bark, may you be more hale than you were yesterday. You have included N, a worthy spirit, in your crew; if you are hale, he will be hale.

O Re in this your name of Re, if you pass by the Eye of seven cubits with a pupil of three cubits, you will make N hale, the worthy spirit in your crew; if you are hale, he will be hale.

O Re in this your name of Re, if you pass by the dead who are upside down, you shall cause N the worthy spirit to stand up on his feet; if you are hale, he will be hale.

O Re in this your name of Re, if the mysteries of the Duat are opened to you in order to guide the hearts of your Ennead, you shall give N's heart to him; if you are hale, he will be hale.

Your body, O Re, is everlasting by reason of the incantation.

To be recited over a strip of royal linen on which this incantation has been written in dried myrrh; to be placed on the throat of the blessed dead on the day of burial. If this protective incantation is placed on his throat for him, praises will be made for him as for the gods, he shall be united with the Followers of Horus; the starry sky shall be made firm for him in the presence of Him who is with Sothis, his corpse shall be a god, together with his relatives, forever, and a bush shall be planted for him over the breast by Menqet. It was the Majesty of Thoth who did this for the Majesty of the vindicated King of Upper and Lower Egypt Osiris through desire that the sunlight should rest on his corpse.

— 102 —

Chapter for going aboard the Bark of Re

O you who are great in your bark, bring me to your bark, so that I may take charge of your navigating in the duty which is allotted to one who is among the Unwearying Stars. What I doubly detest, I will not eat; my detestation is feces, and I will not eat it, I will not consume excrement, I will not approach it with my hands, I will not tread on it with my sandals, because my bread is of white emmer and my beer of red barley. It is the Night-bark and the Day-bark who bring them to me, and the gifts of the towns are emptied onto the altar of the Souls of Heliopolis. Greeting to you, O Great One who acts in the rowing over the sky; the Shens-cake which is in Thinis is that of which the dogs partake. I am not weary; I myself have come that I might save this god from those who would do him evil, namely the pain allotted to thigh, arm, and leg. I have come that I may spit on the thigh, tie up the arm, and raise the leg. 'Go aboard and navigate' is the command of Re.

— 103 —

Chapter for being in the presence of Hathor

I am one who passes by, pure and bald; O Sistrum-player, I will be in the suite of Hathor.

— 104 —

Chapter for sitting among the great gods

I have sat among the great gods, I have passed by the House of the Night-bark; it is the wasp which fetches me to see the great gods who are in the God's Domain, and I am vindicated in their presence, I am pure.

— 105 —

Chapter for propitiating N's Ka for him in the God's Domain

Hail to you, my Ka of my lifetime; behold, I have come to you, I have appeared in glory, I am strong, besouled, and mighty, and I have brought to you natron and incense that I may cleanse you with them, that I may cleanse your slaver with them, even this evil phrase which I have spoken, this evil impurity which I have done, and nothing has been imputed to me, because to me belongs that papyrus-amulet which is on the neck of Re, which was given to those who are in the horizon; if they are white, I will be white, and my Ka will be like them, my Ka's provisions will be like theirs, having been weighed in the balance. May truth be uplifted to the nose of Re, my head being supported by it, for I am an eye which sees and an ear which hears, I am not a bull for butchery, and none shall have an invocation-offering of me.

*Chapter for giving gifts to N
in Memphis and in the God's Domain*

O Great One, Lord of provisions; O Great One who presides over houses; O You who are above, who give bread to Ptah, the Great One who is on the Great Throne; may you give me bread, may you give me beer, may I eat of the shin of beef together with the roasted bread. O Ferryman of the Field of Rushes, bring me these loaves from your polar waters like your father the Great One who travels in the Bark of the God.

Chapter for knowing the Souls of the Westerners

As for that mountain of Bakhu on which the sky rests, it is in the east of the sky; it is three hundred rods long and one hundred and fifty rods broad. Sobk, Lord of Bakhu, is in the east of that mountain; his temple is of carnelian. A serpent is on the top of that mountain; it is thirty cubits long, eight cubits of its forepart are of flint, and its teeth gleam. I know the name of this serpent which is on the mountain; its name is 'He who is in his burning'. Now after a while he will turn his eyes against Re, and a stoppage will occur in the Sacred Bark and a great vision among the crew, for he will swallow up seven cubits of the great waters; Seth will project a lance of iron against him and will make him vomit up all that he has swallowed. Seth will place him before him and will say to him with magic power: 'Get back at the sharp knife which is in my hand! I stand before you, navigating aright and seeing afar. Cover your face, for I ferry across; get back because of me, for I am the Male! Cover your head, cleanse the palm of your hand; I am hale and I remain hale, for I am the great magician, the son of Nut, and power against you has been granted to me. Who is that spirit who goes on his belly, his tail and his spine? See, I have gone against you, and your tail is in my hand, for I am one who exhibits strength. I have come that I may rescue the earth-gods for Re so that he may go to rest for me in the evening. I go round about the sky, but you are in the fetters which were decreed for you in the Presence, and Re will go to rest alive in his horizon.'

I know those who govern the matter by reason of which *Apophis* is repelled; I know the Souls of the Westerners, who are Atum, Sobk the Lord of Bakhu, and Hathor the Lady of the Evening.

Chapter for knowing the Souls of the Easterners

I know the northern gate of the sky; its south is in the Lake of Waterfowl, its north is in the Waters of Geese, the place in which Re navigates by wind or by rowing. I am the whip-master in the Ship of the God, I am one who rows and does not tire in the Bark of Re.

I know those two trees of turquoise between which Re goes forth, which have grown up at the Supports of Shu at that gate of the Lord of the East from which Re goes forth.

I know that Field of Reeds which belongs to Re, the walls of which are iron; the height of the barley is five cubits, its ear is two cubits and its stalk is three cubits; its emmer is seven cubits, its ear is of three cubits and its stalk of four cubits. They are spirits, each nine cubits tall, who reap it in the presence of the Souls of the Easterners.

I know the Souls of the Easterners; they are Horakhty, the sun-calf, and the Morning Star.

N worships the Ennead which is in the Field of Offerings, and he says: Hail to you, you owners of Kas! I have come in peace to your fields in order to receive the provisions which you give; I have come to the Great God in order that I may receive the provisions which his goodwill grants of bread and beer, oxen and fowl. Giving praise to the Ennead, doing homage to the Great God by N.

A boon which the King grants to Osiris and the Ennead which is in the Field of Offerings, that they may give invocation-offerings of bread and beer, oxen and fowl and all things good, and clothing and incense daily, which rest upon the altar every day; to receive Senu-bread and Khenef-bread, Persen-bread, milk, wine, and the provisions of one who follows the god in his procession in his Festival of Rosetjau, bearing the water-jars of the Great God, for the benefit of N.

[Note: The portion of the chapter which occurs at this point appears in the Ani Papyrus on Plate 34.]

O Hotep, I acquire this field of yours which you love, the Lady of Air. I eat and carouse in it, I drink and plow in it, I reap in it, I copulate in it, I make love in it, I do not perish in it, for my magic is powerful in it. I will not be aroused in it, my happy heart is not apprehensive in it, for I know the wooden post of Hotep, which is called Bequtet; it was made firm on the blood of Shu and it was lashed with the Bowstring of the Years on that day when the years were divided; my mouth is hidden and his mouth is silent. I say something mysterious, I bring eternity to an end, and I take possession of everlasting.

Being in Hotep, Lord of the Field of Offerings. This is Horus; he is a falcon a thousand cubits long, life and dominion are in his hand, he comes and goes at will in its waterways and towns, he rises and sets in Qenqenet, the birth-place of the god. He does everything in it as it is done in the Island of Fire; there is no shouting in it, there is nothing evil in it.

This is Hotep who walks throughout this field of his; he partakes of a meal in the birth-place of the god. If he rests in Qenqenet, he will do everything in it as it is done in the Island of Fire; there is no shouting in it, there is nothing evil in it.

I live in Hotep, my bag and my bowl are on me, which I have filled from baskets, being one whom the spirits of the Lord of Plenty guide. I depart and ascend to Him who brings it, and I have power through him, he accepts on my behalf, for I am equipped and content. This great magic of mine is powerful in this body of mine, in these seats of mine; I am one who recalls to himself that of which I have been forgetful. I plow and I reap, and I am content in the City of God. I know the names of the districts, towns, and waterways which are in the Field of Offerings and of those who are in them; I am strong in them and I am a spirit in them; I eat in them and travel about in them. I plow and reap in the Field; I rise early in it and go to rest in it. I am a spirit in it as Hotep; I shoot and travel about in it; at my word I row on its waterways and I arrive at its towns as Hotep. My horns are sharp, I give abundance to the souls and spirits, I allot authoritative utterance to him who can use it. I arrive at its towns, I row on its waterways, I traverse the Field of Offerings as Re who is in the sky, and it is Hotep who satisfies them. I have gone down to the earth, I have made Re content; I have gone up on high and I have caused joy to be made, I have taken power, I have promised peace.

Being in Hotep. O Field, I have come into you, my soul behind me and authority before me. O Lady of the Two Lands, establish my magic power for me, that by means of it I may recall what I had forgotten. I am alive without harm of any kind, and joy is given to me, peace is mine, I create seed, I have received air.

Being in Hotep, Lord of Breezes. I have come into you, having opened up my head and having aroused my body. I close my eye, yet I shine on the day of the Milk-goddess; I have slept by night, I have restored the milk to its proper level, and I am in my town.

O Town of the Great Goddess, I have come into you that I may allot abundance and cause vegetation to flourish; I am the bull of lapis-lazuli, unique and exalted, Lord of the Field, Bull of the Gods. Sothis speaks to me in her good time.

O *Swamp-land,* I have come into you, I have taken the Grey-haired One to the roof, for I am the moon, I have swallowed up the darkness.

O *Town of Fair Offerings,* I have come into you, I eat my meal, I have power over fowl and flesh, and poultry of Shu which attend on my Ka have been given to me.

O *Provision-town,* I have come into you, I have woven the eight-weave cloth, I have donned the fringed cloak as Re in the sky whom the gods who are in the sky serve.

Being in Hotep, Lady of the Two Lands: I have come into you, I have immersed the waterways as Osiris, Lord of Putridity, Lord of the Swamp-lands; as the Oldest One, Bull of vultures. I am a flamingo, which has eaten the like.

O *Qenqenet,* I have come into you, I have seen my father, I have recognized my mother, I have risen early, I have caught fish. I know the deep holes of the snakes, and I am saved. I know the name of this god; He whose mouth is put together, Lord of Holiness, whose hair is in good order, whose horns are sharp. If he reaps, I will plow and I will reap.

O *Town of the Milk-goddess,* I have come into you; those who would oppose me and drive me off and who would follow after me are those who would follow after Horus; heads have been given to me, and I tie on the Head of Horus the blue-eyed, acting according to his desire.

O *Town of Union,* I have come into you; my head is whole and my heart is awake beneath the White Crown; I am guided above and I am hale below, I give joy to the bulls who are in charge of the Enneads, for I am a bull, Lord of the Gods, who proceeds into the place of turquoise.

O *Mighty Woman,* I have come into you, I have taken the Grey-haired One to the roof, I have fashioned Authority, I am in the middle of my Eye.

O *barley and emmer of the District of the God,* I have come into you, I fare upstream, I sail on the Waterway of Horns, Lady of Pure Things, I drive in the mooring-post in the upper waterways. I have borne aloft the storm of the Disturber and I have upheld the Supports of the Old One.

— 112 —
Chapter for knowing the Souls of Pe

O you female Souls of the Night, Marsh-dwellers, Women of Mendes, you of the Fish-nome and of the Mansion of Iapu, Sunshade-bearers of the Adoration, who prepare beer of Nubia, do you know why Pe was given to Horus? You do not know it, but I know it. It was Re who gave it to him in compensation for the mutilation in his Eye; I know it.

It so happened that Re said to Horus: 'Let me see your eye since this has happened to it.' He looked at it and said: 'Look at that black stroke with your hand covering up the sound eye which is there.' Horus looked at that stroke and said: 'Behold, I am seeing it as altogether white.' And that is how the oryx came into being. And Re said: 'Look again at yonder black pig.' And Horus looked at this black pig, and Horus cried out because of the condition of his injured eye, saying: 'Behold, my eye is like that first wound which Seth inflicted on my eye', and Horus fainted before him. Then Re said: 'Put him on his bed until he is well.' It so happened that Seth had transformed himself into a black pig and had projected a wound into his eye, and Re said: 'The pig is detestable to Horus.' 'We wish he were well,' said the gods. That is how the detestation of the pig came about for Horus's sake by the gods who are in the suite.

Now when Horus was a child, his sacrificial animal was a pig before his eye had suffered — Imsety, Hapy, Duamutef and Qebehsenuef, whose father was Horus the Elder and whose mother was Isis — and he said to Re: 'Give me two in Pe and two in Nekhen from this second company. May I be an allotter of eternity, an opener of everlasting and a queller of

strife in this my name of "Horus who is on his papyrus-column".'

I know the Souls of Pe; they are Horus, Imsety and Hapy.

— 113 —
Chapter for knowing the Souls of Nekhen

I know the mystery of Nekhen; it is the hands of Horus of his mother's making which were thrown into the water when she said: 'You shall be the two severed portions of Horus after you have been found.' And Re said, 'This son of Isis is injured by reason of what his own mother has done to him; let us fetch Sobk from the back of the waters, so that he may fish them out and that his mother Isis may cause them to grow again in their proper place.' And Sobk from the back of the waters said: 'I have fished and I have sought; they slipped from my hand on the bank of the waters, but in the end I fished them up with a fish-trap.' *That is how the fish-trap came into being.*

Knowing the mystery of Nekhen. Thus said Re: 'Has Sobk any fish as well as finding Horus's hands for him?' *That is how Fish-worship-town came into being.* Then Re said: 'Hidden are the mysteries concerning this fish-trap which brought Horus's hands to us; the sight is cleared because of it in the monthly festival and the half-monthly festival in Fish-worship-town.' And Re said: 'Nekhen is set in his embrace and the sight is cleared on account of his hands in this Nekhen which I have given to him, and what is in them is shut up in the half-monthly festival.'

Then Horus said: 'Indeed I have placed Duamutef and Qebehsenuef with me so that I may watch over them, for they are a contentious company; further, they are to be there while Nekhen is mine, according to the word of Re, "Place them in the prison of Nekhen, for they have done what used to be done by Her who is in the Broad Hall"; "They are with me", you shall say, and they will end up with you until Seth knows that they are with you and complains.'

O you who are in Nekhen, power is given to me, and I know the mystery of Nekhen; it is the hands of Horus and what is in them, for I have been introduced to the Souls of Nekhen. Open to me, that I may join with Horus.

I know the Souls of Nekhen: they are Horus, Duamutef and Qebehsenuef. Not to be said when eating pig.

— 114 —
Chapter for knowing the Souls of Hermopolis

The plume is stuck into the shoulder of Osiris, the Red Crown shines in the bowl, the Eye is eaten and he who sought it is fetched. I know it, for I have been initiated into it by the Sem-priest, and I have never spoken nor made repetition to the gods. I have come on an errand for Re in order to cause the plume to grow into the shoulder of Osiris, to make complete the Red Crown in the bowl, and to Pacify the Eye for him who numbered it. I have entered as a Power because of what I know, I have not spoken to men, I have not repeated what was said.

Hail to you, Souls of Hermopolis! Know that Re desires the plume which grows and the Red Crown which is complete at this temple, and rejoice at the allotting of what is to be allotted.

I know the Souls of Hermopolis. What is great in the half-month and small in the full month, that is Thoth.

— 115 —
Chapter for ascending to the sky, opening up the tomb, and knowing the Souls of Heliopolis

I have spent yesterday among the great ones, I have become Khepri, I have cleared the vision of the Sole Eye, I have opened up the circle of darkness. I am one of them, I know the Souls of Heliopolis, into which the High-priest of Heliopolis was not initiated through revelation; (I know) the hostile acts by Him who would destroy the heirs of Heliopolis; I know why a braided lock is made for a man.

Re disputed with the serpent, 'Him who is in his burning', and his mouth was injured, and that is how the reduction in the month came about. He said to the serpent: 'I will take my harpoon, which men will inherit', and that is how the harpoon came into being. The serpent said: 'The Two Sisters will come into being', and that is how Re's passing by came into being.

It so happened that He of the red cloth heard, and his arm was not stopped. He transformed himself into a woman with braided hair, and that is how the priest of Heliopolis with braided hair came into being. It so happened that the mighty one was stripped in the temple, and that is how the stripped one of Heliopolis came into being. It so happened that the heritage of the heir came into being, and great will be he who shall see it; he will become High-priest of Heliopolis.

I know the Souls of Heliopolis; they are Re, Shu, and Tefnut.

— 117 —
Chapter for taking the road in Rosetjau

The ways which are above the waters lead to Rosetjau; I am he who clothed my standard which came forth from the Wereret-crown. I have come that I may establish offerings in Abydos, I have opened the ways in Rosetjau, I have assuaged the pains of Osiris. It is I who created water, who discerned my throne, who prepared my way in the valley and on the waterway. O Great One, prepare a way for me, for it is yours. It was I who vindicated Osiris against his enemies, so may I be vindicated against my enemies. May I be like one of you, a friend of the Lord of Eternity, may I walk like you walk, may I stand like you stand, may I sit like you sit, may I speak like you speak before the Great God, Lord of the West.

— 118 —
Chapter for arriving in Rosetjau

I am one who was born in Rosetjau, and benefits have been given to me by those who are among the noble dead, with the pure things of Osiris; I received praise in Rosetjau when I conducted Osiris to the Mounds of Osiris. I am unique, having conducted them to the Mounds of Osiris.

— 119 —
Chapter for going forth from Rosetjau

I am the Great One who created his own light; I have come to you, Osiris, that I may worship you, for pure is the efflux which was drawn from you, the name of which was made in Rosetjau; may you be mighty thereby in Abydos. Raise yourself, Osiris, that you may go round about the sky with Re and see the people; O Unique One, travel around as Re. See, I have spoken to you, Osiris; I have the rank of a god, I say what comes to pass, and I will not be turned away from you, Osiris.

— 122 —
Chapter for entering after coming out

To me belongs everything, and the whole of it has been given to me. I have gone in as a falcon, I have come out as a Benu-bird; the Morning Star has made a path for me, and I enter in peace into the beautiful West. I belong to the garden of Osiris, and a path is made for me so that I may go in and worship Osiris the Lord of Life.

— 123 —
Chapter for entering into the Great Mansion

Hail to you, Atum! I am Thoth who judged between the Rivals. I have stopped their fighting, I have wiped away their mourning, I have seized the buri-fish when it would flee away, I have done what you commanded in the matter, and afterwards I spent the night within my Eye (the moon). I am devoid of ill-will, and I have come that you may see me in the Mansion of Him of the double face in accordance with what was commanded; the old men are under my control and the little ones belong to me.

— 125 —
INTRODUCTION
What should be said when arriving at this Hall of Justice, purging N of all the evil which he has done, and beholding the faces of the gods

Hail to you, great god, Lord of Justice! I have come to you, my lord, that you may bring me so that I may see your beauty, for I know you and I know your name, and I know the names of the forty-two gods of those who are with you in this Hall of Justice, who live on those who cherish evil and who gulp down their blood on that day of the reckoning of characters in the presence of Wennefer. Behold the double son of the Song-stresses; Lord of Truth is your name. Behold, I have come to you, I have brought you truth, I have repelled falsehood for you. I have not done falsehood against men, I have not impoverished my associates, I have done no wrong in the Place of Truth, I have not learnt that which is not, I have done no evil, I have not daily made labor in excess of what was due to be done for me, my name has not reached the offices of those who control slaves, I have not deprived the orphan of his property, I have not done what the gods detest, I have not calumniated a servant to his master, I have not caused pain, I have not made hungry, I have not made to weep, I have not killed, I have not commanded to kill, I have not made suffering for anyone, I have not lessened the food-offering in the temples, I have not destroyed the loaves of the gods, I have not taken away the food of the spirits, I have not copulated, I have not misbehaved, I have not lessened food-supplies, I have not diminished the aroura, I have not encroached upon fields, I have not laid anything upon the weights of the hand-balance, I have not taken anything from the plummet of the standing scales, I have not taken the milk from the mouths of children, I have not deprived the herds of their pastures, I have not trapped the birds from the preserves of the gods, I have not caught the fish of their marshlands, I have not diverted water at its season, I have not built a dam on flowing water, I have not quenched the fire when it is burning, I have not neglected the dates for offering choice meats, I have not withheld cattle from the god's-offerings, I have not opposed a god in his procession.

I am pure, pure, pure, pure! My purity is the purity of that great Benu-bird which is in Heracleopolis, because I am indeed the nose of the Lord of Wind who made all men live on that day of completing the Sacred Eye in Heliopolis *in the 2nd month of winter last day,* in the presence of the lord of this land. I am he who saw the completion of the Sacred Eye in Heliopolis, and nothing evil shall come into being against me in this land in this Hall of Justice, because I know the names of these gods who are in it.

[Note: The Declaration of Innocence appears in the Ani Papyrus on Plate 31.]

ADDRESS TO THE GOD OF THE HALL OF JUSTICE

Thus says N: Hail to you, you gods who are in this Hall of Justice! I know you and I know your names, I will not fall to your knives; you shall not bring the evil in me to this god in whose suite you are, no fault of mine concerning you shall come out, you shall tell the truth about me in the presence of the Lord of All, because I have done what was right in Egypt,

I have not reviled God, and no fault of mine has come out regarding the reigning king.

Hail to you, O you who are in the Hall of Justice, who have no lies in your bodies, who live on truth and gulp down truth in the presence of Horus who is in his disk. Save me from Babai, who lives on the entrails of the old ones on that day of the great reckoning. Behold, I have come to you without falsehood of mine, without crime of mine, without evil of mine, and there is no one who testifies against me, for I have done nothing against him. I live on truth, I gulp down truth, I have done what men say and with which the gods are pleased. I have propitiated God with what he desires; I have given bread to the hungry, water to the thirsty, clothes to the naked, and a boat to him who was boatless, I have given god's-offerings to the gods and invocation-offerings to the spirits. Save me, protect me, without your making report against me in the Presence, for I am pure of mouth and pure of hands, one to whom is said 'Twice welcome!' by those who see him, because I have heard that great word which the noble dead spoke with the Cat in the House of Him whose mouth gapes. He who testifies of me is He whose face is behind him, and he gives the cry. I have seen the dividing of the ished-tree in Rosetjau, I am he who succors the gods, who knows the affairs of their bodies. I have come here to bear witness to truth and to set the balance in its proper place within the Silent Land.

O You who are uplifted on your standard, Lord of the Atef-crown, who made your name as Lord of the Wind, save me from your messengers who shoot forth harm and create punishments and who show no indulgence, because I have done what is right for the Lord of Right. I am pure, my brow is clean, my hinder-parts are cleansed, and my middle is in the Pool of Truth, there is no member in me devoid of truth. I have bathed in the Southern Pool, I have rested in the Northern City, in the pure Field of Grasshoppers, in which is the crew of Re, in this second hour of the night and the third hour of the day, and the gods are calmed when they pass by it by night or day.

THE DEAD MAN IS QUESTIONED

'You have caused him to come,' say they about me. 'Who are you?' they say to me. 'What is your name?' they say to me.

'I am the lower part of the papyrus-plant; "He who is on his moringa-tree" is my name.'

'What have you passed by?' they say to me.

'I have passed by the city north of the moringa-tree.'

'What did you see there?'

'They were the calf and the thigh.'

'What did you say to them?'

'I have seen the rejoicings in these lands of the Fenkhu.'

'What did they give you?'

'A firebrand and a pillar of faience.'

'What did you do with them?'

'I buried them on the riverbank of Maat with the night-ritual.'

'What did you find on it, the riverbank of Maat?'

'It was a staff of flint called "Giver of Breath".'

'What did you do with the firebrand and the pillar of faience after you had buried them?'

'I called out over them, I dug them up, I quenched the fire, I broke the pillar and threw it into a canal.'

'Come and enter by this door of the Hall of Justice, for you know us.'

'We will not let you enter by us,' say the doorposts of this door, 'unless you tell our name.'

'"Plummet of Truth" is your name.'

'I will not let you enter by me,' says the right-hand leaf of this door, 'unless you tell my name.'

'"Scale-pan which weighs Truth" is your name.'

'I will not let you enter by me,' says the left-hand leaf of this door, 'unless you tell my name.'

'"Scale-pan of wine" is your name.'

'I will not let you pass by me,' says the floor of this door, 'unless you tell my name.'

'"Ox of Geb" is your name.'

'I will not open to you,' says the doorbolt of this door, 'unless you tell my name.'

'"Toe of his mother" is your name.'

'I will not let you enter by me,' says the hasp of this door, 'unless you tell my name.'

'"Living Eye of Sobk, Lord of Bakhu" is your name.'

'I will not open to you,' says this door, 'unless you tell my name.'

'"Breast of Shu which he placed as a protection for Osiris" is your name.'

'We will not let you enter by us,' say the cross-timbers, 'unless you tell our names.'

'"Children of uraei" are your names.'

'I will not open to you nor let you enter by me,' says the doorkeeper of this door, 'unless you tell my name.'

'"Ox of Geb" is your name.'

'You know us; pass by us.'

'I will not let you tread on me,' says the floor of this Hall of Justice.

'Why not? I am pure.'

'Because I do not know the names of your feet with which you would tread on me. Tell them to me.'

'"Secret image of Ha" is the name of my right foot; "Flower of Hathor" is the name of my left foot.'

'You know us; enter by us.'

'I will not announce you,' says the doorkeeper of this Hall of Justice, 'unless you tell my name.'

'"Knower of hearts, searcher-out of bodies" is your name.'

'To which god shall I announce you?'

'To him who is now present. Tell it to the Dragoman of the Two Lands.'

'Who is the Dragoman of the Two Lands?'

'He is Thoth.'

'Come!' says Thoth. 'What have you come for?'

'I have come here to report.'

'What is your condition?'

'I am pure from evil, I have excluded myself from the quarrels of those who are now living, I am not among them.'

'To whom shall I announce you?'

'You shall announce me to Him whose roof is fire, whose walls are living uraei, the floor of whose house is the waters.'

'Who is he?'

'He is Osiris.'

'Proceed; behold, you are announced. Your bread is the Sacred Eye, your beer is the Sacred Eye; what goes forth at the voice for you upon earth is the Sacred Eye.'

— 126 —

O you four baboons who sit in the bow of the Bark of Re, who raise up truth to the Lord of All, who judge poor and rich, who propitiate the gods with the breath of your mouths, who give god's-offerings to the gods and invocation-offerings to the spirits, who live on truth and gulp down truth, whose hearts have no lies, who detest falsehood: expel my evil, grip hold of my falsehood, and I will have no guilt in respect of you. Grant that I may open up the tomb, that I may enter into Rosetjau, and that I may pass by the secret portals of the West. There shall be given to me a Shens-cake, a jug of beer, and a Persen-loaf, just like those spirits who go in and out in Rosetjau.

THE BABOONS REPLY: Come, so that we may expel your evil and grip hold of your falsehood so that the dread of you may be on earth, and dispel the evil which was on you on earth. Enter into Rosetjau, pass by the secret portals of the West, and there shall be given to you a Shens-cake, a jug of beer, and a Persen-loaf, and you shall go in and out at your desire, just like those favored spirits who are summoned daily into the horizon.

— 127 —

The book of worshipping the gods of the caverns; what a man should say there when he reaches them in order to go in to see this god in the Great Mansion of the Duat

Hail to you, gods of the caverns which are in the West! Hail to you, door-keepers of the Duat who guard this god and who bring news to the presence of Osiris! May you be alert, may you have power, may you destroy the enemies of Re, may you make brightness, may you dispel your darkness, may you see the holiest of the Great Ones, may you live as he lives, may you give praise to Him who is in his sun-disk, may you guide N to your doors. May his soul pass by your hidden things, for he is one of you. May he strike evil into Apophis, may his wrongdoing be smitten down in the West. You are triumphant over your enemies, O Great God who are in your sun-disk; you are triumphant over your enemies, O Osiris, Foremost of the Westerners; you are triumphant, O N, over your enemies in sky and earth and in the tribunals of every god and every goddess. Osiris, Foremost of the Westerners, speaks in front of the Valley and he is vindicated in the great tribunal.

O you door-keepers who guard your portals, who swallow souls and who gulp down the corpses of the dead who pass by you when they are allotted to the House of Destruction, who cause that the soul of every potent, great, and holy spirit shall be led aright to the place of the Silent Land, even he who is a soul like Re who is praised and like Osiris who is praised. May you guide N, may you open the portals for him, may the earth open its caverns to him, may you make him triumphant over his enemies. So shall he give gifts to Him of the Duat; he shall make the head-cloth potent for its wearer within the hidden chamber as the image of Horakhty. 'May the soul of the potent spirit be led aright; how mighty is that which is in his hands!', say the two great and mighty gods concerning N. They rejoice over him, they acclaim him with what is in their hands, they give him their protection so that he may live. N has appeared as a living one who is in the sky, it has been commanded to him to assume his own shape, he is vindicated in the tribunal, and the gates of sky, earth, and the Netherworld are opened for him as for Re.

N SAYS: Open for me the gates of sky, earth, and the Duat, for I am the soul of Osiris, and I am at peace thereby. I pass by their courts, and they give praise when they see me; I have gone in favored and I have come out beloved; I have journeyed, and no fault of any kind has been found in me.

— 128 —

Worshipping Osiris

Hail to you, Osiris Wennefer, the vindicated, the son of Nut! You are the first-born son of Geb, the Great One who came forth from Nut; King in the Thinite nome; Foremost of the Westerners; Lord of Abydos; Lord of Power, greatly majestic; Lord of the Atef-crown in Heracleopolis; Lord of Might in the Thinite nome; owner of a tomb; greatly powerful in Busiris; Lord of offerings and multiple of festivals in Mendes. Horus exalts his father Osiris in every place which Isis the goddess and her sister Nephthys protect; Thoth speaks with his great incantations which are in his body and which issue from his mouth; and Horus's heart is made more glad than those of all the gods. Raise yourself up, Horus son of Isis, so that you may protect your father Osiris.

Shout with joy, Osiris, for I have come to you; I am Horus, I have saved you alive today, and there are invocation-offerings of bread and beer, oxen and fowl, and all good things for Osiris. Raise yourself up, Osiris; I will smite your enemies for you, for I have saved you from them. I am Horus in this

happy day as one who appears happily in glory with your power.

He exalts you with himself today in your tribunal; shout for joy, Osiris, for your Ka has come to you, accompanying you, that you may be content in this your name of 'Contented Ka'; he glorifies you in this your name of 'Divine Spirit'; he worships you in this your name of 'Magician'; he opens up paths for you in this your name of 'Opener of Paths'.

Shout with joy, Osiris, for I have come to you that I may put your enemies under you in every place where you are vindicated in the tribunals of the Ennead.

Shout with joy, Osiris; take your mace and your staff, with your stairway below you. Control the food of the gods; control the offerings of those who are in their tombs; give your greatness to the gods, O You whom the Great God created. May you be with them in your mummy-form, may you collect yourself because of all the gods, for you have heard the voice of Maat today.

Recite an offering-formula to this god in the Wag-festival.

— 130 —

Another chapter for making a spirit worthy on the birthday of Osiris and for making a soul to live forever

May the sky be opened, may the earth be opened, may the West be opened, may the East be opened, may the chapel of Upper Egypt be opened, may the chapel of Lower Egypt be opened, may the doors be opened, may the eastern portals be thrown open for Re when he ascends from the horizon. May the doors of the Night-bark be opened for him, may the portals of the Day-bark be thrown open for him, may he breathe Shu, may he create Tefnut, may those who are in the suite serve him, may they serve me like Re daily.

I am a follower of Re, who receives his firmament; the god occupies his shrine, Horus having approached his lord, whose seats are secret, whose shrine is pure, messenger of the god to him whom he loved. I am one who takes hold of Maat, having presented her before him; I am he who knots the cord and lashes his shrine together. What I detest is storm, and there will be no heaping up of waters in my presence, I will not be turned back because of Re, I will not be driven off by whoever acts with his hands, I will not go into the Valley of Darkness, I will not enter into the Lake of Criminals, I will not be in the weakening of striking-power, I will not fall as plunder, I will go in among those who are taken before him, behind the slaughter-block of the slaughterhouse of Sopd.

Hail to you, you squatting gods! The seclusion of the god is in the secrecy of the arms of Geb at dawn; who is he who will guide the Great One? He will number the children in his good time, while Thoth is in the secret places; he will make purity for Him who counts the myriads who are to be counted, who opens up the firmament and dispels all cloudiness. I have reached him in his place, I grasp the staff, I receive the head-cloth for Re, whose fair movements are great. Horus flames up around his eye, and his two Enneads are about his throne; if they remove the sore pain which he suffers, then will I remove the pain, that I may be made comfortable thereby. I will open up the horizon for Re, and I have built his ship 'She who proceeds happily'; the face of Thoth will be made bright for me, and I will worship Re, he will hearken to me, for he has implanted an obstacle on my behalf against my enemies. I will not be left boatless, I will not be turned back from the horizon, for I am Re. I will not be left boatless in the great crossing by Him whose face is on his knee and whose hand is bent down, because the name of Re is in my body, his dignity is in my mouth. So he has told me, and I hear his word.

Praise to you, Re, Lord of the Horizon; hail to you for whom the sun-folk are pure, for whom the sky is controlled in the great moment when the hostile oarsmen pass by. See, I have come among those who make truth known, because I am far away in the West; I have broken up the storm of *Apophis*, O

Double Lion, as I promised you. See, I have come; O you who are before the Great Throne, hearken to me. I go down into your tribunal, I rescue Re from *Apophis* every day, and there is no one who can attack him, for those who are about him are awake. I lay hold of the writings, I receive offerings, I equip Thoth with what was made for him, I cause truth to circulate over the Great Bark, I go down vindicated into the tribunal, I establish the Chaos-gods, I lead the Entourage, I grant to them a voyage in utter joy, when the crew of Re goes round about following his beauty. Maat is exalted so that she may reach her lord, and praise is given to the Lord of All.

I take the staff, I sweep the sky with it, and the sun-folk give me praise as to Him who stands and does not tire. I extol Re in what he has made, I dispel cloudiness, I see his beauty, I display the terror of him, I make his oarsmen firm when his Bark travels over the sky at dawn. I am the Great One within his Eye, who kneels at the head of the Great Bark of Khepri. I come into being and what I have said comes into being, I am this one who traverses the sky towards the West, and those who heap up the air stand up in joy; they have taken the bow-warp of Re from his crew, and Re traverses the sky happily in peace by my command; I will not be driven away, the fiery breath of your power will not carry me off, the power of repulsion in your mouth will not go forth against me, I will not walk on the paths of pestilence, for to fall into it is the detestation of my soul; what I detest is the flood, and it shall not attack me. I go aboard your Bark, I occupy your seat, I receive my dignity, I control the paths of Re and the stars, I am he who drives off the Destructive One who comes at the flame of your Bark upon the great plateau. I know them by their names, and they will not attack your Bark, for I am in it, and I am he who prepares the offerings.

To be said over a Bark of Re drawn in ochre on a clean place. When you have placed a likeness of this spirit in front of it, you shall draw a Night-bark on its right side and a Day-bark on its left side. There shall be offered to them in their presence bread and beer and all good things on the birthday of Osiris. If this is done for him, his soul will live forever and he will not die again.

— 131 —
Chapter for being in the presence of Re

I am that Re who shines in the night. As for anyone who is in his suite or who lives in the suite of Thoth, he will give appearance in glory to this Horus in the night and joy to me, because I am one of these, and my enemies will be driven off from the Entourage; I am a follower of Re who has received his firmament. I have come to you, my father Re; I have travelled in the air, I have summoned this Great Goddess, I have adorned the god of Authority, I have passed by that Destructive One who is in the road to Re, and it is well with me. I have reached this Old One who is at the limits of the horizon, whom I have driven off. I take possession of the Great Goddess, I lift up your soul when you have become strong, and my soul is in the dread of you and the awe of you; I am he who enforces the commands of Re in the sky.

Hail to you, Great God in the east of the sky! I go aboard your Bark, O Re; I pass by as a divine falcon, I give orders, I smite with my scepter and govern with my staff. I go aboard your Bark, O Re, in peace; I navigate in peace to the beautiful West, and Atum speaks to me.

[Note: The remainder of this chapter is too corrupt to yield an intelligible text.(ROF)]

— 135 —
Another chapter to be said when the moon is new on the first day of the month

Open, O cloudiness! The bleared Eye of Re is covered, and Horus proceeds happily every day, even he the great of shape

and weighty of striking-power, who dispels bleariness of eye with his fiery breath. Behold, O Re, I have come voyaging, for I am one of these four gods who are at the side of the sky, and I show you Him who is present by day.

Make your cable fast, for there is no opposition to you.

As for him who knows this chapter, he will be a worthy spirit in the God's Domain, and he will not die again in the realm of the dead, and he will eat in the presence of Osiris. As for him who knows it on earth, he will be like Thoth, he will be worshipped by the living, he will not fall to the power of the king or the hot rage of Bastet, and he will proceed to a very happy old age.

— 136A —
Another chapter for making a spirit worthy on the Festival of the Sixth Day

Behold the starry sky is in Heliopolis, and the sun-folk are in Kheraha. The god is born, his fillet is bound on, his oar is grasped, and N gives judgment with them in the lotus-bark at the dockyard of the gods; N takes over the bark in it which has lotus-flowers on its ends; N ascends to the sky, N sails in it to Nut, he sails in it with Re, he sails in it with apes, he repels the waves which are over yonder polar region of Nut at that stairway of Sebeg. Geb and Nut are happy, there is repeated the renewed and rejuvenated name of Wennefer, Re is his power, Wenti is what he is called: 'You are abundance, the greatest of the gods, widespread of sweet savor among all those who are not ignorant of you. Your war-shout is harsh, O swiftest of the Ennead, you being stronger, more besouled and more effective than the gods of Upper and Lower Egypt and their powers. May you grant that N be great and mighty in the sky just as you are greatest of the gods; may you save him from anything that those who hunt with yonder Adversary may do against him. May his heart be valiant, may you make N mightier than all the gods, the spirits, and the dead.'

N is mighty, the Lord of Might; N is the master of righteousness, whom Wadjet made; N's protection is the protection of Re in the sky. May you permit N to pass into your Bark, O Re, in peace; prepare a path for N who navigates the Bark, for N's protection is its protection. N is he who daily drives off the aggressor against Re; N has come like Horus into the holy place of the horizon of the sky; N is he who makes Re known at the gates, and the gods who meet N rejoice over him, for the greatness of a god is on N, the Destroyer will not attack him, the keepers of the gates will not ignore him. N is he whose face is hidden within the Great Mansion, even he the master of the god's shrine; N is he who dispatches the words of the gods to Re; N has come that he may report business to its lord; N is stout of heart and weighty of action among those who prepare offerings.

To be recited over an image of this spirit placed in this bark, you being cleansed, purified, and censed in the presence of Re, with bread, beer, roast meat, and ducks; it means that he will be conveyed in the Bark of Re. As for any spirit for whom this is done, he will be among the living, and he will never perish. He will be a holy god, and nothing evil shall ever harm him; he will be a potent spirit in the West, and he will not die again. He will eat and drink in the presence of Osiris every day; he will be admitted with the kings of Upper Egypt and the kings of Lower Egypt every day, he will drink water from the stream, he will go out into the day like Horus, he will live and be like a god, and he will be worshipped by the living like Re every day. A matter a million times true.

— 136B —
Chapter for sailing in the Great Bark of Re and for passing over the circle of fire

This is the fire which shines behind Re and which is concentrated behind him; the storm is afraid of the shining and splendid Bark of Re. I have come with Him whose face is wiped into his sacred lake, I have seen Him who attains to righteousness, who has fallen among those whose forms are holy, who are in sarcophagi; and the reed-dwellers are many. I have looked there, and we rejoice; their great ones are in joy and their little ones are in happiness. A path is made for me at the head of the Sacred Bark, and I am lifted up as the sun disk; I am bright in its sunshine . . .

Down on your faces, you evil snakes! Let me pass, for I am a mighty one, Lord of the mighty ones; I am a noble of the Lord of Righteousness, whom Wadjet made. My protection is the protection of Re. See, I am he who went round about in the Field of Offerings of the Two Lands; a greater god than you, who reckons up his Enneads among those who give offerings.

— 137A —

Chapter for four torches for the ceremonies which are carried out for a spirit

You shall make four basins of clay beaten up with incense and filled with milk of a white cow; the torches are to be quenched in them.

The torch comes to your Ka, O Osiris, Foremost of the Westerners, and the torch comes to your Ka, O N. There comes he who promises the night after the day; there come the two sisters of Re; there comes she who was manifested in Abydos, for I cause it to come, even that Eye of Horus which was foretold before you, O Osiris, Foremost of the Westerners. It is safe in your outer chamber, having appeared on your brow, for it was foretold before you, O N, and it is safe on your brow.

The Eye of Horus is your protection, O Osiris, Foremost of the Westerners; it spreads its protection over you, it fells all your enemies for you, and your enemies have indeed fallen to you.

The Eye of Horus is your protection, O N, it spreads its protection over you, it fells all your enemies for you, and your enemies have indeed fallen to you.

To your Ka, O Osiris, Foremost of the Westerners! The Eye of Horus is your protection; it spreads its protection over you, it fells all your enemies for you, and your enemies have indeed fallen to you.

To your Ka, O N! The Eye of Horus is your protection; it spreads its protection over you, it fells all your enemies for you, and your enemies have indeed fallen to you.

The Eye of Horus comes intact and shining like Re in the horizon; it covers up the powers of Seth who would possess it, for it is he who would fetch it for himself, and it is hot against him when he is at the feet of the intact Eye of Horus. Eat the food of your body, possessing it, and worship it.

May the four torches go in to your Ka, O Osiris, Foremost of the Westerners; may the four torches go in to your Ka, O N. O you Children of Horus, Imsety, Hapy, Duamutef, Qebeh-senuef, as you spread your protection over your father Osiris, Foremost of the Westerners, so spread your protection over N as when you removed the impediment from Osiris, Foremost of the Westerners, so that he might live with the gods and drive Seth from him; as when at dawn Horus became strong that he himself might protect his father Osiris when wrong was done to your father when you drove Seth off.

To your Ka, Osiris, Foremost of the Westerners! The Eye of Horus is your protector which spreads its protection over you; it fells all your enemies for you, and your enemies have indeed fallen to you. Remove the impediment from N that he may live with the gods; smite the enemies of N and protect N. At dawn may Horus become strong that he may protect N when wrong is done to N, and may you drive Seth off.

To your Ka, N! The Eye of Horus is your protector, it fells all your enemies for you and your enemies have indeed fallen to you.

Osiris, Foremost of the Westerners, is he who causes a

torch to be bright for the potent souls in Heracleopolis; may you make the living soul of N strong with his torch, so that he may not be repelled nor driven off from the portals of the West. Then there will be brought in to him his bread, beer, and clothing among the possessors of offerings; you will send up thanks for power, for N will be restored to his true shape, his true god-like form.

To be spoken over four torches of red linen smeared with best quality Libyan oil in the hands of four men on whose arms are inscribed the names of the Children of Horus. They are to be lighted in broad daylight, in order to give this spirit power over the Imperishable Stars. As for him for whom this incantation is recited, he will never perish, his soul shall live forever, and this torch shall strengthen his spirit like Osiris, Foremost of the Westerners. A matter a million times true.

Beware greatly lest you do this before anyone except yourself, with your father or your son, because it is a great secret of the West, a secret image of the Duat, since the gods, spirits, and dead see it as the shape of the Foremost of the Westerners. He will be mighty like this god, and you shall cause this incantation of these four torches to be recited for him every day, so that his image shall be made to arrive at every gate of these seven gates of Osiris. It means being a god, having power in the company of the gods and spirits for ever and ever, and entering into the secret portals without his being turned away from Osiris. As for him for whom this is done, he shall go in and out without being turned away; he shall not be arrested or left out on the Day of Judgment when he who is detestable to Osiris will suffer. A true matter.

You shall recite this writing when this spirit is pure, made worthy, and cleansed, and when his mouth is opened with a wand of iron. This text was copied when it was found in writing by the king's son Hordedef, being what he found in a secret chest written in the god's own hand in the temple of Wenut, Mistress of Wenut, when he was travelling upstream inspecting the temples in the fields and mounds of the gods. What is done is a secret of the Duat belonging to the Mysteries of the Duat, a secret image in the God's Domain.

— 137B —

Chapter for kindling a torch for N

The bright Eye of Horus comes, the glorious Eye of Horus comes; welcome, O you who shine like Re in the horizon. It drives off the powers of Seth from upon the feet of Him who brings it. It is Seth who would take possession of it, but its heat is against him; the torch comes. When will it arrive? It comes now, traversing the sky behind Re on the hands of your two sisters, O Re. Live, live, O Eye of Horus within the Great Hall! Live, live, O Eye of Horus, for he is the Pillar-of-his-Mother priest.

— 138 —

Chapter for entering into Abydos and being in the suite of Osiris

O you gods who are in Abydos, the whole and complete company, come joyfully to meet me and see my father Osiris whom I have recognized and from whom I have come forth. I am this Horus, Lord of the Black Land and of the Red Land, I have taken possession entirely of Him who cannot be conquered, whose Eye is victorious over his enemies, who protects his father who is saved from the floodwaters and also his mother; who smites his enemies, who drives away the robber thereby, who counters the strength of the Destructive One; ruler of multitudes, monarch of the Two Lands, who smoothly takes possession of his father's house. I have been judged and I have been vindicated, I have power over my enemies, I get the better of those who would harm me, my strength is my protection. I am the son of Osiris, my father is in his own place, his body is in . . .

*Book to be recited in the second month
of winter, last day, when completing the Sacred Eye
in the second month of winter, last day*

The Mighty One appears, the horizon shines, Atum appears on the smell of his censing, the Sunshine-god has risen in the sky, the Mansion of the Pyramidion is in joy and all its inmates are assembled, a voice calls out within the shrine, shouting reverberates around the Duat, obeisance is done at the utterance of Atum-Horakhty. His Majesty gives a command to the Ennead attendant on His Majesty, for His Majesty is happy in contemplating the Sacred Eye: 'Behold my body to which protection has been given and all my members have been made to flourish.' His Majesty's utterance goes forth, his Eye rests in its place upon His Majesty in this fourth hour of the night, and the land is happy in the second month of winter, last day. The Majesty of the Sacred Eye is in front of the Ennead, His Majesty shines as on the First Occasion and the Sacred Eye is in his head; Re, Atum, the Sacred Eye, Shu, Geb, Osiris, Seth and Horus, Mont, Bah, Re the Everlasting, Thoth who travels eternity, Nut, Isis, Nephthys, Hathor the victorious, the two Songstress-goddesses, Maat, Anubis of the land, born of eternity, and the Soul of Mendes: when the Sacred Eye *has been reckoned* up in the presence of the Lord of this land, and it stands complete and content, these gods are joyful on this day; their hands support it and the festival of all the gods is celebrated. They say:

Hail to you and praise to Re! The crew navigate the Sacred Bark and *Apophis* is felled.

Hail to you and praise to Re! The shape of Khepri has been brought into being.

Hail to you and praise to Re! Rejoice over him, for his enemies have been driven off.

Hail to you and praise to Re! The heads of the *Children of Impotence* have been removed.

Worship to you and praise to N!

To be spoken over a Sacred Eye of real lapis-lazuli or carnelian, decorated with gold; there shall be offered to it everything good and pure before it when Re shows himself in the second month, last day; and there shall be made another Sacred Eye of red jasper which is to be placed for a man on every member which he wishes. He who utters this incantation will be in the Bark of Re when it is taken out with these gods, and he will be like one of them, he will be raised up in the God's Domain.

As for him who utters this incantation, also the offerings when the Sacred Eye is complete: four braziers for the Sacred Eye and four for Re-Atum; four braziers for the Sacred Eye and four for these gods, each one of them; five good loaves of white bread, five cones of incense, five thin flat biscuits, one basket of incense, one basket of fruit, and one of roast meat.

*Book which a man should recite for his father
and son: it is an utterance for the festivals of the West.
It means that he will be deemed worthy by Re and by
the gods and that he will be with them. To be spoken
on the day of the Festival of the New Moon.*

An offering of bread and beer, oxen and fowl, roast meat and incense on the fire to Osiris, Foremost of the Westerners; to Re-Horakhty; to Nun; to Maat; to the Bark of Re; to Atum; to the Great Ennead; to the Lesser Ennead; to Horus, Lord of the Wereret-crown; to Shu; to Tefnut; to Geb; to Nut; to Isis; to Nephthys; to the Mansion of Kas, the Mistress of All; to the Storm in the sky which bears the god aloft; to the Silent Land and Her who dwells in its place; to Her of Chemmis, the noble divine Lady; to Her who is greatly beloved, the red-haired; to Her who protects in life, the particolored; to Her whose name has power in her craft; to the Bull, the male of the herd; to the

Good Power, the good steering-oar of the northern sky; to the Wanderer who guides the Two Lands, the good steering-oar of the western sky; to the Sunshine-god who dwells in the Mansion of Images, the good steering-oar of the eastern sky; to Him who dwells in the Mansion of the Red Ones, the good steering-oar of the southern sky; to Imsety; to Hapy; to Duamutef; to Qebhsenuef; to the Southern Conclave; to the Northern Conclave; to the Night-bark; to the Day-bark; to Thoth; to the Southern Gods; to the Northern Gods; to the Western Gods; to the Eastern Gods; to the Squatting Gods; to the Gods of the Offerings; to the Per-wer; to the Per-neser; to the Gods of the Mounds; to the Gods of the Horizon; to the Gods of the Fields; to the Gods of the Houses; to the Gods of the Thrones; to the Southern Roads; to the Northern Roads; to the Eastern Roads; to the Western Roads; to the Gates of the Duat; to the Portals of the Duat; to the Secret Doors; to the Secret Gates; to the Keepers of the Doors of the Duat; to Those with hidden faces who guard the roads; to the Guardians of those who utter cries; to the Guardians of the Deserts who display kindly faces; to Those of the heat who give fire; to Those of the braziers; to Those who open up and quench the flame of fire in the West.

[Note: The first part of this chapter, the description of the gates, occurs in a slightly different form in the Ani Papyrus as Chapter 147 (Plate 11, top). The remainder of Chapter 144 follows.]

O you gates, O you who keep the gates because of Osiris, O you who guard them and who report the affairs of the Two Lands to Osiris every day: I know you and I know your names; I was born in Rosetjau, and the power of the Lord of the horizon was given to me. I was ennobled in Pe like the priest of Osiris; I receive food in Rosetjau and lead the gods in the horizon in the entourage about Osiris; I am one of them as one who leads them. I am a spirit, a master of spirits, a spirit who acts. I am one who celebrates the monthly festival and announces the half-monthly festival, I go round about bearing the fiery Eye of Horus which the hand of Thoth bears on the night when he crosses the sky in vindication. I pass by in peace, I sail in the Bark of Re, and my protection is the protection of the Bark of Re. Mine is a name greater than yours, mightier than yours upon the road of righteousness; I detest any deduction, for my protection is the protection of Horus, the first-born of Re, whom his will created. I will not be arrested, I will not be driven off from the gates of Osiris, I am he who equips the Double Lion, one who is purified daily in the suite of Osiris, Foremost of the Westerners. My lands are in the Field of Offerings among the wise ones, among those who serve me in the presence of Thoth and among those who make offerings. Anubis has commanded those who are among the offerings that my offerings shall be in my possession, and they shall not be taken from me by those who are among the plunderers.

I have come like Horus into the holy place of the horizon of the sky; I announce Re at the gates of the horizon, the gods are joyful at meeting me, and the costly stones of the gods are on me. The Destructive One shall not attack me, and those who keep their gates shall not be ignorant of me. I am one whose face is hidden within the Great Mansion, the Upper Place, the shrine of the god, and I have reached there after the purification of Hathor. I am one who creates a multitude, who raises up Truth to Re and who destroys the might of *Apophis*; I am one who opens up the firmament, who drives off the storm, who makes the crew of Re alive, and who raises up offerings to the place where they are. I have caused the Sacred Bark to make its fair voyages; a way is prepared for me that I may pass on it. My face is that of a Great One, my hinder-parts are the Double Crown, I am a possessor of power, I am content in the horizon, and I am joyful at felling you. O you who are awake, prepare a path for your lord Osiris.

To be recited over these directions which are in writing, and which are to be inscribed in ochre with the two companies of the Bark of Re. Offer to them foodstuffs, poultry, and incense in their presence. It means that a spirit will be made to live and be given power over these gods; it means that he will not be driven off or turned away at the portals of the Duat. You shall make recitation over an image of this spirit in their presence, and he will be permitted to arrive at every gate according to what is written. Make recitation at every gate in accordance with what is written, and make offering to each of them with a foreleg, head, heart, and side of a red bull, and four bowls of blood, not leaving out a heart of costly stone; sixteen white loaves, eight Persen-cakes, eighteen Shens-cakes, eight Khenef-loaves, eight Hebmenet-loaves, eight measures of beer, eight bowls of grain, four clay basins filled with milk of a white cow, green herbs, fresh moringa-oil, green and black eye-paint, first quality unguent and incense on the fire. To be recited and erased, item by item, after reciting these directions, four hours of the day having passed, and taking great care as to the position (of the sun) in the sky. You shall recite this book without letting anyone see it; it means that the movements of a spirit will be extended in the sky, on earth, and in the God's Domain, because it will be more beneficial to a spirit than anything which is done for him, and what is needed will be at hand this day. A matter a million times true.

— 146 —

Here begin the chapters for entering the mysterious portals of the House of Osiris in the Field of Reeds

[Note: The version of this chapter that appears in the Papyrus of Ani includes only ten portals. The full version includes 21 portals, the remaining eleven of which follow.]

What is to be said by N when arriving at the eleventh portal of Osiris. Make a way for me, for I know you, I know your name, and I know who is within you. 'She who always bears knives, who burns up the rebellious; Mistress of every portal, to whom acclamation is made on the day of darkness' is your name. She is under the supervision of Him who veils the Limp One.

What is to be said by N when arriving at the twelfth portal of Osiris. Make a way for me, for I know you, I know your name, and I know who is within you. 'She who summons her Two Lands, who destroys those who come at dawn; Bright One; Mistress of spirits, who hears the voice of her lord' is your name. She is under the supervision of Him who veils the Limp One.

What is to be said by N when arriving at the thirteenth portal of Osiris. Make a way for me, for I know you, I know your name, and I know who is within you. 'She on whom Osiris has extended his hands, who illumines Hapi in his abode' is your name. She is under the supervision of Him who veils the Limp One.

What is to be said by N when arriving at the fourteenth portal of Osiris. Make a way for me, for I know you, I know your name, and I know who is within you. 'Mistress of wrath, who dances in blood, for whom the Haker-festival is celebrated on the day of Her who hears sins' is your name. She is under the supervision of Him who veils the Limp One.

The fifteenth portal. 'She who has a soul, red of plaited hair, dim-eyed when going out by night, who grasps the rebel by his belly, who gives her hand to the Inert One at his critical moment, who makes her comings and goings.' She is under the supervision of Him who veils the Limp One.

The sixteenth portal. 'The terrible One, Lady of Pestilence, who casts away thousands of human souls, who hacks up human dead, who decapitates him who would go out, who creates terror.' She is under the supervision of Him who veils the Limp One.

The seventeenth portal. 'She who dances in blood . . . Mistress of Fire.' She is under the supervision of Him who veils the Limp One.

What is to be said by N when arriving at the eighteenth portal. 'Lover of heat, clean of brand-mark, who loves to cut off heads; the venerated Mistress of the Castle, who quells rebels in the evening.' She is under the supervision of Him who veils the Limp One.

What is to be said by N when arriving at the nineteenth portal. 'She who announces the dawn in her time, flaming hot, Mistress of the powers of the writings of Thoth himself.' She is under the supervision of the veiled ones of the treasury.

What is to be said by N when arriving at the twentieth portal. 'She who is within the cavern of her lord; She whose name is hidden; Mysterious of shape, who takes hearts for food.' She is under the supervision of the veiled ones of the treasury.

What is to be said by N when arriving at the twenty-first portal. 'Sharp of knife against the talker, who acts the slayer, who descends in her own flame.' She is under secret governance.

— 149 —

The first mound; green. *N says:* As for this Mound of the West in which men live on Shens-loaves and jugs of beer, doff your head-cloths at meeting me as at the likeness of the greatest among you. May he knit my bones together, may he make my members firm. May the Sistrum-player, Lord of Hearts, be brought to me that he may shape my bones and establish the Wereret-crown of Atum. Make my head firm for me, O Bestower of Powers; complete and make firm my spine, that you may rule among the gods, O Min the Builder.

The second mound; green. The god who is in it is Re-Horakhty. *N says:* I am one rich in possessions in the Field of Rushes. As for this Field of Reeds, its walls are of iron, the height of its barley is five cubits, its ear is two cubits, and its stalk is three cubits. Its emmer is seven cubits, its ear is three cubits and its stalk is four cubits. They are spirits, each nine cubits tall, who reap it in the presence of Re-Horakhty. I know the gate in the middle of the Field of Reeds from which Re goes out into the east of the sky, of which the south is the Lake of Waterfowl and the north is the Waters of Geese, the place where Re navigates by wind or by rowing. I am the whip-master in the God's Ship, I row and never tire in the Bark of Re. I know those two trees of turquoise between which Re goes forth, and which have grown up at the Supports of Shu at that door of the Lord of the East from which Re goes forth. I know that Field of Reeds which belongs to Re; the height of its barley is five cubits, its ear is two cubits and its stalk is three cubits. Its emmer is seven cubits, its ear is three cubits and its stalk is four cubits. They are spirits nine cubits tall who reap it in the presence of the Souls of the East.

The third mound; green. The Mound of Spirits. *N says:* As for the Mound of Spirits over which none travel, it contains spirits, and its flame is efficient for burning. As for the Mound of Spirits whose faces are downcast, cleanse your mounds, being what it was commanded that you should do for me by Osiris, Lord of Eternity, for I am a Great One. The Red Crown which is between the horns of the Sunshine-god makes the whole world to live with the flame of its mouth, and Re is saved from *Apophis.*

The fourth mound; green. The very high twin mountains. *N says:* As for the Chief of the mysterious mound, as for the very high mountain which is in the God's Domain, on which the sky rests, it is 300 rods long by 150 rods wide, a snake is on it called 'Caster of knives', and it is 70 cubits when it glides; it lives by decapitating the spirits of the dead in the realm of the dead. I rise up against you (the snake), so that navigation may be carried out aright; I have seen the way to you, and I will gather myself together against you, for I am the Male. Cover your head, for I am hale, hale, I am one mighty of magic and my eyes have caused me to benefit therefrom. Who is this spirit who goes on his belly and whose tail is on the mountain? See, I have gone against you, and your tail is in my hand. I am one who displays strength; I have come that I may care for the earth-snakes of Re, so that he will be pleased with me in the evening. I circumambulate the sky, while you are in bonds; that is what was commanded for you upon earth.

The fifth mound; green. N says: As for this Mound of Spirits by which men do not pass, the spirits who are in it are seven cubits from their buttocks, and they live on the shades of the inert ones. As for the Mound of Spirits, open your roads for me until I pass by you when I travel to the beautiful West; that is what was commanded by Osiris, a spirit and master of spirits, so that I might live by my magic power. I am one who celebrates exactly every monthly festival and half-monthly festival; the Eye of Horus which my hand holds goes round about for me in the suite of Thoth. As for any god or any dead who shall lick his lips over me this day, he shall fall into the depths.

The sixth mound; green. N says: As for this cavern sacred to the gods, secret from spirits and inaccessible to the dead, the god who is in it is called 'Feller of the adju-fish'. Hail to you, you cavern! I have come to see the gods who are in you. Clear your vision, doff your head-cloths when meeting me as at the likeness of the greatest among you. I have come to prepare your flat cakes, and the Feller of the adju-fish shall not have power over me, the slayers shall not pursue me, the adversaries shall not pursue me, and I shall live on the offerings which are with you.

The seventh mound; green. The Mountain of the Rerek-snake. N says: As for this town of Ises, which is far out of sight, its breath is fire, and a snake in it is called 'Rerek'. It is seven cubits long over its back, and it lives on spirits, being provided with their power. Get back, Rerek in Ises, biting with your mouth and staring with your eyes! May your bones be broken, may your poison be powerless, for you shall not come against me, your poison shall not enter into me. Fall! Lie down! May your hot rage be in the ground, may your lips remain in the hole! The bull falls to the snake and the snake falls to the bull, but I am protected, for your head is cut off by Mafdet.

The eighth mound; green. The height Hahotep. N says: As for Hahotep, great and mighty, with waves over the water in which none have power, because so great is the terror of the height of its roar, the god in it is called 'High One of Hahotep'; it is he who guards it in order that none may come near it. I am this heron which is over the plateau which is not quiet, I bring the produce of the land to Atum at the time of enriching the crews of the gods. The terror of me has been put into those who are in charge of shrines, and the awe of me has been impressed on the owners of offerings. I will not be taken to the house of the Destroyer, which they desire for me, for I am the guide of the northern horizon.

The ninth mound; yellow. Ikesy-town and the Eye which captures. N says: As for Ikesy, which is hidden from the gods, of which the spirits are afraid to learn the name, from which none goes in or out except that august god who is in his Egg, who puts the fear of him into the gods and the dread of him into the spirits: it opens with fire, and its breath is destruction to noses and mouths. He has made it against those who follow after him in order that they may not breathe the air except that august god who is in his Egg. He has done it against those who are in it in order that none may come near it except on the day of the great celebration. Hail to you, you august god who are in your Egg! I have come to you to be in your suite so that I may go in and out of Ikesy, that its doors may be opened to me, that I may breathe the air in it, and that I may have power through its offerings.

The tenth mound, which is on the plateau; yellow. N says: As for this town of Qahu which has taken possession of the spirits and which has power over the shades who eat what is fresh and gulp down corruption on account of what their eyes see, and who do not watch over the land, who are in their mounds: Put yourselves on your bellies until I have passed by you; no one shall take my spirit, no one shall have power over my shade, for I am a divine falcon and incense shall be burnt for me, offerings shall be presented to me, with Isis before me and Nephthys behind me; the road of the Nau-snake, the bull of the sky, the bestower of powers, shall be cleared for me. I have come to you, you gods; save me and give me my powers for ever.

The eleventh mound; green. N says: As for that town which is in the God's Domain, the body of which is secret, which has power over spirits from which none come out or go in through fear of revealing what is in it: The gods with him (its god) see it as a marvel, the dead with him see it in dread of him, except for those gods who are with him in his mystery as regards the spirits. O Idu-town, let me pass, for I am great of magic, with the knife which issued from Seth, and my legs are mine forever. I have appeared in glory and am strong by means of that Eye of Horus which lifted up my heart after I was limp. One powerful in the sky and mighty on earth, I have flown up as a falcon, I have cackled as a goose, it has been granted to me to alight on the plateau of the lake, so that I stand on it and sit on it. I have appeared as a god, I have eaten the provisions of Him of the Field of Offerings, I have gone down to the Bank of Reeds, I have opened the doors of Maat, I have thrown open the doors of the firmament, I have set up a ladder to the sky among the gods, for I am one of them. I have spoken as a goose until the gods have heard my voice, and I have made repetition for Sothis.

The twelfth mound; green. Isdjedet in the West. N says: As for that Mound of Wenet which is in front of Rosetjau, its breath is fire, and the gods cannot get near it, the spirits cannot associate with it; there are four cobras on it whose names are 'Destruction'. O Mound of Wenet, I am the greatest of the spirits who are in you, I am among the Imperishable Stars who are in you, and I will not perish, nor will my name perish. 'O savor of a god!' say the gods who are in the Mound of Wenet. If you love me more than your gods, I will be with you forever.

The thirteenth mound; green. He who opens his mouth, a basin of water. N says: As for that Mound of Spirits over which no one has power, its water is fire, its waves are fire, its breath is efficient for burning, in order that no one may drink its water to quench their thirst, that being what is in them, because their fear is so great and so towering is its majesty. Gods and spirits see its water from afar, but they cannot quench their thirst and their desires are unsatisfied. In order that no one may approach them, the river is filled with papyrus like the fluid in the efflux which issued from Osiris. May I have power over the water in the flood like that god who is in the Mound of Water. It is he who guards it from fear of the gods who would drink its water when it is removed from the spirits. Hail to you, you god in the Mound of Water! I have come to you that you may give me power over water and that I may drink of the flood, just as you did for that Great God for whom the Nile came, for whom herbage came into being, for whom green-stuff grew up when the same was given to the gods at his coming forth content. May you cause the Nile to come to me, may I have power over green-stuff, for I am your son forever.

The fourteenth mound; yellow. The Mound of Kheraha. N says: As for that Mound of Kheraha which diverts the Nile to Busiris, which causes the Nile to come laden with barley, which guides it to the mouth of the eater, which gives god's-offerings to the gods and invocation-offerings to the spirits: The snake which belongs to it is in the caverns of Elephantine at the source of the Nile; it comes with the water and it halts at that plateau of Kheraha at its assembly which is above the flood in order that it may see in its hour in the silence of the night. O you gods of

Kheraha, assembly which is above the flood, open your water-basins for me, throw open your waterways for me, that I may have power over water, that I may be satisfied with the flood, that I may eat grain, and that I may be satisfied with your provisions. Raise me up, that my heart may be happy, for you are the god who is in Kheraha. Your offerings shall be prepared for me, I shall be provided with the efflux which issued from Osiris, and I will never let go of it.

— 150 —

Note: A summary list of 'Mounds' which does not entirely agree with chapter 149. (ROF)]

The Field of Reeds. The god who is in it is Re-Horakhty.
The Horns of Fire. The god who is in it is Lifter of Braziers.
The Very High Mountain.
The Mound of Spirits.
The Cavern. The god who is in it is Feller of Fish.
Iseset.
Hasret. The god who is in it is He who is on high
The Horns of Qahu.
Idu. The god who is in it is Sothis.
The Mound of Wenet. The god who is in it is Destroyer of Souls.
The Horns of Water. The god who is in it is Greatest of the Mighty Ones.
The Mound of Kheraha. The god who is in it is the Nile.
The River of Flaming Fire.
Ikesy. The god who is in it is He who sees and takes.
The Beautiful West of the gods who live in it on Shens-cakes and beer.

— 151 —
Chapter for the head of mystery

Hail to you whose face is kindly, Lord of vision, one who is knit together for Ptah-Sokar and who is set on high for Anubis, to whom Shu has given the Supports, kindly face who is among the gods! Your right Eye is the Night-bark, your left Eye is the Day-bark, your eyebrows are the Ennead, your vertex is Anubis, the back of your head is Horus, your fingers are Thoth, your braided tress is Ptah-Sokar, and you are before N, who is happy with the Great God, whom he sees in you; lead him on fair roads that he may obstruct the confederacy of Seth for you, and make his enemies fall beneath him before the Great Ennead in the great Mansion of the Prince which is in Heliopolis. May you take a fair road into the presence of Horus, Lord of Patricians, O N.

[Note: The rest of this chapter appears in the Ani Papyrus on Plate 33.]

— 152 —
Chapter for building a mansion on earth

Geb is joyful when I hasten over him on his body, and men, the children of their fathers, give me praise when they see that Seshat brings the Destructive One.

Anubis has summoned me to build a mansion which is on earth, its foundation-plan is in Heliopolis, its circuit is in Kheraha, he who is preeminent in Letopolis is the scribe responsible for making new what belongs to it; men bring to it bowls of water, and the gangs (work at it). Thus said Osiris to the gods who are in his suite: 'Let us go and see the building of this mansion of this equipped spirit who today has come newly among you. Grant that he may be respected and give him the praise due to him who is favored there, and you will see what I have done and spoken.'

Thus said Osiris to this god: 'Today he has come newly

among you; it is Osiris who brings him herds, it is the south wind which brings him barley, it is the north wind which brings him emmer which the earth has ripened.'

The utterance of Osiris has announced me, he who was destroyed has turned himself over from upon his left side and has set himself upon his right side. Men, gods, spirits, and the dead have seen, they spend their time in praise, and I am favored thereby.

— 153A —
Chapter for escaping from the net

O you who look backward, you with power in your heart, you fisherman who net at the river-bank and open up the earth: O you fishermen, children of your fathers, you takers of your catch, who go round about in the abode of the waters, you shall not catch me in this net of yours in which you catch the inert ones, you shall not trap me in this trap in which you trap the wanderers, the floats of which are in the sky and its weights on earth. I have escaped from its snare, and I have rejoiced as Henu; I have escaped from its clutch, and I have appeared as Sobk, I have used my arms for flying from you, even you who fish and net with hidden fingers.

I know the reel in it; it is the middle finger of Sokar.
I know the guard-beam in it; it is the shank of Shesmu.
I know the valve in it; it is the hand of Isis.
I know the cutter in it; it is the knife of Isis with which the navel-string of Horus was cut.
I know the name of the floats in it and of its weight; they are the knee-cap and the knee of the Double Lion.
I know the name of its cords with which it catches fish; they are the sinews of Atum.
I know the names of the fishermen who use it; they are the Earth-gods, the forefathers of the Swallowers.
I know the names of its arms; they are the arms of the Great God who gives judgment in Heliopolis on the night of the half-monthly festival in the Mansion of the Moon . . .
I know the name of the plateau on which it is pulled tight; it is the plateau of the firmament on which the gods stand.
I know the name of the agent who receives its fish; it is 'Marker of jars, the agent of the god'.
I know the name of the table on which he lays it; it is the table of Horus who sits alone in darkness and cannot be seen, of whom those who have not given him praise are afraid.
I have come and have appeared as a great one, I have governed the land, I have gone down to the earth in the two Great Barks, and the Great One has made presentation to me in the midst of the Mansion of the Prince. I have come as a fisherman, with my net and my reel in my hand, my knife in my hand, and my cutter in my hand; I go to and fro and I catch with my net.
I know the name of the reel which closes the mouth of the opening; it is the middle finger of Osiris.
I know the name of the fingers which hold it; they are the fingers which are on the hand of Re and the nails which are on the hand of Hathor.
I know the name of the cords which are on this reel; they are the sinews of the Lord of the Common Folk.
I know the name of its valve; it is the hand of Isis.
I know the name of its draw-rope; it is the draw-rope of the Eldest God.
I know the name of its netting; it is . . . of the day.
I know the names of the fishermen who use it; they are the Earth-gods who are in the presence of Re.
I know the name of . . . ; they are everyone who is in the presence of Geb.
What you have brought and eaten, I have brought and eaten; you have swallowed what Geb and Osiris swallowed. O you who look behind you, O you who have power in your

heart, fish and catch for him who opens the earth, O you fishers, children of your fathers, who entrap within Nefersenet, you shall not catch me in your net, you shall not entrap me in your net in which you catch the inert ones and entrap those who are throughout the earth, for I know it, I know it from its upper floats to its lower weights. Here am I, I have come with my reel in my hand, my peg in my hand, my valve in my hand, and my knife in my hand; I have come and I have entered; I smite and I catch. Do you know that I know the name of the catcher of fledglings? I break his bow. I smite him and I put him in his place. As for the peg which is in my hand, it is the shank of Shesmu; as for the reel which is in my hand, it is the finger of Sokar; as for the valve which is in my hand, it is the hand of Isis; as for the knife which is in my hand, it is the decapitating sword of Shesmu.

Here am I; I have come. Here am I; I sit in the bark of Re, I ferry across the Lake of the Two Knives in the northern sky, I hear the words of the gods, I do as they do, I rejoice as they rejoice over my Ka, I live on what they live on. I ascend on your ladder which my father Re made for me, and Horus and Seth grip my hands.

— 153B —
Chapter for escaping from the catcher of fish

O you net-users, trappers and fishermen, O you children of your fathers, do you know that I know the name of that great and mighty net? 'The All-embracing' is its name.

Do you know that I know the name of its cords? They are the sinews of Isis.

Do you know that I know the name of the peg? It is the shank of Atum.

Do you know that I know the name of its reel? It is the finger of Shesmu.

Do you know that I know the name of its valve? It is the fingernail of Ptah.

Do you know that I know the name of its knife? It is the decapitating sword of Isis.

Do you know that I know the name of its weights? It is the iron in the midst of the sky.

Do you know that I know the name of the floats? They are the feathers of the Falcon.

Do you know that I know the name of its fishermen? They are baboons.

Do you know that I know the name of the plateau on which it is pulled tight? It is the Mansion of the Moon.

Do you know that I know the name of him who uses it for himself? He is the great prince who dwells in the eastern side of the sky.

The Great One shall not eat me, the Great One shall not swallow me, I shall not sit on my haunches by the water, for I have eaten and I have swallowed in his presence, and the food of the dead is in my belly.

I am a guinea-fowl, I am Re who emerged from the Primordial Water, my soul is a god. I am he who created Authority, and falsehood is my detestation. I am Osiris who created righteousness so that Re might live by it daily. I am prayed to as a bull, I am invoked in the Ennead in this my name of the guinea-fowl god. I came into being of myself in company with Nun in this my name of Khepri; I come into being in it daily, for I am the Lord of Light; I appear as Re, Lord of the East, and life is given to me at his risings in the East. I have come to the sky and I have sought out my throne which is in the East. They are the youths and elders who are in the fields who apportion the time when I am born in peace. I have eaten as Shu, I have swallowed as Shu, I have defecated as Shu; the Kings of Upper and Lower Egypt are in me, Khons is in me, the heads of the netters of fish are in me, while the warmth of the earth shall embrace you, you multitudes.

— 154 —
Chapter for not letting the corpse perish

Hail to you, my father Osiris! I have come to you to the intent that you may heal my flesh; I am complete like my father Khepri, who is the like of one who does not perish. Come, that my breath may be stronger than yours, O Lord of Breath; where are the likes of him? May I endure longer than you, for I am fashioned as the possessor of a burial; may you permit me to go down into the earth forever like that one who serves you and your father Atum, and his corpse will not perish; such is he who will not be destroyed. I have not done what you dislike; may your Ka love me and not thrust me aside; take me after you. May I not become corrupt, being like that one who served you better than any god or any goddess, than any herds or any snakes who shall perish. May my soul ascend aloft after death; may it descend only after it has perished. Such is he who is decayed; all his bones are corrupt, his flesh is slain, his bones are softened, his flesh is made into foul water, his corruption stinks and he turns into many worms . . . when he is sent to the Eye of Shu, whether as god, goddess, fowl, fish, snakes, worms, and herds altogether, because they prostrated themselves to me when they recognized me; it is the fear of me which frightens them. Now every mortal is thus, one who will die whether (men), herds, fowl, fish, snakes, or worms; those who live will die. May no worm at all pass by; may they not come against me in their various shapes; you shall not give me over to that slayer who is in his . . . , who kills the body, who rots the hidden one, who destroys a multitude of corpses, who lives by killing the living, who carries out his business and who does what has been commanded to him. You shall not give me over to his fingers, he shall not have power over me, for I am at your command, O Lord of the Gods.

Hail to you, my father Osiris! You shall possess your body; you shall not become corrupt, you shall not have worms, you shall not be distended, you shall not stink, you shall not become putrid, you shall not become worms. I am Khepri; I will possess my body forever, for I will not become corrupt, I will not decay, I will not be putrid, I will not become worms, I will not be faint because of the Eye of Shu, I exist, I am alive, I am strong, I have awaked in peace, I have not decayed, there is no destruction in my viscera, I have not been injured, my eye has not rotted, my skull has not been crushed, my ears are not deaf, my head has not removed itself from my neck, my tongue has not been taken away, my hair has not been cut off, my eyebrows have not been stripped, no injury has happened to me. My corpse is permanent, it will not perish nor be destroyed in this land forever.

— 157 —
Chapter for a golden vulture
to be placed on the neck of the deceased

Isis came, she halted at the town and sought out a hiding-place for Horus when he came out of his marshes . . . awoke in a bad state and painted his eyes in the god's ship. It was commanded to him to rule the Banks, and he assumed the condition of a mighty warrior, for he remembered what had been done, and he engendered fear of him and inspired respect. His great mother protects him and erases those who come against Horus.

To be spoken over a golden vulture with this spell inscribed on it; it is to be set as a protection for this worthy spirit on the day of interment, as a matter a million times true.

— 158 —
Chapter for a golden collar
to be placed on the throat of the deceased

O my father, my brother, and my mother Isis, release me, look at me, for I am one of those who should be released when Geb sees them.

THE BOOK OF GOING FORTH BY DAY

To be spoken over a golden collar with this spell inscribed on it; it is to be set on the throat of the deceased on the day of interment.

— 159 —

Chapter for a papyrus-column of green feldspar to be placed on the throat of the deceased

O you who have come forth today from the god's house, She whose voice is loud goes round about from the door of the Two Houses, she has assumed the power of her father, who is ennobled as Bull of the Nursing Goddess, and she accepts those of her followers who do great deeds to her.

To be spoken over a papyrus-column of green feldspar with this spell inscribed on it; it is to be set on the throat of the deceased.

— 160 —

Giving a papyrus-column of green feldspar

To me belongs a papyrus-column of green feldspar which is not imperfect, and which the hand of Thoth supports, for he detests injury. If it is intact, then I will be hale; if it is uninjured, then will I be uninjured; if it is not struck, then I will not be struck. It is what Thoth has said which knits your spine together.

Welcome, O Elder of Heliopolis, greatest in Pe, to whom Shu has gone; he finds him in Shenmu in this his name of 'Green Feldspar'. He has taken his place opposite the Great God, and Atum is satisfied with his Eye, so that my members will not be damaged.

— 161 —

Chapter for breaking an opening into the sky which Thoth made for Wennefer when he broke into the solar disk

Re lives, the tortoise is dead, the corpse is interred and N's bones are reunited.

Re lives, the tortoise is dead, and he who is in the sarcophagus and in the coffin is stretched out.

[Note: The two remaining paragraphs continue the refrain 'Re lives, the tortoise is dead', but otherwise are unintelligible. A 'rubric' in black follows: (ROF)]

As for any noble dead for whom this ritual is performed over his coffin, there shall be opened for him four openings in the sky, one for the north wind — that is Osiris; another for the south wind — that is Re; another for the west wind — that is Isis; another for the east wind — that is Nephthys. As for each one of these winds which is in its opening, its task is to enter into his nose. No outsider knows, for it is a secret which the common folk do not yet know; you shall not perform it over anyone, not your father or your son, except yourself alone. It is truly a secret, which no one of the people should know.

— 162 —

Chapter to cause to come into being a flame beneath the head of a spirit

Hail to you Lord of Might, tall of plumes, owner of the Wereret-crown, whose possession is the flail. You are lord of the phallus, strong when dawning, a light never ceasing to dawn. You are possessor of (different) forms, rich in hues, one who hides in the Sacred Eye until his birth. You are one powerful of bellow in the Ennead, a mighty runner, swift of steps. You are a powerful god who comes to the aid of one who asks for it, who saves the wretched from affliction. Come at my voice, I am the Ihet-cow; your name is in my mouth and I shall utter it: *Penhaqahagaher* is your name, *Iuriuiaqrsainqrbaty* is your name, tail of the lion-ram is your name, *Kharsati* is your name: I adore your name. I am the Ihet-cow, hear my voice today. You have set the flame under the head of Re and he is in the divine Duat in Heliopolis. May you cause him to appear like one who is on earth: he is your soul, do not forget him. Come to the Osiris N. Cause to come into being a flame beneath his head for he is the soul of that corpse which rests in Heliopolis, Atum is his name, *Barkatitjawa* is his name. Come, cause him to be like one in your following, for he is such a one as you.

Words to be spoken over a statuette of an Ihet-cow made of fine gold and placed at the throat of the deceased; also a drawing of it on a new papyrus scroll placed under his head. A great quantity of flames will envelop him completely like one who is on earth. A very great protection which was made by the Ihet-cow for her son Re when he set. His place will be enclosed by a blaze and he will be a god in the realm of the dead and will not be repulsed from any portal of the Netherworld in very truth. You shall say as you place this goddess at the throat of the deceased 'O you most hidden of hidden gods in heaven, regard the corpse of your son; keep him safe in the God's Domain. This is a book of great secrecy — let no one see it for that would be an abomination. But the one who knows it and keeps it hidden shall continue to exist. The name of this book is "Mistress of the hidden temple".'

— 163 —

Chapters taken from another book, added to the book of coming forth by day. Chapter for preventing a man's corpse from putrefying in the realm of the dead in order to rescue him from the eater of souls who imprisons in the Duat and to prevent accusations of his crimes upon earth being imputed to him; to cause his flesh and bones to be safe from maggots and every god who mutilates in the God's Domain and to allow him to come and go as he wants and to do everything which is in his heart without being restrained

Words to be spoken over a snake with two legs, a sun-disk and two horns; over two Sacred Eyes, each with two legs and wings. In the pupil of one is the figure of Him whose arm is raised and a head of Bes with two plumes, whose back is like a falcon's. In the pupil of the other is a figure of Him whose arm is raised and a head of Neith with two plumes, whose back is like a falcon's. Drawn in dried myrrh mixed with wine, repeated with malachite of Upper Egypt and water from the well west of Egypt on a green bandage with which all a man's limbs are enveloped.

He shall not be repulsed from any portals of the Netherworld; he shall eat and drink, defecate from the hinder-parts as when he was on earth. No complaint shall be raised against him nor the hand of an enemy profit against him forever.

If this text is used on earth he will not be exposed by the messengers who attack those who commit wrong in all the earth. His head shall not be cut off, he shall not be destroyed by the knife of Seth. He shall not be carried off to any prison. But he shall enter the tribunal and come forth justified. He shall be preserved from the fear of wrong-doing which exists in all the earth.

— 164 —

Another chapter

To be said over (a figurine of) Mut having three heads: one being the head of Pakhet wearing plumes, a second being a human head wearing the Double Crown, the third being the head of a vulture wearing plumes. She also has a phallus, wings, and the claws of a lion. Drawn in dried myrrh with fresh incense, repeated in ink upon a red bandage. A dwarf stands before her, another behind her, each facing her and wearing plumes. Each has a raised arm and two heads, one is the head of a falcon, the other a human head.

Wrap the breast therewith: he shall be a god among gods

in the God's Domain. He shall not be repulsed forever. His flesh and bones shall be sound like one who does not die. He shall drink water from the river; land shall be given to him in the Field of Reeds; a star of the sky shall be given to him. He shall be preserved from the serpent, the hot-tempered one who is in the Duat. His soul shall not be imprisoned. The Djeriu-bird shall rescue him from the one at his side and no maggot shall eat him.

— 165 —

Chapter for mooring and not letting the Sacred Eye
be injured, for maintaining the corpse and drinking water

To be said over a divine image with raised arm, plumes on his head, his legs apart, his middle a scarab; drawn with lapis-lazuli and water of gum. Also an image whose head is human, his arms hanging down, the head of a ram on his right shoulder, another on his left shoulder. Draw on a single bandage level with his heart the image of Him with raised arm; draw the other image over his breast without letting Sugady who is in the Duat have knowledge of it. He shall drink water of the river; he shall shine like a star in the sky.

— 167 —

Chapter for bringing a Sacred Eye by N

Thoth has fetched the Sacred Eye, having pacified the Eye after Re had sent it away. It was very angry, but Thoth pacified it from anger after it had been far away. If I be hale, it will be hale, and N will be hale.

— 168 —

Those who lift up their faces to the sky in the bow of the Bark of Re will permit N to see Re when he rises. *A bowl is offered to them on earth by N,* a possessor of gifts in the West within the Field of Offerings.

Those who lift up their faces to the sky in the bow of the Bark of Re will permit Osiris to see Re when he rises. *A bowl is offered to them on earth by N,* a follower of the Great God, the Lord of the beautiful West.

Those who drive Re will cause bread to pass to N as to the suite of Re when he goes to rest. *A bowl will be offered to them on earth by N,* who comes to Horus, Lord of the Mountain-top.

The bearers of gifts will cause N to be like those who are in the Duat. *A bowl will be offered to them on earth by N,* who goes out and comes in with Re forever.

The inert ones will permit N to enter into the Hall of Justice. *A bowl will be offered to them on earth by N,* as a possessor of gifts in the beautiful West.

The snakes will permit N to follow Re into his bark. *A bowl will be offered to them on earth by N,* who travels freely with the gods of the Duat.

The bearers of offerings who give offerings to the gods will give offerings and provisions to N in the God's Domain. *A bowl will be offered to them on earth by N.* May they not stand up against the soul at the portal.

The gods of the eighth cavern of the Duat whose shapes are mysterious, who breathe the air.

The gods who are in their shrines which are about the Primordial Water. May they let N drink. *A bowl will be offered to them on earth by N;* may his soul live and may his corpse be intact in the God's Domain.

The gods who are in the suite of Osiris. May they grant that N be at rest with his mummy. *A bowl is offered to them on earth by N,* in the presence of the Great God who dwells in his bark.

He who stands up. May he permit N to worship Re when he rises. *A bowl is offered to them on earth by N;* he shall be in charge of the braziers.

He who is hidden. May he make N strong in the hall of Geb. *A bowl is offered to them on earth by N,* who knows the secrets of the Lords of the Duat.

He who is mysterious. May he permit N's corpse to be strong and intact on earth and in the God's Domain. *A bowl is offered to them on earth by N,* being a possessor of movement in the God's Domain and in Rosetjau.

He who is concealed. May he give bread and beer to N with you in the House of Osiris. *A bowl is offered to them on earth by N,* who enters into the secrets of the Lords of the Duat.

The mysterious one of Osiris. May he cause N to be a possessor of movement in the sacred place. *A bowl is offered to them on earth by N,* who becomes the owner of a throne in the God's Domain.

Sherem. He shall not let evil draw near to N in the realm of the dead. *A bowl is offered to them on earth by N,* a soul who hears the words of the gods.

The Usher. May he permit N to see Re when he rises and sets. *A bowl is offered to them on earth by N.* May his members live and his body be hale forever.

The Dark One. May he make N to be a spirit on earth and to be strong in the West. *A bowl is offered to them on earth by N,* whose legs have power as a possessor of a throne in the West.

The Eyeless One. May he permit N to be among those who are in charge of braziers. *A bowl is offered to them on earth by N,* who belongs to the Standing One who is in the Duat.

The Embalmers. May they permit N to be in the presence of the Great God, Lord of the West. *A bowl is offered to them on earth by N,* who becomes a possessor of arms and one who is stouthearted in the God's Domain.

The Males whose arms are hidden. May they permit N to be with them forever in the God's Domain. *A bowl is offered to them on earth by N,* who will attain to the throne of Osiris.

The Females whose arms are hidden. May they grant that N be hale and that his offerings endure in his presence. *A bowl is offered to them on earth by N;* he is the two-horned one who hears the words of the gods.

He whose body is hidden. May he grant to N righteousness with Re who is in his Ennead. *A bowl is offered to them on earth by N,* as the possessor of a phallus who takes women forever.

The souls who go forth. May they judge the speech of N among the gods who are with them. *A bowl is offered to them on earth by N* among the living, the lords of eternity.

Those who belong to . . . May they grant that N have power through his offerings on earth like all the gods. *A bowl is offered to them on earth by N,* who benefits from provisions in the God's Domain.

Those who receive. May they permit N to enter into all the secret places of the Duat. *A bowl will be offered to them on earth by N,* who shall have power over offerings upon earth as a possessor of braziers.

The female inert ones. May they grant that N be with the Great God as the possessor of a phallus. *A bowl is offered to them on earth by N,* so that he who is in the secret place in darkness may have light.

Osiris-Anubis. May he grant that N be a possessor of a throne in the Sacred Land. *A bowl is offered to them on earth by N,* who passes the threshold of the portal of Osiris.

The gods of the tenth cavern in the Duat, who cry aloud and whose mysteries are holy.

Those who belong to the sunshine. May they give light to N in darkness. *A bowl is offered to them on earth by N,* who worships the Great God in his place every day.

Those who take hold. May they grant that N be acclaimed. *A bowl is offered to them on earth by N,* on the day of driving off the great encircling serpent.

The Nine Gods who guard those who are in (the cavern).

May they grant the breath of life to N on earth and in the realm of the dead. *A bowl is offered to them on earth by N*, whose hand is extended and who repels him who comes.

The Nine Gods whose arms are hidden. May they grant that N be a spirit like the worthy spirits. *A bowl is offered to them on earth by N*, whose head is hale on earth and in the realm of the dead.

The Hidden Goddess. May she grant that N's soul be strong and his corpse intact like the gods who are in the Duat. *A bowl is offered to them on earth by N;* may his soul rest in the place where it desires to be.

The souls of the gods who have become the members of Osiris. May they grant that N have peace. *A bowl is offered to them on earth by N*, who receives his place on earth and in the God's Domain.

Those who worship Re. N shall not be driven off from any of the portals of the Duat. *A bowl is offered to them on earth by N* when he goes out into the day and is cool in the cool place.

Those whose faces are warlike. May they grant that N be cool in the place of heat. *A bowl is offered to them on earth by N;* may he sit in front in the presence of the Great God.

The gods of the eleventh cavern, covered, . . . hidden, secret.

The Python. May she grant that N be hale before the Great God who is in the Duat. *A bowl is offered to them on earth by N*, who shall come into being as Khepri in the West.

The Soul of the West. May he grant invocation-offerings of bread and beer, oxen and fowl to N on earth and in the realm of the dead. *A bowl is offered to them on earth by N*, a possessor of a throne whose heart is content on the mountain of the God's Domain.

The Souls of Earth. May they grant triumph to N over his enemies in sky and earth. *A bowl is offered to them on earth by N*, who keeps silence regarding all that he has seen.

Those who make offerings. May they grant that N be like the crew (of the solar bark) in the sky. *A bowl is offered to them on earth by N;* may he go in by the secret portal.

The Nine Gods who rule the West. May they permit N to go in by the great secret portal of Osiris. *A bowl is offered to them on earth by N*, who is dominant over the Lords of the Duat.

The Nine Gods who are in the suite of Osiris. May they grant that N have power over his enemies. *A bowl is offered to them on earth by N;* may he become a worthy soul from day to day.

Iqeh. May he grant that N be in the presence of Re and that he may cross the sky forever. *A bowl is offered to them on earth by N*, for he is in the following of Him who dwells in the Place of Embalmment, Lord of the Sacred Land.

The Embalmer of Osiris. May he grant that N's soul shall live; he shall not die again forever. *A bowl is offered to them on earth by N;* mourning shall be decreed for him and for his god.

The Nine Watchers. May they grant wakefulness to N; he shall never be destroyed. *A bowl is offered to them on earth by N*, who is vindicated before Osiris, Lord of the Faiyum.

The Nine Mourners. May they grant mourning for N like what was done for Osiris. *A bowl is offered to them on earth by N* when his soul ascends among the spirits.

He whom Re summoned. May he summon N to Re and his Ennead. *A bowl is offered to them on earth by N* whose soul comes into the secret place and goes up from the earth.

Iqen. May he drive away all evil from N for ever. *A bowl is offered to them on earth by N*, who comes in peace and is vindicated.

Those who are with Her whose head is red. May they permit N to go in and out and to stride forward like the Lords of the Duat. *A bowl is offered to them on earth by N* when he goes in and out of the portal of the Duat.

She whose head is red. May she grant that N have power over the waters. *A bowl is offered to them on earth by N* as one who strides freely up the great stairway.

The Coiled Serpent. May she grant that N be holy in the Duat forever. *A bowl is offered to them on earth by N*, as a worthy soul who is in his cavern.

Those who are with the Coiled Serpent. May they permit N to stride forward freely in the sacred place. *A bowl is offered to them on earth by N*, and he shall be in the presence of the Followers of Horus.

The Nine Gods who hide Osiris. May they grant that N dwell in the place which he desires. *A bowl is offered to them on earth by N*, and he shall be among the Lords of Righteousness.

The Destroyer. May he clear N's vision that he may see the Sunshine-god. *A bowl is offered to them on earth by N*, so that he may be in the following of the serpent guardian of the West.

The gods of the twelfth cavern of the Duat; the gods are united in front of those who guide.

He of the river-bank. May he grant that N be Lord of the Island of the Just. *A bowl is offered to them on earth by N* as a possessor of offerings in the Field of Reeds.

The gods who are in the region of the Duat. May they give justice to N in the Hall of Justice. *A bowl is offered to them on earth by N;* may he plow in the Field of Offerings.

The gods who are with the Coiled Serpent. May they grant that N be in the place which his Ka desires, and he will be there. *A bowl is offered to them on earth by N*, who will come into being at the word of the Lord of the West.

The gods who are on the earth. May they give an island to N in the Field of Reeds. *A bowl is offered to them on earth by N;* may he dwell in the place where he desires to be.

He who is in charge of the earth. May he make a grant of land to N in the Field of Offerings. *A bowl is offered to them on earth by N;* may amulets protect him like the Lords of the Duat.

The gods who are in the earth. May they give food-offerings, provisions, and a portion of meat to N in the realm of the dead. *A bowl is offered to them on earth by N*, when he sets in Manu.

Those who are in charge of the secret things which are in the earth. May they place their walls about N, like what is done for the Inert One. *A bowl is offered to them on earth by N* when he goes in and out of the God's Domain.

The gods who are in the coils of the Serpent. May they cause the sun-disk to look on N. *A bowl is offered to them on earth by N* as a mighty spirit in his firmament.

Yuba. May he grant that N rest in the West. *A bowl is offered to them on earth by N* when going in and out of the West more than anyone.

— 169 —
Chapter for erecting a bier

You are the Lion, you are the Double Lion, you are Horus the protector of his father, you are the fourth of these four mighty gods who belong to those who make acclamation and who make shouting, who bring water by means of their power of . . . Raise yourself upon your right side, lift yourself upon your left side, for Geb will open for you your blind eyes, he will straighten your bent knees, and there will be given to you your heart which you had from your mother, your heart which belongs to your body. Your soul is bound for the sky, your corpse is beneath the ground; there is bread for your belly, water for your throat, and sweet air for your nose. Those who are in their tombs will be kindly to you, those who are in their coffins will be open to you, they will bring to you your members when you are reestablished in your original shape. You shall go up to the sky, the cord shall be knotted for you in the presence of Re, you shall close the net in the river, you shall drink water from it, you shall walk on your feet, you shall not walk upside down. You shall ascend to those who are above the earth, you shall not go out to those who are under the walls; your walls which belong to you, being what your city god made for you, will not be thrown down.

You are pure, your front is pure, your back parts are clean by means of natron, fresh water and incense, and you are pure by means of milk of Apis, by beer of Tjenmyt, and by natron which dispels the evil on you. Tefnut the daughter of Re will feed you in the presence of her father Re; She of the Valley will knit you together as at the burial of her father Osiris, you will bite on something sweet which he gives to you there. Your three portions are above with Re, of barley of Ibu; your four portions are below with Geb, of barley of Upper Egypt; it is the citizens who bring to you Him of the Field of Offerings, and he is set before you. You shall go forth with Re, you shall have power through Re, you shall have power in your legs at all seasons and at any hour.

You shall not be examined, you shall not be imprisoned, you shall not be watched, you shall not be fettered, you shall not be put in the cell for rebels, the sand shall be removed from your face. Beware of him who is heavy against you, let none oppose you; beware that you do not go forth. Take your garment, your sandals, your staff, your loin-cloth, and all your weapons, so that you may cut off the heads and sever the necks of those rebellious enemies who draw near when you are dead. 'Do not go near' is the word of the Great God to you, even he who brings himself on the day of coming into being. The Falcon rejoices at you, the Goose cackles at you, the doors of the sky are opened by Re, the earth is thrown open for you by Geb, because your power is so great and the knowledge of your name is so effective. It is opening up the West for this worthy soul, it is speech which is pleasing to the heart of Re and satisfactory to the heart of his tribunal which watches over men. May the Double Lion lead to the place where N has made his Ka content.

O N, entrap all those who would harm you, for you have life, your soul has health, your corpse is long-enduring, you see the flame, you breathe the air, your vision is clear in the House of Darkness which is set in the entrance (of the sky), without seeing a storm. You serve the ruler of the Two Lands, you refresh yourself at the Meru-tree in the presence of him whose magic is mighty, while Seshat sits before you, Sia protects your body, the Ox-herd milks for you his herd which follows Sekhat-Hor. May you raise yourself at the opening of the waters of Kheraha, may the great ones of Pe and Dep praise you, may you gaze on Thoth the representative of Re in the sky, may you go up and enter into the pillared hall, may the Rivals make report to you. Your Ka is with you because of your joy of heart at your existing. Your happy . . . awaken you, the Ennead makes your heart glad; four loaves are issued to you in Letopolis, four loaves in Hermopolis, and four loaves in Heliopolis, upon the altar of the Lady of Two Lands. May the night of stars awaken you, may the Lords of Heliopolis refresh you, may food be in your mouth, for your feet shall not go astray, your limbs shall have life, you shall grasp a whip in Abydos; you shall guide the collection of the great ones, the full muster of those who are in charge of the company at the jubilee of Osiris at the morning of the Wag-festival, and of the masters of the mysteries. You shall be adorned with gold, your vestment being of fine linen, Hapi shall surge over your breast, the Seter-plant will be beneficial to you, being carved on your offering-stone, and you shall drink beside the Lake of the Two Knives. The gods who are yonder shall favor you, you shall ascend to the sky with the gods who present Truth to Re, you shall be inducted into the presence of the Ennead, and you shall be made like one of them. Yours is the Khar-goose, son of the Ro-goose, and you shall offer it to Ptah South-of-his-Wall.

Chapter for assembling a bier

O N, I have given you your flesh, I have gathered your bones together for you, I have collected your members for you, I have thrown off for you the earth which was on your flesh, for you are Horus within the Egg. Raise yourself that you may see the gods, extend your arm towards the horizon, to the pure place where you desire to be. May men serve you there, may acclamation be made for you, with what is issued from the altar. Horus will raise you up at his appearings, just as he did for Him who was in the Pure Place.

O N, Anubis who is on his mountain will raise you up and will make your bandages strong.

O N, Ptah-Sokar will give you an arm with its temple adornments.

O N, Thoth himself will come to you with the book of the sacred words, and he will set your hand on the horizon, at the place which your Ka desires; he it was who helped you, O Osiris, on that night of death. May your White Crown be firm on your brow, for Shesmu is with you, and he will present you with the choicest of fowl.

O N, raise yourself on your bier that you may go forth. Re will raise you up in the horizon, to the bank of rowers which is in his Bark.

O N, Atum, father of the gods, will cause you to endure forever.

O N, Min of Coptos will raise you up so that gods of the shrine may worship you.

O N, how happy a thing it is that you should cross in peace to your house for eternity, your tomb for everlasting! May you be greeted in Pe and Dep in the shrine which your Ka desires, for your place is preeminent and your power is great. The great bier will raise you up to the Wild Bull whom the gods embrace, for you are a god who begot those who exist, whose shape is better than those of the gods. Your brilliance is greater than that of the spirits, your power is mightier than that of those who are yonder.

O N, Ptah South-of-his-Wall will raise you up and will advance your position above that of the gods.

O N, you are Horus, son of Isis, whom Ptah begot, whom Nut created; may you shine like Re in the horizon when he illumines the Two Lands with his beauty. The gods say to you: 'Welcome! Cross over that you may see your possessions in your house for eternity.' Renenutet will raise you up, even she whom Atum impregnated in the presence of the Ennead.

O Nut, I am the heir of the sky, the companion of Him who created his light; I went forth from the womb when I was orphaned of my father without having the wisdom to answer for my deeds.

Chapter for donning a pure garment

Atum, Shu, Tefnut, Geb, Nut, Osiris, Isis, Seth, Nephthys, Horakhty, Hathor, the Great Mansion, Khepri, Mont the Lord of Thebes, Amun the Lord of the thrones of the Two Lands, the Great Ennead, the Lesser Ennead, the gods and goddesses who are in the Primordial Water, Sobk of Crocodilopolis, Sobk in all his many names in every place of his where his soul desires to be; the southern gods and the northern gods, those who are in the sky and those who are on earth: may you give this pure garment to the worthy spirit N; may you grant that it be beneficial to him; may you remove the evil which is on him. As for this pure garment for N, may it be allotted to him for ever and ever, and may you remove the evil which is on him.

*Here begin the chapters of praising
which are made in the God's Domain*

I am purified with natron, I chew natron, incense . . . I am pure, and pure are the recitations which come forth from my mouth. They are more pure than the fins and scales of the fish in the river, more than the image belonging to the Mansion of Natron; my recitations are pure. How happy am I! Ptah praises me, He who is South-of-his-Wall praises me, every god praises me and every goddess praises me (and they say): 'Your beauty is that of a calm pool, like a quiet water; your beauty is that of a hall of festival wherein every god is extolled; your beauty is like the column of Ptah, indeed like the shaft of Re.' May there be made for me a column for Ptah and a metal jar for Him who is South-of-his-Wall.

See, you are doubly mourned. First stanza. See, you are lamented, you are glorified, you are exalted, you are a spirit, you are mighty. Rise up, for you are indeed risen! Rise up against those who would harm you, male or female, for your enemies are fallen; Ptah has felled your enemies, and you are victorious over them, you have power over them. Your words are heard, orders are carried out for you, for you are risen and vindicated in the tribunals of every god or goddess.

See, you are doubly mourned. Second stanza. Your head, O my lord, is adorned with the tress of a woman of Asia; your face is brighter than the Mansion of the Moon; your upper part is lapis-lazuli; your hair is blacker than all the doors of the Duat on the day of darkness, your hair is bestrewn with lapis-lazuli; the upper part of your face is as the shining of Re; your visage is covered with gold and Horus has inlaid it with lapis-lazuli; your eyebrows are the two sisterly Serpents, and Horus has inlaid them with lapis-lazuli; your nose is in the odor of the place of embalming, your nostrils are like the winds of the sky; your eyes behold Bakhu; your eyelashes are firm every day, being colored with real lapis-lazuli; your eyelids are the bringers of peace, and their corners are full of black eye-paint; your lips give you truth, they repeat truth to Re and make the gods content; your teeth are those of the Coiled Serpent, with which the Two Horuses play; your tongue is wise and sharp when you speak to the kites of the field; your jaw is the starry sky; your breasts are firm in their place when they traverse the western desert.

See, you are doubly mourned. Third stanza. Your neck is adorned with gold and also with fine gold; your throat is great, your windpipe is Anubis; your vertebrae are the Two Cobras; your back is overlaid with gold and also with fine gold; your lungs are Nephthys; your face is Hapi and his flood; your buttocks are eggs of carnelian; your legs are strong in walking; you are seated on your throne, and the gods have given you your eyes.

See, you are doubly mourned. Fourth stanza. Your gullet is Anubis; your body is extended with gold; your breasts are eggs of carnelian which Horus has inlaid with lapis-lazuli; your arms glitter with faience; your shoulders are firm in their places; your heart is happy every day; your heart is the work of the two Mighty Ones; your thighs worship the lower stars, your belly is the peaceful sky; your navel is the Morning Star which makes judgment and promises light in darkness, and whose offerings are the 'life-is-in-it' plant; it worships the Majesty of Thoth. I love its beauty in my tomb which my god decreed for me in the pure place where I desire to be.

See, you are doubly mourned. Fifth stanza. Your arms are a waterway at the fair season of inundation, a waterway which the Children of Water have covered; your knees are enclosed with gold; your breast is a thicket of the swamps; the soles of your feet are firm every day; your toes guide you on fair paths, O N; your hands are the reeds in the water-basins; your fingers are picks of gold and their nails are knives of flint in the faces of those who would harm you.

See, you are doubly mourned. Sixth stanza. You don the pure garment, you discard the thick cloth, you rise up from the bier, the foreleg is cut off for your Ka, O N, the heart is for your mummy, you receive the loin-cloth of fine linen from the hands of the messenger of Re; you eat bread upon a cloth woven by Tayt herself; you eat the foreleg, you devour the haunch. Re glorifies you in his pure abode; you wash your feet in bowls of silver fashioned by the craft of Sokar, while you eat the Shens-bread which was issued from the altar; the two God's-Fathers make presentation, and you eat Persen-bread prepared in the cooking-vessel of the storehouse; in the fear of your heart you chew onions from your offering-stone; the nurse-baboons prepare for you the provisions and food of the Souls of Heliopolis, who themselves bear food to you; fowl and fish are promised to you to be at your feet in the portals of the Great Mansion. You raise up Orion, your hinder-parts reach to the sky; and her hands are on you. That is what Orion said, even he the son of Nut who bore the gods. The two Great Gods of the sky said the one to the other: 'Take on your shoulder him whom I have brought on my shoulder and let us help N on this happy day. May he be glorified, may he be remembered, even he who will be in the mouths of all children.' Raise yourself and listen to your praises in the mouths of all your household.

See, you are doubly mourned. Seventh stanza. May Anubis embalm you, for he has acted on behalf of one whom he has favored. May the Greatest of the Seers make presentation of his clothing, when you go to bathe in the Lake of Perfection, for he is the butler of the Great God. May you make offerings in the Upper Houses, may you propitiate the Lords of Heliopolis, may you present to Re water in a vase and two large jars of milk. May your offering be raised up on the altar; may your feet be washed on a stone of . . . on the slab of the God of the Lake; may you ascend and see Re on the supporting posts of the sky, on the head of Pillar-of-his-Mother, and on the shoulders of Wepwawet; may he open a path for you that you may see the horizon, the pure place where you desire to be.

See, you are doubly mourned. Eighth stanza. Offerings are divided up for you in the presence of Re. You have your front part, you have your back part, being what Horus and Thoth decreed for you. They have summoned you, and you see that whereby you become a spirit. It is caused that the god goes up to you in the neighborhood of the Souls of Heliopolis; may you proceed on the paths, great in your dignity of one who receives the offerings of your father who was before you, being clad in fine linen every day and being guided by the god to the portals of the Great Mansion.

See, you are doubly mourned. Ninth stanza. As for N, there is air for him, air for his nose, air for his nostrils; a thousand geese, and fifty baskets of everything good and pure. Your enemies have fallen and shall exist no longer, O N.

The greetings of Horus to his father when he went in to see his father Osiris when he went up into the great pure place, so that Re might see him as Wennefer, Lord of the Sacred Land; they embraced each other in order that he might be a spirit thereby in the God's Domain.

Worship of Osiris, Foremost of the Westerners, the Great God, Lord of Abydos, King of Eternity and Ruler of Everlasting, the august god in Rosetjau, by N.

I give you praise, O Lord of the Gods, sole god who lives on truth—so says your son Horus. I have come to you that I may greet you, and I have brought truth to you at the place where your Ennead is; may you grant that I be among those who are in your suite and that I may fell all your enemies, for I have perpetuated your offerings on earth forever.

Ho Osiris! I am your son Horus, and I have come to you that I may greet you, my father Osiris.

Ho Osiris! I am your son Horus; I have come, having felled your enemies for you.

Ho Osiris! I am your son Horus; I have come that I may remove all evil which is on you.

Ho Osiris! I am your son Horus; I have come that I may slay for you him who mutilated you.

Ho Osiris! I am your son Horus; I have come, having thrust my hand against those who rebelled against you.

Ho Osiris! I am your son Horus; I have come, having brought to you the confederacy of Seth with their bonds on them.

Ho Osiris! I am your son Horus; I have come, having brought Upper Egypt to you and having bound Lower Egypt together for you.

Ho Osiris! I am your son Horus; I have come, having perpetuated god's-offerings for you in Upper and Lower Egypt.

Ho Osiris! I am your son Horus; I have come, having cultivated fields for you.

Ho Osiris! I am your son Horus; I have come, having flooded the riverbanks for you.

Ho Osiris! I am your son Horus; I have come, having plowed up the lands for you.

Ho Osiris! I am your son Horus; I have come, having constructed canals for you.

Ho Osiris! I am your son Horus; I have come, having cut irrigation channels for you.

Ho Osiris! I am your son Horus; I have come, having made for you a massacre of those who rebelled against you.

Ho Osiris! I am your son Horus; I have come, having made wild bulls and herds into butchery for you.

Ho Osiris! I am your son Horus; I have come, having made provision for you.

Ho Osiris! I am your son Horus; I have come, having brought to you . . .

Ho Osiris! I am your son Horus; I have come, having killed for you . . .

Ho Osiris! I am your son Horus; I have come, having struck down calves for you.

Ho Osiris! I am your son Horus; I have come, having wrung the necks of geese and ducks for you.

Ho Osiris! I am your son Horus; I have come, having lassoed your enemies for you with their own ropes.

Ho Osiris! I am your son Horus; I have come, having got rid of your enemies for you down a drain-pipe.

Ho Osiris! I am your son Horus; I have come, having brought you fresh water from Elephantine so that you may be refreshed with it.

Ho Osiris! I am your son Horus; I have come, having brought you all kinds of fresh vegetables.

Ho Osiris! I am your son Horus; I have come, having perpetuated your offerings on earth like Re.

Ho Osiris! I am your son Horus; I have come, having prepared your bread of red emmer in Pe.

Ho Osiris! I am your son Horus; I have come, having prepared your beer from white Shert-grain in Dep.

Ho Osiris! I am your son Horus; I have come, having cultivated barley and emmer for you in the Field of Reeds.

Ho Osiris! I am your son Horus; I have come, having reaped them there for you.

Ho Osiris! I am your son Horus; I have come that I may glorify you.

Ho Osiris! I am your son Horus; I have come that I may cause you to be a soul.

Ho Osiris! I am your son Horus; I have come that I may make you strong.

Ho Osiris! I am your son Horus; I have come that I may cause . . .

Ho Osiris! I am your son Horus; I have come that I may cause . . .

Ho Osiris! I am your son Horus; I have come that I may make you respected.

Ho Osiris! I am your son Horus; I have come that I may cause you to be feared.

Ho Osiris! I am your son Horus; I have come that I may give you your eyes and the plumes on your head.

Ho Osiris! I am your son Horus; I have come that I may cause Isis and Nephthys to make you enduring.

Ho Osiris! I am your son Horus; I have come, having filled the Eye of Horus with unguent for you.

Ho Osiris! I am your son Horus; I have come, having brought you the Eye of Horus so that your face may be provided with it.

— 174 —

Chapter for letting a spirit go out from the great gate in the sky

Your son has acted on your behalf, and the great ones tremble when they see the sword which is in your hand when you ascend from the Duat. Hail to you, O Wise One! Geb has created you, the Ennead has borne you. Horus is pleased with his Eye, Atum is pleased with his years, the gods of West and East are pleased with the Great Goddess who came into being in the arms of Her who bore the god.

I am reborn, I see, I behold, I will be yonder, I am raised up on my side, I make a decree, I hate sleep, (I detest) limpness, and I who was in Nedit stand up. My bread is prepared in Pe, I receive the scepter in Heliopolis; it was Horus who commanded that I his father be helped. As for the Lord of Storm, the slavering of Seth is forbidden to him.

I will raise up Atum, for my words are great; I have issued from between the thighs of the Ennead, I was conceived by Sekhmet, it was Shesmetet who bore me, a star brilliant and far-travelling, who brings distant products to Re daily. I have come to my throne upon the Vulture and the Cobra, I have appeared as a star.

O you two fighters, tell the Noble One, whoever he may be, that I am this lotus-flower which sprang up from the earth. Pure is he who received me and prepared my place at the nostril of the Great Power. I have come into the Island of Fire, I have set right in the place of wrong, and I am he who guards the linen garments which the Cobra guarded on the night of the great flood. I have appeared as Nefertum, the lotus at the nostril of Re; he issues from the horizon daily, and the gods will be cleansed at the sight of him.

I am he who is vindicated with the Kas, who unites hearts, who is in charge of wisdom, a great one under the god, namely Sia who is at the right hand of Re. I have come to my place among the doubles, I unite hearts because of the wisdom of the Great Goddess, I have become Sia, the god at the right hand of Re. O you who are protected by my hand, it is I who say what is in the heart of the Great Goddess in the Festival of Red Linen. I am Sia who is at the right hand of Re, the haughty one who presides over the Cavern of Nun.

— 176 —

Chapter for not dying again

I abhor the eastern land, I will not enter the place of destruction, none shall bring me offerings of what the gods detest, because I pass pure into the midst of the Milky Way, one to whom the Lord of All granted his power on that day when the Two Lands were united in the presence of the Lord of Things.

As for him who knows this chapter, he will be a worthy spirit and he will not die again in the God's Domain.

Chapter for raising up a spirit and
causing a soul to live in the God's Domain

N: O Nut, Nut, I have cast my father to the earth, with Horus behind me. My wings have grown into those of a falcon, my plumes are those of a sacred falcon, my soul has brought me and its words have equipped me.

Nut: You have opened up your place among the stars of the sky, for you are the Lone Star of the sky; see, O N, fair are the orders which you give to the spirits, for you are a Power; you will not go hungry, you are not among them and you will not be among them. See, upon your head as a soul are horns as of a wild bull, for you are a black ram which a white ewe bore, one who sucked from the four teats. The blue-eyed Horus comes to you; the red-eyed Horus, violent of power, waits for you. He meets his soul, his messengers go, his couriers run, they come to him who is supported above the West; this one goes from you of whom it is said: 'The god who speaks to the Field of the Gods.' Your name is vindicated in the presence of the gods, the Ennead raise you up with their hands, the god speaks to the Field of the Gods. Be strong at the door of the Kas of the horizon-dwellers, for their doors shall be opened to you, they shall praise you and you shall have power over them . . . they go forth and lift up their faces, so that they see you before the Great God. Min . . . your head. Someone stands behind you, and you have power; you shall neither perish nor be destroyed, but you shall act among men and gods.

Chapter for raising the corpse, for having
power in the eyes and ears and for making the head
firm when it has been set in its proper place

Take to yourself the Eye of Horus for which you have asked, namely a funeral meal.

Rejoice, O you who use the hoe! Lift up your heart so as to cleanse the breast, that you may swallow the bright Eye of Horus which is in Heliopolis and drive out what is in the belly of Osiris . . . N shall not be hungry, he shall not be thirsty, for Ha has saved him and removed his hunger, and hearts are filled, are filled.

O you who are in charge of food and attend to supplies of drink, N is commended to the House of Bread . . . Re himself commended him; Re commends him to those who are in charge of food-supplies for this year. They seize and give to him barley and emmer, for this bread of his belongs to the Great Bull. May you give to N five loaves in the temple, for three loaves are in the sky with Re and two loaves are on earth with the Enneads. Nun departs and sees Re, and it goes well with N on this happy day. N is under the command of Shu and Isis and is united happily with his god. They give bread and beer to N, and they make for him everything good and pure on this happy day.

A meal for the guide who travels, a meal of the Eye of Horus! A meal for all who go in and see the god! May you have power over water, may your shin of beef be on the altar of roast meat—four handfuls of water—according to the command of Osiris for N; Shu has ordered meals for N. That is your bread and beer.

Awake, O Judge! Be high, O Thoth! Awake, you sleepers! Rouse up, O you who are within! Offerings shall be given to you in the presence of Thoth, the Great One who went up from the Nile, and of Wepwawet who issued from Tamarisk-town. N's mouth is pure, the Ennead has censed N's mouth, and truly pure are his mouth and the tongue which is in his mouth. What N detests is feces, he rejects urine, even as Seth rejected it. O you two Companions who cross the sky, namely (Re and) Thoth, take N with you, that he may eat of what you eat, that he may drink of what you drink, that he may sit on what you sit on, that he may be strong by means of that whereby you are strong, that he may sail in that wherein you sail. N's booth is plaited with rushes, N's drink-supply is in the Field of Offerings, his food-supplies are with the gods, and N's water is the wine of Re; he goes round about the sky and travels like Thoth.

N detests hunger, and he will not eat it; he detests thirst. Bread is given to him by the Lord of Eternity, who makes an order for him. N was conceived in the night, he was born in the morning, he belongs to those who are in the suite of Re, who are before the Morning Star; he has brought to you the bread which he has found.

The Eye of Horus drips upon the bush of the Djenu-plant, the Foremost of the Westerners comes for him and brings provisions to Horus who presides over the houses. What he lives on, N lives on; what he drinks of, N drinks of; the shin of beef is on the altar of the roast meat, and N is vindicated, even he who is favored by Anubis who is on his mountain.

Ho N! Such is your good repute in which you were held on earth; you are alive and young every day. Your vision is cleared, you are the Lord of the Horizon, and he gives you bread in its due hour, and his nightly portion. Horus has protected you, he has destroyed the jaws of your enemies, he has arrested the thief at the door of his lair.

Ho N! You have no enemies in the Mansion of the Great One, the balance is true as regards your deeds . . . for Osiris, Lord of Provisions for the West. May you go in at will, may you see the Great God in his shape; may there be given to you life for your nose and triumph over your enemies.

Ho N! Your detestation is lies, and the Lords of Offerings will be gracious to you on that night of silence and weeping. Sweet life is given to you from the mouths of the Ennead, and Thoth is pleased about it. May you be triumphant over your enemies, O N; Nut has spread herself over you in her name of Her of Shetpet, and she will cause you to be in the suite of the Great God. You have no enemies, and she will save you from all things evil in her name of 'Great Well', for you are the greatest of her children.

O you who are in charge of the hours, who are before Re, make a path for N that he may pass within the circle of Osiris, Lord of Ankh-tawy, living forever.

O N, be happy in the suite of Nefertum, the lotus-bloom at the nose of Re . . . cleansed in the presence of the gods, that you may see Re forever.

Chapter for leaving yesterday and coming into
today, which he asks for himself and his members

My demise was granted yesterday, I have returned today, I have gone forth in my own shape; I am tousled, having issued from my imet-tree; I am disheveled, having gone forth with my scepter; I am Lord of the Wereret-crown, a third to Nehebkau; I am the Red One whose eye is protected. I died yesterday, I returned today, and a path has been made for me by the doorkeeper of the great arena. I have gone out into the day against my enemy, and I have power over him; he has been given over to me and he will not be taken from me, for an end will be put to him under me in the tribunal, Osiris being in his shroud . . . I am a possessor of blood on the day of coming into being, I am a possessor of knives and I will not be robbed; a path is prepared for me, I am the embalmer-scribe of Her who is in date-wine, and there is brought to me what appertains to the great Red Crown. The great Red Crown has been given to me, and I go out into the day against yonder enemy of mine so that I may fetch him, for I have power over him; he has been given over to me and he shall not be taken from me, for an end will be put to him under me in the tribunal. I will eat him in the Great Field upon the altar of

Wadjet, for I have power over him as Sekhmet the Great. I am a possessor of being, to me belongs the shape of every god when they go round about . . .

— 180 —
*Chapter for going out into the day, worshipping
Re in the West, giving praise to those who are in the
Duat; opening a path for a worthy spirit who is in
the God's Domain, granting him his movements,
extending his strides, going in and out of the realm
of the dead, and taking shape as a living soul*

O Re, you who go to rest as Osiris with all the appearings in glory of the spirits and gods of the West; you are the hidden one of the Duat, the holy soul at the head of the West, Wennefer who shall exist for ever and ever.

How well provided are you, O Dweller in the Netherworld! Your son Horus is pleased about you, and he has taken over the governance; may you permit him to appear to those who are in the Duat, even he the great star who brings what is his to the Duat, and who traverses the place where they are as the son of Re who went forth from Atum.

How well provided are you, O Dweller in the Netherworld! Your stepped throne is in the midst, O Your Majesty the King who rules the Silent Land, great prince of the Wereret-crown, Great God whose throne is secret, Lord of judgment who is over his tribunal.

How well provided are you, O Dweller in the Netherworld! How content are you!

How well provided are you, O Dweller in the Netherworld! The mourners are disheveled because of you, they clap their hands because of you, they cry out because of you, they lament because of you, they weep because of you. But your soul is joyful, your corpse has power, the souls of Re are on high in the West . . . souls when they are set on high in the cavern of the Duat, because of the souls of Re who is in the Duat in the person of the soul of the Angry One, who rests in the person of his soul.

O Osiris, I am a servant of your chapel which is in the middle of your temple. May you give orders that you grant to me appearance in glory to those who are in the Duat, the great star who brings what is his to the Duat, who travels over what is in it, the son of Re who issued from Atum. I rest in the Duat, I have power in the darkness, I go in and out of it. The arms of Tatenen are what receive me and raise me up. O you who are at peace, give me your arms, for I know the chapters for guidance; guide me.

Praise to you who are at peace; give praise joyfully. O Re, be praised through me like Osiris. I have perpetuated your offerings for you, that you may have power through your gifts, just as Re decreed for me. I am the guardian, I am his heir upon earth. Prepare a path for me, O you who are at peace; see, I enter into the Duat, I open up the beautiful West, I make firm the staff of Orion and the Nemes Headdress of Him whose name is hidden. Look at me, O you who are at peace, you gods who guide Him of the Duat. See, I take my powers, having appeared as master of the mysteries; save me from the whipping-posts and the ropes of the whipping-posts; you shall not bind me to your whipping-posts, you shall not give me over to the place of punishment.

I am the heir of Osiris, I have received his Nemes Headdress in the Duat; look at me, for I have appeared in glory in coming forth from your body, I have become his father, and he applauds. Look at me, rejoice over me, for behold, I am on high, I have come into being, one who provides his own shape; open a path to my soul, stand at your proper places, let me be at peace in the beautiful West, open a place for me among you. Open your paths, draw back your bolts. O Re who guides this land, you are the guide of souls, you are the leader of the gods. I am the keeper of the gate, who ushers in those who are to be ushered in; I am one who guards the portals and who sets the gods in their places; I am one who is in his proper place in the Duat; I am the surveyor who is in charge of the surveyors; to me belong the limits of the Duat; I am one who is at peace in the Silent Land, I have made for myself offerings in the West with the souls who are among the gods. I am the guardian of Re, I am the mysterious Benu-bird, I am one who goes in that I may rest in the Duat, and who ascends peacefully to the sky. I am Lord of the Celestial Expanses, I travel through the lower sky in the train of Re; my offerings in the sky are in the Field of Re, my gifts on earth are in the Field of Reeds. I traverse the Duat after the manner of Re, I give judgment like Thoth, I walk and am glad, I run at my own pace in my dignity of one whose affairs are secret, my shape is that of the double god Horus-Seth. I am in charge of the gifts to the gods of the Duat, one who gives food-offerings to the spirits; I am one stout of heart, smiting my enemies. O you gods and spirits who are before Re and who follow after his soul, usher me in at your usherings, for you are those who guide Re, who usher in those who are in the sky, and I am a soul who is holy in the West.

— 181 —
*Chapter for going into the tribunal of Osiris
and the gods who govern the Duat, who guard
their gates, who make report concerning their courts,
who keep the doors of the portals of the West; for taking
shape as a living soul, worshipping Osiris, and
becoming an Elder of the tribunal*

Hail to you, Foremost of the Westerners, Wennefer, Lord of the Sacred Land! You have appeared in glory like Re, and behold, he has come to see you and to rejoice at seeing your beauty.

His sun-disk is your sun-disk;
His rays are your rays;
His crown is your crown;
His greatness is your greatness;
His appearings are your appearings;
His beauty is your beauty;
His majesty is your majesty;
His savor is your savor;
His extent is your extent;
His seat is your seat;
His throne is your throne;
His heritage is your heritage;
His panoply is your panoply;
His destiny is your destiny;
His West is your West;
His goods are your goods;
His wisdom is your wisdom;
His distinction is your distinction;
He who should protect himself does indeed protect himself —
And vice versa.
He will not die and you will not die;
He will triumph over his enemies
And you will triumph over your enemies;
Nothing evil will come into being against him,
And nothing evil will come into being against you for ever and ever.

Hail to you, Osiris, son of Nut, possessor of horns, whose Atef-crown is tall, to whom the Wereret-crown and crook have been given in the presence of the Ennead; the awe of whom Atum created in the hearts of men, gods, spirits, and the dead; to whom the crook was given in Heliopolis; great of shape in Busiris; Lord of Fear in the Two Mounds, greatly dreaded in Rosetjau; Lord of fair remembrance in the Castle, who greatly appeared in glory in Abydos; to whom vindication was given in the presence of the Ennead; who protects the great powers;

THE BOOK OF GOING FORTH BY DAY

the dread of whom pervades the land; on whom men wait, the Elders being on their mats. Monarch of the gods of the Duat, great Power in the sky who rules the living, King of those who are yonder, who glorifies thousands in Kheraha, at whom the sun-folk rejoice; possessor of choice morsels in the Upper Houses, for whom a shin of beef is prepared in Memphis; for whom the night-ritual is performed in Letopolis.

You are a Great One whose strength is mighty, and your son Horus is your protector; he will remove all evil which is on you. Your flesh is knit together for you, your members are recreated for you, your bones are reassembled for you, and there is brought to you . . . Rise up, Osiris; I have given you my hand and have caused you to stand up living forever. Geb has wiped your mouth for you, the Great Ennead calls on you . . . when they travel protected to the gate of the Duat. Your mother Nut has put her arms about you that she may protect you, and she will continually guard you, even you the highborn. Your sisters Isis and Nephthys will come to you, they will enfold you with life, prosperity, and health, and you will be glad through them; they (will rejoice) over you through love of you. They will enclose everything for you within your arms; the gods, the lords of Kas will care for you, and they will worship you for ever.

Happy are you, O Osiris! You have appeared in glory, you have power, you are a spirit; you have made your shape everlasting, and your face is that of Anubis. Re rejoices over you and he is well disposed towards your beauty. You have seated yourself on your pure throne which Geb, who loves you, made for you; you receive him in your arms in the West, you cross the sky daily, you convey him to his mother Nut when he goes to rest daily in the West in the Bark of Re, together with Horus who loves you. The protection of Re is your safeguard, the power of Thoth is behind you, and the incantations of Isis pervade your members.

I have come to you, O Lord of the Sacred Land, Osiris Foremost of the Westerners, Wennefer who will exist for ever and ever. My heart is true, my hands are clean, I bring a meal to its owner and offerings to him who made them. I have come here to your towns, I have done what is good on earth, I have smitten your enemies for you as bulls, I have slain cattle for you, and I cause them to fall on their faces before you. I have purified your pure place, I have cleansed your lustral basin, I have wrung the necks of birds upon your altar for the benefit of your soul, of your powers, and of the gods and goddesses who are in your suite.

As for him who knows this book, nothing evil shall have power over him, he shall not be turned away at the gates of the West; he shall go in and out, and bread and beer and all good things shall be given to him in the presence of those who are in the Duat.

— 182 —

Book for the permanence of Osiris, giving
breath to the Inert One in the presence of Thoth,
and repelling the enemy of Osiris, who comes yonder in
his various shapes; the safeguarding, protection and
defense in the God's Domain which Thoth himself
has carried out in order that the sunlight
might rest on him every day

I am Thoth the skilled scribe whose hands are pure, a possessor of purity, who drives away evil, who writes what is true, who detests falsehood, whose pen defends the Lord of All; master of laws who interprets writings, whose words establish the Two Lands.

I am the Lord of Justice, one truly precise to the gods, who judges a matter so that it may continue in being; who vindicates him whose voice is hushed; who dispels darkness and clears away the storm. I have given the sweet breath of the north wind to Osiris Wennefer as when he went forth from the womb of her who bore him; I cause Re to go to rest as Osiris, Osiris having gone to rest at the going to rest of Re; I cause him to go into the secret cavern in order to revive the heart of the Inert One, the Holy Soul at the head of the West. Acclamation for the Inert One, Wennefer the son of Nut!

I am Thoth, the favored of Re; Lord of strength who ennobles him who made him; great of magic in the Bark of Millions of Years; master of laws who makes the Two Lands content; whose power protects her who bore him; who gets rid of noise and quells uproar; who does what Re in his shrine approves.

I am Thoth who made Osiris triumphant over his enemies.

I am Thoth who foretells the morrow and foresees the future, whose act cannot be brought to naught; who guides sky, earth, and the Duat; who nourishes the sun-folk. I give breath to him who is in the secret places by means of the power which is on my mouth, and Osiris is triumphant over his enemies.

I have come to you, O Lord of the Sacred Land, Osiris the Bull of the West, and I have made you flourishing forever, I grant eternity as a protection for your members.

I have come to you bearing the amulet which is in my hand, my protection for the daily course. Protection and life are about him, namely this god who guards his Ka, King of the Duat, Ruler of the West, who takes possession of the sky in vindication, whose Atef-crown is firm, who appears in the White Crown, having grasped the crook and the flail; whose power is great and whose Wereret-crown is mighty. He has assembled all the gods, for love has pervaded their bodies for Wennefer, who shall exist for ever and ever.

Hail to you, Foremost of Westerners, who refashioned mankind, who comes as one rejuvenated in his time, better than he was formerly! Your son Horus is your protector, in the function of Atum; your face is potent, O Wennefer. Raise yourself, O Bull of the West, be firm as you were firm in the womb of your mother Nut. She enfolds you, even you who issued from her; may your heart be firm in its place, may your heart be like it was before, may your nose endure with life and dominion, you being alive, renewed, and young like Re every day. Great, great in triumph is Osiris — may he endure in life.

I am Thoth; I have pacified Horus, I have calmed the Rivals in their time of raging; I have come and have washed away the blood, I have calmed the tumult and have eliminated everything evil.

I am Thoth; I have performed the night-ritual in Letopolis.

I am Thoth; I have come today from Pe and Dep, I have conducted the oblations, I have given bread-offerings as gifts to the spirits, I have guarded the elbow of Osiris whom I embalmed, and I have sweetened his odor like a pleasant smell.

I am Thoth; I have come today from Kheraha, I have knotted the cord and have put the ferryboat in good order, I have fetched East and West, I am uplifted on my standard higher than any god in this my name of Him whose face is on high; I have opened those things which are good in this my name of Wepwawet; I have given praise and have made homage to Osiris Wennefer, who shall exist for ever and ever.

— 183 —

Worshipping Osiris, giving praise to him and
homage to Wennefer, doing obeisance to the Lord of
the Sacred Land, exalting Him who is on his sand, by N

He says: I have come to you, O Son of Nut, Osiris, Ruler of Eternity; I am in the suite of Thoth, and I am joyful because of all that he has done. He brings to you sweet air for your nose, life and dominion for your face, and fair is the north wind which goes forth from Atum to your nostrils, O Lord of the Sacred Land. He causes the sun to shine on your breast, he illumines the dark way for you, he removes the evil which is on your body by means of the power which is on his mouth. He has pacified the Rival Gods for you, he has stopped the raging and the tumult for you, he has made the Rivals well-disposed to you, and the Two Lands are peacefully reconciled before you; he has driven anger from their hearts for you, and they fraternize with each other. Your son Horus is vindicated in the presence of the entire Ennead; the kingship over the land has been given to him, and his uraeus pervades the entire land. The throne of Geb has been allotted to him, and the potent office of Atum has been confirmed in writing in a testament which has been engraved on a block of sandstone, according as your father Ptah-Tatenen commanded from upon the great throne. His brother has been set for him upon the Supports of Shu, raising up water to the mountains in order to make flourishing what comes out on the desert and the fruit which comes forth on the flat-land, and he gives produce by water and by land. The gods of the sky and the gods of the earth have entrusted the earth to your son Horus, and they follow to his court; all that he has decreed is in their sight, and they perform it immediately.

Your heart is happy; your heart, O Lord of the Gods, possesses all joy. The Black Land and the Red Land are at peace, and they serve your uraeus; the shrines are made firm in their places, towns and nomes are established by name. They make presentation to you with god's-offerings: men make offering to your name forever; men call out praises to you because of your name; men present libations to your Ka and invocation-offerings to the spirits who are in your suite; water is poured over halved bread-cakes for the souls of the dead in this land. Every design of yours is as effective as in its former state; appear, O Son of Nut, as the Lord of All in his glorious appearings, for you are living, permanent, young and real. Your father Re has made your body hale, your Ennead give you praise; Isis is with you and will not forsake you, and there will be no more felling of your enemies. The lords of all the lands worship your beauty like Re when he shines at dawn. You appear as one upraised on his standard, and your beauty is exalted and widespread. The kingship of Geb has been given to you, for he is your father who created your beauty. It was your mother Nut who bore the gods who brought your body into being, who bore you as the greatest of the Five Gods, who made the White Crown firm on your head, and you grasped the crook and the flail while you were yet in the womb, before you had come forth on earth. You have appeared as Lord of the Two Lands, and the Atef-crown of Re is on your brow; the gods come to you bowing down, and the fear of you pervades their bodies; they see you in the dignity of Re, and the dread of Your Majesty is in their hearts. Life is with you, food follows after you, and Truth is presented before you.

May you let me be in Your Majesty's suite as when I was on earth; may my soul be summoned, and may it find you beside the Lords of Truth. I come from the city of the god, the primeval region; soul, Ka, and spirit are what is in this land. Such is its god, namely the Lord of Truth, possessor of provisions, rich in precious things, he to whom every land is drawn. Upper Egypt comes downstream to Lower Egypt with wind and oar to make it festive with gifts, in accordance with what its god commanded; as for anyone who rests within it, he will never have to express a wish. Happy is he who does what is right for the god in it; he will grant old age to him who does it until he reaches the blessed state, and the end of this happy burial in the Sacred Land.

I come to you with my hands bearing Truth, and my heart has no lies in it. I place Truth before you, for I know that you live by it. I have done no wrong in this land, and no man will suffer loss of his possessions.

I am Thoth, the skilled scribe whose hands are pure, the Lord of Purity who drives away evil; who writes what is true, who detests falsehood, whose pen defends the Lord of All; master of laws who interprets writings, and whose words have settled the Two Lands.

I am Thoth, Lord of Justice, who vindicates him whose voice is hushed; protector of the poor man who has suffered loss of his property; who dispels darkness and clears away the storm. I have (given) breath to Wennefer, even the fair breeze of the north wind, as when he came forth from his mother's womb. I have caused him to enter into the secret cavern in order to revive the heart of the Inert One, Wennefer the son of Nut, the vindicated Horus.

— 187 —
Chapter for going in to the Ennead

Hail to you, Ennead of Re! I have come to you, for I am in the suite of Re; prepare a path for me that I may pass among you, for I will not be turned away because of what I have done this day.

— 188 —
Sending a soul, building tomb-chambers, and going out into the day among men

In peace, O Anubis! It goes well with the son of Re at peace with my Sacred Eye; may you glorify my soul and my shade, that they may see Re by means of what he brings. I ask that I may come and go and that I may have power in my feet so that this person may see him in any place where he is, in my nature, in my wisdom, and in the true shape of my equipped and divine spirit. It shines as Re, it travels as Hathor. Therefore you have granted that my soul and my shade may walk on their feet to the place where this person is, so that he may stand, sit, and walk, and enter into his chapel of eternity, because I am one of the entourage of Osiris, who goes by night and returns by day, and no god can be created when I am silent.

— 189 —
Chapter for preventing a man from going upside down and from eating feces

What I doubly detest, I will not eat; what I detest is feces, and I will not eat it; excrement, I will not consume it. It shall not fall from my belly, it shall not come near my fingers, and I will not touch it with my toes.

'What will you live on', say the gods and spirits to me, 'in this place to which you have been brought?'

'I will live on seven loaves which have been brought to me; four loaves are with Horus and three loaves with Thoth.'

'Where is it granted to you to eat?' say the gods and spirits to me.

'I will eat under that sycamore of Hathor, for I have placed my portions there for her minstrels. My fields have been assigned to me in Busiris, my green plants are in Heliopolis, and I will live on bread of white emmer and beer of red barley; there shall be given to me my father's and my mother's families, and my doorkeeper in respect of my land.'

Open to me; may there be space for me, make a path for me, that I may dwell as a living soul in the place which I desire, and I will not be subdued by my enemies. I detest feces and will not eat it, I have not gone infected into Heliopolis. Be far from me, for I am a bull whose throne is provided; I have flown up as a swallow, I have cackled as a goose, I have alighted on the beautiful tree which is in the middle of the island in the flood. I have gone up and have alighted on it, and I will not suffer neglect; as for him who dwells under it, he is a great god.

What I detest, I will not eat it; what I detest is feces, and I will not eat it; what my Ka detests is feces, and it shall not enter into my body, I will not approach it with my hands, I will not tread on it with my sandals. I will not flow for you into a bowl, I will not empty out for you into a basin, . . . I will not take anything from upon the banks of your ponds, I will not depart upside down for you.

Thus says that one who cannot count: 'What will you live on in this land to which you have come so that you may be a spirit?'

'I will live on bread of black barley and beer of white emmer, four loaves being in the Field of Offerings, for I am more distinguished than any god. I will have four loaves daily and four portions of roast meat in Heliopolis, for I am more distinguished than any god.'

Thus says that one who cannot count: 'Who will bring it to you, and where will you eat?'

'Upon that pure river-bank on the day when I have brightened my teeth with myrrh.'

Thus says that one who cannot count: 'What will you live on in this land to which you have come so that you may be a spirit?'

'I will live on those seven loaves; four loaves are brought from the house of Horus and three loaves from the house of Thoth.'

Thus says that one who cannot count: 'Who will bring them to you?'

'A nurse from the house of the Great One and a stewardess from Heliopolis.'

'Where will you eat them?'

'Under the branches of the Djebat-nefret tree beside . . . to which I have been taken.'

Thus says that one who cannot count: 'Will you live on someone else's goods every day?'

I say to him: 'I plow the lands which are in the Field of Rushes.'

Thus says that one who cannot count: 'Who will guard them for you?'

I say to him: 'It is the twin children of the King of Lower Egypt who will look after them.'

'Who will plow them for you?'

'The greatest of the gods of the sky and of the gods of the earth. Men will thresh for me as for the Apis-bull who presides over Sais, men will reap for me as for Seth, Lord of the Northern Sky.'

O you who turn back the ished-tree on your own account, who uproot falsehood, whose faces are pure, shall I be with the confederates of Seth on the mountain of Bakhu? I will dwell with those potent noble dead in order to excavate the pool of Osiris and to rub (his) heart, and there shall be no accusation against me, N, by any living person.

A Commentary

ON THE

Corpus of Literature and Tradition
Which Constitutes

The Book of Going Forth by Day

BY

Dr. Ogden Goelet, Jr.

Department of Near Eastern Studies
New York University

A Preliminary Note
to the Readers of the Commentary

This commentary is divided into two parts. In the first section, I will explain the aspects of Egyptian religion which apply to the *Book of the Dead* (henceforth *BD*). In the second section, there will be a running commentary on the text and vignettes of the Ani Papyrus.

The *BD* is not an easy text to understand. Even for the specialist, there are many parts which are utterly obscure and cannot be explained convincingly. Therefore this commentary is written with rather modest goals in mind. It is not intended to be an all-inclusive explanation of the questions likely to interest the average reader, nor is it intended to explain all the subtleties of Egyptian religion. Meeting those demands would require a highly technical volume, many times the length of this work and certainly unreadable for all but specialists. This is only an *introductory* commentary, intended to describe some of the important principles underlying Egyptian concepts of the afterlife and how these apply specifically to the *BD*. If I can provide original insights into this often perplexing book, it is only because of a century and a half of study done by the true giants in my field.

Four works which proved indispensable in creating this commentary should be mentioned specifically at this point. To begin with, the masterful translation of the Egyptian text by the late Raymond O. Faulkner forms the very basis of this book. The arrangement of our presentation of the Ani Papyrus shows our debt to his work; it acts visually as if it were the textual foundation on which the illustrations of the papyrus rest.

For the explanation of many difficult passages, I am particularly indebted to Erik Hornung, whose *Das altägyptischen Totenbuch* will undoubtedly remain the best all-around introduction to the *BD* for decades to come. He has managed to combine a new translation of the entire work with a brief and invaluable commentary on the text and vignette for every chapter. Like Allen's work mentioned below, Hornung's translation also provides a picture of how a given chapter or its vignettes might compare with other documents. Since Hornung brings to the subject an intimate knowledge of the well-illustrated royal afterlife 'books,' his treatment of the vignettes is unsurpassed when it comes to iconographic parallels. The short commentaries he provides for most chapters are sensible and easy to understand. Particularly useful for specialists are the bibliographical references which appear in the commentary.

I have also consulted Thomas G. Allen's *The Egyptian Book of the Dead*, which critically evaluates the sources used in creating a hypothetical 'ideal' version of the text. Allen has presented us with a group of translations which detail the historical development of the chapters. The many parallels with previous, contemporary, and subsequent religious literature offer the reader both an overview of the history of a text and a better appreciation of how the Egyptians may have viewed the text at any given moment. The index of Egyptian and English words is indispensable for all translators of this difficult group of texts.

Finally, for the Ani Papyrus in particular, Edmund Dondelinger's short commentary (in German) supplied with the Folio Society edition was quite useful, although I have found that I do not agree on several points of interpretation. Dondelinger's study is a fine introduction to the iconography of the *BD* for those with no background in the subject.

In addition to these longer works, I have consulted a great many articles and monographs which illuminated various aspects of either the *BD* or Egyptian mortuary religion. These have been listed in the annotated bibliography at the end of the commentary.

The History of the
Book of the Dead and Its Study

Ancient Egyptian religion was never a unity. Its many aspects — mortuary religion, cult, magical practices, theory, moral and ethical thought — each existed somewhat independently from each other. This is partly because Egyptian religion, unlike Judaism, Christianity, and Islam, was not based on an authori- tative scripture. If we are to discuss the *BD* as a religious text, then, it is important to understand first the general role of texts in Egyptian religion. Since their religion was also not based on divine revelation, the Egyptians apparently never regarded their religious texts as immutable. Instead, from time to time, related material would be gathered into a collection which would serve as a model for scribes or priests, as the case may be. These texts could be used for centuries and would naturally be subjected to theological and cosmological changes. An important characteristic of the Egyptian beliefs concerning the afterlife is overall continuity within a framework of constant development. Themes introduced in the earliest mortuary texts can still be found a thousand years later in the *BD*, and persist, in some cases, into the Christian era.

While the major group of mortuary texts used would change from time to time, the basic pattern of how the various texts related to one another remained fairly constant. Much of the earlier material was dropped or updated to fit current religious thought. Often material which had previously been a royal prerogative would become available for private persons, in the way that, nowadays, old copyrighted material eventually falls into the public domain. Frequently the older material would remain essentially the same, merely shortened. Some scholars have described this phenomenon by the term 'democratization of the afterlife,' but it would be more accurate to view the process as simple diffusion. When new texts appear they often contain not only new chapters, but new religious theories and concerns as well. However, as many spells in the *BD* show, the Egyptians would present new texts in the guise of works of the distant past, only recently brought to light again after being lost for centuries. The conservative nature of the Egyptians was reassured by being behind the times! Regional traditions were another important factor in altering texts so that they might conform better to the needs and beliefs of the dominant local cults. In the end, the result is that each new group of mortuary texts exhibits some degree of overlap with older literature. For example, material from the earliest source, the *Pyramid Texts,* is still found incorporated in mortuary texts of the Ptolemaic period.

The first major group of texts concerning the afterlife was the *Pyramid Texts,* which were inscribed in the royal pyramids of the Fifth and Sixth Dynasties. As their milieu implies, these texts were originally intended only for the benefit of the king or the royal family. Unlike the later religious texts, these inscriptions were not accompanied by illustrations. Images, in fact, were apparently thought to be so potentially dangerous in the proximity of the dead that even the hieroglyphs used in the *Pyramid Texts* were modified so that scorpions, snakes, birds, and people, depicted as signs, could not harm the deceased king in the sarcophagus chamber. Extraordinary precautions needed to be taken because the religious role of the king was unlike that of the private individual in many ways. The king was, after all, the human to whom the gods entrusted the care of Egypt, the jewel of their earthly creation. Although the king was not quite a god, he was certainly godlike and acted as the connecting link between the terrestrial and divine spheres.

Despite the interest in achieving a spiritualized existence in the *Pyramid Texts,* maintaining the integrity of the physical remains is the focus of many chapters. Keeping the corpse intact and revivifying the dead body were the first stages in the deceased's afterlife adventures. Even if the corpse was intact, it needed to be revivified by means of the 'Opening of the Mouth' ceremony. The king's death is frequently denied, and he is ordered to rise up as if he were merely sleeping.

For religious historians, one of the most significant developments in the *Pyramid Texts* is that they contain the first definite appearance of the god Osiris. At this point, the association of the deceased with Osiris is a royal prerogative; Osiris is strongly connected with kingship, particularly the exercise of kingship in the realm of the dead. The view of the afterlife in the *Pyramid Texts* seems to follow patterns that inform much of the rest of Egyptian mortuary literature. The afterlife was predominantly celestial, with an important subterranean complement represented by the Duat. In the *Pyramid Texts*, however, the solar/stellar aspect dominates. Many of these texts are concerned with the methods of getting up to the heavens and becoming an *akh*-soul there. The king hoped that he would eventually join the heavenly retinue of the supreme deity, the sun-god Re. The preferred method was to fly up to the sky, but more down-to-earth methods like ramps, steps, and ladders might also help. The king was theoretically the chief priest of all the local cults and Re and Osiris were the most important of a large array of deities and other supernatural beings who play a role in the next world. The purpose of the *Pyramid Texts* was to aid the king in the many difficulties that he would face, notwithstanding his godlike status, in the afterlife. Whatever gods could possibly help him were called to his aid, even if it meant threatening them or using magic.

The *Pyramid Texts* were later adapted for private use in the First Intermediate Period, becoming the basis for another collection called the *Coffin Texts*. The *Coffin Texts* were more than a simple adaptation of the earlier material. In many instances, the *Coffin Texts* reinterpret the *Pyramid Texts* to conform to contemporary religious beliefs, sometimes so that the new version barely resembles the older model. Perhaps as much as a third of the *BD* chapters can be traced to material in the *Coffin Texts*, far exceeding the proportion of chapters derived from *Pyramid Texts* antecedents. Much of the cosmological structure of the afterlife is presented in *Coffin Text* no. 335, which forms the basis for the later Chapter 17 of the *BD*, one of the most important of all parts of that work. As their name indicates, the *Coffin Texts* were written on the inside walls of wooden coffins of private individuals. This in itself is interesting because it brought the texts with their potentially dangerous signs and symbols in close proximity to the physical remains of the deceased. As in the *Pyramid Texts*, hieroglyphic signs were often modified or truncated to render them harmless. The varying sizes and qualities of the coffins indubitably gave rise to another feature of the *Coffin Texts* which was to continue in later funerary literature — the development of long and short versions of some chapters.

By this period, the Osirian afterlife is offered to non-royal persons, but Osiris has moved into the subterranean realm, which becomes his primary association for the rest of Egyptian history. The Duat, now a definitely chthonic place, often seems more important for the deceased than the celestial regions. Another interesting development in the *Coffin Texts* is that all deceased people can be identified with Osiris. The owners of the coffins bear the title 'The Osiris N,' a privilege which was granted to the king alone during the Old Kingdom. The netherworld becomes populated with even more threatening beings, traps, snares, and nets. Since these private individuals did not enjoy the exalted status of the king, they were faced with more mundane perils, particularly the performance of hard physical labors, which they had probably not experienced during their lifetimes as noble lords and ladies (or at least privileged members of a 'middle class'). For this reason there are numerous chapters aimed at magically avoiding these tasks. The *shabti*, a funerary figurine equipped with agricultural implements, was created to provide the deceased with a substitute worker to perform such afterlife obligations.

Perhaps the most important religious innovation of the *Coffin Texts* is the idea that everyone would be judged in the afterlife on the basis of his or her deeds while alive. Actually there are indications that belief in a final judgment had existed previously, but the *Coffin Texts* provide the first concrete evidence for the procedure in the next world. The judgment takes place before Osiris and a council of gods, but no particular method of trial is spelled out. Allusions to the use of the balance occasionally appear in literary works such as *The Eloquent Peasant*.

During the Middle Kingdom, in addition to the *Coffin Texts*, another remarkable mortuary composition appeared. This work, called the *Book of the Two Ways* by Egyptologists, occurs on the floorboards of a group of wooden coffins from the Bersheh region in Middle Egypt. Many spells from this work are closely related to chapters in the *BD*. More striking, however, is the text's central illustration, which acts essentially as a large vignette for the surrounding text: for the first time Egyptian afterlife literature is supplemented by pictures and the various elements of the next world shown on a map. The work is quite obscure and hard to understand, giving rise to a number of conflicting interpretations by scholars. As the title that they have given it implies, the dominant theme of the work is the land and water routes through the beyond; neither path appears to be more advantageous or more correct than the other. What the two paths represent is subject to much debate, but clearly the deceased must travel before reaching his or her final destination in the next world, a motif which constantly recurs in the *BD*. One school of thought about the *Book of the Two Ways* maintains that in the process of travel the dead is initiated into the secrets of the afterlife. The two paths are separated by the Island of Flame, a place which also plays an important role in the *Coffin Texts* and the *BD*.

Aside from material directly derived from the *Coffin Texts*, the first examples of *BD* chapters do not occur until the late Thirteenth Dynasty, when two versions of Chapter 64 are found on the now lost coffin of a queen named Menthuhotep. The expulsion of the Hyksos and the establishment of the Eighteenth Dynasty seems to have given rise to a great burst of creative activity in many fields, including the writing of funerary literature. The royal tombs of the Eighteenth and Nineteenth Dynasties contain a wide variety of texts whose purpose was to aid the king on his journeys through the afterlife, as well as to put forth explanations of the cosmology of this world and the beyond: the *Litany of the Sun*, the *Amduat* (What is in the Duat), the *Book of Gates*, the *Book of Caverns*, the *Book of Aker* (the Earth), the *Book of Day and Night*, and the *Book of the Divine Cow*. Like the *Book of the Two Ways*, these texts were profusely illustrated, with the paintings executed largely on a yellow background in conscious imitation of the color of an ancient papyrus roll. In keeping with the desire that the royal texts seem as traditional as possible, several chapters are given pseudo-genealogies, tracing their origins to famous monarchs of the past or famous wise men of yesteryear, thus lending an aura of great antiquity. Although these 'books' are found mostly in the great royal tombs in the Theban Valley of the Kings, not all the texts were mortuary by nature, and neither were they all exclusively royal.

To this great corpus of largely funerary literature we should add the *BD*, which seems to have rapidly become one of the most necessary elements of the burial equipment of a well-to-do Egyptian. Sporadic examples of *BD* material have been found in royal contexts: many spells occur on the mummy bandages of Tuthmosis III, Chapter 151 was inscribed on the inside of Tutankhamun's golden mummy mask, and occasional chapters are found on the walls of some royal tombs. However, the *BD* seems to have developed chiefly in the private sphere. While excerpts from its chapters are found on tomb walls, mummy bandages, heart scarabs, and in several other contexts, the most common medium for the *BD* was the papyrus.

THE BOOK OF GOING FORTH BY DAY

Usually the papyrus roll would be placed in the coffin alongside the mummy so it would be at hand when the deceased began his or her journeys into the afterworld. Some papyri were instead placed inside hollow figurines of Osiris, statue bases, or oblong boxes, where they would presumably be readily available after the spirit had arisen.

The *BD* was not the final book in the long tradition of Egyptian afterlife literature, for some of its chapters gave birth to the *Book of Breathings* and similar works during the Late Period. These new funerary books were used either along with or as a supplement to the *BD*, yet it never fell completely out of favor and continued to be used well into the Roman era. One of the most exciting things about the study of ancient Egypt is the opportunity it affords us to observe these centuries-long processes which are only theoretically reconstructed in connection with the Hebrew Bible and the New Testament. For the Bible as we know it today represents a similar confluence of documents and schools of thought. Biblical scholars, of course, know that it was not until the conference at Raphia in 58 c.e. that those works considered authentic and orthodox were gathered together by rabbinical scholars to form the canon of the Hebrew Bible. In the Judeo-Christian tradition, the debate about which works are worthy of inclusion in the Bible still continues.

THE QUESTION OF CANON IN THE *Book of the Dead*

The issue of scriptural canon appears to have had little importance to the Egyptians, in part because their culture was polytheistic. Royal mortuary literature, such as the *Pyramid Texts*, the *Amduat*, and the *Litany of the Sun* shows a remarkable consistency from example to example, although occasionally we can trace some manner of development over the course of years. But in the case of texts made primarily for private persons, such as the *Coffin Texts* and the *BD*, there is not only little textual consistency among the examples of a chapter, but there is also equally little uniformity in the order in which chapters appear on papyri.

One of the most unfortunate legacies of Budge's work on the *BD*, in fact, was that he perpetuated Naville's notion of both a 'Theban' and a 'Saite' recension of the text. Naville had classified all the manuscripts written before the Late Period as belonging to the Theban Recension, because the overwhelming majority of the earlier papyri came from the southern capital of the New Kingdom, located at the place which the Greeks called Thebes. However, *BD* papyri before the Saite period vary so widely that it is meaningless to speak of a 'recension' of the material in any useful sense of the word. Ironically, by the time the *BD* approached a canon in its text and format — the so-called 'Saite Recension' — it had become fossilized to a great extent. The scribal work had already been quite erratic during the Eighteenth and Nineteenth Dynasties, the period of the 'Theban Recension,' and it became very careless in the Saite period. Furthermore, the texts are badly garbled and frequently fail to match their accompanying illustrations, indicating that the scribes were working hastily and usually had poor comprehension of what they were copying. Since it was fundamental in Egyptian religious thought that images by themselves could convey the content of a chapter, the vignettes became the most important part of the *BD* in the Late Period and Ptolemaic era. Although the illustrations were often done with some care, it apparently was sufficient to supply just a few lines of the relevant text, so that often a chapter will break off in the middle of a phrase or even a word.

THE ORGANIZATION OF THE *Book of the Dead*

In the translation that appears beneath the facsimile of the papyrus, each chapter is preceded by a number that does not occur in the Egyptian text. These numbers have been assigned by modern scholars. The numbering system follows that of Naville's seminal 1886 edition of the so-called Saite Recension of the *BD*, based upon a particularly complete papyrus in the Turin Museum. In later years, Egyptologists have added a number of chapters which Naville had not included and have also noted that some chapters were repeated. Whatever imperfections this system of numbering might have, it still remains the chief means of classifying the separate units of the *BD*.

Like many New Kingdom *BDs*, Ani's papyrus begins not with Chapter 1, but with two hymns of praise to Re and Osiris, the chief deities of the afterlife. Directly following these is the key moment of the passage into a successful afterlife — the scene of judgment when the heart of the deceased is weighed against the feather of truth. Often Chapters 30A and 30B, which implore the heart's cooperation in this process, also appear in the initial section of a *BD*. If the deceased were not found worthy, he or she would have been damned and there would have been no use for the remaining chapters in the papyrus. Because they are the focal point of a papyrus, these hymns and the judgment scene are usually the finest parts of any *BD*. In these parts of the Papyrus of Ani, the quality of both the hieroglyphic text and the accompanying vignettes is unquestionably the best in the entire work. Painting these appears to have been the work of the master scribe.

For a long time scholars viewed the *BD* as a collection of disparate spells, with little or no thematic organization. This seemed especially true in the case of papyri belonging to the Theban Recension since, as pointed out above, these manuscripts vary so widely that there is virtually nothing canonical about them. On the other hand, the French religious scholar Barguet recognized that certain chapters of the Saite Recension do have themes in common. Barguet's discovery was significant because he showed that when the Egyptians established a canonical *BD*, they gathered chapters into what they felt were logical or thematic categories. Since some manuscripts may even announce the major groups of chapters with a phrase such as 'Here begin the chapters of . . . ,' we can confidently divide the *BD* into four major sections:

1. Chapters 1–16. The deceased enters the tomb and descends to the underworld. The corpse of the deceased must regain the physical capabilities it had on earth.

2. Chapters 17–63. In this section the components and mythological origin of most of the important places and gods of the beyond are explained. The deceased is made to live again so that he or she might arise as the reborn morning sun.

3. Chapters 64–129. The deceased travels across the sky in the sun-bark as one of the blessed dead. In the evening the deceased continues to travel through the sky in the underworld, eventually appearing before Osiris and the judges of the dead as one already judged worthy.

4. Chapters 130–189. Having been vindicated in judgment, the deceased assumes his power in the universe as one of the gods. This fourth group of chapters may be divided in two subsections: the first containing chapters concerned with travelling in the sun bark with Re and other activities of the blessed dead, and the second containing disparate chapters concerning protective amulets, the provision of food, and important places.

THE MANUFACTURE OF THE PAPYRUS OF ANI

The Papyrus of Ani, like most *BD*'s of the New Kingdom, was a prefabricated product of a funerary workshop. Wealthy Egyptians appear to have provided for their burial well in advance of their demise. The coffin, the tomb, its decorations, and the majority of the objects that went in it were either made or contracted for before the owner's death. In the case of *BD* manuscripts, financial considerations were balanced against religious requirements in deciding what the papyrus would include. Judging from the one source mentioning the cost of a

BD, such documents could be worth approximately half the annual salary of an average laborer. Blank papyrus itself appears to have been relatively expensive; most business documents show traces of prior use. Only the wealthiest clientele could afford to have a custom-made BD papyrus in which a roll of fresh sheets would be inscribed and illustrated specifically for the purchaser.

The usual practice among the 'middle class' was to purchase a papyrus which had been completely or partially prepared in advance. A large number of BD papyri appear to have been drawn up in a template format so that they could quickly be ascribed to *any* purchaser — blank spaces were provided so that the owner's name and titles could be inserted at a later date. Rare examples of unused papyri have been found in which all the spaces for the name and titles remain unfilled. Once Ani (or his survivors) decided how much would be spent on his BD, a manuscript was produced according to his specifications. In the second section of the commentary, I have indicated a few places where one can see how this BD was literally pasted together from different prefabricated papyri.

A careful examination of the hieroglyphic texts in Ani's papyrus quickly reveals a suspicious peculiarity which can be reliably used to identify such 'ready-made' work. Ani's name almost always occurs in one of three circumstances: at the top of a column of text, at the bottom of a column, or immediately following a rubric introducing him as the speaker of the text; significantly, a single scribe seems to have written in Ani's name in nearly all instances. One wonders what Ani, himself a professional scribe, would have felt had he noticed that the person delegated to fill in his name not only omitted it from some chapters, but also misspelled it in the critical scene where the god Horsiese introduces him to Osiris! The inelegant handwriting used for Ani's name is often markedly dissimilar from that used in the rest of the text; at times, the different tone of ink sets it off. A close comparison of the hieroglyphic texts and the accompanying vignettes reveals that the papyrus consists of the work of no fewer than three scribe/artists; at least two different artists painted the vignettes. Moving from sheet to sheet, we can see dramatic shifts in the overall color of the papyrus itself, confirming that Ani's BD was a pastiche in the literal sense of the term.

But these observations hardly diminish the work's quality. This is undoubtedly one of the most beautiful Egyptian manuscripts of any kind. Among BD papyri, it is a masterpiece by any estimation and justifiably gives Ani a touch of the immortality he desired so fervently when he purchased it for himself and his wife.

An Introduction to Egyptian Concepts of the Afterlife

THE GEOGRAPHY OF THE AFTERLIFE

Creation and Nonexistence

Compared to the Egyptians, we have a rather impoverished view of the afterlife. It is ironic that the major religions of the modern world, particularly the great monotheistic religions, seem to have a much more developed concept of Hell than of Paradise. For their part, the Egyptians do not seem to have made much of a distinction between the places where the gods dwelt and the afterworld; these regions seem to blend together at points. They are places whose connection with this world often occurs on a liminal level, in sleep, dreams, visions, and death. In many senses, people encountered the next world in an altered state. The Egyptians' concept of the period between death and transformation in the next world strongly resembles their concept of the dream, in which one was awake while being asleep. For the Egyptians, the transformation into a soul or a spirit after death was an extension of this notion.

Certainly, like the dream world, the realm beyond the grave was the domain of irrationality.

Since the realm of the gods, the cosmos (or ordered universe), and the next world are not always sharply delineated or precisely located, it would be tempting to call these regions collectively 'the Beyond,' were it not for the fact that they touched on Egypt and the land of the living. Egypt was a tolerant, polytheistic society in which several cosmologies and creation myths coexisted. The result was that, like so many other aspects of their religion, the Egyptian concepts of the origin and organization of the universe were not always consistent. Yet there is sufficient congruity to allow us to sketch the relative position of its elements. Many aspects of the Egyptian view of the universe had close parallels in other cosmological systems.

The most influential of all Egyptian cosmological systems seems to have originated with the priests of the solar cult in the town of Heliopolis (located in the north of modern Cairo). In the BD, the Heliopolitan world view appears to predominate. Its creator deity was Atum, whose name has been variously interpreted as meaning 'The Completed One,' 'He Who Is Entirety,' 'The One Not Yet Present,' or 'The Undifferentiated One.' The last rendering seems the most probable because descriptions of the universe before creation state that at that time 'there were not yet two things,' i.e., it was an undifferentiated unity. Atum somehow created himself. By masturbating, Atum was able to bring forth his children Shu (Air) and Tefnut (Moisture), the first male/female pair in creation. Their children were Geb, the god of the earth, and Nut, the goddess of the sky. This pair in turn engendered four children: Osiris, Seth, Isis, and Nephthys. Together these nine deities comprised the ennead (corporation of nine gods) of Heliopolis.

The act of creation brought ordered existence out of nonexistence, the undifferentiated and unordered state which corresponds to the Greek concept of Chaos. Atum's act of creation, then, was comparable to the Greek concept of the cosmos coming into existence out of Chaos. The two principal components of nonexistence were total darkness (*keku*) and limitless primordial waters (*nun*). Perhaps because of their undifferentiated nature, these two elements give rise to the chief characteristics of nonexistence: weariness, inertness, and negation. Osiris's association with these qualities results from his connection with death and from the fact that he had to emerge from a state of nonexistence. Significantly, before Atum's act of creation, not even life and death existed in the undifferentiated mass of nonexistence. It is important to realize that, even after the ordering act of creation, chaos continued to exist and the things which were paradoxically called 'that which does not exist' continued to play an important part in the universe. Chaos and disorder surrounded the universe and constantly impinged upon it. There were even a few places where nonexistence came into direct contact with the cosmos, such as the deserts and the underworld. This cosmology shows how deeply the Egyptian emphasis on complementary dualities is embedded in their conceptual and metaphorical vocabulary.

The Terrestrial Domain and the Horizon

At the center of the universe was the earth, a flat oval-shaped expanse bordered by the oceans. This was the land of the living, the place to which the deceased hoped to return in order that he might 'go forth by day.' Since the tomb was on earth, and since the life-maintaining funerary cult was also located there, the ties with this world were never quite broken. Critical to the entire process of rebirth and transformation were several activities that had to be done on earth: proper treatment of the corpse (mummification), a ritually correct burial ceremony, the performance of the 'Opening of the Mouth' ceremony when the corpse had been placed in the tomb, and maintenance of the spirit through offerings and cult. Although the deceased went on to a new life beyond the grave, it was first necessary to restore the same powers that the mortal body had enjoyed upon earth: the senses, breathing, eating, speech, the mobility of the limbs, and sexual potency.

The necropolis as well as the tomb was seen as an earthly juncture between this world and the next. The Egyptian language is particularly rich in words for 'cemetery.' One of the most telling of these is *khert netjer*, a term which means roughly 'that which belongs to the god' and may be translated 'the God's Domain.' It is an ancient term, attested in some of the earliest Egyptian inscriptions. The phrase shows that there was already a fairly close connection between divinity and the state of death at the earliest stages of Egyptian civilization. Another important word for the necropolis is *Rosetjau*, whose meaning has been the source of much debate. Of the many explanations offered, one of the most likely seems to be 'the place of the dragging,' perhaps an allusion to the first tomb corridor or the ramp leading to the tomb. Originally, the term seems to have had a broader geographic scope, as a name for the great cemeteries of the Old Kingdom located near Memphis. One of the chief mortuary gods of this region, Sokar, seems to have been the origin of the name of the modern town of Saqqara. *Rosetjau* is, however, also used as the name for the necropolis at Giza farther north. By the New Kingdom, it was used on occasion for other cemeteries in Egypt, including the Theban necropolis where Ani was buried.

Another region of great importance for the Egyptian afterlife is the *Akhet*, which lies at the junction between the earth and the sky. For this reason, this word is normally translated 'horizon,' especially since the most frequently employed determinative shows the sun rising (or setting) between two hills. However, as early as the Pyramid Texts, many writings of the word *Akhet* use an elongated oval for its determinative, perhaps as an indication that the *Akhet* is not merely the location of sunrise and sunset, but a much greater expanse. On the other hand, *Akhet* clearly has a close connection with the sun, so a rendering such as 'lightland' or 'the bright place' is probably closer to the mark. The *Akhet* is a place where the gods and spirits come into being. This is significant because there is a strong connection of this region with the *akh*, an important soul-like state of the noble or blessed dead. Perhaps in this form the deceased becomes a pure dazzling light. In the *BD* and other sources the Egyptian word for the funerary prayers, *sakh*, means 'to transform into an *akh*.'

In the Egyptian cosmological system, the gods who personified the various components of the universe frequently had names different from those components. For example, the god Geb was the personification of the earth, called *ta* in Egyptian. Similarly, Nut personified the sky, but the word for 'sky' was *pet*. Between the earth and the sky was the domain of the god Shu, whose name is often rendered 'air' but is probably more accurately translated 'emptiness.' It was said that one of the first events of the creation was the separation of the earth and the sky, an act which is occasionally depicted in scenes showing Shu standing upon the earth and lifting the sky up above him.

The Celestial Sphere

The sky was a particularly important place in the Egyptian cosmology of the afterlife. The sky was the location of the stars, the sun, and other heavenly bodies with which both the gods and the spirits of deceased mortals might be identified. An especially important group of stars were the 'imperishable' or 'indestructible' stars, those circumpolar stars which never dipped below the horizon into the netherworld below. The sky supplied an important medium of travel in the afterlife, where boats were the preferred mode of transportation. The vocabulary of travel through the sky is full of words such as 'row,' 'ferry,' 'traverse' (written with a boat-determinative). An especially important path through the sky was the Milky Way,

whose name in Egyptian means something akin to 'the beaten path,' a delightful and evocative interpretation. In their dualistic conception of the universe, the Egyptians located many aspects of the afterlife in this celestial sphere as well as in the underworld. Particularly important were the Field of Reeds and the Field of Offerings, where the blessed dead could dwell.

The Underworld

Going in the opposite direction, underneath the earth were located the regions of Nun, the primordial waters, sometimes characterized as the 'Abyss,' as in Faulkner's original translation, because of their virtually bottomless quality. These primordial waters were located throughout the underworld. The name 'Nun' itself seems to mean something like 'The Watery One' and occasionally is written with an inverted 'sky' determinative, an indication that Nun may have been considered as a subterranean counterpart to the sky. The waters of Nun were the origin of the forces of chaos. When groundwater was seen seeping upwards through the sand during foundation ceremonies, the Egyptians believed that they had encountered Nun. The Egyptians' characteristic love for balance led them to suppose that nonexistence and Nun had positive as well as negative aspects. Every evening the aged sun entered the underworld and travelled through it, immersed in Nun, only to emerge at dawn as Khepri, the newborn sun. Thus, the waters of Nun had a rejuvenating, baptismal quality essential to rebirth.

Perhaps the most frequent and important of all the components of the afterworld is the *Duat*, the Underworld, a vast region lying under the earth. Already in the *Pyramid Texts* there is a tendency to style the Duat as a chthonic region, but originally it seems to have been connected with the stars. Within the *BD*, the word is most frequently written with a star, or a star in a circle; purely alphabetic spellings are much less common. An explanation for this might lie in the fact that all celestial bodies except for the 'Imperishable Stars' would sometimes cross the Duat. Above all, this was the realm of Osiris and the place through which Re travelled every night in his journey beneath the earth. The royal netherworld books of the Eighteenth to Twentieth Dynasties are texts and scenes showing the night journey of the sun through the underworld, which decorate the Theban royal tombs of the New Kingdom. From these and from their adaptations for private mortuary literature such as the *BD*, we learn that the Duat is a dark, hidden, deep place. It is to some extent connected with the waters of Nun, as well as being the source of the waters of the inundation.

As with the other parts of the universe discussed thus far, the Duat was the abode of many deities, including Anubis, various beings identified as Duat-gods, and Osiris. Of these the most important was Osiris, for this was his own kingdom. He is frequently styled the 'Lord of the Duat.' Even so, the Duat was filled with numerous supernatural beings who were inimical not only to the deceased, but to Osiris as well. In addition to Seth and his associates, who continued to pose a threat to Osiris in the Duat, there were the forces of chaos led by Apophis, who is envisioned as an endless snakelike creature.

THE GODS OF THE *Book of the Dead*

The Gods and 'the God'

It is hard not to be baffled by the bewildering number and forms of gods encountered in the text and vignettes of the *BD*. Most people reading this book come from a monotheistic background, and, whether they are ardent believers or atheists, they probably have an innate bias against polytheism. Yet the Egyptians themselves offer us proof that it is possible to be intelligent, subtle thinkers and still believe in many gods. With the brief and anomalous exception of the reign of the heretic pharaoh Akhenaten, Egyptian religion remained strongly poly-theistic throughout its history. Since not a few of the great scholars of Egyptian religion have been devout ordained ministers and priests, who have sought analogues of their beliefs among the Egyptians, there have been numerous inter-pretations which attempt to explain away the vast number of Egyptian deities, to say nothing of some of their outwardly preposterous appearances. To assert, however, that the intelli-gent elite were really monotheists, or to say that the wide variety of gods actually are aspects of a single deity, is merely wishful thinking. We must beware of trying to impose our intellectual frameworks upon the Egyptians.

One common source of error is the frequent occurrence in Egyptian texts of the phrase 'the god,' implying that the texts were referring to a single supreme god in the sense of the Jewish, Christian, or Muslim usage of the word 'God.' This usage, however, is confined for the most part to a genre of literature which Egyptologists call 'Wisdom Literature' or 'Didactic Literature.' These are the great 'teachings' or 'in-structions' of the great sages of the Egyptian past, such as the *Instruction of Ptahhotep* or the *Instruction of Amenemope*. Be-cause these teachings were primarily intended for the training of young scribes who would serve in a wide variety of situations during their careers, the expression 'the god' was placed in the instructions almost as a blank space in the template ('fill in the name of whichever god you desire'). The same teaching would also employ the phrase 'the gods' and mention specific deities such as Thoth and Re.

This is not to say that there were no tendencies toward monotheism in Egyptian religion. Often such beliefs took the form of henotheism, or the belief in one god's supremacy over many others. For instance, Amun-Re, the chief god of the official state cult of the New Kingdom, bore the epithet 'king of the gods,' an expression asserting his paramount position without denying the existence of other deities. On the local level, many of the major gods were 'solarized' like Amun-Re and said to be the overlord of the rest of the gods. In the reign of Akhenaten this line of thought was taken to its logical extreme, and the Aten became a unique deity, excluding all others. Akhenaten's doctrines appear to have won little sup-port beyond a tiny segment of Egyptian society, and such beliefs did not survive his reign.

A good example of the polytheistic mindset of the average Egyptian is offered by the letters sent home by a late twentieth-dynasty scribe named Thothmose. When his employer, the general (and later High Priest of Amun) Herihor, was sta-tioned near the Faiyum, Thothmose ('Thoth is born') would begin his letters with a salutation invoking the most important local gods: 'I am calling upon Arsaphes, lord of Herakleopolis, Thoth, lord of Hermopolis, and every god and goddess by whom I pass, to give you life, prosperity, and health . . .' Later on in the same letters he would also ask his friends receiving these letters, 'Please call upon Amun, lord of the Thrones of the Two Lands, and Meretseger, to bring me back alive . . .' When Thothmose subsequently followed Herihor on a cam-paign south into Nubia, he would write instead: 'Every single day I am calling upon Horus of Kuban (a Nubian town), who dwells in the mountain, to give you life, prosperity, and health.' Thus, an Egyptian might have a name invoking the protection of one god (Thoth), feel himself primarily a devotee of the god of his hometown temple (Amun), but address prayers to the local deities of the region in which he found himself at the moment (Arsaphes, Thoth, and Horus of Kuban).

Egypt's richly polytheistic culture tended to accommodate rather than to exclude. As a collection of Egyptian thoughts concerning the afterlife, the *BD* reflects several traditions spanning a wide expanse both geographically and chronologi-cally. Chapter 17 of the *BD* shows us that over the course of time various interpretations developed concerning the gods,

their nature, and the cosmologies associated with them, and that these diverse interpretations would coexist side by side within a given text. The case of Thothmose, described above, shows that an Egyptian felt that local deities may have had priority and had to be accommodated into his religious beliefs. When an Egyptian passed from the land of the living to the world beyond the grave, the same variety of traditions per-sisted there.

Gods and Mortals in Egypt

The mere idea that an Egyptian hoped to become one of the gods in the next world sounds like hubris to us. The root of this belief can be found in the meaning of the Egyptian word for 'god,' *netjer,* especially in relation to the afterlife where the word 'god' may have had an extended meaning. Neither the hieroglyphic sign nor any of the suggested etymologies for the word are particularly helpful in explaining what the Egyptians really meant when they spoke of 'god' or 'gods.' The hiero-glyphic sign apparently shows either a pole with cloth stream-ers attached, or a cloth-wrapped pole. In the so-called 'Signs Papyrus,' dating to the Roman era, the hieroglyph is given the gloss 'he is buried.' As strange as this may seem at first, there is evidence from many sources to show that, in addition to the beings we would normally call gods, the word *netjer* could refer to dead people in general. This close relationship between the concepts 'dead' and 'god' in Egyptian appears in a very common term for the necropolis in the *BD*, particularly in the chapter headings: *khert-netjer,* 'the God's Domain.' We should not be taken aback, then, when the deceased says to the gods, 'I am one among you.'

The Aspects of Divinity and the Representations of Gods

There was not only a multiplicity of gods in Egyptian religion, but many of the gods assume a variety of aspects as well. The varying forms of the gods can be manifested in both text and representation. Yet the Egyptians never seem to have felt that these images were the gods' true likenesses. Describing a deity as 'jackal-headed' or as a 'cow goddess' confuses the likeness with the nature. Just as the Egyptians did not believe in a single god, they did not think that their deities were indivisible unities.

In the vignettes of Ani's *BD,* Thoth appears as an ibis, or with an ibis head upon a human body, or in the form of a seated ape. The goddess named 'Hathor' appears in many forms: a cow with a solar disk between her horns, a slender woman with cow horns and a solar disk upon her head, a woman with the sign for 'West' upon her head. Since other goddesses also assume some of the same forms, we can be sure that any given image represents Hathor only if there is a caption to inform us. Hathor is also represented by such symbols as the *menat*-necklace and the head of a musical instrument known as the sistrum, and occasionally these serve as images of the goddess. In general, however, an Egyptian god wears his or her attribute upon the head. The jackal head on Anubis does not show his actual appearance but is his attribute, revealing his association with the deserts, an entirely appropriate image for a god of the necropolis. Perhaps the Egyptian language provides a clearer insight into the underly-ing concept. The spelling of the god's name, the abstraction of the god, remains constant, but the determinative (the hiero-glyphic sign indicating category but contributing nothing to the pronunciation) changes. If we were to ask an Egyptian whether any particular depiction represented a given deity, the reply would probably be that only a certain *aspect* of the god was shown.

The divine names could be important manifestations of the nature of the gods; often the name of a deity appears to be as important as the illustration. The word 'face' is frequently used in the names and epithets of the gods and other supernatural beings encountered in the *BD*. By 'face' the Egyptians meant much more than the mere visage of the deity. The Egyptian word *her*, which we translate as 'face,' has a wide range of meanings: 'head,' 'sight,' 'vision,' 'attention.' There is also an extensive metaphorical usage, as is common with words for parts of the body. With gods, a particularly apt metaphorical extension of 'face' would be the 'aspect' of the deity. It is important to understand, however, that the word *her* should not be taken in the literal sense when used in this fashion. Anubis's jackal head, for instance, is not an indication that the god had an essentially jackal-like character, but rather it is an emblem. It is quite unusual, furthermore, for a representation of Hathor, Anubis, or Thoth to be simply 'animal-headed.' Composite god forms will almost always wear a wig or wig-cover (the *nemes* headdress) both to aid the transition between the human body and the animal head and to stress the divinity of the figure.

Similarly, a depiction of a deity in purely animal form normally has a solar disk, a broad collar, or other jewelry on the body as an indication of supernatural status. The animal form was simply a manifestation of the deity, often one form of many that the god was thought to assume. In this light, we can see in the Egyptian worship of sacred animals something akin to the function that a statue plays in the cult. The Egyptians did not believe that a stone statue of Amun-Re was the god himself any more than a Christian believes that a crucifix is Christ. The divine image in Egyptian religion served as a place in which the deity could momentarily manifest himself or herself. In the same way, the sacred Apis bull was a temporary living manifestation of the god Ptah. As such, it could be used in ceremonies and to procure oracles. Significantly, at the bull's death, it would be buried with great solemnity and quickly replaced by another Apis bull. The deity manifests himself in the living monarch, and when the latter dies another mortal assumes the same function as the chief intermediary between the gods and men.

In contrast to the attention paid to the gods' heads, their bodies were frequently executed in a rather summary manner. Even when they have normal human bodies, their clothing and other ornamentation is seldom as elaborate as that worn by the deceased papyrus owner. More often than not, furthermore, gods are shown as either standing or squatting mummiform figures. This mode of representation does not mean that the gods appeared as mummies in the beyond. The frequent addition of arms and hands to allow the 'mummiform' gods to hold objects is an attribute never found with representations of actual coffins. The intent of the mummy-like shape, rather, was to indicate that the gods' forms were indeterminate and undifferentiated.

Magic in the *Book of the Dead*
Magic and Religion

One of the most problematic aspects of Egyptian religion is the role of magic within it. But our modern distinction between 'religion' and 'magic' would seem strange to the Egyptians. Today, under the influence of science and rationalism, the very word 'magic' has a disreputable aura, evoking images of ignorance, superstition, sleight-of-hand, and fraudulent spiritualism. The major monotheistic religions of the world, partly because of their confessional and pietistic orientation, have a tendency, often rather self-serving, to stigmatize many of the beliefs and practices of other religions as magical and therefore morally and spiritually inferior. All too often one person's religion becomes another person's superstition. Furthermore, in the monotheistic traditions there is a strong historical connection between the concepts 'heretical' and 'magical.'

Since the text of the *BD* constantly uses words which correspond to 'magic,' the subject cannot be avoided. It is quite clear that the Egyptians felt much more positively about magic than we do. According to the *Coffin Texts*, when the creator deity fashioned the universe, one of his first acts was to create magic, his eldest son, named Heka. Some time after this he entrusted both gods and mankind with magic as one of his 'great deeds.' The prominent role the Egyptians gave magic in their religion is a stumbling block for understanding and appreciating their beliefs, particularly when dealing with mortuary texts such as the *BD*. The Egyptians felt that magic was as legitimate as prayer or offerings to the gods, or any other practice which we would consider truly 'religious.' It is not uncommon to find clearly magical incantations existing alongside of prayers within a single chapter in the *BD*. Egyptian religious documents show that it was permissible for mortals to employ magic when dealing with divine forces, although the gods had greater magical powers at their disposal.

Aware of the cultural and theological biases implicit in the tendency to see 'magic' in other peoples' beliefs, anthropologists and scholars of world religions struggled for a long time in the hope of finding more objective criteria for distinguishing between magic and religion. The results of decades of discussion have not been satisfying, particularly with respect to Egyptian religion. It is becoming increasingly apparent to Egyptologists that we have been attempting to impose a modern Western conceptual framework upon an ancient non-Western civilization.

The issue of 'magic' vs. 'religion' can lead to difficulties in such apparently simple problems as the name to give the sections of the *BD*. The Egyptian word that begins most of the subdivisions is *ro*, a term with a wide range of meanings. The basic meaning is 'mouth,' but it can also mean a speech, a chapter in a book, a spell, or a magical incantation. Having to choose among these meanings leaves the translator in a quandary. It would be tempting to vary the translation of this word according to each context, were it not for the constant mixture of the genres within the subdivisions. For this reason the somewhat neutral term 'chapter' has been adopted for the section titles simply on grounds of consistency. Perhaps the intractability of the underlying problem is best illustrated by the observation that, although the Egyptians had several words which would correspond roughly to the English word 'magic,' there does not seem to be an equivalent for 'religion' in their language.

The Vocabulary of Magic

The number of words in the Egyptian language which could be translated as 'magic' is an indication of the complexity of their thoughts concerning magic. The most common and important of these words is *heka*, whose Coptic equivalent was later used to render the Greek word *mageia* in the Coptic New Testament. In Egyptian texts the word was virtually interchangeable with *Heka*, the deity personifying magic. In fact, so close is the identification that translators often have difficulty deciding whether *heka* or *Heka* was intended. Unlike most personifications, Heka could hardly be considered 'a colorless abstraction,' for he frequently appears as the eldest child of the creator deity, or as a personification of the god Re, further evidence of the importance of magic in Egyptian religion.

Heka magic is many things, but, above all, it has a close association with speech and the power of the word. In the realm of Egyptian magic, actions did not necessarily speak louder than words — they were often one and the same thing. Thought, deed, image, and power are theoretically united in the concept of *heka*. The Memphite Theology, which stated that the god Ptah Tatenen brought forth the universe through the spoken word, places the power of the word at the center of the Egyptian world view. This concept is strongly reminiscent of the creation by *logos* in the Greek Gospel of John. The primacy of speech and recitation throughout the *BD* is partially a reflection of the importance of *heka*. Endowed with *heka*, both people and the gods can make words and wishes effective. *Heka* can be used to create or destroy, protect or harm.

Akhu, the other major word for magic, is distinguished from *heka* in that an individual apparently could not exercise *akhu* until after death. The etymology of *akhu* gives us an insight into its nature. The term is derived from a root which can mean both 'to be effective' and 'to be bright.' Puns on these meanings occur, as well as allusions to the *akh*, one of the many aspects of the human 'soul' after death. Otherwise, there is no clear difference in the manner in which *akhu* and *heka* are employed. *Akhu* has the same strong connection with speech, thought, and image, and is also possessed by gods and mortals alike. Several other terms besides *akhu* and *heka* appear with the sense of 'magic' in Egyptian texts, but these are of less importance and will not concern us here.

Magic as a Means of Controlling the Supernatural

Whatever aspect of Egyptian magic was used, most often the Egyptians were attempting to gain control over supernatural forces and irrational forces. Magic and religion, then, have embarrassingly similar objectives. Where magic and religion may differ is the perceived freedom of the divine to act or not. Perhaps one of the characteristic elements of magical practices is that they aim to coerce gods and supernatural beings to perform the will of the deceased. As presumptuous as this may seem, we must bear in mind, first, that magic was a god-given force, and second, that the papyrus owner is identified as being 'true-of-voice' ('vindicated') throughout the *BD*, and thus had been judged morally worthy to participate fully in the rewards of the afterlife. The types of magic in the *BD* are representative of Egyptian magical practices in general: manipulation of images and words; amuletic magic; encircling; eating and drinking; and licking and spitting. Each category of magic is well-attested in the *BD*, but space permits a discussion of only a few examples. The role of images and what might be considered image magic is so pervasive in the *BD* that it is discussed separately in the section immediately following this, entitled 'Word and Image in the Book of the Dead.' For the moment, we will confine our remarks to the closely related topic of amuletic magic.

Amulets and Protection

The easiest type of Egyptian magic to understand is protective magic, for which amulets were used. The wearing of amulets or talismans is a world-wide phenomenon, even in the strictest monotheistic cultures. Much of the jewelry shown in Egyptian art was meant to protect as well as decorate. Because of the intimate relationship between images and words inherent in the hieroglyphic system of writing, an amulet could render a verbal wish into an object that could be worn. Protective magic became especially important in the dangerous climate of the afterlife, where the deceased might not always be able to take an active role in his or her own defense. The time between death and the revival of the corpse was seen as a time when the dead person was especially vulnerable. To protect the body, many amulets of various types were wound into the mummy wrappings, virtually armoring the deceased against harmful forces. In addition to the protective amulets on the body itself, several chapters of the *BD* were concerned with ensuring the potency of amulets. In the Papyrus of Ani, Chapters 155 through 160 and Chapter 166 (see Plate 32) are all concerned with empowering different kinds of amulets. Significantly, in the Ani Papyrus these chapters appear immediately before Chapter 151, which is concerned with protection of the dead in the embalming chamber and in the tomb. The frequent mention of nephrite, a type of green stone, relates to the green color of many amulets, particularly the important 'heart scarab.' The Egyptian word for green also meant 'to flourish,' with all

of its implications of revitalization in the afterlife. The hope of emerging reborn from the earth, just as vegetation does yearly, is written in the green color of Osiris's face in the Ani Papyrus.

The Magical Power of Words

Verbal and image magic are the easiest form of magic to find in the *BD* — so easy, in fact, that one must always be careful not to see magic everywhere. Overly broad criteria could lead one to identify any incomprehensible expression or passage as magical. Should we, for example, consider prayer to be a magical practice because it seeks to influence the gods by words alone? Magic, however, attempts to compel the supernatural and apparently does not require the practitioner either to be morally superior or to show contrition.

The words at the head of many chapters of the *BD* explained the purpose of the following text and were usually written in red — rubrics in the true sense of the word. Here we often encounter striking examples of the Egyptians' belief in the great power of the written word. These titles, as well as rubrics elsewhere in the text, avoid writing the name of either the deceased or any of the gods in red, because this was an inauspicious color associated with both blood and the god Seth: '*Praising* Re *when he rises by the* Osiris Ani . . .' (italics indicate red ink, roman type indicates black). As mentioned above, the introductory word *ro* "mouth" emphasizes that each chapter of the *BD* armed the dead with verbal weapons, and these in turn would be signalled by another rubricized phrase — '*words spoken.*' The mark of the dead practitioner's virtue, furthermore, was the expression 'true of voice,' frequently translated as 'vindicated.'

Similarly, because of the nature of the hieroglyphic system of writing, it is not easy to distinguish between word magic and image magic because the underlying thought is essentially the same in both instances. Most often verbal and image magic seeks to affect someone or something by acting on an image or verbal representation. A rather general term for these practices might be 'magic by analogy' or 'sympathetic magic' — action in one sphere is done in order to bring about a result elsewhere. The classic example of such practices is the wax 'voodoo doll' into which pins are thrust with the desire to inflict harm on a person by 'long distance,' as it were. This type of thinking is hardly unique to the Egyptians and occurs in nearly all cultures. As we shall see later on in the discussion of words and images, most image magic in the *BD* had the more benign purpose of allowing the living to help the dead.

The Relationship of Magic to Myth and Ritual

One of the consequences of the Egyptians' belief that their language was a divine gift was a conviction that a similarity between words did not arise accidentally, but instead reflected an actual relationship which the gods themselves had intended to be discovered by people. Paronomasia was especially important as a means of revealing the hidden connections between this world and the next.

This relationship between the two spheres manifested itself especially in the realm of ritual, where the cult objects and the words used were interpreted as allusions to mythical events. There are many instances where a mythical event has clearly been invented to explain the ritual device or activity, rather than the reverse. We might describe this phenomenon as the 'mythologization of ritual.' For example, in the important 'Opening-of-the-Mouth' ritual during the burial ceremony (illustrated in Plate 6), a priest would strike at the mouth of the mummy case with an adze, a chisel, and other ritual implements, saying phrases such as: 'I open your mouth with the adze (or iron) which split open the mouths of the gods.' Since the funerary arts are attested in Egypt long before the appearance of Osiris, the ritual most likely had its origin among the artisans who carved out the burial equipment. The mythological reference given for the carving tools was undoubtedly a later priestly interpretation. Through the association of myth and object, an action in the earthly realm could be effective in recreating the mythical event which led to the revitalization of Osiris.

The Magical Power of Word Play

Since words were a major category of images for the Egyptians, manipulating the sounds or the signs in a word was thought to affect the object it represented. The goal of such word play, or paronomasia, was far more than the creation of incantations with mysterious sounds. The very phrase 'the god's words,' the most common term for their language, expressed the Egyptians' belief that the divine was implicit in words.

Word play was an important method of linking the earthly realm with the world of the gods. Egyptian puns seem heavy-handed, but they were not intended to amuse. They created an alternate focus which could deflect the power in a word. One example involves the euphemistic substitution of the phrase *mi* "come" for *mut* "death." Most word play in the *BD* either deflects enmity or gives power by a simple reworking of the name of a god or a place: (Chapter 8) 'Hermopolis (*Wenu*) is opened (*wenu*) . . .' The intent is normally to manipulate a name so as to demonstrate the deceased's control over a person or a thing in the beyond. Stating a name, or merely threatening to do so, was often sufficient means for gaining power. A particularly common sort of word play occurs in addresses to the gods in the *BD*. The deceased can sometimes get by the most fearsome of gatekeepers simply by saying: 'I know you, I know your name.' The name was more than 'mere words' — it was an image, a representation of the being or thing to which it was attached. To operate on the image was tantamount to operating on the thing itself. Word play can sometimes be employed in a euphemistic manner, effectively disarming a harmful or unpleasant thing by altering the meaning of its name. A good example of this usage occurs in Chapter 147 (speaking of Osiris): 'the one purified by your own efflux (*setjau*) against (*r*) which the name of Rosetjau was made.' By noting that the word Rosetjau sounds much like the phrase 'against the efflux,' the fluids issuing from Osiris's body were thus made innocuous.

Magic by Consumption

Ani, a scribe by profession, was literate and therefore belonged to an elite among the elite — the very small group of Egyptians who would actually be able to read the *BD* which accompanied them into the afterlife. Considering the strongly verbal nature of this work, the question of how those unable to read were expected to use its spells needs to be addressed. One answer to this problem is given in a passage from the late Demotic tale known as *Setne Khauemwas and Naneferkaptah* (M. Lichtheim, *Ancient Egyptian Literature*, vol. III, p. 131):

'As I could not write — I mean, compared with Naneferkaptah, my brother, who was a good scribe and very wise man — he had a sheet of new papyrus brought to him. He wrote on it every word that was in the book before him. He soaked it in beer, he dissolved it in water. When he knew that it had dissolved, he drank it and knew what had been in it.'

Although there are occasional puns on 'to live on (some type of food)' and 'to live,' and similarly on 'to swallow' (*am*) and 'to know' (*am*), magic by consumption does not play a particularly strong role in the *BD*. There is perhaps an exception in the frequent assertion that the deceased has not eaten filth nor drunk urine. This startling statement may not be a reference to ritual impurity, but rather an allusion to the afterlife of the damned, who are forced to act in complete reversal of their earthly behavior, as the rubric to Chapter 189

explains: '*Chapter for preventing a man from going upside down and from eating feces.*'

The Curative Power of Licking

Another manner in which the mouth could be used magically in assisting the deceased in the next world was to lick or spit upon things. The underlying notion is not as primitive as it may sound at first, for the curative power of saliva has long been recognized. In Chapters 17, 72, and 102, among several others, licking and spitting are employed to heal. In Chapter 146 one of the epithets of a protective goddess is 'She who licks.' The epithet immediately recalls the gesture of a cow toward her young. Spittle also has an important function in a number of Egyptian creation stories where a generative force akin to that of semen is ascribed to it.

The Significance of Encirclement

Processions played an important part in Egyptian religion since they were a public demonstration of devotion to a deity, particularly at festivals. There was often an additional magical aspect of such rituals, for many Egyptian processions would go around an area several times with the intent of rendering malevolent beings and forces harmless by encircling (*pekher*) them. Encircling was such a common method of disarming evil and irrational forces that it is the root of the word for a 'prescription' (*pekhert*) in medical papyri. Indeed, many cures in these papyri supplement the drugs and procedures with magical spells. The most important encircling of all occurred daily when the sun-god Re traversed the firmament above the world, then continued through the night sky beneath the earth. This daily journey, particularly the nocturnal component, was the central theme of most of the royal underworld books. One of the prime objectives of several chapters of the *BD* was to assist the deceased in joining Re in his bark as he established his power over the entire universe daily.

WORD AND IMAGE IN THE *Book of the Dead*

The Significance of the Illustrated Book

Translating Egyptian means more than the usual shift from one language to another. We must move from a writing system based on pictures drawn from objects of everyday life to a system of abstract phonetic characters. This transformation immediately wrests Egyptian words from the cultural references in which they were so deeply embedded. Suddenly we are blinded to the subtle interactions between Egyptian text and image; we can no longer sense the holistic nature of the Egyptians' conceptual universe. It may not seem particularly significant to us that Ani's image appears in the same posture as the verb 'praise' in the opening hymn to Re (Plate 1), nor does it seem important that Ani uses a plow exactly like the determinative of the verb 'plow' when he works in the Field of Reeds (Plate 34). Yet for the Egyptians such coincidences probably seemed like affirmations of the unity of their written words and their world. Art historians have long remarked on the hieroglyphic nature of Egyptian art. To approach the *BD* as a text alone would create an unnecessary conceptual barrier. This is a work that virtually commands us to take account of the profound significance of images in the Egyptians' perception of reality and the forces that controlled their universe. It is not surprising that the Egyptians should have invented the illustrated book, of which the *BD* is the prime example.

In Egypt, the history of illustrated texts by no means begins with the *BD*. In fact, the very first hieroglyphic inscriptions, on ceremonial tablets of the Archaic Period (c. 3200 B.C.E.), exhibit the unification of text with imagery. Throughout Egyptian history most of the relief repertoire of Egyptian temples was essentially illustrated text, in which scenes and captions were more intimately interwoven than on papyri. Virtually all of the temple scenes in which the king and the gods interact with each other were accompanied by dialogues, as if the reliefs were snapshots of Egyptian dramas which could be reenacted eternally simply through their presence on the walls and columns. The phrase used to introduce the speeches in these illustrations was the same as that used for the speeches in the *BD* — *djed medu* "recitation.'"

The first preserved example of an Egyptian illustrated book is the mysterious document known as the Ramesseum Dramatic Papyrus, which dates to the earlier Middle Kingdom. However, it would be surprising if the genre was not already an ancient one by then. Although current scholarship is divided as to the nature of the ritual depicted on this papyrus, it is clearly dramatic in nature. Central to this and most other Egyptian dramas was the theory that reenactment of an activity in the earthly sphere would create some desired effect in the divine sphere. In general, drama and ritual seem to be fundamentally connected to the entire category of illustrated texts. The royal underworld 'books' on the walls of the tombs of New Kingdom monarchs were patterned after illustrated papyri.

The Subordination of Text to Image in the BD

The *BD* was meant to be accompanied by pictures; examples without vignettes are rare. In the format of the *BD* the Egyptians display an attitude that the text was subordinate, a mere subtext. Over the centuries the visual predominance of image above text continued to grow until, during the final stages of the *BD*'s development, the scribes used only as much text as could fit into the ever-diminishing space beneath the vignettes. The text of a chapter might halt abruptly in mid-phrase or mid-word.

We can already see evidence of this cavalier attitude toward the text in several places in the Ani Papyrus. Sometimes a chapter can contain many errors, yet the hieroglyphs used in it will be beautifully rendered. More often the predominance of image manifests itself in the misalignment of text and vignette. In the Ani Papyrus, several chapters and parts of chapters seem to have been written under the wrong vignettes, most notably on Plate 32 where the rubric to Chapter 125 occurs under the unmistakable vignette normally associated with Chapter 126. In Chapter 151, the scribe completely garbled or truncated the text he was copying, sometimes contenting himself with a few representative words from a phrase. Yet, in both instances, the vignettes are first-rate examples of Egyptian book illustration. The displacement of text and image is an important phenomenon which should not simply be ascribed to careless work done on the cheap, for it occurs in material of the highest quality. Helmut Brunner noted in his study of the Divine Birth Legend that even in these royal temple scenes the images do not necessarily relate to the texts accompanying them. These displacements indicate that the vignettes alone evoked the chapter's entire religious and ritual content; the images had an innate potency greater than the power of the text accompanying them.

Several points mentioned above have to do with why the *BD* is so frequently incomprehensible to us today: the significance of spoken rituals in Egyptian religion; the connection between pictures, words, and thought; and above all, the inherent power of images to produce a desired result. It would be far too simplistic to characterize the *BD*'s vignettes as magical and its texts as ritual, but if we view many of the texts as miniature performance pieces, then the reason for many obscurities is partially explained. Unfortunately, it is often difficult to tell whether a chapter represents a ritual or not. In fact, Faulkner uses small capitals in many places to supply continuity where a spell has clearly lost crucial elements such as 'words spoken by,' normally used to introduce speakers in

dramatic or ritual dialogues. Yet the frequency of that very phrase obscures an obvious but important aspect of the *BD* — it is meant to be recited.

Image Magic in the BD

Luckily, the *BD* occasionally supplies us with directions concerning how chapters are to be used, along with instructions for creating the required images and implements. These explanations usually appear in the form of a rubric appended to the end of a chapter; sometimes these 'rubrics' may be written in black rather than in the usual red. A particularly informative example is found in Chapter 100, 'The book of making a soul worthy and of permitting it to go aboard the Bark of Re.' In this case, the terminal rubric states: 'To be said over this written text (i.e., Chapter 100), *which should be written on a clean blank roll with powder of green glaze mixed with water of myrrh. To be placed on the breast of the blessed dead without letting it touch his flesh. As for any blessed dead for whom this is done, he will go aboard the Bark of Re every day, and Thoth will take count of him in daily going and coming. A matter a million times true.'* Without these final remarks, there is nothing in either the vignette or the body of the chapter to reveal that there was a ritual connected with the text. The recitation of the chapter was intended to ensure that the text would be activated at the right moment, enabling the deceased to join Re in his bark. We can understand the function of green, a color the Egyptians associated with Osiris's face, vernal renewal, and rebirth in the afterlife. It is also easy to comprehend why drawing an image in green similar to the chapter's vignette (which shows the deceased standing in the sun's bark) and repeating the accompanying text might be considered effective in bringing about the desired result in the divine sphere. Nevertheless, knowing how the chapter was to be used does not clarify why Sokar, Bebi, and the Egg should be mentioned in this context, nor will this knowledge clarify the sequence of thoughts underlying the incantation. The *rationale* eludes us still.

When T. G. Allen discussed similar rubrics in the *BD*, he remarked that the same rubric sometimes appears in various chapters, just as texts and vignettes occasionally do not relate to each other. He also pointed out that the rubrics are often accompanied by extravagant claims about their effectiveness, reminiscent of those found on modern patent medicines and nostrums. They nonetheless reveal the strong Egyptian belief in the ability of images to affect reality. The strength of the belief in image magic can be seen in the rubrics connected with the amulets placed on the corpse for its protection. The importance of the image is so great in Chapter 165 that the entire text consists of its titular rubric accompanied by a description of how to use the spell: 'To be said over a divine image with raised arm, plumes on his head . . . draw on a single bandage level with his heart the image of Him with raised arm . . . He shall drink water of the river; he shall shine like a star in the sky.'

The instructions in most rubrics connected with image magic indicate that they were part of rituals which the living could perform on behalf of the dead, most likely during the preparation of the corpse or the burial ceremonies. In a few instances the rubric explains how the imagery could be used by the deceased in the next world. The rubric at the end of Chapter 148 (omitted in Ani's papyrus) states that repeating the chapter over a similar vignette in the afterlife can provide the dead with food whenever it is needed: 'To be spoken by a man, when Re manifests himself, over these gods depicted in paint on a writing-board. There shall be given to them offerings and provisions before them, consisting of bread, beer, meat, poultry, and incense. The invocation-offering for his spirit shall be made to them in the presence of Re; it means that this soul will have provision in the realm of the dead . . .'

Image magic in the *BD* is not confined to the rubrics. In

some versions of Chapter 7, the text mentions an 'Apophis of wax,' referring to an image used to control this embodiment of the forces of chaos and harm. The *shabti* figurine mentioned in Chapter 6 is a more benign example of the same type of magic. If the text inscribed on one of these statuettes were recited, the image supposedly would come to life, ready to perform obligatory labor on behalf of the deceased in the next world.

The Myth of Osiris and the *Book of the Dead*

The paramount deity of the Egyptian afterlife is Osiris; he is the very pivotal point of the entire *BD*. No other god appears as often, or takes as many forms, as does Osiris. For most of the other gods in the *BD*, their chief role is either as a cohort or as an enemy of Osiris. In addition to the hundreds of specific references to Osiris, there are nearly as many allusions to him or to his legend.

Although one thinks of Osiris as one of the most important gods in the Egyptian pantheon, he was not always so. In fact, both the meaning of his name and his origins still remain obscure. There are no certain references either to him or his cult until the end of the Fifth Dynasty, when Osiris makes his appearance in the *Pyramid Texts*, the oldest body of Egyptian religious texts that we possess today. From that moment, however, he became the principal deity of the next world and was associated with hope of life beyond the grave. Osiris was also connected with the royal ancestors. The *Pyramid Texts* reveal that there were already several different legends about Osiris even at this early stage of Egyptian history.

Unfortunately, it is not really until the Roman author Plutarch's *De Iside et Osiride,* written in the late second century C.E., that a lengthy consecutive narrative text of the legends surrounding Osiris is attested. Indeed, this is true of most myths and legends from ancient Egypt. Myths, or stories about the gods, were seldom gathered into narrative passages of any length. In most cases when a book on ancient Egypt mentions a myth about a certain deity, what is actually meant is a series of facts and events which modern scholars have been able to compile from a wide variety of sources. There is, moreover, evidence that the Egyptians tended to invent myths to explain the origins of rituals and ritual instruments, rather than inventing rituals in order to reenact mythical events. Although we probably know more about the legends concerning Osiris than about any other god, even this myth is essentially a scholarly reconstruction from many texts. Like most such reconstructions, it is occasionally uncertain which elements belong to which version of the myth.

By the time the *BD* was formulated, the basic framework of the contemporary myth of Osiris might have been as follows. The divine pair Geb and Nut had four children: Osiris, Isis, Nephthys, and Seth. At the dawn of Egypt's history Osiris ruled as a living king of Egypt, with his sister Isis as his wife. Osiris's jealous brother Seth wished to rule in his stead and murdered Osiris, dismembering him and tossing his remains into the Nile. For this reason, Osiris had cult places throughout Egypt, each of these towns supposedly being where a part of his dismembered body washed up; his most important cults were at Abydos and Busiris. It fell to his sister/wife Isis, a goddess endowed with great magical powers, to gather his scattered parts and to reassemble them. A less common version of the Osiris legend has him merely dying or drowning. Throughout the night after his death, both Isis and Nephthys mourned over their brother. Thoth, and frequently Horus as well, assisted the two goddesses in the revitalization of Osiris. The means for bringing him back to life vary from one version to another.

Once revitalized, he usually appears as Wennefer, an epithet which perhaps means 'he who is always perfect.' When Osiris comes back to life, however, he never returns to the land of the living, but remains in the Underworld, the Duat, where he rules as King of Eternity and supreme judge of the dead. His resurrection was limited to the next world and so he passed on the rights of kingship to his son and avenger, Horus. Significantly, he is always depicted in a mummiform costume with only his head and arms free of his tight-fitting garment, unlike the deceased person when he is called 'the Osiris N,' who is shown as a normal human being. Osiris often wears the *atef*-crown, which is formed of the White Crown of Upper Egypt at its center, two ostrich feathers at the sides, and, normally, a pair of ram's horns at the base. He holds in his hands a flail and a shepherd's crook, two other attributes of kingship. Ironically, unlike noble deceased mortals such as Ani, Osiris is a chthonic being who never will 'go forth by day.'

This fragmentary narrative cannot do justice to the richness of the Osiris legend, reconstructed from hundreds of allusions scattered through the *BD*. The order and nature of events, as well as the participants, varies not only from chapter to chapter, but within different sections of some of the longer chapters. Some of these references were derived from moments and places in local Osiris festivals which varied from place to place in Egypt. However confusing it may seem, we must bear in mind that Egyptian religious texts tend to collect rather than edit; no attempt was made to reconcile contradictions or to form a continuous tale. It is not surprising that the numerous local traditions should have given birth to a wide range of phrases, words, and allusions.

Among the epithets of Osiris, such as 'the Weary One,' 'the Inert One,' or 'the Dismembered One,' we can see allusions to the death and murder of Osiris. While many of the epithets of Osiris have a euphemistic quality, there are several which refer explicitly to funerals, mummification, decay, putrefaction, and his corpse. But Osiris does not take things lying down, to make an apt pun. Instead, he is often said to hate or combat these aspects of his death. The places where the actions in the legend occur also vary: Nedyt, Abydos, Busiris, to mention just a few.

The Role of Re in the Afterlife

The very title of the *BD* in Egyptian, 'The Chapters of Going Forth by Day,' evokes an image of the soul emerging into the restorative rays of the sun's light after revival during the nighttime in the underworld. Most Egyptian mortuary texts are like the *BD* in this respect — they view the life beyond the grave as combining a chthonic Osirian afterlife with a solar or stellar afterlife. The Egyptian sense of balance meant that both aspects of life beyond the grave were necessary for the survival of the dead.

The chief celestial deity, the sun-god Re, was therefore a major figure in the Egyptian concepts of the afterlife, second only to Osiris. The influence of the priesthood of Re's chief city, Heliopolis, is felt almost everywhere in the *BD*. The worship of Re or another form of the sun was one of the most important of all Egyptian cults ever since the very beginning of recorded history. The belief in Re may have reached one peak in the Fifth Dynasty and then another peak approximately a millennium later during the reign of Akhenaten, but Re's influence on all religious thought was paramount throughout Egyptian history.

The influence of Re is manifested in the many ways in which both people and gods were associated with his name. A very high percentage of the personal names (the name in the first of the two cartouches) of the pharaohs were compounded with Re, and theophoric names containing Re were also quite common among non-royal individuals. Moreover, several of the most important gods in Egypt were 'solarized' to some extent, by syncretizing them with Re. The most outstanding example of such syncretisms was the chief deity and state god of the Middle and New Kingdoms, Amun-Re. Other important Re-syncretisms were Sobk-Re, Khnum-Re, Min-Re, and

Re-Horakhty. The basic concept underlying such combinations was to identify a local god with the chief creator deity. In the religious texts that adorned the Theban royal tombs of the New Kingdom, a new, important god of the afterlife makes his first appearance — Osiris-Re.

Although Re had a role in the afterlife from the earliest periods of Egyptian history, it was not until the Eighteenth Dynasty that belief in a solar afterlife became widespread among private individuals. At this time, there was also a change in Re's role in the next world, which no longer limited him to the celestial sphere. In the 'underworld books' that decorate the walls of the Theban royal tombs, the sun was given an important function in the nether regions that had previously been the territory of such gods as Osiris, Sokar, and Anubis. In the *BD*, Re had three major aspects: Re, Khepri, and Atum. Atum was seen as the aged Re who entered the *Duat* at sunset, travelling beneath the earth (from west to east) until his rebirth at dawn as Khepri, the morning sun.

While in the subterranean world, Re would awaken and rejuvenate the deserving dead. But his journey was fraught with difficulty and danger, since he faced continual opposition from his enemies, particularly the Apophis monster, the representative of the forces of chaos. The Apophis monster had many forms, but the most common in the *BD* and the royal afterlife books was an endless serpent. Since Re and his daughter Maat together represented the ordering principles of the universe, naturally Re must triumph over Apophis. The story of Re's struggle and eventual victory, however, has a disconcerting implication — it means that, in the next world, even a mighty deity such as Re could expect to battle against the forces of chaos and would need to recruit whatever aid he could enlist among the gods. These forces of chaos, who are identified with weariness, impotence, and weakness, seem to be some of the opponents of Osiris as well. In addition to sharing some enemies, Re and Osiris had similar roles in the cosmos. Re was seen as the ruler of eternity in its form *neheh,* while Osiris was the ruler of *djet*-eternity. The god with whom Re was most closely associated in mortuary literature was Horus, particularly in his form of Horakhty. Horus, of course, was also considered to be the son of Osiris and the god who avenged his father's death.

In the *BD* Re's importance is felt everywhere. It is significant that the Papyrus of Ani begins with a hymn to Re, directly before the hymn to Osiris Wennefer, a clear indication that these two gods are the main gods of the afterlife. Nonetheless, the main sphere of activity for Re in the *BD* remained the celestial realms. There the deceased, particularly in the form of an *akh*-soul, wished to enter Re's entourage, either to sail in one of his celestial barks or to join his allies in fighting off the encroachments of Apophis. The *BD* constantly identified the deceased with Re, and hoped that he or she, like Re, would be reborn daily at dawn.

EGYPTIAN CONCEPTS OF THE SOUL AND THE AFTERLIFE

For the Egyptians existence after death was first and foremost a series of transformations; we could borrow the name of Richard Strauss's great symphony *Death and Transfiguration* to describe their afterlife experience. But, unlike a symphonic work or a novel, the *BD* is primarily a collection of themes, not a consecutive narrative. Written from a polytheistic standpoint, it did not have to conform to a single editorial overview. Death may have been inevitable, but the course of events following it was not. As a result, we encounter a bewildering number of forms that human spirits can assume as they travel through the next world. Yet the deceased are not tourists, expected to move sequentially through a prescribed course of events. The dead had to adapt their forms constantly according to the circumstances. The notion of transformation in the next world was so

fundamental that it is the basis for the usual term for a mortuary prayer, *sakh*. This word is sometimes translated as 'glorification' or 'extollation,' but its literal meaning is 'that which transforms (one) into an *akh*,' referring to one of the forms of the soul. The *BD* uses several terms to describe the otherworld form of the deceased: *ba, ka, akh,* the Shadow (*shut*), and others. In addition to these spirit forms, the personality of the deceased could be embodied in the heart, *ib,* and the name, *ren*.

Coexisting with the predominant concept of the transformation of the human spirit in the next world was another line of thought, which envisioned life beyond the grave as essentially a continuation of earthly life. According to this viewpoint, the deceased could look forward to a rebirth after death. This is perhaps the reason for the repeated desire to regain the physical capabilities of a living person.

The Denial of Death

In the *Pyramid Texts* (§657e), phrases such as 'Rise up, O Pepi! You have not died' abound. Throughout Egyptian religious history such denials of death were a constant theme in mortuary literature. As in many other cultures, the Egyptian dead would be treated as if they were merely in a deep sleep and needed to awaken and go about their business. In the *BD* the denial of death appears mostly in the form of euphemism, beginning with the very name given to the funerary workshops where the *BD* and other funerary equipment were produced — *Per-Ankh,* 'The House of Life.' The idea behind such euphemisms involved more than not speaking ill of the dead: an effort was made not to even speak of a person's death at all. People who are called simply 'dead' in Egyptian religious contexts often seem to be the damned or unhappy dead. To mention death would be to confirm death's power over the departed; so we today euphemistically speak of 'the departed' or say that someone has 'passed away.' The *BD* seldom mentions that the papyrus owner has died, but rather calls him 'the Osiris N' and 'vindicated' even before his judgment has taken place. Similarly, other dead persons who had gone on before are often called 'those who are yonder.' Instead of speaking of dying, texts use phrases such as 'to moor' or 'to unite with the land.' The day of death became 'the day of mooring,' the 'good day,' or 'that day of come hither.' The last phrase, which appears in Chapter 17 and elsewhere, is particularly interesting since it contains the play on words between *mi* "come!" and *mut* "death," mentioned above. Another stratagem of avoidance was to refer to the dead by using a term for a form of the soul.

The denial of death was, nonetheless, not complete. There are many references to the methods to avoid 'dying a second time.' Most *BD* papyri begin with Chapter 1, whose vignette shows the procession to the grave and the ceremonies at the tomb door. This is one of the few times that we see the deceased as a dead person in his coffin. Most of the time the deceased person appears either as a living person, elegantly dressed, as if conducting official business, or as a human-headed *ba*-soul.

The Importance of the Corpse and the Tomb in the Afterlife

On a theoretical level, the enormous care an Egyptian took to acquire a completely outfitted tomb and the attention to the preservation of the body seem contradictory. If one wished to be transfigured in the next life, and the corpse was deemed to be merely temporary housing before moving on to more permanent and acceptable quarters, what was the reason for the vast expense on a tomb, its outfitting, and mummification? If one was ultimately judged on the content of one's character, why wouldn't a simple burial be sufficient?

Judging from the way they buried their dead even in prehistoric times, the Egyptians always clung to a fundamental belief in a connection between this world and the next. The most important nexus between these two worlds was the tomb, or a funerary stela, because commemoration of the dead on monuments was considered to be crucial to preservation in the afterlife. The lavishness of some burials suggests that the Egyptians believed that one could really 'take it with you.' If this thought sounds primitive to us, we should consider how well the Egyptian practice has actually worked. After all, because of tombs and grave goods, many ancient Egyptians, great and small alike, continue to live vividly in our imaginations.

All transformations of the soul began with a reawakening of the corpse in the tomb. Although there are numerous references to the corpse, even it does not seem void of life. Efforts are constantly maintained to preserve the body intact. Several chapters in the *BD* deal with the problems of preserving the corpse from beings who might decapitate the dead, or rip out the heart, and otherwise damage the corpse. In addition to the importance of maintaining the integrity of the physical remains, a sizable proportion of the tomb equipment of a wealthy Egyptian was intended to help in the transformation of the soul: statues, coffins, mummy cases, relief images, and the mummy case could all provide the soul with temporary resting places, particularly if the spirit should momentarily return to the world from time to time — a home away from home, so to speak. In addition, a tomb or a funerary stela served as the focus of the deceased's cult upon earth. Prayers and offerings to the departed were performed by a priest — often a male family member — before the offering slab. Food would be presented in support of the spirit in the next world. In return for such services, the priest would receive income from the funerary estate, usually an endowment in the form of land. Just as the living helped the dead, so too did the dead help the living.

On another level, the Egyptian mind probably related the lavishness of burial to the deceased's chances of achieving a successful afterlife. Like purchasing expensive seats at a political banquet, an elaborate burial was at least partially intended to buy the dead a higher level of access in the next life.

A major reason that we have problems understanding why the Egyptians considered tombs and the preservation of the physical remains so important for the afterlife is that the Egyptians and modern monotheists hold diametrically opposed views on the relationship between the corpse and the soul. The mummy-shape is used as a determinative in the Egyptian word *qi* "form, shape, nature." Notice the accumulation of meanings here — 'form, shape, nature.' The Egyptians conceived the preservation of the corpse as the preservation of the person's essence, while we look upon the body as a hollow shell, devoid of the soul which is the very essence of the personality that the corpse once housed. Unlike the view that appears from time to time among Christian ascetics, the Egyptians did not have the negative concept of the living physical body as a prison for the soul.

It is quite significant that sometimes the Egyptians used a mummiform figure as a determinative for their word *netjer* "god." The same word could on occasion simply mean 'dead person.' On the so-called Signs Papyrus, which dates to the end of ancient Egyptian history, the gloss for the *netjer*-sign is 'he is buried.' The mummiform image may appear in this context because the Egyptians thought that the corpse was in some manner divine. Not only was the deceased identified with Osiris, each part of his body was identified with a god. In fact, according to the *BD* and a great number of other Egyptian texts, the blessed dead become full-fledged members of the company of the gods.

We shall begin our description of the aspects of the human personality after death with two things which are not strictly speaking spirit forms, but which still can retain some of the vital force of being: the heart and the name.

The Heart

The *BD* was very concerned with the survival of the heart. Preservation and protection of the heart was the theme of several chapters (26–30B). The heart's importance was reflected in burial practices as well. Alone of the major organs, the heart was left inside the corpse. For additional protection a separate heart in the form of a heart scarab was often provided in case something should happen to the deceased's heart. The heart is mentioned frequently throughout the rest of the *BD* in a wide variety of contexts because, among other things, the heart was considered to be the seat of the emotions and the intellect. In short, the heart was the Egyptian equivalent of the mind, a notion perhaps best seen in the so-called Memphite Theology, in which Ptah creates the world through heart and tongue, i.e., intellect and *logos*. 'Heart and Tongue have power over all other organs.' In *The Tale of Sinuhe*, the phrase 'my heart was not in my body' seems to be a way of saying that the hero had completely lost his wits. The heart makes its most dramatic appearance in the key scene in the *BD* when it is weighed against the feather symbolizing *maat* at the judgment of the dead. The text of Chapter 30B, which relates to the judgment scene and was inscribed on the large heart scarabs mentioned above, indicates that the heart was felt to have a will and an existence of its own.

The Name

A dramatic illustration of the importance of commemoration and the name is the practice known by the Latin term *damnatio memoriae*. Sometimes, if a person fell into great disfavor, his tomb would be entered and his offending name and image would be effaced everywhere. This practice is a form of image magic discussed above. By damaging the name, the Egyptians felt that they were attacking an aspect of the human spirit. A particularly impressive instance of *damnatio memoriae* occurred in the reign of the 'Heretic Pharaoh' Akhenaten, who had the name of Amun, the chief deity of the land, erased from monuments all over Egypt. After his death, it seems that outraged Egyptians returned the favor, so to speak, and effaced Akhenaten's name wherever it was visible. Commemoration, particularly through one's name, was a very significant motif in Egyptian civilization. Name changes marked important changes in a king's career. As we can see in many places throughout the *BD,* one of the ways in which one could gain power over another being was through knowledge of its name. A telling phrase in this respect is the frequent statement which the deceased makes to threatening beings in the afterworld: 'I know you, I know your name.' The implication is clear — knowing the name of someone or something gives one a certain amount of control and power.

Transformation or Resurrection and Transmigration?

Whatever form the transformation of the spirit might eventually take, it involved a movement from this world into another realm of existence beyond. Contrary to a common misconception about their ideas of life after death, the Egyptians neither believed in the transmigration of the soul on earth in the Hindu or Pythagorean manner, nor hoped for a resurrection in this world. Rather, they believed in *transfiguration* in the next world. Except in dreams or visions, the dead did not reappear on earth. The notion of a ghost, a *revenant*, was foreign to the Egyptians.

Nonetheless, it is easy to see how some misconceptions about their afterlife beliefs arose. The Egyptians did not think that the dead would assume their transformations automatically — their active participation was required. To accomplish these changes, the *BD* contained various 'transformation spells,' giving the deceased the ability to change temporarily into a different form. These transformation spells, however, particularly the longer ones, are firmly connected with the afterlife. Such texts frequently mention Osiris, or other deities in an afterlife context. Any locations mentioned are usually parts of the afterworld: the heavens, the celestial and under-world barks of the gods, the Duat, the 'God's Domain' (*khert netjer*), the West, the Field of Reeds, etc. For the most part, it is the earth, the world of the living, which seems to be far removed and secondary. The *BD* is not invalid in this world, but a typical instance in which a chapter is effective on earth as well shows the priority of the two spheres distinctly. The end of Chapter 135 reads:

> *'As for him who knows this spell, he will be a worthy spirit in the realm of the dead, and he will not die again in the realm of the dead, and he will eat in the presence of Osiris. As for him who knows it on earth, he will be like Thoth, he will be worshipped by the living, he will not fall to the power of the king or the hot rage of Bastet, and he will proceed to a very happy old age.'*

The most important transformations a deceased person could expect to make, however, were spiritual in nature. These were the aspects of the afterlife personality which correspond most closely to our concepts of a soul: the *akh*, the *ka*, the *ba*, and the Shadow.

The Akh

If there was such a thing as a hierarchy of souls in the next world, the *akh* would probably be at the top. The term is frequently translated by Egyptologists as 'blessed dead.' Although *akh*-hood is the ultimate goal of the solar conception of the afterlife, there is little that we can say about this form of the soul. When depicted in Egyptian art, the *akh* only occasionally appears as a Created Ibis, the sign used in the hieroglyphic writing of the term. As with other forms of the soul, the *akh* is usually depicted as a mummy, the generalized form for gods. The word *akh* means something like 'the effective one' or 'the radiant one.' As an *akh* the deceased was truly transfigured, in an essentially incorporeal state, having become a stellar or solar being. Unlike the *ka* or the *ba*, the *akh* does not seem to have much to do with the earthly realm.

The Ka

Perhaps the most commonly mentioned form which the human personality could assume after death was the *ka*. It would be overhasty, however, to translate this complex word simply as 'the soul.' Unlike the *akh*, the *ka* could exist separately from an individual's physical being while he or she was still alive. In this manner the *ka* could function as the person's Doppelgänger. In Egyptian reliefs and paintings, the *ka* is shown standing protectively behind the king, acting as a sort of guardian angel in life. Examples of this sort have led to an interesting interpretation of the *ka* as the spiritual body within the physical body. The *ka* is also represented as a pair of upstretched arms, frequently placed on a standard or an offering stand and embracing food offerings. In the plural, the term *ka* can also mean 'food, victuals,' a frequent play on words. In this instance, the word play may actually derive from an innate quality of the *ka* — it was thought to represent the 'vital energy' of a human being. Without a *ka*, life was not possible, as shown by a common euphemism for death — 'to go to one's *ka*.' The *ka* was the force which vivifies statues and images.

Although humans seem to possess only one *ka*, some gods were thought to have many *ka*s. The sun-god and creator deity Re, for example, had no less than fourteen *ka*s. These *ka*s are personifications of qualities such as strength, prosperity, nour-ishment, glory, respect, effectiveness, permanence, creativity, magical power. The most important of Re's personifications

were Perception (Sia), Authoritative Utterance (Hu), and Rightful Order/Truth (Maat).

The Shadow

The notion that a person's personality or soul could be embodied in the insubstantial form of a shadow is not confined to Egypt — but appears in European culture as well, for example, in *Peter Schlemiels wundersame Geschichte*, a tale by the romantic German author Chammiso, and the opera *Die Frau ohne Schatten*. Several passages in the *BD* talk of the deceased moving 'with the swiftness of a shadow,' possibly a reference to the speed with which a shadow is created upon the ground. The shadow is connected, naturally enough, with the sun and daylight. In many *BD* papyri and tombs the deceased is depicted emerging from the tomb by day in shadow form, a thin, black, featureless silhouette of a person. The person in this form is, as we would put it, a mere shadow of his former existence, yet nonetheless still existing. Another form the shadow assumes in the *BD*, especially in connection with gods, is an ostrich-feather sun-shade, an object which would create a shadow.

The Ba

The *ba* flies around in the form of a bird (a Jabairu stork), usually shown with the human head of the deceased. We see Ani and his wife Tutu perched on top of a shrine-shaped tomb in this form, with human arms upraised in a gesture of prayer. This form of the *ba* recalls the creatures mentioned in a monument of Seti I which have the faces of humans and talk in an unintelligible language. With the *ba*, there appears to be a special emphasis on its mobility — one might say it is 'free as a bird.' Funerary stelae request that the *ba* be granted the power to 'go forth and (re)enter (the tomb) in the manner in which it did on earth.' Apparently it was the form in which a deceased person could expect to return temporarily to earth and receive offerings. The *ba* appears to have manifested itself only when the body containing it was deceased, at which point it assumed its normal form as a human-headed bird, often depicted flying above the coffin. Such representations recall the name of the god Buchis, whose Egyptian name *Ba-her-khat* means literally 'the *ba* on (or over) a dead body.' The *ba*, like the *ka*, was connected with the statue and other images, as described in a fascinating text of the Late Period that mentions its relationship with other aspects of the soul (S. Morenz, *Egyptian Religion*, pp. 151–152):

> 'Osiris . . . he appears as a spirit (*akh*) to join his form in his sanctuary. He comes flying out of the heavens like a sparrow-hawk with glittering plumage, and the *ba*s of the gods are together with him. He soars like a falcon to his chamber at Dendera. He beholds his sanctuary . . . In peace he moves into his magnificent chamber with the *ba*s of the gods which are about him. He sees his secret form painted at its place, his figure engraved upon the wall; then he enters his secret aspect, installs himself upon his image . . . The *ba*s take their places at his side.'

Hornung cites a similar example in his commentary on Chapter 89: 'See that my *ba* comes to me from wherever it may be . . . that it may see its body once more and alight on its mummy.' This quote is important because it connects the *ba* with the mummy. The vignette associated with this chapter is also significant, for this is the illustration of the *ba* bird hovering over the recumbent mummy. *Ba* images were placed in the tomb behind the corpse of the deceased, as shown in the vignette of Chapter 151.

Rebirth and Regeneration

The goddess Nut had a significant role as a mother goddess in Egyptian religion. According to the Heliopolitan cosmology, she and her consort Geb were the parents of Osiris, Isis, Seth, and Nephthys. In addition, Nut appears on a great number of papyri, coffin lids, and tomb ceilings as the mother of Re. The sun is shown entering her mouth and emerging again from between her thighs. The presence of this common scene on coffin lids confirms a point made repeatedly in a wide variety of textual sources — the coffin itself is conceived as a celestial womb from which one is reborn into the next world. This theme of rebirth is one of the reasons for the frequent identification of the deceased with Re. Here lay the hope not for mere rebirth, but for a *daily* rebirth in the manner of the sun. The sun entered the Duat in the evening as the aging, ram-headed Atum and reemerged transformed into the youthful Khepri at the following dawn. While in the underworld, the sun would be rejuvenated by the water of Nun. Not only the coffin, but statues and other images as well were seen as places where the soul of the dead could take substance and reemerge into the afterlife. More often than not, most of the deceased's statuary will show him or her not just reborn, but rejuvenated as well.

Initiation and Restricted Knowledge for the Afterlife

There is a vast corpus of non-Egyptological literature which claims that there is a hidden meaning to the *BD* and many other Egyptian religious texts. On the whole, Egyptologists have been quick to dismiss these theories, which are far too complex and numerous even to list here. Yet virtually all the same Egyptologists admit that not everyone in Egypt had equal access to or participation in their religion. This should hardly be surprising in a society in which only a very small percentage of the population was literate. Even within the priesthood, only a specialized priest, the 'lector priest,' handled the spoken and written elements of ritual.

All modern reconstructions of Egyptian temples and their priestly staffs have noted that not only were the temple complexes divided into public and restricted sections, but also that levels of access within the priesthood itself were differentiated. Only the upper level of the permanent priesthood seems to have been allowed to come in close contact with the divine image, for example. Such restrictions are encountered in a wide range of religions.

Restricted knowledge and secret, esoteric knowledge are not the same thing. The possibility that works such as the *BD* were intended for a select audience of initiates, however, seems to be a problematic proposition. First of all, although we may think of the *BD* as being a widespread document, it was accessible only to a small segment of Egyptian society. Knowledge was power, and the elite wished to keep that power among themselves. Chapter 137A of the *BD* says in its rubric: '*Beware greatly lest you do this before anyone except yourself, with your father or your son, because it is a great secret of the West, a secret image of the Netherworld . . .*' Given the hundreds and hundreds of *BD* papyri that were made, this plea for confidentiality does not quite ring true. Instead the desire was for secrets to be kept among a select few. In the same vein, it should be pointed out that once the king had been buried, the *Pyramid Texts* were definitely meant never to see the light of day again. Yet within a few generations that material, rewritten in the form of the *Coffin Texts,* was made available to a fairly wide audience among the nobility of the First Intermediate Period.

Much of the *BD* is frankly incomprehensible, even for experts. No amount of exegesis can explain many passages. Images and allusions follow one another with bewildering force and frequency, lacking thematic and logical connection. The same can be said for much of the rest of Egyptian mortuary literature. Yet the endurance of the well-administered Egyptian state and its monumental undertakings are proof that the Egyptians were a fundamentally rational people. Their Greek contemporaries assure us that the Egyptians' religion was deeply imbued with profound theological doctrines.

This contrast between the seeming nonsense of much of the *BD* and virtually everything else we know about these matter-of-fact, down-to-earth people has led to a belief that the *BD* and other Egyptian mortuary texts must have a hidden meaning, perhaps only known to a few initiates among the priesthood. Certainly this would be in keeping with later developments in early Egyptian Christianity, which had a long struggle with esoteric Gnostic heresies within its ranks.

The quote from Chapter 137A above illustrates an important aspect of Egyptian views of the afterlife. Survival and success in both this and the next world required special, often hidden, knowledge. Indeed, one of the outstanding features of the next world was its secret aspects. Consequently, one of the most frequently encountered themes in all Egyptian mortuary literature is the deceased's assertion of belonging to a select group in the afterlife. This gives rise to a feeling that one had to be *initiated* into the world of the dead, as if one were becoming a member of a secret society in the cosmic sphere. The motif of initiation is best illustrated by a frequent type of obstacle that the deceased faces in the *BD,* namely gaining the right of entry to a place. In this situation, the dead can overcome the difficulty only by displaying knowledge: addressing a fearsome gatekeeper by his bizarre name, answering a god's mysterious question with an equally cryptic answer, alluding to obscure events in the mythological past. After providing the correct answer and thereby showing that he or she was actually one of the gods, the deceased is allowed to proceed. Thus we are left with the paradoxical result of a secret society whose inner workings are known to anyone with the resources to obtain a *BD*.

The Judgment of the Dead

Egyptian biographies contained fulsome praise of the dead and proclaimed their charitable deeds on behalf of the poor and weak. Underlying all such protestations of virtue was a strong and consistent belief that people would be judged after death according to their deeds in this life. This meant that the Egyptian concepts of the afterlife were deeply imbued with a moral sense. The fear of that final judgment haunted Egyptian mortuary literature. Since probably no Egyptian entered the next world entirely spotless, one of the *BD*'s purposes was to magically purge the deceased of sin. In this respect, however, it is only fair to remember that in the perilous environment of the beyond, there were many dangers which could threaten the gods as well as the purest of souls. At the same time it is also notable that the most 'magical' parts of the *BD* sometimes also contain numerous assertions that the deceased is 'true-of-voice' (*ma'a-kheru*) and has been found worthy at the Weighing of the Heart.

The first indications of a belief in a divine judgment for one's lifetime deeds appear in a genre of Old Kingdom tomb inscriptions, warning those who might violate the purity of the tomb that 'the god will judge it against him,' or 'it will be judged against him,' or, using a more colorful threat, 'Thoth will wring his neck like a duck.' It is unclear, though, whether the revenge will come in this life or the next. Definite references to a tribunal in the afterlife appear as early as the *Coffin Texts*. At the time the *BD* became the chief mortuary text, the judgment was seen as the key event of the passage into the next existence. As we pointed out above, the most important scene in the majority of *BD* papyri was the Weighing of the Heart before Osiris and the Great Council of Gods 'who hear cases.'

Damnation and Punishment

The very presence of Ammit, 'the Swallower of the Dead,' at the base of the scales shows that the Egyptians believed in some form of damnation. Yet there was a constant threat that harm could befall even pure and innocent souls in the next world. One of the purposes of Egyptian mortuary literature was to give the dead the information necessary to steer his or her way past such dangers. Just as eternal life took many forms in the beyond, so did eternal punishment.

The Egyptians could be as sadistically imaginative as any hellfire-and-brimstone preacher when it came to the eternal punishment of evildoers. Vignettes and fearsome names of gods and other supernatural beings reveal some of the fates which could befall the condemned. Sometimes they were to suffer forms of earthly capital punishment and were tortured, decapitated, or burned in fiery pits. More often the damned are treated like sacrificial animals and slaughtered with knives, dismembered, their blood drained away; they could be cooked and eaten by such creatures as Ammit. But destruction need not be so gory to be ominous and terrifying. Souls could be consigned to a lightless and watery limbo — presumably the waters of Nun — to float there forever as the 'Drowned Ones.' These fates can be summarized in the expression 'to die a second death,' or become nonexistent, thus losing all hope of eternal life.

One of the more disturbing aspects of the next world was the constant presence of the irrational, which meant that the afterlife was threatened by an element of caprice and randomness. For this reason, magic was needed in addition to the more traditional means of insuring one's fate through purity and pious behavior before the gods. If the gods did not behave the way they should, then it was necessary to provide the soul with esoteric knowledge, including both defensive and offensive magic.

The Ani Papyrus

PLATE I

The first vignette of the papyrus shows Ani as a living man; yet, since he is given the epithets 'the Osiris' and 'vindicated' (lit. 'true-of-voice') in the accompanying text, he is unquestionably considered to be deceased and in the next world. Ani and Tutu stand before two offering-stands and gesture respectfully toward Re-Osiris in the first vignette of Plate 2 Ani appears here as he does in nearly every other scene in the papyrus, alive and nattily dressed in his best official linens; with his little chin beard and elaborate fringed wig, he could change into modern clothes and walk the streets of Greenwich Village, looking very much *au courant*. Ani's posture, with both arms bent slightly and raised in front, is the gesture of prayer. This first vignette shows a fair amount of damage, which is to be expected since it would have been the outermost part of the papyrus roll on which Ani's *BD* was written.

A stick figure of a man in more or less the same posture as Ani appears at the top of the right-hand column of the hieroglyphic text on the plate. (The canonical direction in which Egyptian papyri were written was from right to left, against the direction in which the signs face.) This sign is one of the determinatives (signs indicating meaning) belonging to the verb *dua* "to pray to, worship" in the rubric to the Hymn to Re that the vignette accompanies: 'Worship of Re when he rises in the eastern horizon of the sky.' Ani in the vignette has thus adopted the posture of the introductory verb in the text. Egyptian art and language constantly interlock in this fashion. Indeed one of the most striking characteristics of Egyptian culture is that it made no distinction between art and language. Although the Egyptian script was not picture writing in the true sense of the phrase, Egyptian was written pictorially.

Ani's wife, Tutu, is outfitted equally lavishly. On her head she wears a cone of scented fat that women and men used at banquets and other indoor ceremonial affairs where it was necessary to perfume the body. An open flower has been fixed into the cone for decoration. She carries a *menat* in one hand and brandishes a sistrum in the other, two instruments which made a rattling, rustling sound and were used to accompany ritual singing and recitations. Tutu is probably making music as her husband recites this hymn, inasmuch as the primary roles of women in Egyptian religious ceremonies were to sing and provide musical accompaniment. Whether Tutu was alive or dead at the time the papyrus was prepared is not absolutely certain. However the fact that her name, in the captions, is never followed by the epithet 'vindicated' indicates that she was still alive, as does her appearance mourning her husband in the vignette for Chapter 1 (Plates 5–6). Although this papyrus was prepared primarily for Ani, it was probably intended to assist Tutu in her afterlife as well, in view of the prominent role Egyptian women played in decorating their husbands' tombs.

The hymn stresses two of the most important goals of the entire *BD:* to be accepted into the presence of Osiris, where the judgment would take place, and ultimately to join Re in his various sun barks, in order to accompany the god there forever. Osiris was the predominant deity of the *Duat,* the netherworld, but a stellar and solar afterlife in the company of Re was the more desirable form of eternal life. The appearance of a sun-hymn as the first text in Ani's papyrus is consonant with the hope embodied in the very title of the *BD,* 'Book of Going Forth by Day.'

The scene to the right of the hymn belongs to a genre of similar scenes which scholars in the early days of study of the BD misnamed 'Chapter 16,' despite the fact that the pictures were never accompanied by text. What this 'chapter' has actually proved to be is an additional vignette for hymns to the rising sun. Yet the designation of this elaborate picture as a chapter is not entirely erroneous since the iconography of such vignettes is so rich that they clearly were intended to convey additional theological concepts concerning the rising sun.

An elongated and arched form of the sign *pet* "sky" stretches across the top of the entire vignette. The same blue-green sign is found in several other parts of the papyrus — for example, above the two lions in Chapter 17 (Plate 7) and underneath the solar barks throughout the papyrus. Directly beneath this is a personified sign for 'life,' the well-known *ankh,* whose two arms seem to be lifting the large red disk of the sun into the sky above. The *ankh* stands upon a *djed*-pillar. The disk, *ankh,* and *djed*-pillar are combined into a motif, whose origin and meaning have not been satisfactorily explained, associated with the god Osiris. As a word the motif means 'endurance,' and therefore was extensively used as an allegorical figure, especially on amulets. In effect, the tripartite motif is a form of Osiris-Re, the syncretized deity who combines the chthonic and celestial aspects of the afterlife. Significantly, the text to the right of this vignette is a hymn to Osiris Wennefer, so that the scene is enclosed by praises to Osiris-Re's components. Flanking the Osiris-Re motif are the goddesses Isis (left) and Nephthys (right), who are both shown in the posture of adoration and squatting upon the sign *nub* "gold". Like most Egyptian goddesses, they are distinguishable only by the attributes (really their names in hieroglyphs) that they wear on their heads. The 'gold' signs are themselves resting upon a reed mat. Beneath the mat and flanking it is a form of the sign for 'mountain' (*dju*). Thus, while showing the temporary dissolution of the syncretized Osiris-Re into his component deities, the scene illustrates the beginning of the sun's daily journey through the sky, when it emerges out of the desert horizon after its nighttime journey underneath the earth and through the Duat. The entire vignette is framed by the image of the rolling desert on which stand six baboons worshipping the sun. Other variants of the same vignette show the complete cycle in one scene, with the sun being received into the arms of a goddess representing the underworld.

PLATE 2

This plate displays the vignette and text of the Hymn to Osiris Wennefer. Tutu and Ani are once again shown before two stands heaped with offerings being presented to Osiris. The couple is shown worshipping in the usual manner. Ani stands with his arms bent in prayer while Tutu accompanies him with the rattling sounds of the *menat* and the sistrum. The hymn is rather direct in its language and relatively free of the obscurities which occur in so much of the *BD;* it describes Osiris by his many epithets and qualities, and closes with a number of wishes on Ani's behalf.

PLATE 3

The critical moment of Ani's *BD,* the Judgment of the Dead, occurs in Plate 3, directly following the Hymn to Osiris Wennefer in the preceding plate. Normally Chapter 125, the 'Negative Confession,' is associated with this scene. In this papyrus, however, that chapter does not occur until much further on in the last third of the roll (Plate 31), where it incorporates a miniature version of the weighing scene. In Plate 3 we find instead Chapter 30B, written in the group of vertical columns beginning above and to the left of the scales and continuing over the figures of Ani and Tutu. Chapter 30B is often called the 'Heart Scarab' spell because it is known primarily as the text which appears on large funerary scarab-shaped amulets which were placed within the mummy bandages near the heart. Many *BD* papyri contain a longer version of this chapter, but the short form is the one used in Ani's papyrus. On the right side of the plate appears a speech of the Great Ennead, a speech by Thoth, and a brief speech by Anubis.

The dramatic focus of the entire vignette is on the scales in the center, with Ani's heart on the left pan and the feather of *maat* "Truth, Rightful Order" standing upright on the right pan. Adorning the top of the scales is a small image of a baboon, a form of the god Thoth, who is associated in the afterlife with the judgment of the dead. Thoth himself, in his usual ibis-headed form, stands to the right of the activity. He wears a white sash diagonally across his chest, indicating that he is assuming the role of lector priest, the official who reads (and writes) the rituals. In his hands he holds the tools of his (and Ani's) scribal trade, a reed brush and a scribal palette. He is ready to record the results of Ani's judgment.

In the event that Ani should be found wanting, his soul will be fed to the almost humorously grotesque, composite beast waiting with a dog-like eagerness on a reed mat behind Thoth. Although her name does not appear in the captions, we know from hundreds of other examples that this is Ammit, whose name means 'she who swallows the dead.' However, a homophonous verb *am* means 'to know,' which adds another dimension to Ammit's character. The beast has the head of a crocodile and wears the tricolored wig-cover (*nemes* headdress), an attribute of divinity often worn by divine beings in Egyptian art. The wig-cover is an effective device for joining head and body on composite creatures, for instance the animal-headed anthropoid deities such as Thoth or Anubis in this same scene. Ammit's forefront is that of a lioness, while her hindquarters are those of a hippopotamus. We need not take her tripartite nature literally, since the number three is often merely a way of conveying plurality in Egyptian language and iconography.

Kneeling at the base of the scales is the jackal-headed Anubis, the god of the dead and of embalming, acting here as the Guardian of the Scales, another of his important functions. There is something almost frightening about his red eye, as he steadies the right-hand pan with one hand and the plumb bob with the other. In the small text above his head, he alerts the expectant onlookers to pay attention to the decision of the scales and the plumb bob. On his torso he wears a strapped vest decorated with a fish-scale pattern. Gods are shown in such archaic and unfashionable garments as a way of indicating their great antiquity.

Immediately to the left of the base of the scales stands the figure of Shai, one of the three personifications of what we would call 'Fate.' Above him is a small shrine surmounted by a rectangular object with a woman's head. This is Meskhenet, the personification of the birth-brick. Egyptian women gave birth squatting over two bricks, so Meskhenet represented the place where a person first touched the earth; thus she is another aspect of Fate. Standing behind Shai is a pair of female figures who, according to the caption above them, are Meskhenet (again) and Renenutet, a third aspect of Fate. The distinction between these three forms of Fate is not really important for understanding their presence here. Simply put, they convey the message that a person's fate and fortune would be present at this portentous moment of the afterlife. Whether they merely serve as witnesses, or affect the turn of events in some manner, is unclear. The group of figures by the scale is completed by the bird-like form of Ani's *ba* perched on a shrine watching the event on which his future literally balanced. Ani thus appears twice here, once in a human form and once in a spiritual form. Both are nevertheless merely different aspects of the same deceased Ani.

The 'Great Tribunal' mentioned in Chapter 30B is shown in the upper register which runs almost the entire length of the scene. The eleven seated mummiform figures are Re and a modified version of the Great Ennead in the Heliopolis creation myth, minus Osiris and his evil brother Seth. Moving from right to left we see: Re-in-the-Midst-of-his-Bark, Atum, Shu, Tefnut, Geb, Nut-Mistress-of-the-Sky, Isis and Nephthys, Horus the Great God, Hathor-Mistress-of-the-West, and finally Hu (Authoritative Utterance) and Sia (Perception). The last two deities are important manifestations of the sun-god Re. Each deity clasps a *was*-scepter in front, symbolizing power and good fortune. Osiris, as the ruler of the Duat, appears on the continuation of this scene in the next plate.

Ani and Tutu bow in respectful anticipation at the left of the entire scene. As in the previous vignettes, Ani appears as a living man, dressed and adorned in a fine costume. His hand-on-shoulder gesture and slight bow are found in scenes where officials pay their respect to superiors. Tutu is equally well outfitted and carries the sistrum in her hand.

Chapter 30B is concerned with pacifying the heart, so that it will not act as a witness against Ani in the weighing ceremony. The apparent intent of the text was to prevent the heart from blurting out the sins which the deceased had committed on earth, but at the same time to dissuade the heart from telling falsehoods. It is unclear why the heart would wish to sabotage the dead, yet the afterworld was a place where the irrational was a commonplace occurrence. And it is, after all, our irrational subconscious that leads us to blurt out hidden feelings in slips of the tongue.

Some versions of this text ascribe its authorship to one of the great sages of Egyptian history, Prince Hordedef, the son of Mycerinos, the Fourth Dynasty monarch who built the smallest of the Great Pyramids at Giza. This attribution is highly suspect, since scarabs of any form are not attested until the First Intermediate Period, and Heart Scarabs are not found until the Seventeenth Dynasty. The Egyptians frequently attempted to lend their innovations borrowed glory by means of an invented connection with honored individuals of the past.

PLATE 4

Now that Ani has been found vindicated, he is introduced to Osiris Wennefer by the falcon-headed Horsiese, 'Horus-son-of-

Isis.' One hopes that this introduction will go smoothly because, in an amusingly ironic touch, the copyist has misspelled Ani's name as 'Ai' here. Horsiese makes the important announcement that 'Osiris Ani' has been vindicated on the scales before the gods. Although Ani has been judged favorably, there are many things that can go wrong in the next world before he can join Re in the sun-bark, and most of the remaining parts of the *BD* are provided to protect Ani against the chaotic forces in the beyond.

Even something as seemingly simple as the representation of Horsiese is actually iconographically rich. Horsiese is shown wearing the *pshent,* the Double Crown, which combines the White Crown of Upper Egypt with the Red Crown of Lower Egypt. The god raises his hand in greeting before the enthroned Osiris, assuming the same posture as is found in the determinative for the verb *nis* "to call, to summon." The god's kilt, with its yellow pleating and white front panel, has been tightened about his waist by means of the *tiyet* or 'Isis-knot,' probably derived from the *ankh.* A bull's tail, an indication of both fertility and great physical power, has been fastened at the back of the god's elaborate kilt. The kilt, crowns, and bull's tail are all standard royal regalia in the earthly realm.

The middle scene depicts Ani kneeling respectfully on a reed mat before Osiris in his booth and wearing a type of white wig that officials of the Ramesside period wear from time to time. The wand he holds upright in his hand is a visual pun, for not only is it a symbol of official status in Egypt and a common hieroglyphic sign meaning 'power' or 'direct,' but it can also represent the verb 'to offer,' the very activity Ani is performing here. He is seated amid an extensive array of offerings, many of which are mentioned in the standard offering formula of Ani's time: 'An offering which the King gives Osiris . . . consisting of bread and beer, oxen and fowl, clothes and alabaster . . .' We can see an ox's foreleg, a plucked and roasted duck, tall jars of unguents, perfumes, and — as in every offering scene — bouquets of flowers, especially lilies and lotuses. These last two flowers belong to the vast rebirth imagery of the Egyptians, whence their popularity as a decorative motif in mortuary contexts.

The most important and most complex section in the whole vignette is the depiction of the enthroned Osiris. The kiosk in which Osiris sits has green-striped walls in the shape of the *Per-wer,* the archaic shrine of Lower Egypt. The shape of this shrine is also a common sarcophagus form, a clearer example of which can be seen in Plate 8. This would certainly be a fitting place for the lord of the underworld. Osiris's audience chamber is surmounted by the recumbent mummiform figure of the hawk-headed god Sokar, originally the chief god of the vast Old Kingdom necropolis at Saqqara and a major deity of the Egyptian afterlife. During the New Kingdom, Sokar plays an important role in the royal underworld books illustrating the nighttime journey of the sun, and perhaps his presence here is an allusion to that aspect of the underworld. Sokar sits amid an array of rising cobras which protect the shrine.

Osiris sits on a seat over whose low backrest a piece of red cloth has been draped as a cushion. The sides are decorated to resemble a shrine of the type that appears on Plate 8 in the vignette to Chapter 17. The two door panels may indicate that Osiris's throne represents the gateway to the Duat. The pattern on the garment which Osiris wears may represent fish scales, a possible reference to the myth in which Osiris drowns and gets eaten by a fish.

Before the god are numerous symbols of preservation of the corpse and of rejuvenation in the next world. Immediately in front of Osiris is a lotus, a common symbol of rebirth, upon which the mummiform Four Sons of Horus stand. Between the lotus and the pillar hangs the *imyut,* an enigmatic object in the shape of a hanging, headless goat skin. The two deities

attending Osiris are Isis and Nephthys, who mourned him at his death and were instrumental in reviving him.

PLATES 5–6

Chapter 1, which appears on Plates 5 and 6, is one of the longest chapters, and certainly among the most popular judging from the large number of exemplars preserved in both papyri and tombs. We shall take this opportunity to introduce many issues and themes fundamental to the rest of the *BD.* This chapter, significantly, was one of those most frequently found on contemporary tomb walls. It was perhaps a guarantee that the funeral had been properly performed. One unusual hieratic exemplar of this chapter, found on the verso of a papyrus fragment of the Eighteenth or Nineteenth Dynasty, contains red 'verse-points,' which are normally associated with literary texts and other didactic material; this suggests that Chapter 1 may have even been used to train scribes.

The subtle communication between imagery and text is characteristic of ancient Egyptian culture. Sometimes the connection between text and image has an allusive character, and the present case has an interesting illustration of this phenomenon in the direction in which the text runs. Instead of writing the columns from right to left, which is the normal direction of Egyptian writing, the columns are written from left to right, yet the signs still face right. The term for this backwards orientation is 'retrograde.' The phenomenon of retrograde texts in the *BD* has long intrigued scholars. It is an arrangement encountered in material other than Egyptian mortuary literature, but is rather rare. One explanation for retrograde writing is that the left-to-right orientation signified that the deceased would be both moving and directed toward the West, the land of the dead — for according to the Egyptian sense of direction, the West was 'right.' The orientation of the columns of text thus corresponds to the left-to-right progression of the vignettes across the top of the papyrus roll. Unfortunately, since there is quite a bit of inconsistency in the writing direction of many papyri, such as Ani's *BD,* this explanation is not entirely satisfactory. Indeed, there are numerous *BDs* in which there is no retrograde writing. As we shall see in several places in other plates, retrograde writing could lead to various kinds of blunders by the copyists, especially since most of them were naturally more used to writing in the canonical right-to-left direction.

The length of Chapter 1 meant that the accompanying illustration, whether it appeared on a papyrus or a tomb wall, was usually extensive and detailed. In tombs the *BD* vignettes appear on a yellow background which imitated the color of aged papyrus, so that the walls would look like an old papyrus. The subject matter here is the funeral ceremony, which consisted of several stages and dramatic moments and offered artists a rare occasion for a narrative presentation. The ultimate purpose of the funeral was to place the intact corpse in the tomb so that it would be revitalized in the afterlife. On another level, an Egyptian funeral was a ritualization of some of the mythological events that took place when Osiris was murdered, mourned, and buried; several events in the 'passion of Osiris' are mentioned in the text. In the 'Opening of the Mouth' ceremony shown at the end of the vignette (Plate 6), the theme was the revitalization of the body. The chapter which follows this one, Chapter 22, may be more directly associated with that ceremony, but its performance is shown only here and in the vignette accompanying Chapter 23 in Plate 15.

From the standpoint of its dramatic composition, the vignette is divisible into four unequal portions. The largest section appears almost in the center of the entire vignette. On each side of the major scene are two smaller sections, which are divided into two registers. At the right side of the whole scene appears the final portion, accounting for about a quarter of the entire length. The action, which moves from left to right, narrates and summarizes Ani's burial. Although the vignette is idealized, the veracity of the events and objects portrayed in it has been confirmed by archaeological finds in several tombs of the New Kingdom, particularly the intact burial of the architect Kha, now on view in the Turin Museum. The scene, also vividly and poignantly described in the Harpers' Songs, is worth describing in detail because several of the items and activities shown here reappear in later chapters of the *BD*.

The double register at the beginning of the vignette (Plate 5) represents the tail end of the funeral cortege. At the top we see four simply dressed men, probably servants, carrying various things to be placed in the tomb shown at the far right side of the vignette (Plate 6): the tools of Ani's profession, a scribe's palette and document case; a chair; a bed; his walking-stick; a *tiyet* (or Isis-knot) and a *djed*-pillar, two amulets representing protection and endurance in the afterlife. In the lower register appear important individuals, some of Ani's mourners to judge from their costumes. These people attend to a large box surmounted by a black figure of Anubis, the god of death and mummification. This chest holds the four canopic jars containing Ani's internal organs, which were removed from his body during the process of embalming and mummification. The sides of this chest are decorated with a pattern of inlaid *djed*- and *tiyet*-signs. An elaborate example of such a chest was in fact found in the tomb of King Tutankhamun.

Next we see the main part of the procession. The focus of this section, indeed of the entirety of Plates 5–6, is the bier with Ani's mummiform coffin resting on a ceremonial boat with raised prow and stern, imitating the barks on which gods travel. Beside this kneels Ani's grieving widow Tutu, who squats bare-breasted on the runners of the sledge. The chief male mourners follow behind in their elegant clothes, showing their sorrow. The coffin, its surmounting shrine, the mourning Tutu, and the boat have all been placed on a sledge which is being dragged toward the tomb, as has the canopic chest following behind. Just as Osiris's body had sailed to his final resting place, so too would Ani's. The Osirian connection is further emphasized by the presence of the two small flanking mummiform figures of Isis and Nephthys, who are sometimes represented as two kites. Even though the procession moved across the sandy ground, the coffin would then be theoretically travelling by water. Here we can see a fine example of the Egyptian love for *symbolic* reenactment of the mythological past which underlies their rituals. The bouquets of lotus flowers festooning both the bier and the canopic chest represent wishes for rebirth.

Directly in front of the sledge appears a priest who wears a panther-skin cloak over his garment. As he walks, he turns slightly backwards to offer incense in a typical arm-shaped censer and to make a libation offering. Before him are four men who guide the tow-rope and the four oxen pulling the bier along. Finally, at the very head of the procession (Plate 6) are three men carrying various grave goods as they arrive at the tomb site. Looking ahead, we can see that all these objects would be piled up outside the tomb during the rituals performed at the door.

The group of women, some of whom kneel upon the ground in bereavement, are Ani's female mourners who have been waiting there for the arrival of the cortege. They have bared their breasts in a characteristic attitude of mourning, and unlike the more stoic men, their faces are tear-streaked. In front of this group the final ceremonies outside the tomb door are shown. As a wealthy man, Ani seems to have been able to afford the services of three priests. One, a lector priest, holds a roll of papyrus before him as he recites various prayers and ritual texts. The two priests in panther skins are performing the 'Opening of the Mouth' ceremony. During this rite various objects are placed at or struck against the head of the coffin, thus magically opening and restoring the deceased's mouth, eyes, and ears to use in the afterlife. This was how the god

Thoth had restored Osiris. Thus Ani would be able to respond confidently with all the capabilities of a living man at the weighing of his soul (which has already been shown in Plate 3) and other events of the afterlife. Many papyri illustrate a larger number of the implements of the ritual at this point. One of the more commonly depicted objects employed in the Opening of the Mouth was a freshly severed foreleg of a calf. The leg's removal is depicted in the poignant scene behind the officiating priests. The mutilated and bleeding calf is shown bleating with its distressed mother behind it.

Although one might expect that some of the 'Opening of the Mouth' ceremony would appear in the text below, it does not. Instead, a series of allusions to the ritual's desired effects appears at the end of Chapter 1. Other papyri contain several chapters specifically connected with the ritual, but Ani's contains only Chapter 22. The ritual objects were of great importance to the restoration of the dead, and so play a constantly recurring role in the *BD*.

At the far right of the vignette (Plate 6) stands the tomb pylon and the tomb itself surmounted by a pyramid, a type of monument known to have existed at Deir el-Medineh during the Nineteenth Dynasty (roughly contemporaneous with Ani). In the final scene of the funeral, Tutu pays her last respects as the coffin is grasped from behind by a priest in the guise of Anubis, shortly before it is placed in its final resting place. At the very end of the papyrus, this same tomb is shown again under much more happy, triumphant circumstances.

The text of Chapter 1 introduces us to one of the central problems of interpreting Egyptian religious material — the often puzzling relationship between text and illustration. The entire scene is an abridged representation of Ani's funeral, leading us to believe that the text would describe his burial ritual. The accompanying text, however, alludes to the mythical events surrounding the death, dismemberment, and burial of Osiris, followed by his eventual vindication chiefly through the aid of Horus and Thoth, who have a major role in the *BD* as the defenders of Osiris and, by extension, of the dead in general.

Like most rituals in Egypt, one essential function of a funeral was to reenact mythical and allegorical events through ceremony. The relationship between myth, symbol, and ritual in Egyptian religion is problematic. Are ceremonies such as the Opening of the Mouth the rendering of myth into ritual, or are myths merely stories created to explain ritual activity? This may be a riddle with no single solution in any culture. Within the context of the *BD,* this unanswerable question at least offers an explanation of why many passages in Egyptian funerary literature appear to be non sequiturs.

As complicated as the events in this text may seem, the overall theme is rather simple: by identifying himself with those who defended Osiris and assisted in his burial, revival, and final vindication, the deceased hopes that the same events will transpire after his funeral. The frequent references to Osiris and his dismembered body reflect the concern for corporeal integrity in the next world. The deceased clearly hoped that his mummy would remain intact, and if not, that it would be restored magically as the corpse of Osiris was. At the close of the chapter, the deceased expresses the wish that his form in the afterlife might be capable of all the physical activities of earthly existence. Some versions of the chapter also include the wish to be capable of intercourse and hence to be fertile in the next world.

With the words '*Here begin the spells of going out into the day* . . .' (Plate 5, rubric to Chapter 1), the parts of the *BD* concerned with protecting Ani in his post-mortem life begin. Because of its great complexity and careless editing by the Egyptians themselves, modern scholars have sometimes felt that the *BD* was merely a motley collection of magical spells. The rubric to this chapter, however, shows that the Egyptians felt that certain chapters had a thematic consistency and should be grouped together. This rubric is more than the title to Chapter 1 — it served as the heading for the entire *BD*. The full Egyptian name for this collection was '*(The chapters of) going forth by day and by night . . . to the place he might desire to be.*' It is significant that the Egyptian title does not say 'coming forth by day,' for the work was written from the viewpoint of the deceased, not of the living.

It is typically Egyptian that the dead should be styled as 'the Osiris N' and as Osiris's rescuer simultaneously. The dead hoped not to remain in the tomb and the Osirian underworld, but rather to travel about freely as an *akh,* a spiritual form associated particularly with the solar, celestial aspects of the afterlife. Since the world after death was essentially a confrontation with the forces of nonexistence and, therefore, of irrationality, the *Book of Going Forth by Day* was conceived as a guide to aid the deceased to deal with the dangers of the afterlife *that even the gods Osiris and Re had to thwart.* One might say that the whole purpose of the *BD* is encapsulated in the rubric of this spell. One of the goals of this commentary is to indicate the rational basis that the Egyptians saw in the world beyond the grave.

'Bull of the West' (Chapter 1, first paragraph) is an epithet of Osiris, attested in several other places in the *BD*. Osiris and his brother Seth were the children of Nut, the goddess of the sky, and Geb, the god of the earth. Underlying these lines is the process of identification of the deceased with various gods and with the myth of the restoration of Osiris. To those raised in the Judeo-Christian or Islamic traditions, such identifications seem to be terribly presumptuous, virtually blasphemies, until one realizes that the Egyptians assumed such divine roles in order that mythical history would repeat itself for their benefit. The assumption of such roles was not confined to the afterlife. We know from several sources, particularly the stela of a twelfth-dynasty official named Ikhernofret, that a 'Passion Play' of Osiris was performed at Abydos, that god's chief city. Ikhernofret informs us that during this festival he was honored to act out the role of some of the gods in addition to the usual priestly functions of attendance on Osiris's cult statue. The gods, via the priests playing their parts, thus had an active role in Egyptian festivals, similar to the one performed by the priest in the guise of Anubis in the vignette to the present chapter.

It is most significant that Chapter 1 should close with the lines '. . . may no fault be found in him, for the balance is voided of his misdoings,' an explicit reference to the judgment scene in Plate 3. These words are a subtle indication that the *BD* should not be dismissed as a collection of magical spells without moral content. This phrase reminds the gods that Ani has been found morally satisfactory at the weighing of his heart, and therefore should not be denied his rights in the afterlife.

Although the vignette for Plates 5–6 shows only the burial ceremony and, as is standard, is accompanied by Chapter 1, three other texts appear here as well: Chapter 22, followed by Chapter 21 and the rubric normally connected with Chapter 72. The scribe writing in the text for Chapter 1 came to the end of the spell nearly at the end of the fourteenth column from the left, close to the middle of the vignette. With so much space remaining on the sheet, he began writing in the rubricized title to Chapter 22, filling out the line, rather than beginning the chapter at the top of the following column, as is usually done.

Chapters 22 and 21 are both concerned with restoring the deceased's mouth in the God's Domain. In order to survive in the next world, the deceased would need his mouth to eat, drink, and breathe, just as he had done on earth. Equally important, but easily overlooked, would be the ability to speak, mentioned at the end of Chapter 21. The *BD* is intended primarily as an oral work and its texts were effective only when read aloud. The frequent rubricized phrases '*He says:*' or '*Words spoken by . . .*' emphasizes throughout the *BD* that the deceased needed to recite the texts in it.

The scribe chose to end the plate with the terminal rubric of Chapter 72. This choice is puzzling on grounds of consistency, especially since neither the text of the chapter nor the accompanying title appears here. This chapter, furthermore, generally has no relationship to any of the three other chapters accompanying the vignette. If we consider the words of this rubric, however, its text was quite appropriate since its purpose was clearly to ensure that the deceased would have the magical means to acquire the necessary food and drink in the afterworld. The text also states that if Ani knew this chapter *before* his death ('on earth') it would guarantee his success in the beyond. Although several chapters are said to have validity on earth as well as in the God's Domain, similar references to the afterlife effectiveness of information acquired while alive are quite rare in the *BD*.

PLATES 7–10

When it is included in a papyrus, Chapter 17 usually is one of the longest and most profusely illustrated of all the chapters of the *BD*. This is true of the Ani Papyrus, even though its version of Chapter 17 is missing approximately one-third of a hypothetical complete text. In a sense this chapter functions as a generalized description of the *BD*. These pictures serve that purpose better than the text and introduce many iconographic elements seen elsewhere in the *BD*. Chapter 17 was intended to be an introduction to many of the important features of the next world in both words and pictures. There seems to have been a conscious effort to accompany most items in the text with an illustration in the vignette, even if the connection between them was occasionally tenuous. As with the material on the previous two plates, the text and illustrations are written retrograde, left to right.

The leftmost scene of Plate 7 shows Ani and his wife seated under a type of canopy which is known by the generic word *seh* 'tent, booth.' Tutu raises one arm in a gesture of prayer or praise, while the other, preternaturally long, extends behind her husband's back and grasps his shoulder. Ani is shown moving a piece in a game called *senet,* frequently but erroneously identified as 'chess' or 'draughts.' This scene is one of the many indications that this papyrus dates to the Nineteenth Dynasty, when *senet* had acquired a symbolic value.

Senet was basically a game of chase and not a game of strategy. Pieces were moved over a grid of 30 squares, decorated with words and signs of mythological and religious import — some auspicious like the word *neferu* "beauty," some ominous like a watery pit or a net. Many elements of *senet* play a role in the *BD* and other religious texts. On the final square of the board, the god Osiris appears, who is also a major goal of the passage into the next world. In the *BD* the deceased is shown moving a piece, but there is almost never an opponent present, unlike representations of this game in scenes of daily life from the Old Kingdom. Clearly, *senet* is no longer merely a game; it is an allegory for the successful transition into the afterlife. Yet, as important as the *senet* game may seem, it is mentioned only summarily in the rubric below: '*playing at senet, sitting in a booth.*'

The *senet*-playing scene is immediately followed by a depiction of both Tutu and Ani as *ba*-birds with candles before them, in effect forming the hieroglyph for *ba;* together they are perched upon a stylized shrine or tomb. In front of Ani's *ba*, there is the caption: 'The *ba* of the Osiris.' Usually, the name of the deceased appears as well, but not in this instance. The scene represents the ultimate purpose and very title of the *BD*, 'going forth by day,' the successful emergence from the tomb as a spirit. This event, too, is mentioned briefly in the rubric to the chapter and is otherwise not really mentioned in the text. Perhaps the juxtaposition of the first two scenes is an allegory conveying the beginning and end results of the metaphorical game of *senet*. Before the shrine is an offering-stand with a watering can and two open lotus flowers crossed over it.

Directly after the offering-stand is a group composed of two lions standing back-to-back with the *akhet*-sign "horizon, bright place" between them, resting on their backs. The sign *pet* "sky" is stretched out over the entire group. The short captions by the pair of lions contain an interpretation rather than a simple identification of the two lions. The right-hand text states briefly 'yesterday,' while the left reads 'tomorrow,' most likely referring both to the endpoints of the sun's passage from west to east under the earth and to the time span during which Ani would be underground himself, before he was able to 'go forth by day.' In the text below, the line which applies to this scene is 'To me belongs yesterday, I know tomorrow' followed by a gloss identifying Osiris with yesterday and Re with tomorrow. The picture of the two lions, then, is to be read from right to left — that is, from west to east, yesterday to tomorrow — whereas the chapter text is written retrograde, moving westward (see the commentary on Chapter 1, Plates 5 and 6). In fact, we may observe that in this papyrus most of the texts concerning Re are not retrograde, and are therefore oriented toward the eastern horizon, while most of the texts concerning Osiris and the netherworld are retrograde, and are thus oriented westward in keeping with Osiris's identification with yesterday. In the final scene on the papyrus, the tomb and the tomb door are oriented in such a fashion that Ani would be emerging into the east, going in the same direction in which the daytime sun travels.

These two lions appear to represent not Ruty 'Double Lion,' but Shu and Tefnut, who were worshipped together in a shrine at Leontopolis ('Lion-town') in the Delta. In the text of the chapter the Supports of Shu are mentioned, perhaps alluding to the lions in the vignette above. A modified form of this scene appears on a headrest found in the tomb of Tutankhamun in which the back-to-back lions are separated by an image of Shu, who acts as a pillar and holds up the headrest.

The next representation is of a heron standing before an offering-stand with a flower on top. The accompanying caption identifies this bird as *benu* "the heron," a Heliopolitan deity associated with the beginnings of creation as a manifestation of Atum, or Re as a creator deity. The Benu is often described as the 'Egyptian Phoenix,' an error which may derive from Herodotus, who has transmitted a faulty description of a legend he claimed to have heard from the priests of Heliopolis. In the Egyptian legends, however, the Benu is not reborn from his ashes after a fiery death; rather, the Benu made his appearance on the primordial mound when the land emerged from the water, bringing the light with him, a concept fundamental to Heliopolitan religion. As an example of how puzzling the glosses in the accompanying text can be, the Benu is said to be Osiris in one explanation and Osiris's corpse in the other, two associations the Benu does not seem to have outside this chapter.

Directly following the heron is a representation of a mummiform coffin, with Ani's body inside, lying on a lion bed in a shrine or a shrine-like coffin. Both the bed and the equipment underneath it are essentially the same things that were seen being carried in the upper left register of the vignette for Chapter 1 (Plate 5). To the sides of the bier stand the 'Two Kites,' representations of Isis (left) and Nephthys (right) in the form of a common raptor whose plaintive cries made while hovering were interpreted by the Egyptians as the sounds of mourning. The two explanations in the text mention the Two Kites, Horus, Atum, and the god Min, but refer to neither Osiris nor the coffin. The pennants streaming at either corner of the bier may signal the presence of the 'breath of life.'

The two figures at the left of Plate 8 represent two cosmological beings, Heh "Millions" (rendered by Faulkner as 'Chaos-god') and Wadj-wer "Sea." They are depicted as 'fecundity figures,' with portly, androgynous bodies and drooping breasts, and with no clothes save a cloth sash about their waists from which pendants hang down to cover their genitals. In older Egyptological scholarship they are erroneously termed 'Nile Gods' because their iconography was frequently associated with water. The larger kneeling figure of Heh is colored blue with ripple lines to convey his watery aspects. He holds a notched rib of a palm frond in his hand and wears a similar object in his headband. This is the *renpet*-sign, which means 'year,' so we may read his image as meaning 'Millions of years.' He extends his arm over an oval in which there is a *wadjet*-eye. The other fecundity figure, Wadj-wer, is accompanied by three inscriptions: the first says, 'Sea is his name'; the second, 'the lake of natron,' applies to the small rectangle behind him over which his hand is placed protectively; the third text pertains to the other small rectangle, identifying it as 'the lake of *maet*,' referring to an unknown substance (spelled differently from the term *maat* "truth, rightful order"). Natron was used in the embalming process and perhaps so was *maet*. The two deities and the two lakes are mentioned in the text below, and Re is said to dwell in the water.

The brightly colored shrine appearing next is labeled 'Rosetjau,' a generic name for 'necropolis.' The central element in the shrine is a double-leaf door. Since the first element (*ro*) of Rosetjau means 'gateway,' the picture probably represents a gateway into the afterlife. This interpretation seems to be supported by the text below, which speaks of knowing the Road of the Just and of various gates. This 'gateway' is also represented on the throne of Osiris depicted in Plate 4.

The next scene shows the full form of the *wadjet*-eye atop a small tomb or shrine and corresponds to the several citations of the eye in the associated text. In the explanations given in the text, the eye is an element of mythological cycles pertaining to both Horus and Re. The two differing interpretations are among the many indications that texts such as Chapter 17 represent collections of opinions formed over a long period of time and were not meant as definitive statements of religious dogma.

Next appears the figure of a recumbent mummiform cow with a sun-disk between her horns and wearing the *menat* associated with Hathor. Like many deities associated with the preservation of the king in the afterlife, this figure has a royal flagellum projecting from her back. The figure lies atop a shrine stand, which in turn is upon a reed mat. The identifying inscription in front of the cow says, 'Mehetweret (The Great Flood Water), the Eye of Re,' a deity also known as Hesat, or the Celestial Cow. This goddess, who is mentioned in the text beneath this scene, is sometimes depicted resting on a pool of water, rather than on a shrine. Cows are frequently part of the religious iconography of deities who play an important role as mother-goddesses, as is the case with Hathor. In some papyri, though not this one, Mehetweret is identified with Hathor. Mehetweret is also the central figure in the vignette for Chapter 71.

Following the representation of the Celestial Cow, there is a scene showing the mummiform Four Sons of Horus, the deities personifying the canopic jars in which the organs of the deceased are stored, standing beside a coffin-like chest. In reality, the canopic jars, roughly in the same form and usually made of alabaster, were placed inside a box similar to this one or the one depicted in Plate 5. The Four Sons of Horus are mentioned in the accompanying text immediately following the segment concerning Mehetweret, the Celestial Cow; they appear frequently in the *BD*. Their forms and names are, moving from left to right, the ape-headed Hapy, the human-headed Imsety, the jackal-headed Duamutef, and the falcon-headed Qebehsenuef. The same deities are depicted again on the side of the chest. A head and two hands, each clasping an *ankh*, emerge from the center of the rounded top of the coffin. This odd representation, which may be intended to show that the object is actually a personification of such chests, is accompanied by a brief inscription before the head reading: 'the mound of Abydos.' Mounds in religious contexts usually refer to the mound which emerged from the primordial waters at the creation. The illustration and the accompanying text almost certainly represent an attempt to give the funerary equipment a fanciful mythological origin. It does not seem probable that the reverse was true, i.e., that the Egyptians created canopic chests in order to reenact a mythological event.

Proceeding from the chest and the canopic deities to Plate 9, we see a row of eleven minor gods squatting on a reed mat. This is somewhat at variance with the main text below, which mentions only seven gods. The names of the gods in the vignette's captions, furthermore, seem to have been miscopied in a few instances, particularly at the end of the row, where a single deity's compound name, 'He who sees by night what he shall bring by day,' has been distributed erroneously between the last two divine figures.

The scene at the left of Plate 10 shows two *djed*-pillars flanking a shrine surmounted by the god Re in falcon form confronted by a human-headed bird wearing the White Crown of Upper Egypt. These represent the 'Two Fledglings' mentioned in the text below. Since the scene is bracketed by two *djed*-pillars, in effect forming the name *Djedu* 'Busiris,' the town of Osiris in the Delta, the other deity is certainly Osiris. Once again the two chief gods of the afterlife appear together in the same scene.

This scene marks an important juncture in the papyrus in both a textual and a literal sense. Even a cursory examination of the document shows that sheets from two different versions of Chapter 17 have been joined here. The area taken up by the columns of text suddenly widens, the handwriting changes, and the colors used in the double border at the bottom differ. As mentioned above, the version of this chapter in the papyrus of Ani is missing roughly a third of the 'ideal' text, preserved in its entirety on only a small number of manuscripts. Like spliced film strips from an edited movie, the text breaks off abruptly at the end of a column, then picks up at the top of the following column *in medias res*. The join runs through the middle of the text column between Tutu and the group of three seated deities.

When the two sheets of papyrus were joined, the scribe had apparently decided not to include any of the text pertaining to the next scene, which shows the 'Great Cat,' a manifestation of the sun-god, killing a snake with a knife at the base of a tree. If that text had been included, it would discuss the *ished*-tree of Heliopolis, which was split on the night of making war between Re and his enemies (see the Theban Recension section of this volume for the omitted parts of Chapter 17). The snake in the illustration is not a cobra, who normally functions as the guardian of gateways and shrines. Instead we have a more generic snake type often used to depict harmful creatures such as Apophis, the enemy of Re and the chief representative of the forces of chaos and nonexistence. The identity of the three gods armed with knives who sit behind the Apophis-snake is uncertain.

The next illustration in the vignette is associated with a text which would appear much further along if this chapter were in its theoretically complete form. The central element of the scene is the sun bark, which has a decorated mat affixed to its prow. In the middle of this boat sits Re, shown here in his form as Khepri, the scarab beetle who represents the morning sun. The boat is shown travelling not on water but upon the sign *pet* "sky." The boat is bracketed by the kneeling figures of Ani and his wife at the prow and two baboons at the stern, all of whom raise their arms in the posture of adoration. The two stars in front of the baboons are the hieroglyphic sign for 'adore, praise,' the very action they are performing.

Directly following and marked off by a vertical bar is a depiction of the god Atum in a solar disk. As the deity representing the evening sun, Atum acts as a complement to the last scene. His boat is also travelling across the sky, but in the opposite direction from the bark in the previous scene. In front of Atum is an object which has been identified as a packet of instruments lashed together, the 'execution tools' of the sun-god.

The last scene in the vignette for Chapter 17, the scene most often found ending the illustrations for this chapter, represents a lion resting upon a shrine-like plinth and surmounted by a uraeus serpent, a bouquet of lotus flowers, and a flaming brazier. In front is an open lotus blossom on an offering-stand. The text below identifies this animal as Rehu "the Lion," whom more complete versions of the chapter say is the 'phallus of Re.'

Chapter 17 is one of the longest and most important of all chapters of the *BD*; it is also one of the oldest, with a close antecedent in Chapter 335 of the *Coffin Texts*. Because of the chapter's length, it is hardly surprising that there are many versions of both the text and the accompanying vignettes. The importance of this chapter was that it offered a detailed theological overview of the relationship between the sun-god and other important deities of the next world. The lengthy and often rubricized introduction to this chapter, in fact, almost sounds as if it could serve as a general introduction to the entire work, and many *BDs* begin with Chapter 17.

The text offers a particularly good example of one of the most important motifs and purposes of the *BD* — namely, providing the deceased with esoteric knowledge necessary for the afterlife. The structure of much of the chapter, with its question-and-answer format, indicates that it should be understood as initiation literature. In order to pass into the next world, the dead would need to know what was there and could expect to be examined on that knowledge. After some statements there appears a rubricized question *'Who is he?'* or *'What does it mean?'* followed by an explanation, frequently in the form, 'It means . . .' In some cases there will be one or more additional explanations, *'Otherwise said:* It means that . . .' When we look at Chapter 17 antecedents in *Coffin Text* 335, it is interesting that there are versions both with and without such explanatory glosses. Chapter 17, however, always includes the explanations. Chapter 17 instructs the deceased on many of the most important aspects and personages of the world which he would encounter beyond the grave.

For Egyptologists, the special interest of Chapter 17 is that it is one of the few instances when the Egyptians supply *their* commentary on a religious text. Unfortunately, in most cases that commentary is as obscure as the text it purports to explain. Since it supplies two or more alternative explanations, it could be that parts of this chapter were as confusing to the Egyptians as they are for the modern reader. It has also been suggested that when alternative interpretations of the text appear, these might represent the views of different theological schools, stressing the importance of a particular god or gods. An examination of the commentary in the Papyrus of Ani, however, does not seem to reveal any cohesive groups of opinions. In fact, the different explanations usually have no thematic consistency, or are diametrically opposed.

One of the more intriguing lines in the entire chapter appears in the terminal rubric of some manuscripts: *'(It goes well) with one who recites them (i.e. the verses) on earth.'* Several other chapters have similar claims that a spell is equally useful and valid for both the afterlife and this world (usually in that order). Since references to material from the *BD* are quite rare in non-mortuary contexts, some scholars feel that such statements are yet another indication that the *BD* is at least partially a form of initiation literature. The deceased acquired knowledge, in some chapters, in order to show his or her specialized competence. To be highly effective was, after all, the very essence of being an *akh*-spirit. The German scholar Jan Assmann, one of the proponents of this view, points out that in many chapters the deceased wished both to assert their personal identity and to gain the approval of the gods, as if attempting to join the 'guild' of the divine and the glorified dead. In this instance, the text of Chapter 17 is informative since it presents the parts of the text in a question-and-answer format that one would expect in an examination. This explanation for the glosses and their alternatives seems more satisfying than ascribing them all simply to confusion among the Egyptians.

PLATE 11

The two chapters on this plate share with Chapter 17 a general concern with esoteric knowledge and the performance of ritual. After the conclusion of Chapter 17, the scribes assembling Ani's *BD* affixed the next group of sheets without really adapting the mismatched borders at the top or the bottom. The retrograde direction of the text is maintained.

This plate is split into two registers, with Chapter 147 above and Chapter 146 below; in both chapters there is no separation of text and vignette. Each register begins at the left with the figures of Ani and Tutu standing in adoration before a series of various kinds of entrances, which will eventually lead to the 'Domain of Osiris in the Field of Reeds,' as versions of these chapters in other papyri inform us. The first entrance illustrated in each chapter is the largest and most elaborate. In Chapter 147 these entrances are called *aryt* "gates" and are guarded by three squatting figures, which the text identifies as a 'gatekeeper,' a 'guardian,' and an 'announcer.' In Chapter 146 the entrances are called *sebkhet,* which can mean either 'pylon' or 'gateway,' but which is here translated as 'portal.' In contrast to the upper register, each entrance in Chapter 146 has only one 'gatekeeper.'

Ani's versions of Chapters 146 and 147 are simplified versions of much longer texts which portray as many as 21 entrances, each of which can be passed only after a brief dialogue with each being blocking the way. In the present case, however, this exchange is merely implied. Knowing the names of the gatekeepers appears to be sufficient to give the deceased power over these creatures and thus gain entrance. The complex and threatening names of these beings, as well as Ani's arcane declarations at his arrival before each entrance, connect these two chapters with a genre of texts in which the deceased demonstrate their acquisition of special knowledge and thereby prove their fitness for membership in the community of gods. As noted at the end of the commentary to the preceding plate, Jan Assmann has suggested that such texts may be based upon initiation rituals among Egyptian craft and professional groups. In Chapter 147, Ani demands passage so that he might assist Osiris, presumably because he has succeeded in joining the gods.

PLATES 12–14

Like Chapters 17, 146, and 147 on the preceding plates, Chapter 18 on these three plates is concerned with ritual and the display of knowledge. After the conclusion of Chapters 146 and 147 the scribes assembling Ani's *BD* affixed the noticeably lighter sheets that comprise Chapter 18 and its unique introductory scenes, which are not found in any other *BD* papyrus. The respectful posture of Ani and Tutu, who are shown twice standing behind priests officiating in panther-skin robes, again implies that the couple is participating in a ritual. The priest in the upper register is identified as a 'Pillar-of-his-Mother' priest, and the one in the lower register as a 'Son-whom-he-loves' priest. One of the major functions of both offices was to perform the 'Opening of the Mouth' ceremony, in which ritual equipment, the mummy of the deceased, and the *BD* itself are made effective. In this case, however, the priests are shown making a gesture of speech toward the doorways that appear to the right of the priests' invocations. For his part Ani merely

recites two brief praises of Osiris as the god in charge of both Rosetjau and the God's Domain, and as judge of the dead.

Chapter 18 is concerned with instructing the deceased about various aspects of the afterworld. For unknown reasons, this lengthy chapter occurs twice in Ani's *BD* — here and again on Plates 23–24. The main purpose of this chapter is to describe some of the councils which judge the dead and mythological events with which each council is connected. The two priests merely introduce 'Osiris Ani' to the *djadjats* or 'Councils' of gods belonging to the God's Domain and Rosetjau. (In the lower register, Ani's name has been carelessly omitted in the space provided for it directly behind the priest's leg.) Like Chapter 17 this chapter introduces ancient commentary and explanations in the form of rubricized questions followed by an explanation. In the present case, however, the questions are answered with only one interpretation. Unlike the beings who appeared in Chapters 146 and 147 the gods who are mentioned in Chapter 18 are mostly important deities with significant cults in Egypt: Atum, Osiris, Anubis, Isis, Horus, Nephthys, Wepwawet, etc.

Generally speaking there is no fixed vignette for Chapter 18 whose text appears in between the vertical strips illustrating the divine members of the councils. Ani's papyrus leads us into the retrograde text, so to speak, through the two doorways, which are mentioned neither in the chapter nor in its introduction. The upper doorway is surmounted by a frieze of erect cobras and ostrich feathers, both of which can mean *maat.* Above the lower doorway is the recumbent figure of Anubis, behind whom the *wadjet*-eye appears.

The text of Chapter 18 follows a general pattern. First comes an address to Thoth, asking him to vindicate Ani against his afterlife enemies in the presence of a succession of councils, each belonging to a major Egyptian cult center. In each instance Thoth's vindication of Osiris (and of the Osiris Ani) is also connected with an event or a ritual in the mythical past. In all but the final section, each block of text concludes with an explanation of either the council or the mythical occasion in answer to a rubricized question. The purpose of Chapter 18 is simple. It allows Ani to get Thoth's favorable introduction to the major bodies which might be called upon to pass judgment on him in the next world.

Directly after the double doorways, the chapter begins with a commentary on the members of the first council. Each of the next ten sections of Chapter 18 faces a representation of those gods who are said to be in the corresponding council, with the text running in the retrograde fashion of most *BD* chapters. When Chapter 18 is repeated in the papyrus (see Plates 23 and 24), the same text is used but with the vignette in the normal position at the top. The translation for this chapter begins on Plate 12 with the address to Thoth and a description of both the Council of Heliopolis and a mythical event. However, both versions of Chapter 18 on the Ani Papyrus omit this introductory material and begin instead with the gloss 'As to 'the Great Council which is in Heliopolis': . . .'

The fact that the same error occurs twice offers us a fascinating insight into scribal practices and how manuscripts such as Ani's *BD* were fashioned. The textual material in the two examples of Chapter 18 is not only virtually identical, glyph for glyph, but was also executed by the same scribe. The text on Plates 12–14 seems ill-adapted to the allotted space in several places, with stretched out writing and noticeable gaps at the bottom of some columns. The version on Plates 23–24 is evenly spaced and fits much better. For these reasons it seems almost certain that the text on Plates 23–24 was the model on which the present version of Chapter 18 was based.

The omission of the chapter's beginning most likely occurred when the scribe was writing in the text beneath the long vignette on Plates 23–24. The scribe, especially if he found most of the material he was copying incomprehensible, probably decided to work as much as possible according to his normal customs. Since the canonical direction of non-religious texts is right-to-left, he began copying the material from his master copy at the far right column of Plate 24 and proceeded to write the text in backwards, starting at the end of the chapter. The result of this practice was that he ran out of space at the left-hand column of Plate 23 and thus truncated the text at its beginning rather than at its end. Due to the different format of illustration and text in the second version on Plates 12–14 he could not use the same procedure and attempted to put in the text, block by block, moving from left to right as he should have in the first instance. Ideally, each block of columns should have begun with the invocation to Thoth and ended with a gloss on the council. Unfortunately, with the start of the chapter missing, each group of columns began instead with a comment on the council and contained parts of two sections of Chapter 18. Even with this makeshift, the text in the rightmost column of several blocks nevertheless could not fill out the space.

These are the groups of the gods as they appear in the vignettes, from top to bottom, moving from left to right:

1. Atum, Shu, and Tefnut — the three gods cited in the gloss as the Council of Heliopolis — plus Osiris and Thoth.

2. Osiris, Isis, Nephthys, and Horus — the Council of Busiris.

3. Osiris (not mentioned in the gloss), Horus, two *wadjet*-eyes above shrines, and Thoth — the Council of Letopolis.

4. Horus, Isis, Imsety, and Hapy — the Council of Pe and Dep.

5. Osiris, Isis, Anubis, Imsety, and Thoth — Osiris, Anubis, and Thoth are not part of the relevant council on the Banks of the Washerman; on the other hand, Horus, who should appear here, does not.

6. Osiris, Isis, Wepwawet, and a large *djed*-pillar — the Council of Wepwawet.

7. Thoth, Osiris, Anubis, and Isdes — the Council of Judging the Dead.

8. Three squatting male deities, presumably representing 'gods' in general — the Council at the hacking up of the earth of Busiris.

9. Re, Osiris, Shu, and Bebi — the Council of Naref, with the addition of Osiris.

10. Horus, Osiris, Isis(?), and an unidentifiable god — the Council of Rosetjau.

At the far right edge of the plate, we can see where the different sheets of papyrus have been joined. The artificiality of the join is emphasized by the inward tapering of the top and bottom double borders. There are even remains of an empty vertical column at the edge of Chapter 23, the first text on the next sheet.

PLATE 15

The text under the first two vignettes on Plate 15 contains four chapters — 23, 24, 26, and 30B — written continuously as a single running text. This is the second appearance of Chapter 30B in this papyrus (see Plate 3). The way in which text and vignette are arranged does not conform to the usual pattern of beginning each chapter at the top of a vertical column, adjacent to the relevant illustration.

Chapter 23 contains some of the words of the 'Opening of the Mouth' ritual, which was performed on the deceased's mummy, statues, amulets, *Book of the Dead* papyri, and virtually all other objects connected with the burial. The ceremony activated all the images and words necessary for the maintenance of the dead in the next world. We have already encountered another representation of this ritual at the end of the

vignette for Chapter 1. In the present case, the vignette shows Ani as a statue squatting on a base which resembles the *maat*-sign often found under representations of divine statues. On the right of the scene the *sem*-priest, wearing a panther skin over his garment, is shown in the act of striking the statue with a snake-shaped adze, one of the many implements employed in this complex ritual. Between the statue and the priest are a chest and some of the other objects used in the 'Opening of the Mouth' — a double-feathered implement and three more adzes. This chapter is followed directly by Chapter 24, which is concerned with giving Ani the magic requisite for his survival in the next world.

The text of Chapter 23 may explain why so many chapters and passages in the *BD* are completely obscure to us. Were it not for the title of the chapter and the accompanying vignette, there would be no indication from the text alone that the words are connected with a specific ceremony called the 'Opening of the Mouth.' There are certainly many other rituals hidden away in the *BD*, but given our skimpy knowledge of Egyptian rituals, they escape our attention.

The second vignette in this group of chapters depicts Ani holding his heart in his right hand, a scene which would be appropriate to both Chapters 26 and 30B. Anubis stands at the right of the scene holding a *was*-scepter. Between Ani and Anubis is a large and elaborate pectoral plaque attached to an equally ornate bead necklace, which Ani seems to be offering to the god. Plaques of this sort sometimes were provided with shallow depressions for a heart scarab, the type of large amulet on which the text of Chapter 30B was normally written. The scarab form was chosen for the amulet because this beetle was the verb 'to become, to grow,' and thus represented a wish for rebirth. In the center of the plaque is a representation of the scarab-headed Khepri, the morning sun, travelling in a divine bark. In fact, Ani most likely is not holding his actual heart but a heart scarab in his right hand.

The first text associated with the vignette, Chapter 26, was intended to ensure that Ani's heart would be returned to him should it be lost. The closing lines of this chapter seem to imply that the body derived its power from the heart and would be inert and inoperative without it. For the Egyptians the heart was not just the engine which ran the body, it was the seat of the emotions and intelligence as well. Losing the heart would prevent one from surviving in the God's Domain. Another danger posed by the heart was that it could testify against Ani when he was judged, an eventuality Chapter 30B was designed to protect against. Since the heart plays such an important role in the Egyptian afterlife, it is not surprising that Chapter 30B appears twice.

The frequent pattern of separating chapters with yellow column markers resumes with Chapter 61 in the middle of the plate, but is abruptly dropped for the next few chapters. The scene depicts Ani holding his *ba*, shown here in its normal form as a human-headed bird. There seems to be little connection between the text and the chapter's purpose since the *ba* is not mentioned even in more extensive versions of the text.

The rubric of the following Chapter 54 informs us that the chapter was intended to give Ani breath in the God's Domain. The vignette depicts Ani holding a small billowing sail, which is a symbol of the desired breath and air mentioned in the text.

The next-to-last chapter on Plate 15 uses a rather unassuming vignette which shows Ani standing with a handkerchief in his left hand while his right clasps a walking stick before him. This is essentially nothing more than the hieroglyph for 'official.' The text is that of Chapter 29, returning us to the subject of protecting the heart. Since the text of Chapter 29 fits the space beneath it poorly and since the vignette which normally accompanies this chapter depicts the deceased holding his heart protectively, it seems likely that the scribe has entered the wrong chapter here.

Plate 15 ends with Chapter 27. The vignette shows Ani

standing in a posture of adoration before a large heart placed on the type of standard used for gods or divine images. Behind the standard is a group of four mummiform deities squatting on a plinth in the shape of a *maat*-sign. Like the previous chapter, this chapter is intended to prevent harm from befalling Ani's heart. As we have seen in Chapter 30B, the heart was even thought to have a will of its own, separate from its owner. The text of Chapter 27 also appears on heart scarabs. The chapter addresses unspecified deities who seize and destroy hearts in the God's Domain, as well as 'founders of everlasting,' presumably the four beings depicted here. Technically speaking, the Egyptian text differentiates between *haty*, which means the chest in the sense of the more archaic and poetical 'bosom,' and the word *ib*, which refers to the heart proper.

PLATE 16

The leftmost vignette on Plate 16 depicts Ani and Tutu standing together in a tree-lined pool of water from which they are drinking. This scene accompanies Chapter 58, whose purpose is to guarantee that the deceased will be provided with food and water in the God's Domain. The text begins with a dialogue, presumably between Ani and an unknown deity. The interchange is typical of many in the *BD*, for it involves a question from the god which Ani must answer correctly. Such dialogues may derive from initiation rituals connected with Egyptian professional life, as has been discussed for Chapters 17, 146, and 147. As he would in the earthly ritual, Ani shows that he belongs among the gods by supplying the correct answers and demonstrating the arcane knowledge necessary for passage across the water.

Chapter 59, which has the same rubric as the preceding chapter, appears next. The vignette depicts a tree goddess emerging from a tree trunk and pouring water into the extended hands of the kneeling Ani. This scene was a favorite in contemporary tombs of the Theban nobility of the Eighteenth and Nineteenth Dynasties. The 'sycamore of the sky' mentioned here apparently can guarantee that the deceased will have water and be able to breathe in the afterlife.

After the yellow demarcation stripe, Chapter 44 occurs, yet its introductory line appears on the left side of the marker rather than on the right as one would expect. Several other chapters on this plate show the same misalignment of the first line with the division markers on the sheet. The vignette for Chapter 44 shows Ani sitting before an offering table stacked with bread loaves in the form of reed leaves, a very frequent motif which appears in tombs, stelae, and papyri from the Old Kingdom on. Ani holds a walking stick and a wandlike scepter, two common marks of official status. The object of this chapter is to prevent Ani from dying a second death in the God's Domain. The reference to the Imperishable Stars connects the most desirable afterlife with an existence in the realm beyond earth and sky. The short dialogue accomplishes this purpose by presumably showing Re that not only is the deceased his son, but also that he knows the god's secrets.

Chapter 45 follows with its vignette depicting Anubis attending to the standing mummy of Ani. Since Anubis was the deity responsible for embalming and the preservation of the corpse, his presence here might have been felt to be essential to the stated purpose of the chapter, which is to prevent the putrefaction of the corpse. Anubis, however, is not mentioned in the text, which seeks to identify Ani with Osiris, the god who overcame putrefaction in the afterworld.

In the vignette for the following Chapter 46, we encounter a doorway flanked by a heron, presumably the Benu, and Ani's *ba* in the form of a human-headed bird. The rubric states that this chapter, like the preceding one, is intended to ensure that Ani shall live and not perish in the God's Domain. The text that accompanies this chapter varies greatly among the papyri

containing it. Some versions, but not the one which appears here, mention the doorway.

The next vignette belongs to Chapter 50. The scene shows Ani striding away from a highly stylized representation of a chopping block whose two poles are set in the base of a mountain. This is the *nemet* or slaughterhouse of the god mentioned in the text. Above the chopping block is a knife dribbling blood. The text begins by speaking of four knots which are tied about Ani, a reference to a magical practice in which enemies are disarmed by tying representations of them into knots. In this case the knots are tied about Ani protectively, and their potency is increased by including pieces of hair. Seth, who so often is a negative figure in the *BD*, appears here in a positive role as one of Ani's protectors. It is typically Egyptian that even that which is generally negative should have positive aspects as well.

The next rubric, '*Chapter for not letting Ani be ferried over to the East in the God's Domain*,' and the accompanying text belong to Chapter 93. Since a boat appears in the adjoining vignette, but not here, some manner of copyist's error seems possible. Instead, the vignette shows Ani in a posture of adoration facing a row of three striding gods, each holding a *was*-scepter and an *ankh*-sign, a scene having no apparent thematic connection with travel. There is, however, a possible reference to the East in Ani's unusual position in the scene, the only time in the entire papyrus when he is shown on the right side of the scene and facing left. As explained in commentary for Plates 5–6, the left represents the east in the papyrus. Since other papyri have different versions of the vignette for this chapter, the significance of the scene and reasons for its orientation remain uncertain. Up to this point Ani has been shown facing right, and is presumably progressing further towards the west and his ultimate goal. Perhaps the scribe who composed this papyrus chose this vignette for Chapter 93 simply because it offered more space for inscribing the text.

The three gods shown in the vignette are not mentioned in the text of Chapter 93, so their number might merely be a way of expressing plurality, i.e., 'the gods.' The tone of the chapter is magical throughout. Ani asserts that he possesses great powers and that he will bring harm to Re, Osiris, Khepri, and Atum should any harm be done against him. The notion of threatening the gods is completely alien to our religious consciousness but occasionally appears in Egyptian religious material. The beginning of the text, with its reference to the phallus of Re and its connection with the god Bebi, is actually quite unclear in the translation presented here.

Judging from where its title appears, the next vignette accompanies Chapter 43, which, as noted above, may have been erroneously applied to the previous Chapter 93. The title of this chapter informs us that its purpose was to prevent the deceased from having his head taken from him in the God's Domain. In this case, however, we encounter a scene in which Ani is depicted holding his scribal palette in one hand while the other is raised and extended out in front of him in a gesture of invocation. In front of Ani is a small ferryboat with a divine being squatting in it. This figure holds a flail and his head is reversed upon his body, as if he must look backwards perpetually. This personage is obviously the querulous and quarrelsome divine ferryman known from a number of other chapters of the *BD*, particularly Chapter 99, which is not present in Ani's papyrus. The name of the backwards-looking ferryman in the vignette is known from Chapter 99 as Mahaf, 'He who looks behind himself,' a misinterpretation of his original name, 'The Stern is Behind Him.'

PLATE 17

The first text on this plate belongs to Chapter 89, whose first column begins on the wrong side of the division line, as do the first columns of several other chapters on this and the previous plate. The purpose of this chapter was to enable the *ba* of the deceased to rejoin his corpse in the God's Domain. The vignette depicts Ani's *ba* clutching a *shen*-symbol and hovering over the coffin. The *shen* was ring-shaped with a flat base; it signified both cyclical eternity and protection. The cartouche in which kings' (and rarely gods') names are placed is a specialized form of the *shen*. The coffin lies on a bier with a lion's head and tail, a type of bed which may be associated with embalming. The bed is flanked by two lamps on stands placed at its head and foot. The burial ceremony in Chapter 1 (Plate 5), the Opening of the Mouth ceremony in Chapter 23 (Plate 16), and the present vignette are the only occasions that the corpse of the deceased is depicted in any form in this papyrus. Normally Ani appears as if he were alive and functioning exactly as he did on earth. The scene and the text represent one of the most important moments in an individual's after-death existence. The reunion of spirit and physical body marks the moment after which the corpse of the deceased will be completely reawakened.

The next vignette accompanies Chapter 91. The scene is a simple one, showing Ani's *ba* in the form of a human-headed bird outside a doorway. The purpose of this chapter is to ensure that the *ba* of the deceased will be able to move about freely in the God's Domain. According to the text, the chapter applies to the *akh*, the *ba*, and the Shadow of the deceased. The reference to 'going forth' in the rubric means that the deceased will be able not only to move freely in the beyond, but to enter this world temporarily and return afterwards. Although the *BD* focuses on the God's Domain and the Duat, it was also important that the spirit of the deceased should be able to move back and forth, to 'go forth by day' into this world as well.

There are many variants of the vignette in other papyri, yet the underlying theme is fairly constant; in fact, it is essentially a continuation of the subject matter of the previous Chapter 91. Both chapters aim at ensuring the deceased's free movement in the next world and to extend the movement into this world as well. In the various versions of this vignette in other papyri, the deceased is shown emerging from the tomb either as a *ba*, as a black, wraithlike Shadow, or as a normal human. In Ani's *BD*, he is shown twice, once on each side of the door. Since his *ba* accompanies him on the right side of the scene, at that point Ani has passed from the beyond and is emerging from either the door of the West or the door of his tomb. The vignette in this papyrus clearly illustrates the desired result of Chapter 92 — Ani has gained power over his legs again and is 'going forth by day,' using the phrase which is the *BD*'s title in Egyptian.

PLATE 18

The leftmost vignette on Plate 18, the first in a series of three linked scenes, depicts Ani kneeling respectfully before a divine bark while pulling taut the rope holding it on its sledge. This illustrates Chapter 74. The text continues the motif of enabling the deceased to 'go forth by day,' the topic of the previous Chapters 91 and 92. The central image is the bark of the god Sokar, one of the most important mortuary gods of Egypt. Sokar is often associated with the necropolis by his common epithet 'Lord of Rosetjau.' The focal point of Sokar's cult was the elaborate portable bark shown here. This is called the *henu*-bark and was carried by priests in processional rituals. The bark is affixed to a sled, which in turn rests on a repository stone, just as it would during the intervals between the occasions when the god paraded about in public. The two carrying-poles, which would rest on the shoulders of the priests, jut out in front and in back. The elaborate prow with the reversed antelope head is the chief characteristic of the bark. Sokar is usually depicted as a recumbent falcon bound in mummy bindings so that only his head is visible, as on Plates 4 and 19. In this scene, the god's head is shown protruding from the shrine in which his image is kept. The same falcon's

head appears as an emblem at the top of his shrine. The rubric of Chapter 74 expresses the intent to make the deceased 'swift-footed when going forth by day,' but it is not clear how this wish relates to the accompanying scene.

The next vignette in the series belongs to both Chapter 8 and Chapter 2. The scene shows Ani standing at the left holding his staff before him in one hand while the other grasps a handkerchief. Dominating the right-hand portion of the vignette is a large-scale rendition of the hieroglyph for 'West,' a falcon perched on a round-topped standard with a feather protruding in front. The base of the standard is fixed into the hieroglyph for 'mountain' or 'desert.' Two jars flank this hieroglyph. A similar scene sometimes occurs as the initial scene among the vignettes which accompany Chapter 17, appearing before the *senet*-playing scene. The title of Chapter 8 is '*Chapter for opening up the West by day,*' presumably ensuring that the deceased will be able to move about in the beyond by day as well as by night. The opening phrase of the chapter contains a play on words in Egyptian: 'Hermopolis (*Wenu*) is opened (*wenu*).' The title of Chapter 2 states that it is intended for '*going out into the day and living after death.*' The relationship between the chapter texts, their rubrics, and accompanying vignette is obscure.

The last of the three linked vignettes on this plate belongs to Chapter 9. The scene is something of a visual pun. The ram standing on a plinth-like shrine with a small lamp before him is actually another form of the word *ba*. The shrine represents a stylized tomb at whose center is an open door comparable to the Rosetjau-shrine in the vignette for Chapter 17 (Plate 8). This suits the chapter's title, '*Chapter for going out into the day after opening the tomb.*' The image of the ram, then, serves roughly the same purpose as the *ba*-bird in the vignette for Chapter 92 at the end of the previous plate.

The next two vignettes are separated from the three previous ones by a single column of text. These two pictures also are linked, although their texts are not thematically similar. The first vignette, which accompanies Chapter 132, depicts Ani approaching a doorway. This is apparently the activity which is mentioned in the rubric '*Chapter for causing a man to turn about in order to see his house upon earth.*' Once more, unfortunately, the text seems to have little to do with either its title or its vignette. The words may be those from a magical incantation.

The following vignette shows Ani treading upon a snake as he spears it. There is something incongruous about the detached manner in which Ani performs this dramatic activity. The text belongs to Chapter 10, whose purpose is to enable the deceased to '*go out into the day against his enemies in the God's Domain,*' the land of the dead. Although there is no demarcation line at this point, the column of text to the right of this vignette actually belongs to the next chapter.

The last vignette on Plate 18 shows Re as a falcon-headed god with a large sun-disk on his head, sitting in one of the many barks in which he travels. As befits Re, the bark is shown on top of the sign for 'sky.' This boat has an elaborate rectangular mat affixed to its prow. On top of the mat a small figure of a nude child sits with his finger to his mouth. This child is the deity Horus-the-Child, or Harpocrates as the Greeks called him. The accompanying text is one of many sun hymns that modern scholars have lumped together under the overly broad heading 'Chapter 15.' The text varies so much that virtually no two versions are alike, so that a more accurate term would be simply 'Sun Hymn.'

PLATE 19

The material on this plate is essentially a continuation of the themes of 'Chapter 15' on the previous plate, except that the text honors Osiris instead, addressing him in various forms and aspects. Unlike many of the other texts connected with Osiris, this one is not written retrograde. On the left side of the plate is a large-scale vignette of Ani and Tutu in postures of adoration which have been encountered several times previously in this papyrus. Above them are their names and titles; in the case of Tutu, this is the only place in the papyrus where her titulary appears.

The right-hand illustration shows Osiris and Isis standing in a kiosk and facing Ani and Tutu on the opposite side of the plate. In this vignette we encounter a depiction of Osiris not only as king of the dead, but as 'King of Upper and Lower Egypt'; his cartouche appears in the second column to the right of Ani's hand. The same scribe who drew the masterful rendition of Ani and Tutu at the left also executed this scene. Osiris is standing on the *maat*-sign. He holds three implements associated with earthly kingship in his hands: the *was*-sceptre, the flagellum, and the shepherd's crook. Although he is a god, it appears that Osiris's beard has been fastened by a chin-strap, as if it were the false beard of a pharaoh, another feature that parallels Osiris's representation with that of a living Egyptian monarch. He wears the standard White Crown of Upper Egypt, but unlike any other representations of his crown thus far, the royal uraeus is affixed to its front. Behind Osiris stands Isis, who grasps her husband and brother with one hand. Isis's vulture headdress with the uraeus affixed in front indicates her role as earthly queen of Egypt, matching her husband's depiction as king; on top of her headdress is the throne which is her normal divine attribute. At the top of the kiosk is the image of Sokar, which reveals the true nature of this structure as an elaborate representation of a sarcophagus. The overall outline of this kiosk should be compared with the shrine illustrated on Plate 4 and the coffin illustrated on Plate 5.

Plate 20–21

At this point the papyrus resumes the series of sun hymns, written retrograde. The close juxtaposition of Osiris and Re hymns brings the chthonic and solar elements of the afterlife together roughly at the midpoint of the papyrus. There are no vignettes on Plate 20.

The single vignette on Plate 21 depicts the falcon-headed Re in his day bark, similar to the last vignette of Plate 18. In this representation, however, Ani has joined Re in the boat and stands before the god in a gesture of adoration. Instead of Harpocrates on the prow of the boat, a figure of Horus in his normal falcon form appears. Re is shown sitting on a *maat*-sign, grasping an *ankh* in his hand, and wearing an enormous sun-disk on his head. As on Plate 18, the bark is riding on top of the *pet*-sign "sky." The sun hymn ends just three columns after this representation.

Directly after the yellow vertical separation line, Chapter 133 begins; it continues into the next plate, where its illustration appears. In the Ani Papyrus, this chapter is entitled '*To be recited on the (first) day of the month,*' one of several variant rubrics that are given for this chapter. Thematically speaking, the text is much like the sun hymns encountered in this papyrus and others, which is probably the reason for its appearance here. It is also one of the few chapters in the *BD* whose origins can be traced back to the *Book of the Two Ways* (discussed on p. 140). The chapter identifies the deceased extensively with Re and expresses the wish that he join the god and his company on the sun bark. The text concludes on the next plate with a lengthy rubric describing how to construct a magical model of the vignette depicting the sun bark and the starry sky. By means of such magic, it is claimed that the deceased Ani will acquire great powers among the gods, including Re himself.

Plate 22

The vignette for Chapter 133 shows the falcon-headed Re seated in his sun bark, both boat and god looking much as they did in Plate 21, but without the presence of Ani and without the colorful mat at its prow. The divine boat is shown approaching a rectangular blue panel of stars, presumably representing the night sky.

Chapter 134 begins directly after the demarcation line. Like Chapters 15 and 133, its purpose is to ensure that Ani shall join Re in the sun bark, although Ani is not shown in the vignette. The vignette shows Re once again, with an enormous sun-disk before him in the front of the boat. Although the title says '*Praising Re on the (first) day of the month,*' the text is much more reminiscent of a magical text than of hymnic material. Like the previous chapter, it is connected with the first day of the month. The large blank spot in the middle of the sixth column is one of several places in this papyrus where the scribes carelessly forgot to write Ani's name into the blanks provided for it. As with the previous chapter, the text concludes with a lengthy rubric detailing image magic which can be performed to ensure that Ani will assume his place on the sacred bark and ward off the enemies of Re.

Plate 23–24

On the right edge of Plate 23 appears one leaf of a large yellow door which has swung open, so as to reveal what is inside. We are in effect passing into Chapter 18, which appears for a second time in the papyrus on Plates 23 and 24. A more successful representation of the 'revealing doorway' motif appears on Plates 30 and 31 in connection with Chapter 125.

Ani is shown kneeling in adoration before a long row of seated deities, who face him. In the version found on Plates 12–14, Chapter 18 was introduced by two priests making an invocation before two portals; that scene does not appear in the version found here, nor does Tutu appear with her husband. Also, there are slight differences in the number and order of the gods shown, as well as in the manner in which the deities are depicted. None of these differences is significant, however. Unlike the previous version of this chapter, the text and the accompanying illustration are presented separately and continuously.

After the yellow division line at the center of Plate 24, the text for Chapter 124 appears. The vignette shown here is one of several variants found among contemporary *BD* papyri. In this case, Ani and Tutu stand before three gods on the top of a shrine-like plinth. According to the title, the chapter is concerned with descending to the tribunal of Osiris. The body of the chapter, however, appears to have little to do with the stated purpose, but rather is concerned mainly with the purity of what Ani hopes to eat in the afterlife. Ani would guarantee that his food be wholesome by accepting it only from certain gods. The repeated statement in the *BD* and other Egyptian mortuary texts that the deceased will not eat excrement may seem bizarre, but in the next world it was possible to end up in a situation where normal positions and processes were inverted — compare, for instance, the rubric for Chapter 189 (Theban Recension): '*Chapter for preventing a man from going upside down and from eating feces.*' In Chapter 124 there is also a hint of some manner of ritual concerned with food. As Ani puts certain morsels of food in his mouth, he becomes one of the gods and thereby gains control over gods and situations that he may encounter in the beyond.

Plates 25–28

As the rubrics inform us, Chapter 86 and the next ten chapters constitute a series of 'transformation spells,' beginning on Plate 25 and extending to the end of Plate 28. These chapters were essentially magical spells intended to aid the souls of the blessed dead in assuming the forms of different beings. The Ani Papyrus is particularly rich in such material, containing nearly all of the chapters of this type. This genre of texts has a long history within Egyptian mortuary literature, beginning with the Pyramid Texts. Transformation into many other beings is a particular characteristic of the protean sun/creator deity. That god is frequently mentioned in the transformation spells, presumably as the entity with whom the deceased wishes to identify himself.

The purpose of such chapters is frequently misunderstood, giving rise to the popular misconception that the Egyptians believed in a doctrine of transmigration of the soul similar to the one associated with Indian religion. Many variants of these chapters, however, make it quite clear that these transformations all occur in the God's Domain; for instance, one never encounters those terminal remarks which state that the text has equal validity or power in this world as in the next. 'Transformation spells' remain firmly connected with the afterlife. In addition, the transformations were meant to be temporary and did not occur automatically or involuntarily according to a set principle. Instead, the transformations were to be made when the deceased had to overcome certain obstructions in the next world. Erik Hornung has pointed out that the forms which the deceased assumes are also associated with rebirth and regeneration, and are often employed in amulets and their decoration.

The artist who drew the vignettes accompanying these chapters was particularly skilled at drawing birds and flowers. In Plates 25–28 the vignettes are accordingly done with far greater naturalism than any other scenes in the papyrus.

Of the animals and birds in the transformation spells, the swallow in Chapter 86 is probably the most accurately drawn. The restlessly soaring swallow represented the notion of 'wandering' for the Egyptians. The multicolored mound on which the swallow is perched is presumably the primordial mound on which the creator deity first made his appearance on earth. The terminal rubric appearing on the plate is absent in the Ani Papyrus.

The next vignette belongs to Chapter 77, the transformation into a golden falcon. The vignette shows a gold-colored falcon standing, appropriately, on the hieroglyph for 'gold.' There is a flagellum projecting from his back, a common attribute of deities in theriomorphic form.

The third vignette on Plate 25 is associated with Chapter 78, which continues through Plate 26; this chapter is intended to transform the deceased into a divine falcon. The illustration shows a green-feathered falcon with a flagellum projecting from his back as in the previous example. The falcon is perched on a small shrine-like plinth. The text that accompanies this vignette is one of many that may contain the text of a temple or initiation ritual. The scholars who have studied this chapter have felt that it is essentially a dramatic text, with at least two people performing the various roles which Faulkner has indicated in small capital letters.

The first vignette on Plate 27 is associated with Chapter 87, a spell for transforming the deceased's soul into a 'son of the earth,' i.e., a snake. The manner in which the snake is depicted is a wonderful example of the Egyptians' fertile iconographic imagination. The snake is shown walking on a pair of human legs attached to its belly. The intent may be to remind us that inside the image of the snake, so often feared and detested, is Ani's soul undergoing a temporary transformation. The first lines of the chapter allude to the reason why Ani should desire to transform himself into this creature in the first place — its apparent long life and connection with cyclical rebirth.

The vignette for Chapter 88 shows a crocodile perched upon a shrine. In this case, the image of the crocodile, so often a negative one among the Egyptians, seems to have been chosen as a temporary transformation because of the animal's fearsomeness. This would help in the face of Ani's potential enemies in the afterlife.

The vignette for Chapter 82, whose rubric identifies it as a spell for transformation into Ptah, depicts that god in his shrine; before the shrine is an offering stand with an open lotus blossom. Actually, the text of this chapter is not particularly concerned with Ptah at all. The chapter begins with the deceased's announcement that he has been transformed into a bird. After that, a dialogue between Ani and the gods takes place, and only then does the text mention identification with gods. At that point we can see that the title of the chapter is somewhat misleading, for the deceased does not become Ptah, rather only his tongue becomes the tongue of Ptah. The piecemeal identification of the parts of the deceased's body with parts of the body of several different gods is a theme that often occurs in the *BD*. The most complete example of this '*e pluribus unum*' motif appears in Chapter 42 in Plate 32, near the end of this papyrus.

Normally the title of Chapter 85, the next spell on this plate, is '*Chapter for being transformed into a living soul* (ba) *and not entering into the place of execution,*' but in Ani's papyrus the title speaks of transformation into the 'soul (*ba*) of Atum.' The vignette depicts a striding ram on top of a shrine-like plinth, representing a tomb, with a candle or lamp before it. The combination of ram and candle are, for unknown reasons, a writing for *ba* (see commentary on Chapter 9, Plate 18). The *ba* can be depicted as either a ram, as it is here, or more commonly as a human-headed bird. The reason for the slight alteration in Ani's rubric may be the association of the ram-headed Atum with the setting sun. In the only part of this chapter that this papyrus contains, the deceased identifies himself with Re and Khepri, the sun at its rebirth at dawn; the continuation of the chapter is suddenly interrupted by the title of the next chapter, which begins about three-quarters of the way down the column preceding the yellow division line. This is another instance where the scribes who copied out this papyrus edited it 'on the fly.'

Chapter 83, entitled '*Being transformed into a Benu-bird,*' is appropriately illustrated in the accompanying vignette by a very dignified-looking heron with two breeding plumes at the back of his head. (See Chapter 17, Plate 7, for discussion of the Benu-bird.) The text associated with this title and vignette, however, has nothing to do with either. Ani identifies himself here with several gods, including Horus, Re, Thoth, and Khons.

Plate 28 begins with Chapter 84 and its vignette, a heron, this time without breeding plumes. Once again, the text of the chapter apparently has nothing to do with either its vignette or its title, '*Chapter for being transformed into a heron.*' The 'magician' which this text mentions is the personification of *heka*-magic. The scribe whose job it was to insert Ani's name everywhere in the papyrus has again omitted it from the last column before the next chapter.

The vignette for Chapter 81A shows Ani's head emerging from a lotus blossom on a pool, a scene that brings to mind the god Nefertem, who is also depicted in this manner, and who is mentioned in the longer versions of this chapter (81B). The lotus was a particularly popular symbol of rebirth and rejuvenation among the Egyptians. As is the case in most of the other transformation spells, the lotus and Nefertem have a close association with Re in his aspect as the creator deity.

In fact, it is Re himself who illustrates the final transformation spell on Ani's papyrus, Chapter 80. Re is depicted as a squatting anthropomorphic deity with a sun-disk on his head. As stated previously, Re has a protean quality. He is also the god with whom other deities most frequently were syncretized, perhaps because he has so many attributes. The title of this chapter, '*Making transformation into a god and giving light and darkness,*' alludes to this quality. The intent is most likely to enable the deceased to transform himself or herself into any deity desired.

PLATE 29

Chapter 175, a relatively long retrograde text, appears on Plate 29. The vignette depicts Ani and Tutu standing before Thoth, who squats on a plinth representing a tomb. The title, '*Chapter for not dying again*,' presents one of the major themes of the *BD*. The problem of understanding the nature of this text is made harder by the wide variation among its exemplars. The Papyrus of Ani preserves one of the more interesting examples. In Ani's version, he has a conversation with Atum, who seems to reassure him that he will be content in the afterlife. This contrasts oddly with the overwhelming majority of the chapters where Ani seeks to use virtually any means possible to gain entrance into the company of the gods, even to the extent of threatening them. Ani's protestation that there may not be lovemaking in the afterlife seems natural enough, considering that Tutu is standing behind him as he speaks. The view of the afterlife as a place in which one becomes a spiritualized being beyond all earthly needs and desires sharply contradicts a very common motif in which the deceased asserts or wishes that his body may function exactly as it did on earth. Another striking aspect of the chapter is that Atum, who created the universe, describes how the universe will end by his destroying it and returning the earth to the waters of Nun. Only the creator and a few of the gods will survive.

PLATE 30

This plate presents the introduction of Chapter 125, one of the most important of all texts in the *BD* corpus, judging from the high proportion of papyri which include it. The text of this chapter runs in the canonical right-to-left direction. On a closer examination of the papyrus, we can see that the reason for this peculiar switch in direction between the two chapters is very simple — the material on this plate is actually from two different papyrus sheets which have been pasted together almost seamlessly.

Ani and Tutu are shown, as on Plates 1 and 2, in their most elegant costumes, in postures of adoration before two offering stands heaped with a profusion of food and flower offerings. These are being presented to Osiris, who appears with Isis in a shrine on the right side of the plate; the same scene, in varying degrees of elaboration, also appears on Plates 4 and 19.

The chapter is divided into several sections. The first part, which appears on this plate, provides the deceased with the correct speech to give when arriving at the Hall of the Two Truths, the place where the judgment takes place. Since Ani's heart has already been weighed and he has been vindicated, declared 'true-of-voice,' the placement of Chapter 125 in this part of the papyrus might seem incongruous. The purpose of the first part of the chapter is to demonstrate to the divine council that Ani is knowledgeable about affairs of their realm and should therefore be accepted by the gods as one of their own. Texts of this sort often involve a question-and-answer dialogue with the gods, as is the case here.

PLATE 31

It is fitting to present this part of Chapter 125 as a single gatefold plate, for this is the very metaphor intended by the Egyptian scribes themselves when they illustrated Ani's *BD*. The vignette shows a shrine whose doors have been thrown open, revealing the deities who judge the deceased sitting inside. We should imagine that the small doorways at each side of the shrine were actually big enough to meet at the center of the structure when closed. Each deity, if they can all truly be called such, appears in a column of text. These beings are arranged in a long horizontal band, so that a brief text appears both above and below each figure. The shrine is surmounted by a frieze of alternating cobras and *maat*-feathers. Since under certain circumstances the cobras can be read *maat* as well, this decorative feature might be an allusion to the Two Maats.

At the far right side of the shrine is a wider column of scenes separated from the judges by a yellow division marker.

This column has been divided into four small scenes. The top register shows the two Maat goddesses, identifiable by the large feathers tucked into their hair-fillets. They are sitting on thrones, each holding a *was*-scepter and an *ankh*. Beneath them is a scene showing Ani adoring Osiris before a small altar surmounted by a large lotus blossom. The third scene contains an abbreviated version of the weighing ceremony, showing Ani's heart being weighed against the feather symbolizing Maat (compare Plate 3). In this version of the scene only Anubis attends the scale, while Ammit eagerly awaits a bad verdict. The bottom register in the column depicts Thoth painting a large Maat-feather, presumably an indication that Ani has passed his trial successfully. Since the weighing scene is such an important part of any *BD* papyrus, it is improbable that this is a second weighing of the soul. The scene is essentially a reminder of the context of the chapter.

Chapter 125 is sometimes called 'the Negative Confession,' since the deceased denies a long series of sins in his earthly existence. As Faulkner points out, the expression 'negative confession' is self-contradictory, and a more accurate description would be 'the Declarations of Innocence.' Most often Chapter 125 will be found in conjunction with the weighing of the heart, the scene of judgment, but in this papyrus the weighing scene illustrates Chapter 30B (Plate 3), while Chapter 125 is located near the end of the papyrus. From the standpoint of both logic and our ethical sense, placing the introduction to the gods and the declaration of innocence *after* the judgment scene stands more to reason. In the papyri where the judgment and this chapter appear close together, the question arises whether the text might not have been intended as a magical purge of the deceased's earthly sins. On the other hand, one could interpret this chapter as an attempt to reaffirm the innocence which has already been proven before. This would be just as reasonable a precaution to take as guarding against the removal of one's head or heart in the chaotic world of the afterlife, where even the gods must struggle constantly against irrationality. Nevertheless, the magical character of much of the *BD* indicates that a magical or ritual purgation is the most likely purpose of Chapter 125.

The version of the chapter presented in Ani's papyrus consists of an address to the forty-two gods of the tribunal. Some commentators have tried to connect this number with the nomes of Egypt, those small city-states into which the country was divided administratively. Actually, the number of nomes varied throughout Egypt's history, yet the number of deities in the council of Chapter 125 remained constant. A more plausible explanation is that the number forty-two was chosen because it is a multiple of seven, a number which had an important role in Egyptian magical thought.

There are often two declarations of innocence within Chapter 125, only one of which is found in Ani's papyrus. The first group of denials is normally presented in a narrative form and has a larger proportion of sins involving civil and economic transgression. The second series of declarations, which is the one found here, addresses each denial of a sin to a specific deity. This second set tends to mention a higher proportion of cultic and moral transgressions.

At the top of each text column is the vocative particle *i* "O," followed by a god's name. Most of these beings occur only in this text and are never known to have temples, cults, or priests. As with the fearsome guardians in Chapters 146 and 147 (see Plate 11), many of the god names appearing here allude to the frightening, threatening nature of those who witness Ani's judgment.

PLATE 32

Chapter 42, which appears on the left half of Plate 32, has been reduced here to the section containing the deification of the members. Each of the twenty-one columns of text identifies a part of Ani's body with the god mentioned in the third and fourth registers from the top. The number twenty-one was chosen here most likely for the same reason as the number forty-two in the previous chapter — it is a multiple of the magical number seven.

The intent of this text has already been encountered in several other places in the *BD*. By identifying himself with a deity or deities, the deceased would thus automatically enlist the aid of the gods invoked in achieving a place within the company of gods. In this chapter Ani tries to attain this objective by associating each part of his body with a god. The text follows the pattern of medical papyri, beginning with Ani's hair and ending with his toes. We can see that the text is retrograde, since Nun, with whom Ani's hair is identified, appears in the leftmost column, and the uraei with which his toes are identified appear in the rightmost column of the chapter.

The next vignette is a well-known illustration that normally belongs to Chapter 126. However, the accompanying text is one of the standard terminal rubrics for Chapter 125. As the modern numbering system implies, Chapter 126 would normally appear directly after Chapter 125, yet its vignette is preceded by Chapter 42. The sequence of texts and vignettes makes it clear that either a copyist's error has been made or, more likely, that a mistake was introduced in the funerary workshop while pasting the sheets together. Once the scribe realized that the prefabricated vignette had been placed out of sequence, he probably decided to continue with the text for Chapter 125, even though the replacement did not quite fit the space allotted. Interestingly enough, he continued to write the text in the canonical direction in which the preamble to Chapter 125 reads (125A, Plate 30). The rubric belongs to a genre of texts which explain the ritual requirements for reciting the spell.

The scene shows four cynocephalous baboons sitting at the corners of a rectangular pool. On each side of this pool is a flaming brazier. The pool's red color indicates that it is filled with a fiery liquid, reminding one of the 'Lake of Fire' frequently mentioned in the *BD*. Had the correct chapter been written here, it would have probably begun by addressing the baboons 'who sit in the bark of Re.'

The next four vignettes depict types of amulets commonly placed in the mummy bandages of contemporary burials. Moving from left to right we have: the *djed*-pillar (Chapter 155); the *tiyet*, or 'Isis-knot' (Chapter 156); the heart (Chapter 29B); and the headrest (Chapter 166). Amulets of these types, which have many religious, mythical, and iconographic associations, helped protect the corpse in the period between death and its reawakening in the tomb, when it would be defenseless against a variety of inimical forces. The translations presented here for Chapters 155 and 156 include long terminal rubrics, not found on the Ani papyrus, which give detailed instructions for the use of the amulets. Since the scribe apparently allotted only two columns per amulet for the accompanying texts, he also had to truncate Chapter 166; this entailed the omission of all the references to the head, which the chapter was intended to protect.

Plate 33

Chapter 151 is one of the most variable of all chapters of the *BD* in respect to its text and vignette. Its component scenes are an attempt to represent the mummy of Ani lying in the burial chamber along with all the elements necessary for the protection of the corpse inside the tomb. This composite vignette is certainly one of the most iconographically rich representations in the entire papyrus. Since Egyptian art is essentially aspectual, the illustration shows the most characteristic view of things rather than their appearance in reality. The vignette is a schematic representation of Ani's burial chamber with its furnishings and attendant deities, who will protect Ani at this critical moment. Each component vignette, except for the central one and the one below it, is accompanied by a text; the general purpose is to ensure the preservation of Ani's physical remains.

The central scene depicts Anubis attending Ani's mummy as it lies under the embalming tent, shown here as a striped canopy. The appearance of the mummy rather than Ani's actual corpse in this context can be considered a form of visual euphemism. Underneath the lion-headed bier, a piece of funerary furniture connected with the embalming of the dead, are three jars which presumably contain material needed for Ani's mummification. To the left of this central scene is a figure of Isis kneeling with her hands upon a *shen*-sign, a symbol of both protection and infinite repetition. The Egyptian name is derived from a word which means 'to encircle, to go around,' used extensively to describe the eternal circuit of the sun. The cartouche which protects royal names is essentially an elongated *shen*-sign. At the right the goddess Nephthys kneels in an identical posture. In the three divine personages there is an allusion to the legend of Osiris wherein these gods protected and revived Osiris after he had died.

The four standing figures at the corners of the block of nine interior scenes on this plate are the Four Sons of Horus, the personifications of the Canopic jars in which the internal organs of the deceased are kept; they are, of course, deities who protected the corpse. Unlike their uniform appearance here, in the other instances where these deities occur in this papyrus they have four different heads, allowing one to distinguish them without reading the accompanying texts. Moving clockwise we have: Hapy (upper left); Imsety (upper right); Duamutef (lower right); and finally, Qebehsenuef (lower left).

Directly above the mummification scene is a *djed*-pillar, an object associated with Osiris and signifying endurance. The accompanying text mentions not only Osiris, but also his protection, perhaps a reference to the various protective amulets placed about the mummy. The scene below depicts Anubis recumbent on a shrine with a flagellum emerging from his back. This is Anubis in his aspect of 'He-who-is-over-the-Secrets,' an epithet which refers to his concern with embalming equipment. The collar about his neck is a stylized form of the *sa*-sign, which means 'protection,' particularly magical protection. This word appears several times in the chapters for the amulets on the preceding plate. In front of Anubis is a sceptre which means 'power' or 'might' with two *menat*-collars dangling from its sides.

To each side of the central block of nine scenes are two roughly symmetrical strips, both containing representations of three subsidiary figures. In the middle of each group is a representation of a burning torch, formed by an oil-soaked piece of twisted cloth which is lit. In the top register are two representations of Ani's *ba* perched on a plinth-like shrine and facing outwards in a gesture of adoration. At the bottom, facing inwards, are two *shabtis*, or funerary figurines. The text that accompanies these objects is a version of Chapter 6 (Theban Recension), the same spell normally inscribed on actual figurines of this type. When the deceased recited these words, the *shabti* would presumably become animated and perform certain obligatory labors in the afterlife on behalf of the deceased.

More complete versions of this chapter contain an introduction. Also missing from Ani's version are the texts associated with 'magical bricks,' protective objects placed in the walls of the burial chamber. The title given for this chapter in several papyri, 'Chapter for the head of mystery,' refers to the mummy mask. In fact, there is an unpublished exemplar of Chapter 151 inscribed on Tutankhamun's gold mummy mask. The preservation of the head was considered to be as critical to one's afterlife survival as keeping one's heart. The various brief texts that accompany the component vignettes are sometimes quite garbled in Ani's papyrus, and have required a translation based on several other versions.

PLATE 34

The vignette which accompanies the text on the left of Plate 34, portraying Ani and Tutu offering bouquets, resembles several other scenes found with hymns in this papyrus. Chapter 110 is one of the most popular of the chapters of the *BD*, and is also found in many contemporary tombs of the New Kingdom. The texts and the vignette have a long history with precursors dating back to the *Coffin Texts*. The arrangement in which the figures stand on the baseline and the text flows around the scene occurs with other hymns in this document. From this point on, Ani has presumably passed safely into the beyond, for the vignettes and their accompanying texts become distinctly more benign in tone. As the rubric to this spell indicates, Ani is now about to enter the 'Field of Hotep.' The word '*hotep*' is most likely a deliberate play on words, since it means both 'peace' and 'offering' simultaneously — as well as being the name of the god personifying offerings.

It is unclear whether at the time when Ani's papyrus was written, the Field of Hotep was thought to be separate from the Field of Reeds. In either case the Egyptian word *sekhet* "field" might be better translated as 'marshland' or 'wetland.' Both Fields were thought to lie in the next world in the regions near the horizon, a transition point before one entered the celestial sphere. The two Fields represented a type of paradise, formed of immense expanses of peaceful reed-marshes or farmland. For the Egyptian, especially if he enjoyed hunting, marshlands had the same attraction that lush woods had for the deer-hunting English nobility of the eighteenth century. In these fields, the deceased would travel about and perform some of the obligatory labors associated with the afterworld. The accompanying text seems to treat Ani as if he were one of the blessed dead at this point, for he claims to assist and protect other deities.

As with most of the really complicated illustrations in the *BD*, there are approximately as many versions of the scenes on the right side of this plate as there are papyri and tomb walls where it has been found. Generally speaking, there is not much relationship between the elements of the vignette and the text of Chapter 110. Nearly all representations of the scenes agree that this part of the afterworld is vast in size and surrounded by water. In the midst of this watery expanse, Ani's papyrus shows the Fields of Hotep divided into four unnamed islands, each of which constitutes one pictorial register. It is hard to tell whether there is any chronological scheme implied in this complex representation.

The top island depicts Ani bowing deferentially in such a manner that his forelock dangles down almost touching his outstretched palms. Behind him stands Thoth, who is writing something on the back of his palette with a reed brush. The significance of these two figures is hard to understand, especially since the god is not mentioned in either the vignette or in the text on the left side of the plate. Immediately to the right of these figures, Ani appears again, respectfully offering to three sitting gods with animal heads. The first is rabbit-headed, the second snake-headed, and the third cow-headed. The caption identifies them as 'the two enneads.' The visual evidence need not be taken literally, for the word 'ennead' does not mean literally nine gods. The number three was for the Egyptians the expression of plurality, and nine, as the plurality of plurality, was a way of saying 'very many'; 'the two enneads' would have been a way of saying 'very, very many gods.' In the middle of the island, Ani is shown paddling himself in a boat, which looks like a divine bark of the sort which Re uses to convey himself across the firmament. In front of him is a small pile of offerings. Following this scene we encounter Ani in the

posture of invoking, his arm directed toward the falcon-god perched on the top of a shrine. Facing this falcon deity is a mummiform figure standing before a lotus placed on an offering-stand. The three ovals behind this group are given obscure names in many other papyri, but not in this case. The text behind the mummiform figure may serve as a summarizing description for all the scenes on this island: 'being in the Field of Hotep with breath at the nose.' The sense of this phrase seems to be that Ani has been admitted into the company of gods and lives and breathes in the world beyond.

The second island shows Ani engaged in agricultural activities. Although Ani works here in the beyond, the *BD* makes it clear that this is a temporary activity, before he moves on to his most glorious stage of existence in the celestial sphere. He is shown both harvesting flax and threshing grain by driving cattle over the grain. In the scene immediately after the threshing, Ani is shown in a posture of prayer and adoration before a heron on a standard, which is actually the Egyptian hieroglyph for 'abundance.' Like any paradise, the Field of Offerings is a richly abundant region. In the final scene on the island, Ani is shown kneeling with a wandlike scepter in his hand. The scepter is more than an insignia of office and power, it can be the Egyptian word for 'making an offering' as well. The mounds and ovals in front of him have a caption above them which says, 'the food of the *akhu*.' The scene may thus show Ani offering his rich harvest to the blessed spirits he is about to join.

The third island shows Ani plowing in a field, which the inscription informs us is vast. The connection between this and the harvest which Ani is presenting in the scene above is uncertain, but perhaps some of his offering was derived from his labors on this island. The agricultural scenes in Chapter 110 are sometimes connected with the labors which one wishes to avoid by having a *shabti* perform them. The labors described in Chapter 6, however, seem very much harsher. Furthermore, it seems improbable that the *BD* would show anything untoward happening to the papyrus owner.

It is hard to explain the various waterways, texts, and boats shown on the fourth island at the bottom. One caption states that these are places associated with the *akhu*, the blessed dead. The snake-headed boat appears to be connected with Osiris here, whereas texts at Deir el-Medineh state that this is the boat of Re-Harakhte.

PLATE 35

Like Chapter 110 on the preceding plate, Chapter 148 with its vignette is among the most popular of the chapters in the *BD* repertoire during this period. The scene is found in private tombs, temples, and even royal tombs. In private tombs, this chapter usually appears in connection with the false door stela where the offerings are presented on behalf of the deceased; this is fitting since the seven celestial cows and their bull are identified as donors of bread and beer to the souls of the dead. In Ani's *BD*, furthermore, Chapter 148 appears directly after the description of the Field of Offerings. Chapter 148 is presented here in the same fashion as the vignette for Chapter 125. We see the scene as if it had been kept hidden inside of this shrine-like place until the front doors were flung open on Ani's behalf.

Ani's texts represent a much shorter version than the translation that appears on this plate, but the omitted material is too informative to pass over, especially because the abridged text in the papyrus left out the names of the cows and the bulls. Ani's version simply presents the opening speech and the brief addresses to the four steering oars of the sky and to the three standing deities behind each oar. Perhaps the scribe who composed this scene for Ani felt that the names of the seven celestial cows were so familiar that there was no need to supply them. In the lower left corner Ani presents open lotus flowers which have been placed on top of the two offering stands. He stands with his hands raised in prayer before a hawk-headed deity who wears a sun-disk on his head with a pendant uraeus. This is certainly Re since he is the god addressed in the short retrograde prayer above the scene. Other sources identify this god as Re-Harakhty.

The cows are depicted as mummiform animals, each with a solar disk between her horns and a *menat*-collar around her neck, like the Mehetweret cow in Chapter 17 (Plate 8). Before each cow and the bull is a group of offerings. The introductory text indicates that the motherly cows might also serve as the means of Ani's rebirth in the next world. The cow is one of the most common manifestations of the goddess Hathor, and goddesses known as the Seven Hathors have an important role in Egyptian religion as deities connected with fate. The bull at the bottom of the column bears no aspects of divinity and is identified as the husband of the cows.

According to the texts the four steering-oars are also seen as providers of both protection and food for the deceased. Perhaps it was for this reason that ten similar oars were placed alongside the shrines containing Tutankhamun's sarcophagus. After the description of the steering-oars, more complete versions include a prayer addressed to the mothers and fathers of the gods, then close with a lengthy rubric; both have been omitted in Ani's papyrus. The rubric, like several others, seems to describe the image magic that is to be used in connection with this chapter. The text insists that the chapter is to be said by the deceased on his behalf alone, and that by reciting the spell, he will be protected and provisioned in the God's Domain.

PLATE 36

Ani and Tutu are depicted presenting an elaborate offering, as on Plates 1, 2, 30, and 34, and giving praise before a hawk-headed mummiform god who stands facing them in a coffin-like shrine, similar to that appearing on Plates 4, 8, 19, and 30. The shrine is surmounted by an image of the mummiform Sokar and a frieze of uraei wearing sun-disks. We should imagine that the fringed curtain hanging across the shrine was actually draped across the front, allowing only the god's head and double-plumed *atef*-crown to be seen by the adoring couple. In his hands the god clutches a *was*-scepter along with the two usual attributes of Osiris and of Egyptian kings, the flagellum and shepherd's crook, as on Plate 30. The caption by the deity identifies him as 'Sokar-Osiris, the Lord of the Secret Place, the great god, Lord of the God's Domain.'

The accompanying text — in the canonical direction like most hymns on the papyrus — is Chapter 185, which like 'Chapter 15' is a designation given not to a fixed chapter, but rather to a collection of similar hymns. In this case 'Chapter 185' designates Osiris hymns found in the end scenes of *BDs*. Although the hymn here is addressed to Osiris, the god in the shrine is really his syncretized form, Sokar-Osiris. In some versions of these hymns, there are poetical statements that all beings past, present, and future come to Osiris, and that there is no remaining in the Beloved Land (Egypt). Such sentiments also appear in a contemporary genre of poems known as the Harpers' Songs, some of which implore banquet audiences to 'follow your heart' and enjoy life, for no one can tarry in Egypt.

PLATE 37

We should consider this concluding scene to be a continuation of the preceding plate. The key element of the entire vignette is the unassuming representation of Ani's tomb with its pyramidal top in the bottom right corner. At this point in the papyrus, Ani certainly has achieved the goal of the document and will soon be 'going forth by day' through the doorway. The tomb is shown nestled against the Western Mountain of Thebes into which the tomb shafts were cut. Towering above the tomb is the slope of the desert cliff, indicated by the striped and dotted pinkish soil.

The mountain is incongruously surrounded by a papyrus thicket. The papyrus stalks are connected not with the mountain, but with the goddess Hathor whose head is shown emerging from the slope. The thicket symbolizes the marshlands where the undomesticated cattle roamed in primordial times. The goddess's eye is in the form of the *wadjet*-eye of Horus or Re, and she wears the *menat*-collar about her neck. Between her horns is a sun-disk surmounted by two ostrich feathers. In addition to her other attributes, Hathor became a major deity of the afterlife in the New Kingdom. At Thebes, she was particularly associated with the Western Mountain where the royal and private tombs were located. At Deir el-Bahri, the section of the Theban necropolis where the splendid mortuary temple of the eighteenth-dynasty Queen Hatshepsut was located, there was a cult of Hathor, who according to legend had appeared there in a cave. Hathor, then, is shown emerging into the light just as Ani hoped to do himself. This illustration is a striking testament to the allusive character of Egyptian religious art.

On the left side of the plate we see a most luxuriant and elaborate pile of offerings placed on two offering stands. Floral garlands have been draped about the columns of the stands, and bouquets appear both on top and directly in front, completing the most lavish presentation of this kind in the papyrus. There is a celebratory, triumphant feeling implicit in these abundant offerings; they seem to be intended both to mark Ani's successful passage through the beyond and to thank the gods for helping him safely through.

These offerings appear directly before the odd figure of the goddess known as Tawaret, standing erect upon a shrine-like plinth. Her name, which means simply 'the Great One,' belongs to a group of divine names such as Sekhmet "the Powerful," Wosret "the Mighty," and Amun, "Hidden," which are circumlocutions for names considered too holy or too portentous for mere mortals to pronounce. This is akin to the substitution of 'Adonai' or 'Elohim' for the tetragrammaton YHWH in the reciting of the Torah. Tawaret is a composite being: her body and head are those of a pregnant hippopotamus, but she has the fore and hind legs of a lioness, and a crocodile's tail at her back. She is often shown with pendulous human breasts, which are indistinct in this representation. On her head she wears a low diadem-shaped headdress known as a modius, on which cow horns with a sun-disk are affixed. She wears an elaborate necklace about her throat. In one of her forepaws she holds a lit torch, while the other paw holds an *ankh* and rests upon a large *sa*-sign meaning 'protection.'

The main function of Tawaret is as a protector of women and children, especially in the dangerous moments of childbirth. Her appearance in this context is hard to fathom, unless it has something to do with her occasional epithet 'Mistress of the Horizon,' her generally protective nature, or the rebirth implicit in the Egyptian conception of the afterlife.

Chapter 186, which normally appears here, is actually not present and has been replaced by the string of epithets of the goddess Hathor. Eventually women would claim the title 'the Hathor N,' as a feminine parallel to the male 'the Osiris N,' as a designation of the deceased in *BD*'s and other mortuary literature.

Selected Bibliography

The following bibliography is not a comprehensive listing of major works on the *Book of the Dead*, nor is it even a listing of all the work which were consulted in writing this book. The list below represents a selection of some of the most useful studies on the *BD* and important aspects of Egyptian mortuary religion. Some of these books have already been discusssed previously in the introduction and those remarks will not be repeated here.

Allen, J., *Genesis in Egypt. The Philosophy of Ancient Egyptian Creation Accounts. Yale Egyptological Studies* 2 (New Haven 1988).

A good overview of Egyptian cosmological doctrines, with some application to the afterlife.

Allen, J., 'The Cosmology of the Pyramid Texts,' *Yale Egyptological Studies* 3 (New Haven 1988) 1–28.

Although this paper is addressed to the problems of the royal afterlife as it appears in the *Pyramid Texts,* it is quite useful for understanding the *BD.*

Allen, T.G., *The Book of the Dead or Going Forth By Day. Ideas of the ancient Egyptians concerning the Hereafter as expressed in their own Terms,* E.B. Hauser, ed. *Studies in Ancient Oriental Civilization* 37 (Chicago 1974).

Assmann, J., 'Death and Initation in Ancient Egypt,' *Yale Egyptological Studies* 3 (1989) 135–159.

A discussion of the relationship between initiation rituals and several parts of the *BD.*

Barguet, P., *Le livre des morts des anciens Égyptiens* (Paris 1967).

A pioneering study of the *BD* which contains a discussion of the thematic groups to which the chapters belong.

Bonnet, H., *Reallexikon der ägyptischen Religionsgeschichte* (Berlin 1952).

Somewhat out of date today, but still a most useful one-volume study of many aspects of Egyptian religion.

Brunner, H., 'Illustrierte Bücher im Alten Ägypten,' in *Wort und Bild,* 201–218.

Cerny, J., *Paper and Books in Ancient Egypt* (London 1952).

An invaluable study of Egyptian scribal practices and the manufacture of papyri of all sorts.

Dondelinger, E., *Papyrus Ani. BM 10.470. Vollständige Faksimile-Ausgabe im Originalformat der Totenbuches aus dem Besitz der British Museum. Kommentar* (Graz 1978).

Faulkner, R.O., *The Ancient Egyptian Book of the Dead,* rev. ed. C. Andrews, ed. (Austin 1990).

Faulkner, R.O., *A Concise Dictionary of Middle Egyptian* (Oxford 1962).

Friedman, F., 'The Root Meaning of 3h: Effectiveness or Luminosity,' *Serapis* 8 (Chicago 1984–85) 39–46.

Goyon, J.-C., 'La littérature funéraire tardive,' in *Textes et langages* 3. (Paris 1972).

A discussion of the later developments of Egyptian funerary literature and how these documents relate to the *BD.*

Hornung, E., *Das Totenbuch der Ägypter. Bibliothek der Alten Welt* (Zürich 1979).

Hornung, E., 'Die Totenbücher des Neuen Reiches,' in *Textes et langages de l'Égypte pharaonique. Bibliotèque d'Etude* 64.3 (1974) 65–71.

Hornung, E., 'Jenseitsführer,' in *Lexikon der Ägyptologie* III (1977) 246–249.

Hornung, E., *The Valley of the Kings. Horizon of Eternity,* D. Warburton, trans. (New York 1990).

A profusely illustrated commentary on the Egyptian concepts of the royal afterlife during the New Kingdom. The best non-technical study of the representations of the next world as they appear in the Theban royal tombs.

Keller, C.A., 'A Late Book of the Dead in the Emory University Museum,' *BES* 6 (1985) 55–67.

Merkelbach, R., 'Ein ägyptischer Priestereid,' *Zeitschrift für Papyrologie und Epigraphik* 2 (1968) 7–30.

A brief article which shows the connection between Egyptian priestly initiation oaths of the Ptolemaic period and the 'Negative Confession' of Chapter 125 of the *BD.*

Milde, H., *The Vignettes in the Book of the Dead of Neferrenpet. Egyptologische Uitgaven* 7 (Leiden 1991).

A complete study of the vignettes of a representative papyrus of the New Kingdom. This work is an excellent and comprehesive study of the use of vignettes in mortuary literature.

Mosher, M., 'Theban and Memphite Book of the Dead Traditions in the Late Period,' *Journal of the American Research Center in Egypt* 29 (1992) 143–172.

An intriguing study of the *BD* canon in the later periods of Egyptian history.

Munro, I., *Untersuchungen zu den Totenbuch-Papyri der 18 Dynastie,* London and New York 1987).

A detailed study of *BD* papyri of the New Kingdom with particular attention devoted to dating criteria.

Naville, E.H., *Das ägyptische Totenbuch der XVIII.–XX. Dynastie aus verschiedenen Urkunden zusammengestellt* (Berlin 1886).

Still the standard collection of parallel versions from some of the better *BD* manuscripts of the New Kingdom. An indispensable work for those who must translate or work with the actual Egyptian text.

Niwinski, A., *Studies on the Illustrated Theban Funerary Papyri of the 11th and 10th Centuries B.C. Orbis Biblicus et Orientalis* 86 (Freiburg, Switzerland and Göttingen 1989).

A highly technical but fascinating discussion of the iconography of the *BD* in the Third Intermediate Period.

Posener, G., 'Les signes noirs dans les rubriques,' *Journal of Egyptian Archaeology* 35 (1949) 77–81.

Ritner, R., *The Mechanics of Ancient Egyptian Magical Practice. Studies in Ancient Oriental Civilization* 54 (Chicago 1993).

The best study of Egyptian magical practice today. Quite readible and with extensive references to the relevant Chapters in the *BD* and other funerary literature.

Rössler-Köhler, U., 'Jenszeitsvorstellungen,' in Lexikon der Ägyptologie III (1977) 252–267.

Rössler-Köhler, U., *Kapitel 17 des ägyptischen Totenbuches. Untersuchungen zur Textgeschichte und Funktion eines Textes der altägyptischen Totenliteratur. Göttingen Orientstudien* 10 (Wiesbaden 1979).

The best study thus far of one of the lengthiest and most important of all Chapters of the *BD.*

Saleh, M., *Das Totenbuch in den thebanischen Privatgräbern des Neuen Reichs. ADAIK* 46 (Mainz am Rhein 1984).

An overview of the use, illustration and placement of *BD* Chapters on the walls of Theban tombs in the New Kingdom.

Seeber, C., 'Jenseitsgericht,' in *Lexikon der Ägyptologie* III (1977) 249–252.

Seeber, C., *Untersuchungen zur Darstellung des Totengerichts im Alten Ägypten. Münchner Ägyptologischen Studien* 35 (Berlin 1976).

A comprehesive study of the all-important judgement scene in the *BD.* Extensively illustrated.

Yoyotte, J., 'Le jugement des morts dans l'Égypte ancienne,' in *Le jugements des Morts. Sources Orientales* 4 (Paris 1961).

A Glossary of Common Terms and Concepts

ABDJU-FISH: A form of the god Horus which accompanies the sun-bark and, along with the Djeseru-fish, defends the boat against the enemies of Re.

ABYDOS: Ancient town in Upper Egypt, especially sacred to Osiris.

AKER: Earth-god represented as a pair of lions or sphinxes back-to-back.

AKERU-SPIRITS: Spirits connected with the earth.

AMMIT: Hybrid monster present at the Weighing of the Heart, ready to gobble up those hearts weighed down with sin.

AMUN: Theban god who became state god of Egypt from the New Kingdom onwards.

ANDJET: Ninth nome of Lower Egypt in the central Delta; ancient religious center.

ANKH-TAWY: 'Life-of-the-Two-Lands': Memphis.

ANTINAIOPOLIS: A town in Middle Egypt.

ANUBIS: Jackal-headed god of embalming, closely associated with Osiris.

APIS: Sacred bull worshipped at Memphis, earthly manifestation of Ptah.

APOPHIS: Serpent-demon, arch enemy of the sun-god and representative of the forces of chaos.

AROURA: Area of land, about two-thirds of an acre.

ASH: Libyan god closely associated with Seth.

ASYUT: Ancient town in Middle Egypt.

ATEF: Tall, white crown flanked with ostrich feathers and horns, worn especially by Osiris.

ATHRIBIS: The town in Lower Egypt sacred to the Kemwer (Great Black Bull) and to the god Khentikhai.

ATUM: Primeval sun-god worshipped at Heliopolis; also the aged sun at its setting.

BA: One of the forms of the soul in the afterlife, often in the form of a human-headed bird; the *ba* has no separate existence from a person until after death.

BABAI: Minor deity, usually malevolent but also connected with the crowns of Egypt.

BAH: Heron-god symbolic of abundance and plenty.

BAKHU: Eastern mountain where the sun rises.

BASTET: Cat-goddess of festivity and fertility with cult center at Bubastis.

BATY: A minor bull-god.

BENU-BIRD: A form of the creator deity as a Great Blue Heron which rested upon the primordial mound when it first emerged from the waters (the so-called phoenix of ancient Egypt).

BES: Benevolent dwarf-demon with lion-like features.

BLACK LAND: The fertile Nile Valley as opposed to the flanking Red Land; Egypt.

BUBASTIS: Cult city of Bastet in the eastern Delta.

BUSIRIS: City in the central Delta sacred to Osiris.

BUTO: City in the northern Delta sacred to the serpent-goddess Wadjet.

CHAOS-GODS: Deities of the primeval chaos.

CHEMMIS: The hidden place in the Delta where Isis hid from Seth and brought up the infant Horus.

CHILDREN OF IMPOTENCE: Opprobrious epithet of evil spirits.

CONCLAVES: Assemblies of the gods, one of Upper Egypt and one of Lower Egypt.

COPTOS: Town of Upper Egypt, center of the worship of Min.

CROCODILOPOLIS: Cult center in the Faiyum of the crocodile-god Sobk.

CUBIT: Linear measure of 20.6 inches.

DAY-BARK: Boat in which the sun-god crosses the sky above the earth.

DEP: One of the two towns (with Pe) which, united, formed the Delta city of Buto, predynastic capital of Lower Egypt.

DJATY: Minor deity, son of Hathor.

DJED-PILLAR: Cult object resembling a tree trunk with lopped-off horizontal branches, sacred to Osiris, Ptah, and Sokar.

DJESERU-FISH: The red fish which accompanied the Abdju-fish in protecting the sun-bark.

DISMEMBERED ONE: The dead Osiris before resurrection.

DOUBLE LION: Form of the sun-god as two lions back-to-back, whose name in Egyptian is Ruty.

DUAMUTEF: Jackal-headed Canopic deity, one of the Four Sons of Horus.

EDFU: Cult center of Horus in Upper Egypt.

ELEPHANTINE: Island at the First Cataract; southernmost border of Egypt proper; source of the Nile in Egypt.

EMMER: A form of wheat.

ENNEAD: Company of Nine Gods.

EYE OF HORUS: Torn out by Seth, restored by Thoth, symbolic of everything good, beneficial, and pleasant; the Egyptian name for Horus's eye is the Wadjet-eye.

FAIYUM: Inland lake and marsh area west of the Nile in Middle Egypt, center of the worship of the crocodile-god Sobk.

FENKHU: People of Syria.

FIELD OF OFFERINGS, FIELD OF REEDS: The fields in which the blessed dead hoped to sojourn in the journey through the afterlife.

FIVE GODS: Gods of the five epagomenal days at the end of the 360-day year, namely Osiris, Horus, Seth, Isis, and Nephthys.

FLAIL: Whip-like part of the royal insignia.

FOREMOST OF THE WESTERNERS: An epithet of Osiris.

GEB: Earth-god, consort of Nut; one of the Ennead of Heliopolis.

GOD'S FATHER: Priestly rank.

GREAT CACKLER: Epithet of the creator-god in the form of a goose.

HA: God of the West.

HAKER-FESTIVAL: A festival connected with the death and rebirth of Osiris.

HAPI: God of the Nile, symbolic of abundance.

HAPY: Ape-headed Canopic deity, one of the Four Sons of Horus.

HATHOR: Cow-goddess of love; patroness of the West.

HELIOPOLIS: Ancient center of the sun-cult, now part of modern Cairo.

HEMEN: Falcon-god worshipped near Esna in Upper Egypt.

HENU: The Sacred Bark of Sokar; Sokar himself.

HERACLEOPOLIS: A religious and political center on the west bank in Middle Egypt near the Faiyum.

HERMOPOLIS: Ancient religious center of Middle Egypt, especially associated with Thoth.

HOGGING-BEAM: Beam running the length of a vessel at deck level to lend rigidity to the hull.

HORAKHTY: 'Horus-of-the-Horizon': sun-god, usually falcon-headed; often combined with Re as Re-Horakhty.

HORDEDEF: Son of King Khufu (Cheops) of the Fourth Dynasty who built the Great Pyramid; later revered as a wise man.

HORUS: Falcon-god; ancient creator-god; opponent of Seth; son of Osiris (and Isis) and his successor to the kingship of Egypt.

HOTEP: God personifying the Field of Offerings.

HU: Authority personified as a god.

IGAU: Another name for Anubis.

IHET: Sky-cow who gave birth to the sun.

IHY: The god who represents the sound made by the sistrum and *menat* instrument; the child of Hathor.

IMAU: Cult-place in the western Delta.

IMPERISHABLE STARS: The circumpolar stars, which never set, in contrast to the Unwearying Stars.

IMSETY: Human-headed Canopic deity, one of the Four Sons of Horus.

INERT ONE: The dead Osiris before resurrection.

INET-FISH: A fish which symbolized both fertility and re-birth.

IQEN: God associated with the celestial ferryman.

ISDES: Form of the god Thoth.

ISHED-TREE: The tree in Heliopolis which was cracked in the fight between Re and his enemies; also the tree on whose leaves the King inscribes his titulary.

ISIS: Mother-goddess, sister and wife of Osiris, mother of the young Horus.

ISLE OF FIRE: The place in the afterlife where the blessed dead are refreshed but the sinners are tortured and destroyed.

KA: The vital life-force or genius of a person, born with him and resembling him exactly; attendant on him in life and especially death.

KHEPRI: Scarab or dung beetle representing the young sun.

KHERAHA: Religious center south of modern Cairo.

KHNUM: Ram-god who created man on a potter's wheel.

KHONS: Theban moon-god.

LAKE OF THE TWO KNIVES: Sacred water at Hermopolis where the sun-god came into being.

LETOPOLIS: Religious center at the apex of the Delta, cult place of Horus.

LIMP ONE: The dead Osiris, before resurrection.

MAAT: Goddess of truth, justice, and cosmic order; often depicted as a small seated woman with an ostrich feather on her head being presented to a god by a worshipper.

MAFDET: Protective goddess, killer of snakes, in the form of a civet or ocelot.

MANSION OF THE PRINCE: Palace at Heliopolis where divine justice is dispensed.

MANSION OF THE PYRAMIDION: Temple of the sun-god in Heliopolis.

MANU: Western mountain where the sun sets.

MASTER CRAFTSMAN: Title of the High Priest of Ptah at Memphis.

MEMPHIS: First capital of Dynastic Egypt; cult center of Ptah; almost opposite modern Cairo.

MENAT: A musical instrument in the form of a necklace-counterweight and associated with Hathor.

MENDES: Religious center in the central Delta.

MENQET: Goddess of beer.

MIN: Ithyphallic fertility god of Coptos.

MNEVIS: Bull sacred to the sun-god, worshipped at Heliopolis.

MONT: Falcon-headed Theban war-god.

MOUNDS: The fourteen mounds or regions of the Elysian Fields.

MUT: Vulture mother-goddess of Thebes; consort of Amun.

NAREF: Necropolis near Heracleopolis associated with the Osiris myth.

NATRON: A mineral salt used in the embalming process.

NEDIT: Place near Abydos where Osiris was murdered.

NEDJEFET: Place in the region of Asyut.

NEFERTUM: God of the lotus, son of Ptah.

NEHEBKAU: Serpent-god, a form of Re.

NEITH: Ancient creator-goddess, worshipped especially at Sais in the Delta.

NEKHEN: Ancient capital of Upper Egypt, cult center of Horus .

NEMES-HEADDRESS: The striped royal wig cover which is normally worn by the gods as well as the pharaohs.

NEPHTHYS: Sister of Isis and Osiris, consort of Seth, mother of Anubis.

NESHMET-BARK: Sacred Bark of Osiris.

NETJERU: Ancient town in the twelfth Lower Egyptian nome, in the northern central Delta.

NIGHT-BARK: Boat in which the sun-god sails through the Netherworld.

NOME: One of the forty-two administrative and religious districts into which Egypt was divided, twenty-two in Upper Egypt, twenty in Lower Egypt.

NUBIA: The land south of Egypt proper; the area between the First and Second Cataracts.

NUN: The primordial waters, the Abyss; god personifying the same.

NUT: Sky-goddess whose arched body formed the vault of heaven, consort of the earth-god Geb; one of the Heliopolitan Ennead.

OMBITE: He of the Upper Egyptian town of Ombos: epithet of Seth.

OSIRIS: God of the dead; legendary primeval king of Egypt slain by his brother Seth; also a title commonly prefixed to the name of the deceased, who thus became identified with the god.

PAKHET: Lioness-goddess of Middle Egypt.

PE: One of the two towns (with Dep) which, united, formed the Delta city of Buto, predynastic capital of Lower Egypt.

PELICAN: As goddess, advocate of the dead, mother of the dead, or even the deceased himself.

PER-NESER: National shrine of Lower Egypt.

PER-WER: National shrine of Upper Egypt.

PILLAR-OF-HIS-MOTHER: Her sole support, god of the Thinite nome; a grade of funerary priest.

PTAH: Human-form creator-god of Memphis.

PUNT: Also called God's Land, source of aromatic resins for incense, probably in the region of modern Somalia.

QEBEHSENUEF: Falcon-headed Canopic deity, one of the four Sons of Horus.

RE: Form of the sun-god at his noonday strength, often falcon-headed.

RED CROWN: Distinctive royal crown of the kingdom of Lower Egypt.

RED LAND: The desert flanking Egypt, as opposed to the Black Land of Egypt proper.

RENENUTET: Harvest-goddess and nurse in serpent form.

RIVALS, THE: Horus and Seth when they contended for the kingship of Egypt after the murder of Osiris.

ROD: Linear measure of 100 cubits, approximately 172 feet.

ROSETJAU: Name of the Necropolis of Giza or Memphis, later extended to mean the Other World in general.

SACRED EYE: Eye of Horus torn out by Seth and restored by Thoth, symbolic of everything good, beneficial, and pleasant; the Egyptian name is Wadjet. Also the eye of the sun-god symbolizing the sun's destructive power.

SACRED LAND: The necropolis.

SAIS: Ancient city in the north-central Delta, cult center of Neith.

SATIS: Goddess of Elephantine associated with Khnum.

SEBEG: The planet Mercury as a god.

SEKHAT-HOR: She-who-remembered-Horus: cow-goddess.

SEKHMET: Lioness-goddess symbolic of destructive power, consort of Ptah at Memphis.

SELKET: Scorpion-goddess, protectress of the dead.

SEM-PRIEST: Funerary priest; supervisor of the burial rites.

SENET: A popular Egyptian board game having an allegorical meaning for the afterlife (often wrongly connected with chess or checkers).

SEPA: Town in the Heliopolitan nome sacred to Anubis.

SESHAT: Goddess of writing and reckoning.

SETH: God of storms and the desert; brother and murderer of Osiris and rival of Horus; also the god who guards the sun-god Re from the evil serpent Apophis.

SHABTI: Magical figurine, servant of the deceased, which will carry out on behalf of its dead master all the hard work required of him in the other life.

SHESMETET: Lioness-goddess, personification of divine power.

SHESMU: God of the winepress.

SHETYT-SHRINE: Sanctuary of Sokar at Memphis.

SHORES OF THE WASHERMAN: Place in the extreme north of Egypt.

SHU: God of the air, consort of Tefnut; one of the Heliopolitan Ennead.

SIA: Intelligence personified as a god.

SILENT LAND: Realm of the dead.

SISTRUM-PLAYER: Musician-priest of Hathor (a sistrum is a Near Eastern rattle or percussion instrument); see also Ihy.

SOBK: Crocodile-god, son of Neith.

SOKAR: Falcon-headed god of the dead in the Memphite area; often combined with Ptah as Ptah-Sokar.

SOPD: God of the eastern Delta.

SOTHIS: Sirius the Dog-star as a goddess; sometimes takes the role of Isis.

SUPPORTS OF SHU: The columns of air supporting the sky at the four cardinal points.

TATENEN: Memphite creation-god assimilated to Ptah.

TAYT: Goddess of weaving.

TEFNUT: Lioness-goddess, consort of Shu; one of the Heliopolitan Ennead.

THINIS, THINITE NOME: Religious center of Upper Egypt where Osiris was worshipped; also the district of which it was the capital.

THOTH: Scribe of the gods, god of wisdom and learning represented as an ibis or a baboon; mediator between Seth and Horus; restorer of the Sacred Eye to Horus.

TJEBU: Ancient town in the tenth Upper Egyptian nome.

TJEKEM: Name of the sun-god.

TJENENET-SHRINE: Originally the holy-of-holies at Memphis.

TJENMYT: Goddess of beer.

TWO BANKS, TWO LANDS: Name for Egypt.

TWO FLEDGLINGS: Horus the Protector of his father and Horus the Eyeless.

THE TWO KITES: Isis and Nephthys as birds lamenting the death of Osiris.

UNWEARYING STARS: Stars which rise and set, in contrast to the Imperishable Stars.

URAEUS: Upreared cobra, symbol of royalty.

WADJET: Serpent-goddess worshipped at Buto; protectress of Lower Egypt.

WENIS: Ancient town in the nineteenth Upper Egyptian nome, on the west bank in Middle Egypt.

WENNEFER: Name of Osiris which is especially associated with resurrection in the next world.

WENTI: Name of the sun-god.

WENU, WENUT: Religious center near Hermopolis and its goddess in the form of a hare.

WEPWAWET: Opener-of-the-paths: wolf-god of Asyut, closely connected with Osiris.

WERERET: A name of the White Crown of Upper Egypt.

WEST: The region where the sun sets, hence the land of the dead.

WESTERNERS: The dead.

WHITE CROWN: The crown of Upper Egypt.

XOIS: Religious center in the central Delta.

Professional Acknowledgments

Book Design and Typography
Studio 31

Color Prepress
Studio 31
Daniel Herman — Photoshop Artist

Photography
Rick Young, Inc.
Tom Mackiel — Photographic Consultant

Color Separations
Color by Pergament
Thanks especially to
Dave Brody, Joe Caravella, and Frank Marino

Printing and binding
Asia Pacific Offset, Inc.
Thanks especially to Tim Linn

Bookbinding of facsimile volume
Amistad Enterprises
Penny Sherred

Text input
Kathryn Kurtz

This book was produced
utilizing a dual platform of traditional
typography and state-of-the-art computer graphics.
The text is typeset in ITC Galliard with a Linotron 202,
driven by Bestinfo Pagewright composition software, running
on a PC-based computer, and Marcus Interface Box. Manual pasteup
was used to produce camera-ready mechanicals. The 1890 facsimile volume
was photographed on 8 × 10 Fuji film, and scanned and separated on a
Crossfield Scantex drum scanner. The high resolution images were
reassembled on a Macintosh Quadra 840AV running Adobe
Photoshop. Final film output was done on an Agfa
Selectset 5000. The Map Key to the Papyrus
was assembled with Photoshop
and Quark Xpress.

Note: All products names are either registered trademarks
of the companies referenced, registered trademarks of the products
mentioned, or not. Thorough investigation of copyright and trademark
should be undertaken prior to the use of any of the above names.